White Men's God

White Men's God

The Extraordinary Story of Missionaries in Africa

Martin Ballard

Greenwood World Publishing
Oxford / Westport, Connecticut
2008

First published in 2008 by Greenwood World Publishing

1 2 3 4 5 6 7 8 9 10

Greenwood World Publishing
Wilkinson House
Jordan Hill
Oxford OX2 8EJ
An imprint of Greenwood Publishing Group, Inc
www.greenwood.com

Library of Congress Cataloging-in-Publication Data

Ballard, Martin.
    White men's God : the extraordinary story of missionaries in Africa / Martin Ballard.
       p. cm.
    Includes bibliographical references and index.
    ISBN 978-1-84645-032-7 (alk. paper)
       1.   Missions – Africa – History. I. Title.
    BV3500.B24 2008
    266.0096 – dc22

                                                                2008027474

ISBN 978-1-84645-032-7

Designed by Fraser Muggeridge studio
Typeset by TexTech International
Printed and bound by South China Printing Company

Contents

Acknowledgements

My thanks are first and foremost due to librarian Terry Barringer. I first met her after she had brought the invaluable Royal Commonwealth Society Library to its new home in the Cambridge University Library. Apart from being an expert on missionary sources, she is also widely read in the field, and she has supported me consistently throughout the project, while leaving me free to draw my own conclusions from this mass of material.

Without the help of Karin Attar and my old friend Geoff Rainbow, I would have had no access to German language texts. Carla Zipoli also provided assistance with Fr Sapeto's Italian memoirs. I am also grateful to Nick Godfrey for advice on the Rwandan genocide. Finally, I must thank my wife Eva for her unfailing support and patience.

Preface

In 1444, Prince Henry the Navigator of Portugal despatched his ships down the West African coast. At their mastheads flew the banner of the Order of Christ, and the pious prince instructed his captains to plant a cross on every African headland. In the following years, priests opened stations down the western coast of Africa, while others remained on board their vessels as they rounded the Cape of Good Hope, to settle on the continent's remote eastern shore. These pioneer missionaries, who had been recruited in the Iberian peninsula at a time when the Inquisition was at the height of its power, carried a package of medieval attitudes and practices of appeal to those living within traditional African society. In 1491, Mvemba Nzinga, chief of the Nsundi people, whose lands were sandwiched between the great Congo river and Portuguese Angola, offered himself for baptism. In the following years, he assumed the title of King Afonso I, renamed his capital city San Salvador, distributed European names and titles among his chiefs and despatched his son Henry to Portugal for training in the priesthood. The young man later returned as the first black bishop in the western church since antiquity. When Afonso died at the end of a long reign, a Portuguese priest penned his glowing obituary.

> His Christian life is such that he appears to me not as a man but as an angel sent by the Lord to this kingdom to convert it … He studies the Holy Gospel and when the priest finishes the Mass he asks for benediction. When he has received it he begins to preach to the people with great skill great charity … He punishes with rigour those that worship idols and he has them burned along with these idols.[1]

After his death, the Jesuits ran a college in San Salvador which successfully turned out generations of indigenous clergy and lay workers, and Kongo remained an independent Catholic state for another 140 years.

From the beginning, however, the Christian message to West Africa was fatally corrupted by the all-pervasive business of slavery. When Henry the Navigator's first expedition returned with some 200 Africans, the prince attended their sale and donated a fifth of his share of the proceeds to the Church. Later, Popes would buy slaves to propel their galleys, and Vatican policy routinely promoted key interests of the slaving empires of Spain and Portugal. Perversely, the efforts of committed priests to ease the suffering of the native people in North and South America only increased the demand for imported Africans. By the seventeenth century, Angola's only recognised function was to serve as a reservoir for Brazilian slaves, and as Portuguese ships set out for the New World, they received a blessing from the bishop of Luanda, sitting on a marble throne beside the waterfront. By mid-century, the Angolan interior had become largely depopulated by slave raids, and in 1665, the armies of the Catholic king of Portugal snuffed out the independence of its neighbouring Catholic kingdom of Kongo when the African king and virtually all his followers died on the battlefield of Ambuila. By the beginning of the next century, travellers could find no trace of Christianity in the region 'except crucifixes and relics, which were not distinguished by the people from their amulets and fetishes'.

By now, Angola served as a punishment station for immoral and unruly priests, most of whom lived openly with concubines and were in some way involved in the slave trade. As if to draw the Catholic *missio antiqa* to an end, Capuchin monks burnt the charismatic prophetess Dona Beatriz Kimpa for the sin of teaching that San Salvador was the true Bethlehem; that Jesus, the Madonna and St. Francis had all been black people; that God recognised no distinction of colour; and that Africans would find a place in the heavenly kingdom.[2]

* * *

During these centuries (see Chapter 7), Catholics had also been seeking to bring the Ethiopian church into obedience to the Pope in Rome, though here too the enterprise had ended in bloodshed and failure. But if the Catholic record was deeply flawed, Protestants could show nothing at all. Across northern Europe, not a single voice had been raised in audible protest, and no churchman had even suggested that European Christians might carry some responsibility for African souls. The white men who manned the slaving castles were bizarre ambassadors for reformed piety. A British naval officer described the bedraggled set of wretches that met his ship at Cape Coast: 'Here was a mixed bag of factors, writers, artificers and soldiers – sick, hopeless and drained of both health and dignity.' They had 'lank bodies, a pale visage, their pockets sewn up, or of no use, and their tongues tied'. Paid in false currency, they were forced to purchase supplies from company stores, at company prices, and were fined for every misdemeanour. Instead of making their fortune, they lapsed deep into debt and sought oblivion in sex, drink and early death.[3] Such men knew nothing of the continent on whose borders they perched and told stories of how African women took apes as lovers, to produce a race that could scarcely be called human.

Devout Protestants found no problem in reconciling their faith with active participation in the trade. Hymn writer John Newton, who would later be converted to the anti-slavery cause, recalled the time when he worked as a slaver on the coast: 'I never knew sweeter or more frequent hours of divine communion, than in my last two voyages to Guinea … During the time I was engaged in the slave trade I never had the least scruple as to its lawfulness. I was on the whole satisfied with it, as the appointment Providence had marked out for me.'[4] It was said that Newton composed words for the hymn 'How Sweet the Name of Jesus Sounds' as he watched slaves being brought aboard his vessel, and his opinions remained unchanged when he later wrote 'Amazing Grace'.[5] While merchants at home and planters in the Caribbean prospered hugely, their clergy could justify the whole awful business on the grounds that Africans had no immortal souls.

In 1688, 244 years after Henry the Navigator first set his ships to Africa, four Dutch Quakers from Germanstown, Pennsylvania, presented the first recorded protest against African slavery to their local meeting: 'Tho they are black we cannot conceive there is more liberty to have them slaves as to have other white ones. There is a saying that we shall doe to all men like as we will be done to ourselves; making no difference of what descent, generation or colour they are. And those who steal and rob men, and those who buy and purchase them, are they not alike?'[6]

Twelve years later, a pamphlet, *The Selling of Joseph*, published by lawyer Samuel Sewell who had himself been a prime mover in the Salem witchcraft trials, circulated in New England. A tiny number of impoverished Pennsylvanian Quakers then began to make waves around the fringes of their own community, though there was as yet little sign of change. In 1701, the Church of England set up the Society for the Propagation of the Gospel (SPG), with a remit to care for the spiritual health of British citizens living overseas, and just eight years later, colonial governor and plantation owner Christopher Codrington bequeathed his large Barbados estates to the society. It was reported that, from then on, church slaves on the SPG estates could only be

distinguished from their secular neighbours by the word SOCIETY
that was branded on their backs.

* * *

Across Europe, the seventeenth century had been a time of hardship
and religious fanaticism; even as slaves were being shipped across the
Atlantic in increasing numbers, more women than ever before were
being executed on the charge of witchcraft, and wars of religious origin
brought famine and death on a scale that reduced the population in the
worst-hit areas to half its peacetime number. During those same years,
however, a strand of 'enlightened' thought was also gathering strength.
In the late sixteenth century, Frenchman Michel de Montaigne had posed
two fundamental questions – 'what do I know?' and 'how do I know it?'
Galileo Galilei and Isaac Newton took up his challenge, using experi-
mentation to explore the workings of the natural world, while René
Descartes and John Locke applied the same techniques to philosophy
and political science. Facing the moral problem of how to distinguish
right from wrong without recourse to a higher authority, enlightenment
thinkers rediscovered *natural law*. While the concept had both classical
and medieval Christian roots, it was now used to defend those 'inalienable
rights' that were common to humanity regardless of national legal
systems or revealed religion. Whether these rights extended to slaves
would remain an issue to divide 'enlightened' opinion.

By the early eighteenth century, most philosophers and many
churchmen had adopted a fashionable deism that stripped religion of any
'magical' element and pushed back the boundaries of divine intervention.
English man of letters, Joseph Addison, proclaimed the existence of
a remote unmoved mover:

> The spacious firmament on high
> With all the blue ethereal sky,
> And spangled heavens, a shining frame
> Their great Original proclaim.

From this point it was only a short step to Voltaire's challenge to the core
Christian doctrines of incarnation, redemption and biblical authority.
At least among the intellectual elite, human reason and experiment had
replaced tradition and authority as arbiters of those questions – 'what do
I know?' and 'how do I know it?' Working from these new criteria, some,

but by no means all, enlightenment thinkers reached the conclusion that trading in slaves was indefensible – though none took the further step of becoming activists in an anti-slavery cause. Fashioned by enlightenment ideas, the eighteenth century would become a watershed in human self-consciousness.

Before taking up the narrative of the modern missionary movement at the turn of the eighteenth and nineteenth centuries, we will briefly disentangle the core beliefs of different Protestant groups, follow Christian activists' involvement in the anti-slavery cause and identify some of the – often conflicting – currents within contemporary society, which were to influence the working assumptions of those who offered to serve in Africa.

Chapter 1
White Men's God

Pietists and Evangelicals

In 1731, the pious young Count Zinzendorf was summoned to attend the coronation of Christian VI, king of Denmark, and during the celebrations, he got into conversation with a black servant, Anthony Ulrich. After listening with horror as this ex-slave described the conditions under which his people lived and worked on the West Indian island of St. Thomas, Zinzendorf returned to his estate at Herrenhut to share Ulrich's story with members of a Christian community (which included a number of refugees from Moravia) who had settled on his land.

After a year's debate and heart searching, potter Leonard Dober and carpenter David Nitschmann left Herrenhut on 21 August 1732, bound for Ulrich's island of St. Thomas. They travelled to Copenhagen on foot, wearing working-men's clothes, with just thirty shillings in their pocket, planning to work in the Caribbean 'as slaves amongst slaves'. In the years before the count died in 1760, a further 226 missionaries followed the two Moravian pioneers out of Herrenhut. Among their more far-flung destinations were 'Greenland, St. Croix, St. Thomas, St. Jan, Barbice, Palestine, Surinam, Savannah in Georgia, among the negroes in Carolina, among the savages in Irene, in Pennsylvania, among the Hottentots, in Guinea, in Litvonia … Isle of Man, Shetland, in Prison, on the journey to Ceylon, Ethiopia, Persia … and otherwise on Land and Sea.'[1] The listing of Guinea and Hottentots highlights two abortive attempts to settle in Africa. The 'Guinea' party's landing on the Danish Gold Coast was abandoned after nine brethren died in the space of a few months. The 'Hottentot' party settled in 1737 at Genadendal, near the Cape of Good Hope, where the climate was kinder, but they became demoralised by the vicious verbal assaults of Dutch Reformed Church *predikants* and the apparent apathy of Africans and left after just seven years. This settlement stood empty until it was reoccupied later in the century by another generation of Moravians.

Zinzendorf's Moravians were a semi-detached part of a much larger group within the Lutheran church, known – originally mockingly – as pietists. This movement, which began to spread across German-speaking lands in the late seventeenth century, had in a tradition of piety that drew inspiration from earlier Mennonites and Anabaptists. Although pietists could be found in the noble courts of Germany and the banking houses of Switzerland, the largest number were concentrated in the desperately poor rural state of Württemburg. The mood of their 'heart religion' can be accessed through their devotional poetry that was set to music by fellow-believer Johann Sebastian Bach.

> I want to give my heart to you
> sink in it, O my saviour
> I want to lose myself in you
> and if the world is too small for you
> ah, for me alone you shall
> be more than earth and heaven.

Those who sought to achieve perfection by introspective devotion struggled to separate themselves from a society that they perceived to be irredeemably corrupt, and it followed from this that the secular state was an ephemeral institution that would one day be swept away. Since humans could expect only suffering in this life, political affairs – even fundamental issues of justice – were viewed as matters of indifference. Within pietist communities, the state of a woman's soul could be measured by the cleanliness of her house, and children would be beaten for any misdemeanour at home or school. In their search for isolation and purity, some followed Mennonite forerunners to the North American frontier, while others looked to overseas mission fields for refuge from sinful society. Visitors to German stations would be fascinated to be confronted by old-fashioned, industrious people – not unlike those who would be found today in a North American Amish community.

> They bustle about in the cool of the day – then sleep all the hottest part. They knit every pair of stockings or socks they wear and never wear such a thing as a woven pair – moreover great thick worsted-like cord, requiring in consequence huge shoes or boots which give a clumsy appearance. Beautiful needlework – every stitch of which they do themselves in every line – & all like Baby linen, so beautifully fine.[2]

* * *

By the early eighteenth century, the Church of England had reached a
condition characterised by critics as 'soul extinct, stomach well alive';
it was even said that those listening in the pews could be hard-pressed to
decide whether the preacher was 'a follower of Confucius, Mohammed
or Christ'. The Moravians worked wherever souls needed saving, and
unsettled Anglican clergyman John Wesley was their most celebrated
European convert. The moment in May 1738, when he 'felt his heart
strangely warmed', was a classic Moravian conversion, achieved
under the spiritual direction of one of Zinzendorf's missionaries. After
Wesley had spent three months at Herrenhut, he organised his English
followers on the community model, and even after he had cut links with
Zinzendorf, he continued to preach a doctrine of Christian perfectionism
that was close to the pietist model. Since he pronounced a message that
Christ had died for all, it followed that all must be free to accept or refuse
the call to salvation. His brother Charles made this proclamation in one
of his earliest hymns.

> Come, sinners to the gospel feast,
> Let every soul be Jesus' guest
> Ye need not one be left behind,
> For God hath bid for all mankind.

Apparently innocent enough today, the words 'God hath bid for all
mankind' was then interpreted by Protestants of the Calvinist tradition
as a rebirth of the heresy which asserted that humans could achieve
salvation by the exercise of their own free will.

One of Wesley's earliest followers, Selina, Countess of Huntington,
broke from her mentor on this issue of free will. Fired by the Calvinist
cause, she founded the splinter Countess of Huntington's Connexion and
used her wealth to build and support chapels and ordain her own clergy.
She also sent letters of admonition to those whom she perceived to be
in danger of backsliding into heresy – one of which was directed at Henry
Venn, curate in the parish of Clapham. His conversion would prove
a key event in the birth of the Church of England's own evangelical wing.
While Wesley was going his separate way, Venn and fellow 'awakeners'
remained within the Anglican fold to deliver their message of conversion,
personal salvation and biblical authority. As the years progressed,
differences of emphasis began to emerge. Venn was first and foremost

a preacher, who delivered his very direct message to those who packed his Huddersfield church. The younger Augustus Toplady, in contrast, was a hard-line Calvinist, who was more concerned with launching bitter attacks on the 'Satanic shamelessness' of even the smallest concession to the doctrine of free will. His famous hymn – 'Rock of Ages' – was packed tight with the message of original sin, predestination and the coming judgement.

> Nothing in my hand I bring
> Simply to thy cross I cling
> Naked come to thee for dress
> Helpless look to thee for grace
> Foul I to the fountain I fly,
> Wash me saviour or I die.

Tensions between the two wings of evangelical belief would become ever more marked during the following nineteenth century. A variety of organisations, often operating independently, each with its own agenda and belief structure, set in train a chain of events that would start a powerful new missionary movement to Africa.

Anti-Slavers and Settlers

Quakers were expected to live by strict rules of justice and truth, but in practice, many became deeply involved in the business of slavery. After the restoration of Charles II, parliament laid penalties on all who would not conform to the established church, and in the following years, obdurate Quakers were shipped to work as indentured labourers on the sugar island of Barbados. Other members of the society took refuge in the American colonies, where most settled in the colony of Pennsylvania. As conditions improved at home, London-based Quakers set up businesses with bases in London, Philadelphia and Barbados. Although comparatively few of them operated ships on the middle passage, many became slave-owners, and huge Quaker fortunes were built in the support operations of banking and the carrying trade, as well as in iron production, which provided metal for the chains of slavery, and confectionary manufacture, which used the products of plantation sugar. Early Pennsylvanian protests against any kind of Quaker involvement could be dismissed as the ravings of a lunatic fringe, but the message had to be taken more seriously when delivered by respected Philadelphia schoolmaster Anthony Benezet. At about this time, the anti-slavery cause had also found its first serious advocate in London. Outraged at the abuse of black people that he saw around him in the London streets and docks, broad church Anglican Granville Sharp launched a long and ultimately successful campaign in the courts for the emancipation of all Africans who lived in England. After establishing a correspondence, Benezet and Sharp started to publish one another's works on opposite sides of the Atlantic.

From time to time the Society for the Propagation of the Gospel sent chaplains to provide spiritual guidance for those who were working in and around the slaving stations, and in 1745, the society recruited Cambridge graduate Thomas Thompson as chaplain to Cape Coast Castle. He claimed to have accepted the position 'out of pure zeal to become a missionary'. 'Having considered of the properest method I could take for the instruction of the blacks, I considered it best, not to insist much at first upon points of Christian doctrine, but to strike at their false worship, and endeavour to convince them of their absurd notions, and expose the folly of their absurd and superstitious rites.'[3]

After returning to a comfortable English rectory, Thompson produced a pamphlet, *The African Trade for Negro Slaves shown to be Consistent with the Principles of Humanity, and with the Laws of Revealed Religion.* His case was constructed from pages of texts from Leviticus to the epistles of St. Paul. With not a single clear-cut anti-slavery text to be found between the covers of his Bible, Granville Sharp built his response on the concept of Christian love, reinforced by the enlightenment concept of natural law.

> We must not, for the sake of Old-England, and its Africa trade, or for supposed advantage, or imaginary necessities of our American colonies, lay aside our Christian charity, which we owe to the rest of mankind: because, whenever we do so, we certainly deserve to be considered in no better light than as a society of robbers, a mere banditti, who, perhaps, may love one another, but at the same time are at enmity with all the rest of the world. Is this according to the law of nature? – For shame Mr. Thompson![4]

Parallel protests from Benezet only provoked the SPG directors into stout defence of Thompson's position. Far from being immoral, slavery was on 'the contrary very plainly implied in the precepts given by the Apostles.... Though the Society is fully satisfied that your intention in this matter is perfectly good, yet they most earnestly beg you not to go further in publishing your Notions, but rather retract them.'[5]

In London, Bristol and Liverpool, clerks still kept their ledgers tidy. Items of expenditure were entered in one column; there were goods for barter – Barbados rum and calicoes, old clothes and coloured beads; there were also entries for the replacement of essential equipment – tools for forcible feeding, thumb screws, leg irons and whips; wages for captain and crew and the cost of repairing vessels. Assets were listed across the page – male slaves (fit), female slaves (fit), children, sickly slaves (unlikely to live). Everything fetched a price, big or small.

While working for a Quaker master in America, Olaudah Equiano managed to put together the money to buy his freedom and achieve a good standard of education; then, after crossing the Atlantic, he became acknowledged as a leader of London's black community and published an autobiography that would become a key text for the abolitionist movement.[6] In 1783, Equiano called on Sharp to seek help in publicising a case on insurance liability that was going through the commercial courts. On the one side, the owners of the slave ship *Zong* were trying to secure compensation on the value of 132 sick slaves, who had been thrown overboard on the middle passage, while, on the other, the insurers were denying liability on the grounds that the deaths had been a result of the captain's deliberate act. When presenting the case, the solicitor general pointed out that morality had no bearing on the law of liability. 'This is a case of chattels or goods. It really is so: it is a case of throwing over goods.... Whether right or wrong, we have nothing to do with it.'[7] Although the owners received their compensation, victory came at a high cost as, from that time on, biblical texts seemed poor justification for the scale of human suffering that had been exposed in open court. The case of the slave ship *Zong* brought a rush of converts to the anti-slavery cause. After following proceedings closely with Quaker friends, young evangelical member of parliament William Wilberforce immersed himself in two decades of parliamentary campaign, while Cambridge student Thomas Clarkson started to research a book that would demolish all claims that the Atlantic trade was conducted in a humane manner.

Equiano now took Sharp on a tour of London, showing him how hundreds of – overwhelmingly male – blacks had to scavenge on the streets for a wretched living. Some had been discharged from the army or navy, while others had been turned onto the streets by disgruntled owners. Under the Poor Law, responsibility for relief lay with the parish where the applicant was born and, to nobody's surprise, there was no parish in England that would accept responsibility for destitute people who had been born either in Africa or on American plantations. Besides being a social reformer, Sharp was also a political radical, and he grasped at the chance of creating an African colony that would bring together his two life passions – the emancipation of slaves and the creation of a form of government that was truly accountable to its own people. He drew up plans for an ideal multi-racial colony, democratically structured on the Anglo-Saxon model of hundredors and tythingmen, which would bring civilisation and Christianity to the suffering continent of Africa. Government backers were more attracted by the fact that his projected colony would export the growing social problem of 'indigent blacks' to a distant continent. A Swedish traveller recommended a fertile site at the mouth of the Sierra Leone River – home to the supposedly friendly Mende people – that the Portuguese had called Sierra Leone (Mountains of the Lion).

> Disorders … prevail chiefly among the class of people, who suffer their brutal passions to get the upper hand of their reason, and whose will the affections always govern their intellectual faculties. Nothing is more common and fatal among this class, than excess in drinking. Nevertheless there are remedies on the spot well known to the negroes, which effectually cure the diseases that cannot be escaped.[8]

Sharp's undoubted idealism was not balanced by administrative competence, and the venture was a disaster from the start. As soon as the settlers were on board, rumour spread that the convoy was bound for the penal settlements in New South Wales and the 'free settlers' had to be locked below decks to prevent them from jumping ship. Of some 400 who left London in April 1787, more than fifty were dead by the time they reached Plymouth. When the party finally landed on a startlingly beautiful shore, food ran short and reassurances on disease proved calamitously ill-founded, and the enterprise foundered until local chiefs finally drove some sixty survivors into the bush. If the operation was to be salvaged, it clearly needed to be brought under professional management.

* * *

In retirement, 'awakener' Henry Venn the Elder returned to Clapham, where his son John was now rector, and here father and son acted as spiritual advisers to a group of philanthropically minded evangelical lay people. Although most were barely thirty years old, members of this 'Clapham Sect' were already making their names in a variety of fields. If any one man set the mould for what would become known as Victorian virtues, it was their acknowledged leader, Henry Thornton. Successful banker and member of parliament, he was both frugal and authoritarian by nature, and once he had adopted a cause, he pursued it relentlessly. Alongside him were anti-slaver William Wilberforce, future East India Company chairman Charles Grant and later Master in Chancery James Stephen. Although school-reformer Hannah Moore, and husband and wife Thomas and Jean Babbington, lived outside the parish, they too kept in close touch with the group. As a broad churchman who lived in central London, Granville Sharp was never on particularly close personal terms with members of this 'Clapham Sect', but the younger men did respect his pioneering stand on slavery and they rallied to rescue his failing enterprise. Together they formed the Sierra Leone Company, whose humanitarian and commercial objectives and aims were laid out in a formal declaration.

> Every measure will be taken for laying a foundation of happiness to the natives, by the promotion of industry, the discouragement of polygamy, the setting up of schools, and the gradual introduction of religious and moral instruction among them.... The most general and wide diffusion of European light, knowledge and improvement, the Home committee members hope, through the medium of this Company, may thus be introduced into the continent of Africa.[9]

As a symbol of this high aspiration, the settlement was renamed Freetown, and Anglican clergyman Melville Horne was recruited to serve as chaplain to the reformed colony. On returning home just one year later, he published a sad volume of *Letters on Missions*. 'I felt I had acted precipitately – I charged my self with folly and vanity – I lamented having left my Parish in England – and having placed myself in the situation to which I began to think divine providence had never called me.... My spirits were broken, sleep and appetite forsook me.'[10] Despite the fact that Horne had contacted no Africans outside the colony, his book rapidly became accepted as a manual for missionary work. According to his recommendation, a mixed party of ten or twelve people – and ideally three or four times that number – should be recruited for every venture, and their objective should be to bring Christianity to the heathen, rather than 'to make them Church of England men, Dissenters, or Methodists'.[11] While Horne suffered his agonies of self-doubt, Thornton was constructing a sound capital base for his new company. With this accomplished, his immediate challenge was to find a new supply of settlers, who could carry on the enterprise that had been started by Sharp's ill-fated pioneers.

The Turning Point

The year 1792 stood at a time in human history when everything that had previously been immutable seemed to be under threat. In that summer, the Paris mob stormed the Tuillery Palace, and France was declared a republic a few months later. As printing presses ran off accounts of voyages to distant parts of the world alongside copies of Tom Paine's *Rights of Man* and Mary Wollstonecraft's *Vindication of the Rights of Woman*, it appeared that the enlightenment had carried all before it. As scientists explored ever-new fields, the factories of Lancashire and Yorkshire were beginning to turn out fabrics in previously inconceivable quantities. Quoting the economic doctrines of Scottish economist Adam Smith, philanthropists could even argue that slavery was an inefficient method of production, which distorted the free market by keeping millions in deepest poverty, when they should rightly have been working for a wage and buying British goods. At just this time, even the enlightenment itself was coming under challenge from a new romantic movement, which was inspired by writers such as Swiss-born Jean Jacques Rousseau, German Johanne von Goethe and English poets Samuel Taylor Coleridge and William Wordsworth. Within this ferment of ideas, people of widely different political and religious views and of divergent social background started to look beyond personal survival; fired by a conviction that life could be better, anti-slavery societies competed for public attention with pressure groups that sought to reform schools, hospitals and the penal code.

During the second half of the eighteenth century, the powerful tide of religious emotion known as the Great Awakening had helped propel Methodist and Moravian missionaries deep into the African populations of the Caribbean and North America. As black congregations appointed pastors from among their own ranks, the story of how Moses led his Israelites out of Egypt emerged as the driving metaphor for emancipation. In that same year of 1792, William Carey threw a pile of magazines in front of a group of like-minded younger Baptist ministers. 'See what the Moravians are doing', he challenged, 'and some of them British like us and many only artisan and poor.'[12] His colleagues agreed to set up the Baptist Missionary Society (BMS), with Carey as its first missionary and his friend Andrew Fuller as home secretary. Carey had taught himself Latin, Greek and Hebrew, while earning his living as a cobbler; Fuller had started adult life as a wrestler in the East Anglian fens, and even after ordination, this huge man still enjoyed testing strength against worthy competition.

The London Missionary Society (LMS) was established two years later. Originally designed according to Melville Horne's principles as a broadly based body that would recruit from all parts of the evangelical spectrum, it came increasingly under the supervision of Congregationalists, who traced their line of descent back to Cromwell's New Model Army.[13] Like the Baptists, they followed a democratic system of church order, in which ultimate authority lay with the individual congregation, so that any authority the home committee members might possess would lie in their control of financial resources.

The Scots were divided over the value of foreign missions. While some Presbyterians supported movements south of the border, the majority argued that preaching to uncivilised people was a waste of time and effort and even a breach of the divine order, but in 1796, societies were set up in both Edinburgh and Glasgow. Both were underfunded, and for the next half century, the LMS continued to recruit many of its leading missionaries from north of the border. In 1799, the same members of the Clapham Sect who controlled the Sierra Leone Society established the Church Missionary Society (CMS), which quickly established a close collaboration with evangelical activists in the University of Cambridge. Five years later, the same people would also take an active part in founding the British and Foreign Bible Society. In all its forms, Protestantism was a religion of the book, and missionaries were settling

in many areas across the world where the spoken language had never
been committed to writing. After establishing verbal communication,
they first needed to define an agreed grammar and orthography before
undertaking – with widely varying competence – the long process
of translating the Bible and other religious texts, and this new society
assumed responsibility for printing and distributing their work.

Enthusiasm carried beyond Britain. In 1810, a group of graduates
from Williams College, Massachusetts, established the American
Board of Commissioners for Foreign Missions (ABCFM). New England
Congregationalist in origin, it functioned both as a society in its own right
and as the co-ordinating body for smaller American bodies. Then in 1815,
wealthy Swiss pietists set up a college in Basel where aspiring pietists –
most recruited from Württemburg – would be trained to work for the
more affluent British societies. Six years later, the Basel Missionary Society
sent workers to the Danish Gold Coast on its own responsibility.

All had global ambitions. William Carey set off for India, LMS recruits
sailed for the South Seas and the CMS sent Cambridge graduates to
confront the sophisticated cultures of the Orient. This was a time of
fervour. Young Calvinist Reginald Herber, later to be Anglican Bishop
of Calcutta, took barely twenty minutes to dash off the words of a hymn
that would become the anthem of the fledgling Protestant missionary
movement:

> From Greenland's icy mountains,
> From India's coral strand,
> Where Afric's sunny fountains
> Roll down their golden sand,
> From many an ancient river,
> From many a palmy plain,
> They call us to deliver
> Their land from error's chain…

Christian Missions and the Enlightenment

Historians debate whether the modern Protestant missionary movement
should be seen as an affirmation of or a reaction against the spirit of the
age.[14] For German-speaking pietists – as later for Catholics – there could
be no equivocation; both were hostile to the enlightenment and all its

works, and both went to great lengths to distance themselves from the
civilisation that it had spawned. It will be seen, however, that German
missionaries would later be significantly influenced by ideas that
flourished within their national romantic movement. The position
of English-speaking Protestants was more ambiguous. Unlike the
Germans, recruits had come of age within a post-enlightenment society
and had absorbed its key assumptions on the meaning of civilisation.
Most accepted that Christian Africans would be recognised by the
fact that they rejected traditional art, dancing and drumming; built
rectangular houses; dressed in modest western clothing; and ate their
food with cutlery, sitting at the table. It followed that such tokens of
salvation could never be achieved until Africa had a cash economy
that was driven by 'legitimate trade' with the industrialising nations
of Europe. At the same time, missionary thought processes were far
removed from anything that their contemporaries would have recognised
as 'enlightened'. While some home churchmen struggled to reconcile faith
with the new empirical thinking, those who volunteered for missionary
work – almost without exception – clung to a pre-enlightenment
acceptance of the literal authority of scripture. When his own faith was
in crisis, Bishop John Colenso of Natal described his earlier acceptance
of the Bible as

> None other than the voice of Him that sitteth upon the Throne.
> Every book of it – every chapter of it – every verse of it (where do
> we stop?) every letter of it – is the direct utterance of the Most High!
> The Bible is none other than the Word of God – not some part of it
> more, some part of it less, but all alike, the utterance of Him who
> sitteth upon the Throne – absolute – faultless – unerring –
> supreme.[15]

At the end of the seventeenth century, however, a literal approach
to scripture could even persist among those who were involved in
exploring new ideas. No less a figure than Isaac Newton, pioneer of the
new scientific method, dabbled in alchemy and turned his mathematical
skills to the task of predicting the date of the second coming of Christ –
finally settling on the year 1948. Earlier missionaries were inclined
to consign the end of the world to a distant future, when their own
preaching would usher in a glorious divine rule. As the nineteenth
century progressed, this perspective would come increasingly under

challenge from more literal interpreters, who anticipated the 'end time' as both an immanent and a cataclysmic event. While most of these new 'fundamentalists' continued to promote European manners, they would continue to trust scriptural authority over reason and experiment.

Workers in the field, along with those on home committees who sent them out, also rejected the findings of medical science when these came into conflict with their own confidence that sickness and health were a gift of God, to be bestowed on those who lived a pious, chaste and cleanly life. When explorer John Baikie led an expedition to the Niger in 1854, he rejected the traditional practice of using quinine as a cure for those who were already ill and instead distributed a daily prophylactic dose to all on the expedition. The result was triumphant: 'we had the same number and the same men, twelve Europeans and fifty-four Africans ... that we had on board when leaving'. Although missionaries witnessed the success as they travelled on his expedition, some fifty death-scarred years would pass before either Catholic or Protestant societies would routinely use quinine as a prophylactic against malaria.[16]

On their remote stations, missionaries inhabited a pre-enlightenment – even Old Testament – world. As late as the early twentieth century, almost every society working in Northern Rhodesia (modern Zambia) passed down tales of how their workers had, like the prophet Elijah of old, matched the power of prayer against traditional custom.

> There was a period of great drought, and the people were in want. They had made offerings to the spirits and had for days been praying for rain. I was led to put God to the test. Going up to the people and addressing the spirit-medium, I said, 'We will ask for a sign to prove who is able to give rain, the spirits or God. We believe that God alone can send it, and that it is useless to pray to the spirits. The sign shall be, if rain is sent before the end of the week (this was on Monday) that the spirits have sent it, but if no rain falls until early next week, that shall be the proof that the spirits cannot help you, but that God can.'[17]

Through the coming days, the people watched as lightning flashed and rain fell across the surrounding countryside, until the Christians' faith was rewarded on Sunday with a downpour. 'Our prayers were answered. Jehovah was vindicated. Superstition, witchcraft, and spirit-worship must crumble away before the faithful declaration of the good news.'

Few, if any, missionaries who worked within the mosquito's killing zone sought to intellectualise the varied pressures that had formed their pre-enlightenment attitudes to life and religion. Those who faced inevitable sickness and a likely early death for both themselves and their families could perhaps only function from the foundation of a very simple faith.

Chapter 2

The Foundation of Happiness

The Return to Africa – Sierra Leone

In 1790, ex-slave Thomas Peters landed in London off a ship from
Halifax, Nova Scotia, carrying a petition that he had been charged with
delivering to the British government. Alone in the bewildering city,
he somehow found his way to Granville Sharp, who, in turn, guided
him to Henry Thornton's office and into the presence of the secretary
of state. Peters told an extraordinary story. After the outbreak of
hostilities between Britain and her American colonists fifteen years earlier,
runaway slaves had been encouraged to form a battalion in the loyalist
army, and Peters had been among many who fought in the king's cause.
When the colonists emerged as victors, the British refused to abandon
their black allies to their fate and shipped them to Canada, where they
were to receive both land and freedom. In the event, promised farms
turned out to be stretches of virgin forest in cold and alien Nova Scotia.
Abandoned, without money or tools, some were reduced to rooting
up trees with their bare hands, while others sank back into a condition
close to slavery, working without pay for white landowners.[1] Now,
community leader Thomas Peters had been sent to seek help for this
suffering, but religious and law-abiding, people.

Finding it hard to believe his good fortune, Thornton assured Peters
that his Nova Scotians would be welcome in Sierra Leone, and fellow
members of the Clapham Sect constructed ambitious plans on how
so many colonists could be usefully employed in building and running
a chain of mission stations that would stretch along the length of the
Sierra Leone River and deep into the heart of Africa. The British
government committed funds to provide the fleet of ships that would
be needed for the journey, and Peters agreed that he would return to
Canada to rally his people's support for the great enterprise. Thornton's
fellow anti-slavery activist Thomas Clarkson offered the services of his
brother John, who was a naval officer on half pay, to lead the expedition.
Before he left for Canada, Sharp briefed the young man on the high ideals
on which the colony had been founded, recommending that he should

call the Nova Scotians 'Africans' rather than 'blacks' or 'negroes', as both those terms already carried pejorative overtones. 'You will be disposed on all occasions to conduct yourself towards black and white men not only with the same impartial justice in your public capacities, but with the same condescension and familiarity in all the intercourse of private life.'[2]

In Nova Scotia, John Clarkson found a deeply religious people, who wore modest clothing, made regular marriages, treated adultery as an offence and had little problem with alcohol. There were Baptists who grouped themselves around Pastor David George and Methodists who looked to the ecstatic blind preacher Moses Wilkinson. Most surprisingly, there was also a flourishing congregation established by black sailor John Marrant, who had been personally ordained by the Countess of Huntingdon to work as an overseas missionary for her Connexion.[3] Although warm and friendly, the Nova Scotians had followed events in France and had taken on board the three revolutionary principles of liberty, equality and fraternity that cemented their determination that those of African inheritance must never again be treated as a lower branch of the human race. Clarkson formed a strong and lasting bond with these future settlers, and they had no reason to doubt his promise that every family would receive rent-free land beside the ocean in their new African homeland. Peters also assumed that, as the community leader, he would eventually be given charge of the colony.

In early 1792, a fleet of fifteen ships, carrying some 1,200 men, women and children, arrived off the coast of Sierra Leone. A handful of Sharp's original settlers watched the newcomers land on Freetown beach. They gathered behind their ministers, opened their hymn books and marched forward singing:

> Awake and sing the song,
> Of Moses and the Lamb,
> Wake! every heart and every tongue
> To praise the Saviour's name.

By the standards of the day, the Sierra Leone Company governed by enlightened laws; according to the constitution, half of any jury had to be of the same race as the accused, and at least in aspiration, capital punishment was to be prohibited. But Thornton had jettisoned Sharp's utopian plans to create a fully participatory democratic society on African soil, and to Peters's fury, all executive power was bestowed on Clarkson and a council, recruited from a motley collection of disillusioned and alcoholic whites. Even more seriously, the settlers discovered that the company had also disowned Clarkson's promise that everyone would receive rent-free land beside the ocean. Any aspiration that Sierra Leone would become a model democratic society was extinguished when Peters died of malaria and John Clarkson was recalled to London, to be replaced by the bluff military man, Captain Dawes. As discontent rumbled into rebellion, settlers found ways to remind their inflexible governor 'of the recent melancholy fate of Louis XVI', advising him to 'take it into his head to be disgusted and march off'. In time, the Nova Scotians settled into some form of order within their tight community. Visitors, who heard the sound of hymns rising from the chapels at all times, commented that these had to be from some intensely religious people in the world; but the long-term plan that John Clarkson's Nova Scotians would provide staff for inland mission stations had quickly become lost to sight.

* * *

At the time when order was crumbling into open rebellion, Thornton needed to recruit a governor who could restore order and convert philanthropic aspiration into financial profit. For several years, Zacharay Macaulay had been working as overseer on a Jamaican plantation, 'in a field of canes, amidst perhaps a hundred of the sable race, cursing and bawling and noise of the whip resounding on their shoulders'.[4] He confessed that he was still 'tottering on the brink of eternity' at the time when he arrived in London to visit his sister Jean Babbington. After his pious hosts had guided him through an evangelical conversion and convinced him of slavery's evils, Thornton offered him the vacant position in Sierra Leone. Macaulay would later face accusations of having a hand in slavery, but in his defence, another fifteen years would pass before Wilberforce's Act for the Abolition of the Atlantic Slave finally became law, and during that period, trading in slaves remained a legal occupation for British subjects. In any case, it was virtually impossible to conduct any trade from his base on the edge of a slaving continent without some measure of involvement in the business.

As governor, Macaulay was responsible for implementing both the company's commercial and religious objectives; according to settled

strategy, trade and religion were to advance up the rivers, hand in
hand, with company posts doubling as mission stations. This project
immediately created conflicts of interest with those who were already
trading in the area. Each Mende chief controlled his stretch of riverbank
and leased out land to slaving factories that were operated by European
and mixed-race traders, and both chief and trader had a vested interest
in preventing the governor's Sierra Leone Company from establishing
direct contact with inland markets. At the same time, they were interested
in accessing any mission education that would prepare their children for
the task of making a living in a rapidly changing environment.

Since the same members of the Clapham Sect sat on committees
of the Sierra Leone Company and the CMS, it should have followed that
the first missionary initiatives would be Anglican, but even fervently
evangelical clergy in Jane Austen's England found good reason why
they should not leave comfortable parsonages for the fever-ridden West
African coast. Any suggestion that the society should ordain men from
the lower orders aroused fierce opposition among the established clergy;
ordination into the Church of England confirmed a man's place in
society, and objectors feared that unsuitable candidates would use a few
years of overseas service as a back-door means of advancement. English
non-conformists and Free Church Scots, who acknowledged no social
divide between minister and flock, were therefore first in the field. None
had been trained in African culture, and all were ignorant of even
the most basic tenets of the Muslim religion that they were now
commissioned to confront.[5]

Disaster followed disaster. As soon as a party of Methodist families
arrived in Freetown, the women started to complain that the town had
no pastry shops where they could buy gingerbread for their children,
and Macaulay was glad to see them on the next boat home before they
could bring further shame on the Christian cause. Methodist operations
depended on donations from some very poor people, and this failed
enterprise would be remembered with dismay for many years. The
society continued to send out ministers and teachers, most of whom had
been snatched out of remote country circuits. Despite their lowly origins,
they failed to treat members of the Nova Scotian community with even
elementary respect, and many died within weeks of arriving in the
colony.[6] One minister, who was given special charge to start work
on the Gambia River, was shocked to discover that Africans really did
have black skins and doubted whether such fearsome creatures could

possibly be included in the covenant of grace.7 Other denominations fared little better. A joint party of Scots from the Edinburgh and Glasgow societies began to quarrel among themselves as soon as they boarded ship and bad feeling persisted after they had reached Freetown. Their women caused particular outrage to colonial society by going about barefoot and insisting on doing their own domestic work. One Baptist schoolmaster plunged into radical settler politics, until he too was sent home to face Andrew Fuller's awesome wrath, and from that time, it was drummed into all aspiring Baptist missionaries that they must not, under any circumstances, involve themselves in secular politics.

If the Christian enterprise in Sierra Leone was not to end in total disaster, the established church, however belatedly, needed to succeed where others had failed. Recruitment problems eased when pietist graduates, first from the Basel training college and then from the Berlin Lutheran Mission, began to apply for positions within this Anglican society. Early German recruits were little better prepared than the Free Churchmen who had gone before them. 'So narrow was my upbringing that I really thought that a heathen land must be even in its very outward appearance basically different from a Christian country, the one cultivated and organised, the other a wild chaos marked from the start by the characteristics of paganism. But lo, it was a very beautiful country.'8

Some remained within the colony, while others were dispatched to run schools at lonely sites on the Sierra Leone River. All fell victim to tropical diseases – often barely settling before they or their wives fell ill and died. Deaths of adults were recorded at missionary headquarters; child mortality can only be inferred. Still these pietists kept writing messages of stoicism and faith.

> Our meetings together were more frequent last year than they have been during this; but they were of a different nature; we either met to pay the last respects to departed friends, or to settle their little affairs; and we parted with but faint hopes, at times, of seeing one another again on this side eternity. Blessed be the Father of all Mercies, this present year we have but twice looked into the gaping grave.9

Their sense of self-sacrifice was striking. Although they had by now concluded that German lives were held in lower account at headquarters than those of English colleagues who sailed for more salubrious fields, they still told each other how, like knights of old, they had to fill the enemy moat with their dead bodies, so that those who came after could scale the walls and take the castle. They were indeed crucial to the whole African venture, and the mission's seventy-year dependence on Basel recruits would become formalised when, in 1825, the society opened a college in Islington, where the recruits were taught English and pietist doctrinal deviations were rooted out.

By the time the once penniless Zacharay Macaulay returned home in 1799, he had somehow amassed a fortune large enough for his family to live in a fine London house, fit for raising his precocious son Thomas Babbington Macaulay. On the same boat, he took with him four black girls and twenty-one black boys, who were children of leading settlers and local chiefs. While the boys learnt printing, carpentry and mechanics in Clapham, the girls were boarded with a 'generous woman' in Battersea. All were entertained in local houses, and they played with John Venn's children – including one lad, who had been named Henry in his grand-father's honour – and regularly attended the parish church. Fourteen were baptised by the rector, with the charge that they must take up the task of converting their country people. Unhappily, Europe turned out to be the black man's grave and only six ever returned home.

* * *

In 1804, Fulani Sheikh Uthman dan Fodio raised the standard of the *jihad* in his capital of Sokoto, and in the following years, his horsemen carried an uncompromising version of Islam south across the Hausa emirates to the confluence of the Niger and Benue rivers and the Yoruba city of Ilorin. Towards the west, the shock waves of Uthman's *jihad* would fan out some 1,500 miles to the Atlantic coast. Europeans had long heard tales of how a 'higher race' of Africans would one day be discovered deep within the continent. When news spread that the Fulani had slim noses and thin lips, it was easy to conclude that the quest was at an end. If only such a fine race of people could be convinced that the Islamic faith was a lesser religious path, they would surely turn to Christ and Africa would be won. But even as strategists looked to revive the early plans to build chains of mission stations, their ambitions had to be placed on hold in the face of a new and more urgent challenge.

Just a year after parliament finally passed the Abolition Bill, ships from the Africa Squadron began to patrol the West African coast and,

between 1808 and 1830, some 30,000 're-captive' men, women and
children, who had been rescued from slaving ships, were handed over
to the care of the colonial governor of Sierra Leone. When the new
governor Sir Charles McCarthy took up the post in 1814, he found these
re-captives living in makeshift villages, without any support: 'feeble bulbs
set in the soil, with scarce enough life to survive'. Facing a humanitarian
crisis, he urged the CMS to abandon its river stations to concentrate on
providing care for this vulnerable community. McCarthy proposed that
each village would have its missionary, who would combine the roles of
magistrate, teacher, parish priest and development officer. No detail was
too small for his personal attention as he planned to construct his version
of the homeland on the shores of Africa (importing church towers, bells,
clocks and weathercocks from England). 'Quill-pens and copy-books,
prayer books and arithmetic books were ordered for the schools, with tin
cases for the children to carry them in, lamps to read them by. Hats were
ordered for the men, bonnets for the women, shoes for all; gowns and
petticoats, trousers and braces-buttons, too, with needles, thread and
thimbles, soap and smoothing-irons, even clothes-brushes, nothing was
forgotten.'[10]

Charge of the receptive village of Regent was given to a German, who
was known by the anglicised name of William Johnson. At one moment,
this driven man would be consumed with manic energy, at the next, he
would plunge into deepest despair. Perhaps his mental health problems
struck a chord with people who had suffered so much, but the Regent
villagers certainly responded to their missionary and his devoted assistant
William Tamba with huge enthusiasm.[11] Whenever a naval vessel
docked in Freetown, people from Regent would line the road, to identify
re-captives from their area and welcome them into their homes. His
villagers became known for their skills as farmers, blacksmiths, masons,
carpenters and shopkeepers, and four years on, Johnson could report
that Regent had a flourishing cash economy. So many children had been
baptised with his name that, in later years, Johnsons across West Africa
needed to be identified by nicknames. Then in 1823, just as the work had
reached a peak of success, the community was devastated by the colony's
worst yellow fever epidemic; 12 of 28 CMS workers died in that one year
and others, including Johnson, followed in 1824. Until that time, the
CMS home committee had invested heavily in Sierra Leone, but in the
wake of the tragedy, resources were diverted into more promising fields.
Continuing CMS money was concentrated on the Fourah Bay Institute

of Higher Education, and when the college opened in 1827, the first
student through its doors was a promising Yoruba re-captive named
Samuel Ajayi Crowther, who would later play such an important role
in the missionary story. Although the CMS pulled out of secondary
education, this work was taken over by the community, and by mid-
century, the colony could boast a self-supporting structure of secondary
education that delivered a significantly higher literacy rate for the colony
than was currently achieved in either Britain or Germany.[12]

At just this time, a woman of unusual talents took it on herself to
scrutinise the whole structure of missionary education. Orphaned in
childhood and then becoming a young widow, Hannah Kilham joined
the Quakers and, while working in one of their hostels for African
sailors, picked up the basics of both the Wolof and the Mandingo
languages. On three journeys to West Africa, she was shocked to discover
the low standard of missionary education. In Sierra Leonian schools,
where German teachers still had difficulty handling English, let alone any
African language, even the most gifted children achieved little, and
Kilham concluded that the basic problem was that pupils were trying
to learn in a foreign tongue.

> What would be the consequence, if we gave to an English child, at
> home, a Latin book to learn without any English translation, and
> just taught it to spell and read the Latin words? Would the child,
> by practising in this way, acquire a knowledge of that language?
> Assuredly not: and it would be very unjust to complain of the want
> of capacity in the Africans in Sierra Leone, as the cause of their not
> having advanced more than they have.[13]

After opening a school for re-captive girls in the beautiful Freetown
village of Charlotte, she set about recording key words and numerals
in twenty-five African languages. In 1830, she left to examine educational
practise in neighbouring Liberia and was killed when her ship was struck
by lightning on the return journey. Her belief in the value of first-language
education had, however, aroused interest at the Basel seminary, and from
that time, the Germans would rapidly win a high reputation for their
language skills. The CMS took full advantage of this development, and
a Basel recruit was despatched to Freetown with a sole remit to work
on African languages.

The Return to Africa – Captain Cuffee's Vision

In England, the earliest case for repatriation was argued by white philanthropists; in the United States, its origin can be identified within the black community. For all their good deeds, American Quakers were reluctant to welcome blacks into their tight communities, and it was an unusual event when the meeting at Westport, Massachusetts, accepted the son of a freed slave and a Native American woman into full membership. While keeping his Fanti name to demonstrate pride in his African inheritance, Paul Cuffee embraced the Quaker work ethic and, ultimately, became master of his ship.

In 1811, 'finding his property sufficient to warrant the undertaking, and believing it to be his duty to appropriate part of what God had given him to the benefit of his and our unhappy race, he embarked on board of his brig, manned entirely by 'persons of colour', and sailed to the land of his forefathers, in the hope of benefiting its natives and descendants.'[14]

On arrival in Freetown, Cuffee took advice from respected Nova Scotian settler John Kilzell. Born a local Mende, he had been shipped to America as a slave and had now returned to set himself up as an independent trader. Kilzell explained that however much the Sierra Leone Company might extol the virtues of free and legitimate trade, it was in practise busy monopolising the import and export business on the Sierra Leone River. The two men agreed on a plan of action: while Kilzell's Methodist congregation formed itself into a trading co-operative, Cuffee would sail for England to find a businessman who would distribute the society's exports across Europe. On the voyage, he urged his crew to show everyone in Liverpool that 'people of colour' could live by the highest possible standards. The arrival of his trim vessel did indeed create a stir in that slaving port, though once ashore, his crew only managed to demonstrate that black sailors were likely to behave much like any others. After recruiting a London Quaker businessman to handle the distribution, Cuffee returned to Freetown, where he bought a house as a token of his commitment to the venture. Back in America, he then set about promoting the causes of trade, colonisation and the Christian mission. Speaking to black audiences across the northern states, he insisted that settlers needed to set an example of regular worship, legal monogamy, temperance and justice to all men and avoid 'frolicking and amusements that lead to expense and idleness'. He planned to introduce

Africans to a sound educational system that would embrace both literacy and practical skills.

It was a bold vision, but Cuffee was not to realise it. He returned to Freetown in 1815 with thirty-eight 'people of the despised race of Africa' but was forced to leave in a hurry when he discovered that company agents were planning to seize his ship. Three years later, he died of malaria picked up on the coast. His funeral orator laid out the beliefs that had driven his whole enterprise.

> Captain Cuffee was an advocate of African colonisation. He wished to see that part of our nation, which are despised and kept in a state of bondage and degradation in Christian countries, returning to the land of their ancestors, carrying with them the light of science and religion and diffusing it through those vast benighted regions. By this means, he hoped that our curse would be converted into a blessing, and Africa speedily brought to enjoy all the advantages of civilisation and Christianity.[15]

These beliefs would inspire future generations.

The Return to Africa – Liberia

Along the east coast of the United States, there was no summer in the year 1816. From Maine to Carolinas, crops failed, and people called the year 'eighteen hundred and froze to death'. Scientists would later discover that the conditions had been caused by the most powerful volcanic eruption in recorded history on the Pacific island of Tabora, but at the time, many interpreted them as a portent of the end of time. As preachers roamed the country, stirring up religious revival, all kinds of organisations were formed for the improvement of the lot of man – and among these was the American Colonization Society (ACS). It was in that year of famine that Elias Caldwell, clerk of the Supreme Court, called the first meeting of the ACS in Washington, DC. Both Caldwell and Secretary Ralph Gurley were convinced abolitionists, but for reasons of self-interest, their committees soon fell under the control of plantation owners.

Across both free and slave states, whites saw the free-black community as a terrifying threat to their security. Since plantation owners often chose to emancipate their children, many were light in colour, but even the most liberal-minded whites refused to look on them as equals. At the same time, free but poor ex-slaves placed a strain on charitable resources: 'granted that eminent American clergymen still denied that Negroes have souls, nobody could deny that they have stomachs'.[16] Planters, who lived constantly under the perceived threat of black rebellion, therefore became increasingly drawn to the cause of African colonisation.

Gurley identified two 'missionaries' to undertake the task of finding a suitable site for a new colony. Rev Samuel Mills had made his name as a preacher in the remote south-west, while his companion Ebenezer Burgess was a Professor of Mathematics and Natural Science. On arrival in Freetown in 1818, like Cuffee before them, they took advice from John Kilzell, and he recommended that they should negotiate for a site on Sherboro Island. Across most of Africa, land did not belong to the ruler but to all his people and – to complicate the issue – this included not only the living but also the dead and those yet to be born. For all their faults, slavers had never claimed to own the land on which their forts were built, and indeed, they paid rents that were interpreted as a token of submission. Sherboro chiefs became alarmed when they realised that these particular white men would only be content with outright purchase and they remained unimpressed by the promise that 'wise and good men' in America would bring knowledge and trade to their land. When negotiations broke down, the two Americans spent time touring villages, singing 'From Greenland's Icy Mountain' and collecting specimens of the island flora, before finally setting off for home. When Mills died on board ship, Burgess felt free to deliver the kind of report that could unlock congressional funds. Dispensing with the truth, he painted a picture of fertile land, with excellent trading prospects, where everything was ripe for colonisation and trade. The society would have been well advised to give attention instead to a report delivered by a naval officer who had travelled with the party. 'Should the Society finally succeed in getting the land I cannot flatter them with the enjoyment of peaceable possession without the protection of a military establishment, as they will always have diffi-culties to encounter with the natives (whose jealousies are easily excited) until they become sufficiently strong to bear down on all opposition.'[17]

Burgess did succeed in raising funds; less successful were the attempts to attract settlers. Free blacks, those who had supported the cause of repatriation when preached by their Paul Cuffee, were justifiably suspicious of a venture that was being enthusiastically promoted by their old masters. A party of eighty-six settlers, of whom just twenty-eight were adult males, led by an Episcopal clergyman and a black druggist, landed on Sherboro Island in 1820 – only to discover that the site which Kilzell had prepared for them was shut in by forest on all sides and had no fresh water. Both leaders and many colonists died within weeks; then to compound the disaster, a relief party managed to arrive in Freetown at its height of the great yellow fever epidemic.

The Americans did not give up. President Monroe had been steering a bill for the abolition of the US slave trade through congress, and with an American naval squadron patrolling the West African coast, the society entrusted the next round of negotiations to robust naval men – Squadron Surgeon Eli Ayres and Lt Robert Stockton. After selecting a site further down the coast, known to the Portuguese as Cape Mesurado, they arranged a meeting with local dignitary King Peter and all his chiefs. After Stockton had painted a bright future in which local people would grow rich trading yams and beeswax for tobacco, rum and sugar, and their children would learn to read and write in missionary schools, King Peter explained that Mesurado was sacred territory, and if any white man settled there, the king 'would die, and his women would cry aplenty'. Despite these reservations, Ayres was soon able to report home that every one of their objectives had been achieved.

> We have purchased a tract of country containing $1,000,000 worth of land, with the best harbour between Gibraltar and the Cape of Good Hope, and Island containing nine houses, and six others to be built; there are excellent springs of water near the site we have selected for the city; and at the pitch of the Cape, there is an excellent place for watering ships. All this we have purchased in fee simple for little more than was stipulated to be given for the annual rent of Bassa, and not amounting to more than $300.[18]

He did not bother to explain how these reservations had been overcome. Stockton finally had lost patience. Giving Ayers a pistol, with instructions to use it if necessary, he held his weapon at the King Peter's head while he put his mark on the treaty. By the lieutenant's interpretation, Peter had signed away all his people's ancestral lands, and from that time, colonists would claim sovereignty, not only over the narrow boundaries of the settlement, but over the whole hinterland inhabited by people who had taken no part in the negotiations.

After naming the new settlement Monrovia in the President's honour, the society set about recruiting emigrants. One tall middle-aged man stood out among the volunteers. Before gaining his freedom and being ordained as a Baptist minister, Lott Cary had been born a slave on a Virginia plantation, and he now explained to the congregation that he had received the call to be a missionary.

> I am about to leave you and expect to see your faces no more. I long to preach to the poor Africans the way of life and salvation. I do not know what may befall me, whether I may find a grave in the ocean or among savage men, or more savage wild beasts on the Coast of Africa; nor am I anxious what may become of me. I feel it my duty to go.[19]

Once he got there, he found the colonists and local Africans in a state of open warfare and was immediately called on to take part in digging defences and mounting cannon on the barricades. As in so many later colonial wars, sophisticated weapons outbalanced superiority of numbers, and when the fighting was over, just two settlers lay dead, against more than 100 Africans. With uneasy peace restored, Cary directed his vast energy at building up a flourishing Baptist Church in Monrovia, in running his trading house and serving as his people's political leader – even rising to the rank of acting governor. His missionary enterprise ended in 1828, when he was killed in an explosion while filling cartridges for a task force that was preparing to attack a local township.[20]

Other American societies had their eye on this part of Africa. In the wake of a slave revolt in neighbouring Virginia, the Maryland state legislature voted $20,000 a year to help its local colonisation society set up Maryland in Africa to accommodate the state's 'surplus' free black population. A site was chosen over 100 miles down the coast from Monrovia, Cape Palmas, home to the Grebo people, who had long provided sailors (Krumen) for the white men's ships. The treaty was another loosely worded document. Descriptions of the territory acquired were inexact, and it was never clear whether the Grebo had surrendered sovereignty over the land. Nevertheless, villages were flattened to provide the colony with room for expansion, and Africans were forced to adopt western behaviour and dress within the colony after settlers protested that they could not be expected to walk past naked savages on their way to church on Sunday.

Among other dangers, disease remained a deadly hazard for settlers.
Home committees, which operated on the assumption that people of
African descent must carry natural defences against African ailments,
were puzzled to receive reports of the deaths of African-American settlers
from both Monrovia and Cape Palmas. Twenty-four from the brig Doris
died within a month of arrival and, within a year, this total had risen
to forty-eight. The story of Francis Paxton was typical. Though she
implored her ten children to leave her behind in America, they refused
to emigrate without her, and though her spirits rose when she saw
friendly faces waiting on the quayside at Monrovia, her life ended
in desolation after eight family members rapidly died. Still the society
kept on promoting its cause:

> Colonisation must be written on the door-posts of every dwelling of
> free coloured people in our country. It may be ridiculed, the climate
> may be arrayed in all its mortality – the natives may be a subject of
> sport; the distance to the country may be magnified; the self denial
> to be made, be spread out in all its details.... All these things may
> be related over and over again, but the inscription must be on the
> door-post. African colonisation is our only security from social and
> political death.[21]

High mortality changed thinking within the Colonisation Society. The
idea that they could expect freed slaves from the New World to serve –
and survive – as missionaries in Africa was now exposed as unrealistic.
As white missionaries arrived in increasing numbers, a pattern of
mortality began to emerge; whatever their skin colour, emigrants from
the northern states were vulnerable to malaria, while those from the
south had a better chance of survival. The reason can now be understood;
malaria was then endemic in the West Indies and across large areas of the
southern states and – at high cost in infant mortality – this did provide
some measure of immunity to the adult population. White Methodist
clergyman and politician John Says, born and raised in the West Indies,
survived into old age, but he buried four New England – born children
in Liberia. It is estimated that some two-thirds of the sixty-one white
missionaries who arrived in Cape Palmas between 1836 and 1846 would
die there, and of those who survived, a disproportionate number had
been raised in the south. Facing this disparity, the American Board and
other northern-based societies became uncomfortable with the idea that

anybody from a slave-owning family could be allowed to preach in
Africa. The problem would not be resolved until mainstream missionary
societies split into separate northern and southern bodies in the bitter
aftermath of the American Civil War.

If disease was one obstacle to missionary work, commerce proved
to be another. Paul Cuffee had already discovered that, in practise,
'legitimate trade' favoured those who started with the largest resources.
The colonists planned to monopolise all coastal business, buying African
primary products from the interior and selling them on to the ships at the
largest possible profit. Since American companies would not risk their
own staff in such dangerous postings, settlers could set themselves up as
exclusive agents for the import of manufactured goods and any attempt
by Africans to trade directly with the white men's ships was likely to
provoke a punitive raid by the colonists. One American officer reported
that, whenever the navy became involved in the colony's affairs, it
generally turned out that the local Africans were victims rather than
aggressors. An American Board worker went so far as to suggest that
home supporters were contributing to the overthrow of the African
people by the very act of contributing money to missionary societies.
'If the Dutch and English settlers have injured the Kaffres and
Hottentots, then you must expect the American colonists to carry
on the work of oppression here as soon as their numerical strength
would warrant with two-fold fury.'[22]

Facing evidence of escalating violence, anti-slavery activists separated
themselves from the colonial cause. After reading the society's journal,
anti-slavery activist William Lloyd Garrison concluded that the whole
enterprise had been conceived in the blood of the poor natives.

The Episcopal Church was also shaken by racial conflict. At a time
when the Liberian president and virtually all the members of his
government were black, adherents pressed that their bishop at Cape
Palmas should be of the same colour. This was a step too far for home
supporters, and in 1851, preferment was bestowed on the racist son
of a slave-owning Virginian family.[23] Bishop John Payne offered cash
for boys and dowries for girls as incentives to fill mission schools. Once
inside, students were dressed in western clothes, named after mission
benefactors and taught a curriculum of 'grammar, geography, arithmetic
and the elements of astronomy'. At the end of their course, a favoured
few found employment in the mission compound, while virtually all the
rest abandoned Christian ways.[24] Payne's colleague Colden Hoffman

arrived on the coast with substantial private means, acquired as a New York businessman. During his seventeen years at Cape Palmas, he funded the construction of a church, an orphan asylum, a home for the blind and a hospital – all of which were open free to colonists, local Africans and seamen – and even in a community much given to backbiting, nobody had a bad word for the mission's 'beloved Barnabas'. Recognising that Payne's system had produced no lasting results, he turned his Hoffman Station into a community of whole families. But this too had unforeseen consequences. Shut off from the outside world, his converts grew increasingly isolated from both colonists and Grebos – in their words, they became bats, who did not know whether they were beasts or birds. In the end, both Payne and Hoffman failed to understand that, however they approached the task of conversion, their efforts could only appear to Africans as an integral part of the larger colonial oppression.

Others took up the challenge. In 1859, Hoffman and mission Schoolmistress Mary Bell visited Basel missionaries at Akropong on the Gold Coast, where she met her future husband, the German Lutheran, Johann Gottleib Auer. When it became clear that his young New England wife would never settle in what she experienced as a suffocating pietist environment, Auer applied to Payne for a position in Liberia, and after being re-ordained into Episcopal orders, he took up work as controller of mission schools there. Quickly mastering the Grebo language, he discovered that pupils could repeat long passages of the New Testament in English parrot-fashion, without understanding even such a simple word as 'father' and that Payne's translations of the liturgy, the Bible and schoolbooks – which not a single white colleague had ever been able to read – were riddled with mistakes. In the post-bellum division of mission fields, Liberia was allocated to the south, and now more than ever, the home committee would not countenance the idea of appointing a black bishop. But at the time when Payne retired in 1869, every other white priest either had been lost to malaria or had returned home, leaving the committee with no other choice but Auer. Now bereaved of his wife Mary, the new bishop energetically set about a programme of radical reform. First, he closed down all Payne's boarding institutions, replacing them with village schools, where converts could keep on living within their families and communities; then, he set about advising tribal people on how to increase the production of coffee and cotton and sell their products direct into overseas markets. A clash with the colonists was inevitable. Just a year after Auer died, his mission graduates led an uprising against the Cape Palmas settlers, who cared nothing for Auer's reforms. Had Bishop Auer still been alive, they angrily declared, he would surely have been hanged as a traitor.

A Failed Strategy

One attempt to successfully establish missionaries in West Africa came directly out of an incident reported sensationally in the American press. Around 1836, a group of Africans from Mende country were purchased in Havana by an American plantation owner. While travelling north in the Spanish vessel *Amistad*, they had managed to break free from their shackles, kill the captain and cook, and seize the ship. When these 'mutineers' finally landed on American soil, New England abolitionists formed a committee to argue the case that they should be freed on the grounds that their original capture had been illegal. Newspapers followed proceedings as the case went through the legal system, up to the Supreme Court. When it finally declared them free, the Africans wanted only to return home as quickly as possible, but their humanitarian patrons had other plans. After reforming the committee as the African Missionary Association (AMA), their benefactors announced that they would be turned into missionaries, who would establish the long-planned chain of stations into the heart of Africa. After being subjected to an intensive course of religious indoctrination and missionary training, the *Amistad* survivors were dressed in modest puritan clothing and sent out to make their testimony at endless fund-raising meetings. In Broadway Tabernacle, New York, they were exhibited at fifty cents a look; elsewhere, mothers gathered up their children and promised to contribute if the organisers would only take the 'cannibals' away. Meanwhile, the committee was recruiting experienced white and African-American staff to lead their new missionary operation. When the party of thirty-five, mostly male, freed slaves finally landed at Freetown in August 1839, the expedition leaders followed the Nova Scotian model and lined up their charges to sing 'From Greenland's Icy Mountain'. But this would prove to be the shortest-lived missionary enterprise in recorded history; even before the first verse was finished, the 'Merica men' were ripping off their shirts to expose their Mende tribal markings and plunging into the crowd. Through the evening, the Americans tried to shut out the hated sound of drumming and dancing that rose from the town as their charges celebrated the return home. Just one girl, who was adjudged to have 'remained faithful', was sent back to America for further training. It was yet another failure.

With the 'Merica men' gone, the AMA started to recruit in the American Midwest, where pioneers were proving their toughness. Some volunteers were young couples; others single white women who planned to work as teachers and evangelists – a few were freed slaves. After settling beyond the colonial frontier, wives built houses and planted crops alongside their menfolk. Reared in virgin territory at a time when great cities were rising from nothing on the North American plain, these pioneers saw no reason why the same could not happen in Africa. Their leader George Thompson imported a new brand of Protestantism, which combined religion with a passionate adherence to the teetotal cause. On his way through Freetown, he was horrified to discover that even the clergy had a relaxed attitude to alcohol. He recalled the evening when he was entertained at the Baptist minister's table alongside the colonial governor, 'Brother P called the boy to bring bottles and glasses. The Governor said, "I will take a little if Mr Thompson will excuse me." I answered, "You must take it on your own responsibility. I have no excuse for you."'

Thompson proclaimed an uncompromising message: 'No strong drink! No coffee! No tea! No tobacco! Oh! only WATER!' He assured workers that 'pure, cold water, rightly administered' was more effective against the most violent attack of fever than quinine and 'the whole list of medicines'.[25] In the villages, his staff used 'Colossal Drawings of the Human Stomach' to demonstrate the damage inflicted by drink on the inner organs and preached an apocalyptic message with revivalist fervour.

> On the 19th March, as Bro. Condit had been shut out of Barmah, he went in his boat to a town beyond and preached. The king and his people gave him a very warm reception, listened eagerly; some weeping; and they had a glorious meeting. Bro. C. felt God was there, and that a lasting impression was made. They freely gave up and stripped themselves of their charms and ornaments, and broke down their idol house on the spot, saying 'We will have no more to do with such things. The Gospel has come to us and we must now obey it.'[26]

But such emotional responses (even if accurately reported) always proved ephemeral and the high investment in both money and human life brought meagre return. The task of converting Africa to Christianity was proving more difficult than had been foreseen by the British, Germans and American Protestants in the more optimistic early years.

Half a century after Granville Sharp's pioneers had landed on the west coast of Africa, it had become very clear that the whole experiment of converting Africa through colonies of freed slaves had failed. White churchmen could argue that the fault lay with unreliable and uncommitted settlers, but in reality, the attempt to combine colonisation with mission work had exposed irreconcilable conflicts of interest with indigenous people. At the same time, white missionaries not only suffered unacceptable levels of mortality but also remained deeply at odds with local society. Only the Americans had escaped the colonial enclaves – and then with little success; imprisoned within formal dress, avoiding physical exertion and often carried around the countryside in chairs by black porters, most white missionaries seemed like alien creatures to those Africans that they had sailed out to convert. In 1841, the same Henry Venn the younger who had played with Macaulay's children in the Clapham vicarage became secretary of the CMS. With so little progress achieved, it seemed clear to him that the whole method of operation needed to be re-examined. Venn was not the only, or even the first, strategist to reach the conclusion that missionaries from overseas should assume the role of auxiliary to native Africans who had been born and educated in their homeland. He did, however, have the advantage over others in that the potential frontline recruits were already living in the re-captive villages of Freetown. Venn nursed particularly high hopes for Fourah Bay graduate Samuel Ajayi Crowther. Accepting the risks inherent in bringing Africans to unhealthy London, he invited Crowther to London to study at the CMS College in Islington and meet home supporters.

During those years when Crowther was coming to maturity, two men of mixed race – one born in England and the other in Africa – were, however, already making a significant impact in Fanti country, behind the slaving epicentre of Cape Coast Castle.

Chapter 3
Knowing One's Place as a Negro

The Gold Coast

The Methodists

When William Wilberforce retired from politics in 1823, leadership
of the parliamentary anti-slavery movement passed to Thomas Fowell
Buxton; ten years later he succeeded in steering a bill through parliament,
which abolished slavery throughout British possessions. Under his
leadership, humanitarians of all Protestant denominations organised
themselves into a coherent lobby, identified by the name of Exeter Hall
in London's Strand, where like-minded bodies held their annual
meetings. To add to the humanitarians' frustration, the export of slaves
from West Africa had flourished – even grown – since 1807, and Buxton's
1839 work *The Slave Trade and Its Remedy* expanded on the thesis
that slave trading would never be finally rooted out until Christianity,
legitimate trade and civilisation advanced together into the interior.

As Buxton was addressing a Methodist meeting, he told a story
designed to strike at the hearts of his audience. When Thomas Thompson
had returned home from Cape Coast some seventy years earlier, he
had handed the care of a small group of converts from the mixed race
community around the castle walls over to his ordained African assistant
Philip Quarque. At the end of a long life, Quarque in turn passed the same
group's successors over to schoolmaster Joseph Smith. When Governor
McCarthy discovered that a later generation of young men were still
meeting for Bible study, he arranged for the Society for the Promotion of
Christian Knowledge (SPCK), the publishing arm of the Anglican Church,
to send them some books. Taking their name from the imprint, they now
named themselves the Gold Coast Society for the Promotion of Christian
Knowledge. Using this faithful band as his parable, Buxton delivered
a summons: 'Remember the wrongs of Africa; and remember that the
only compensation you can offer is religious instruction.… I conclude
by saying again, one hundred missionaries, if you please! I cannot
be content with one less than a hundred from this Society.'[1]

Just one – James Dunwell – responded to the call. On landing at Cape
Coast on New Year's Day 1835, this 'godly though not overgifted youth'

received the warmest possible welcome; Africans shook him by the hand, and even the European traders were friendly. Most movingly – he received a formal letter of welcome, signed by thirteen members of the Gold Coast SPCK. Surrounded by goodwill, Dunwell felt inadequate to the task – 'the people are thirsting for the word of life' he wrote, 'and I am dry'. Within just a few months he was dead.

More Methodists arrived in the following year – first the Wrigleys and then the Harrops. One by one they died; first Mrs Wrigley, then both the Harrops. Wrigley's cry of dereliction puts flesh onto bald mortality statistics.

> With feelings of unutterable sorrow I have to announce the heart-rendering fact that Mr and Mrs Harrop and my beloved partner are no more. O may God teach me the resignation to that which my human reason would say is utterly unaccountable and inexplicably mysterious, to acknowledge thine hand; to revere thy sovereign will, and to submit to thy righteous dispensation. Such a state confounds all my reasonings and levels me with the dust …
>
> This was too much for me or my mind or my soul to bear – my mind already enfeebled by loss of rest was completely prostrated – I could no longer control myself and I was reduced to a state of complete frenzy for the space of half an hour, while all around me were bathed in tears.[2]

Before he too followed his wife and friends to the grave, Wrigley advised his society that only married men should be appointed missionary and that they must travel with their wives. While his stated reason was that the mission needed women to work as teachers, it is likely that he feared single men would fall to the temptations of all too visible African flesh.

Even after all the expatriates had been struck down by malaria, Methodist churches and schools continued to flourish under African leadership. Elizabeth Waldron, daughter of an African woman and an Irish merchant, was primarily responsible for building a schooling system, and a generation later, it would be said that she had trained every influential man and woman on the coast. Still, nobody doubted that the young Christian community needed a superintendent to harness this extraordinary energy. Son of an African father and English mother, Thomas Birch Freeman was born into deep poverty in a village near

Winchester, and despite having little formal schooling, he grew up to
be fluently, if barely legibly, literate – though he would always remain
out of his depth when confronted with figures. Freeman volunteered
for work on the Gold Coast in the belief that he might have inherited
some immunity against the dreaded African diseases from his father;
to be considered for the job under Wrigley's rules, he proposed to,
and was accepted by, his employer's housekeeper Elizabeth Boot.

Within weeks of their arrival on the Gold Coast (modern Ghana),
Elizabeth was nursing her husband through malaria, until she too fell ill
and died. Her husband, however, survived and remained on the Gold
Coast until he died in 1890, at the age of eighty. Although Thomas
Freeman's reputation at home would rest on accounts of travels to strange
and disturbing places, his success in the field came from a rare ability to
bring out the talents of people around him. After he had ordained SPCK
member William DeGraft, the two men travelled tirelessly – sometimes
separately and sometimes together. They reached Lagos and Abeokuta
before the Anglicans did, and Porto Novo and Dahomey before the
Catholics, wherever possible leaving behind Methodist cells, staffed
by Fanti Christians. Freeman was not a linguist, and throughout his long
life he never succeeded in preaching a sermon in any African language.
But on that multi-lingual coast, the mission's educational effort was not
directed towards first-language literacy but to producing the English-
speaking commercial clerks who were so much in demand.

Just 100 miles inland from Cape Coast was Kumasi, capital of the
slaving confederacy of Ashanti. A decade earlier a small British force
under Sir Charles McCarthy had been destroyed by Ashanti warriors,
and rumour had it that the governor's skull still hung from Ashantehene
Kwaku Dua's golden stool. Now Freeman was excited to receive a report
that Methodist trader and SPCK member James Hayford had so far won
the ruler's confidence that he had been allowed to conduct a Christian
service within the royal palace. He set off for Kumasi, and before long
Kwaku Dua received news that a strange fetish man was approaching his
capital. It was not an auspicious time, however. Even as Freeman waited
in a neighbouring village for permission to enter Kumasi, the sister of
a local chief died, prompting ritual blood-letting, which profoundly
shocked the missionary: 'As I walked out early in the morning, I saw the
mangled corpse of a poor female slave, who had been beheaded during
the night, lying in the public street.... In the course of the day I saw
groups of the natives dancing around this victim of superstitious cruelty,

with numerous frantic gestures, and who seemed to be in the very zenith of their happiness.'3

The young Methodist found it hard to reconcile this experience with the welcome and gifts that were poured on him when he finally arrived in Kumasi. He could only conclude that, while the common folk wanted the ritual killing to stop, their rulers were still sunk deep in pagan superstition.

As Freeman's narrative circulated in Britain, he, DeGraft and two young Ashanti princes were brought to Britain to promote the opening of an exciting Ashanti venture. In Methodist churches across England, the two coloured ministers performed a powerful double-act, with DeGraft's spell-binding sermons, in particular, providing unequivocal proof of how the gospel could even transform a benighted African savage. When the two princes received an audience with Queen Victoria, they were reminded of their duty to carry the benefits of civilisation back to their homeland. Importantly, the money flowed in. A white missionary did spend some time in Kumasi, but Freeman found it impossible to keep the station staffed, and in the end, his Methodists left no impression on Ashanti society.

Still, Freeman enjoyed other successes. He was always at ease with Africans, be they the educated elite on the coast or tribal people of the interior, and this sense of affinity grew stronger when he married an African woman and began to raise an African family. He remained a popular figure with the white community, and he brought black and white together in lively (and well-lubricated) parties.4 Methodist home churches were at that time becoming aligned with the temperance cause, and an account of one such event caused no little alarm, which was heightened when a passing Presbyterian published memoirs that described how he had been served at this superintendent's table by a young man and a girl, 'each in a state of semi-nudity', having on 'only the waist cloth, being from the waist upwards and from the knee downwards naked, and that in the presence of ladies'.5 For his part, Freeman believed that the home committee's only useful role was to raise the funds needed to support advances in the field. It was his habit, in fact, to assume commitments without thought for the financial implications. Debt was the result. Called home to repeat his fund-raising operations, he proved unsuccessful, and he resigned in 1857 to take up the government post of civil commander of Accra – from which he was dismissed two years later with his accounts in impenetrable confusion.

Local preacher, smallholder and amateur botanist, Thomas Birch Freeman became a legendary figure on the coast. Furthermore, his colleague DeGraft's family would provide leaders for both the British colony and independent Ghana. The Gold Coast Methodist Church's unique tradition of non-white leadership was also maintained as Freeman's title of superintendent passed to his Jamaican assistant, Henry Wharton.

The Pietists

Four young Basel missionaries received a frosty welcome when they presented their credentials to the commandant of the Danish trading fort of Christiansborg Castle in 1827. 'The Basel Mission takes servants, shoemakers, clerks and God knows what sort of people into their service' he declared. 'In the course of a few years, these peoples' poor heads are crammed with the crudest orthodoxy. Lacking psychology, manners and even the most simple erudition, they are sent out to the Coast, where they are more likely to turn Christians into pagans than pagans into Christians.'[6]

After suffering the familiar litany of casualties from malaria, sole survivor Danish pietist Andreas Riis finally managed to establish a station at Akropong, some 30 miles inland. Here he 'slept on palm branches and lived on pepper soup, snails and fish from which the worms crept',[7] before returning home after twelve years to report the death of eight colleagues, without the compensation of a single convert. After his return to Africa, the operation was reinforced by a party of Moravians from Jamaica, but Riis quarrelled endlessly with both black and white colleagues and he was finally dismissed on the accusation of buying a plantation, complete with slaves, and trading in powder and muskets on his own account.

As local people refused to leave their tribal communities to settle on mission land, the Basel pietists filled their stations with ransomed debtors, who accepted Swiss money to pay off creditors – all of whom were perceived, both by the wider community and by themselves, as slaves of the mission. After serving their time, a few stayed on as teachers, catechists, workers and Christian wives, but most left as soon as their ransom or debts were paid off. Some West Indians took up the option of returning home when their contract had expired. Others remained to make a memorable contribution to the local economy. The Rochesters, husband and wife, are given credit for the introduction of the cocoyam and the earliest manufacture of groundnut oil in West Africa. Working alongside the German artisan Joseph Mohi, the Jamaicans also hugely expanded the range of African farming – introducing orange and mango trees, bananas, yams, beans, groundnuts, coffee, tobacco, cotton, sugar cane and breadfruit. In the religious field, second-generation Jamaican Nicholas 'Nico' Clerk survived a gruelling education in Germany to be ordained as a Lutheran clergyman.

Two sharply contrasting ideologies can be identified within the German tradition and both had their period of dominance in the Basel mission. On the one side were those who stressed stereotypical Teutonic virtues of 'discipline, authority and subordination'; on the other were those who drew inspiration from the writings of Goethe's friend and collaborator Johann Herder, a romantic philosopher who had likened society to an organism bound together by a common language, which he described as the 'soul of the *volk*'. 'Climate, water and air, food and drink, they all affect language.... Viewed in this way, language is indeed a magnificent treasure store, a collection of thought and activities of the mind of the most diverse nature.'[8] While the word *volk* would later gather sinister overtones, Herder himself rejected any suggestion that his philosophy could justify slavery, colonialism and trading exploitation.

Under the influence of both Johann Herder and the English Hannah Kilham, Basel seminarians now concluded that Africans could only be approached through their own languages. S.G. Christaller and Johannes Zimmermann became fluent in the related languages of, respectively, Twi and Ga. While Christaller set about collecting regional stories and proverbs that would influence later works of anthropology, Zimmerman married a divorced lady from the Jamaican community and dreamed of populating the land with Germano-Africans, who would be equipped with the best characteristics of both races. As the two men penetrated deeper into traditional life, they became increasingly convinced that their fellow missionaries should not try to draw individuals out of traditional society but should instead attempt to transform whole communities. Arguing that African society should be judged by its own standards, Zimmerman pointed out that domestic slavery could stand comparison with European treatment of the old and infirm.

There are absolutely no 'free' and lonely, abandoned persons in Africa. The structure of the clans and domestic slavery prevents old people, widows, orphans, criminals, neglected children and lazy rascals from forming a proletariat. Everybody belongs to somebody.[9]

However, both men faced the accusation that, in their anxiety to accommodate traditional society, they were prepared to condone sinful behaviour, and when they started accepting polygamists into church membership, the whole Basel Mission acquired a lasting reputation for being lax on church discipline.

Inevitably, there was a backlash. The appointment of Joseph Josenhans as mission inspector in 1849 signalled the authoritarian party's return into the ascendancy. As the inspector exercised absolute rule over the whole mission, so, he declared, every pastor had a duty to do the same within his sphere of influence. In an attempt to impose order on the ground, Josenhans introduced a dedicated postal service between stations and imported master craftsmen from Germany to open a wide range of workshops. Each station now had its own trading arm to manage a two-way business in primary products and German manufactured goods. In time, Johansen's initiatives began to unsettle the whole balance of trade and society in the region. While Methodist businessmen complained that the Germans were distorting competition by using the unpaid labour of debtors and ex-slaves, local chiefs protested that the Basel stations were undermining traditional society. Closed off behind defensive walls and offering refuge to all who were at odds with their rulers, the pietists were building miniature European colonies, planted deep within the host communities.

The Jamaicans – and the Baptists in Nigeria and Cameroon

Across the Atlantic in Jamaica, frightened planters barricaded themselves inside their homes as the clock approached midnight on 1 August 1838. But as the midnight hour of freedom for slaves approached, their workers were packed into their churches. Presbyterian carpenter Andrew Chisholm, teacher Edward Miller and slave boy George looked up at Scottish *dominee* Hope Wadell. Black Methodist minister Henry Wharton waited with his congregation, while in the nearby Baptist Church, printer Joseph Merrick sat with his family and Alexander Fuller's children clung to their mother's knee. Never had there been such anticipation as the people counted down the minutes. When the clock struck midnight they hugged one another and cried with joy. Freedom was powerful medicine and West Africa was in their thoughts.

The Baptists, in particular, lost no time in addressing the issue of how they might take the faith that they had discovered as slaves back to their homeland as free people. Just a year later, Thomas Keith sailed for Africa, carrying nothing but a letter of introduction from his minister; a rumour would later come back that he reached his destination, but nothing more was heard of him. Then James Keats sailed for Sierra Leone, and he was last seen boarding ship for the Congo. Across the island, Baptist congregations started collecting money to mount a coordinated enterprise and even those with no cash donated a week's labour to the cause.

The very idea that freed black slaves might set themselves up as missionaries outraged many English Baptists, but they finally became reconciled to the project – on the condition that it be under white leadership. So, in 1844, newly ordained admiralty draughtsman Alfred Saker joined a party of forty-two Jamaicans on the Spanish island of Fernando Po. While Saker remained on the Spanish island, Merrick set up a mainland station in one of the wettest places on earth, beneath Mount Cameroon, where he set about committing the Isubu language to writing, translating hymns and Bible passages and printing his work on a press that he had brought from the new world. Once again, African inheritance provided no immunity from African diseases, as Merrick and his children died. When the Spanish announced that all the Baptists must leave Fernando Po, Saker set up his headquarters in Merrick's abandoned station, which he renamed Victoria, and planned to turn it into a flourishing port that would monopolise the regional trade. He reasoned that, once this was achieved, Victoria, like Lagos, would be claimed as a British crown colony, and he would be confirmed as its consul.

But West Indian Baptists, who had travelled out with such high hopes, quickly came to detest their abrasive leader. Those who had the means returned to their Caribbean Island, while others watched helplessly as, pursuing his ambition of personal advancement, Saker extinguished their dream of a Christian mission run by blacks for blacks. In 1859, white missionary Alexander Innes published an indictment of the way that his superior had set about achieving his objectives.

When I arrived out at the Cameroons, instead of meeting with a Christian Mission and a Christian Missionary, as I had fondly anticipated, I was introduced to something more like a Treadmill ... (Mr Saker) I found to be a complete Tyrant. Instead of devoting himself to missionary work he was engaged in keeping a store, by which he monopolised the legitimate trade on the credit of the Baptist Missionary Society.

He attached a letter signed by sixteen West Indian residents:

> Dear Fathers, we wish you to know that Mr Saker has been
> persecuting us very much for a long time; he does not act like a
> father and a friend to us poor Africans … but he treats us with great
> cruelty – he gets into great passions with us … and makes use of
> very bad language to us, calling us names, such as – 'damn you, you
> black brutes', and 'black beasts' and 'devils', and other things which
> we do not like to write.[10]

Innes' revelations provoked a major dispute within the home Union,
and many leading ministers and lay people publicly withdrew support
from their own society. Meanwhile, Saker's advocates insisted that his
detractors were out of touch with the realities of African life. When he
was called home to defend his actions, Saker defied his critics by refusing
to answer any charges. Bolstered by the unwavering support of mission
secretary Alfred Baynes, he returned to Victoria, where he retained
his position as mission superintendent until he retired in 1876, after
thirty-two years on the coast.

The Scots

At the time of emancipation in Jamaica, Scottish moderator Hope
Wadell circulated copies of Buxton's influential book around all his
churches, and soon the same excitement for an African mission was
running in the Presbyterian community. Once again, however, the
enthusiasts received only a stinging rebuke from the home kirk. The
very proposal was 'premature, displaying more zeal than judgement,
not accordant with the state of dependence in which our Jamaica church
stood, both for means and missionaries, and as highly presumptuous,
after the failure of vastly greater efforts by others than we could possibly
put forth'.[11]

But when the islanders refused to let the matter rest, the new and
comparatively small United Presbyterians agreed to adopt the Jamaica
Africa Mission as its first overseas venture. And so, in January 1846,
Hope and Agnes Waddell set out from Liverpool with 'Mr Samuel Edgerly,
printer and catechist … with his wife; Andrew Chisholm, carpenter,
a brown man; Edward Miller, teacher, a Negro of African descent; and the
ex-slave boy George'. In Africa, the party set up a base among the Efik
people who lived on the waterways, known as the Oil Rivers, that formed

the mouth of the Cross River. In slaving days, ships from Liverpool had anchored in these hot, damp inlets, dismantled their superstructure and laid up the vessels until the hold was full of slaves. Although these 'supercargoes' had long ceased trading in slaves, demand for soap in grimy industrial cities had created a strong demand for palm oil. While the cargo had changed, the pattern of trade remained the same.

The need for missionaries certainly appeared great. The settlement of Calabar was made up of a group of trading settlements, dominated by the palm-oil traders – known as kings – 'Eyamba V of Duke Town' and 'Eyo Nsa II of Creek Town'. Eyamba lived in a famous iron palace, which had been imported from Liverpool in prefabricated form. At one time, Eyo had served as a deckhand on a slaving ship; now he owned 400 canoes, a coach and horses and thousands of slaves. But the royal titles were misleading; real power lay with the Ekpe 'leopard society', whose messengers travelled silently through the dark forest. To outside eyes it appeared a strange and evil world. Religion focused on shrines and watercourses, and the sound of animals crying in the dark indicated that witches were abroad, carrying evil and death. Any woman who bore twins was thought to have consorted with an evil spirit; since nobody could tell which was the spirit baby, both were killed and the mother was driven into the bush. It was also said that cannibal practices still flourished further upriver. When home supporters read riveting accounts, they responded by sending cash donations (if they were affluent enough) or 'decent clothes' (if they were poorer) for the civilising of Calabar. As a gesture of belief in a better future, Hope Waddell built his headquarters on the spot where the bodies of slaves and twin babies had been exposed to the vultures, and Chisholm and Miller were given the gruesome task of supervising the clearing of human remains before building work could begin. Wives and slaves accompanied people of rank into the next world. Although, here as elsewhere, missionaries may have exaggerated some tales of human suffering for home consumption, the days after Eyamba's death do seem to have been very bloody.

> Every night the work of death went on in the river, and the screams of the victims were heard both in the ships and the mission-house. Some were sent out, bound in canoes and deliberately drowned. Others returning from distant markets, chanting their paddle song and glad to get home, but ignorant of what had taken place, were waylaid, knocked on the head and tumbled into the river. Corpses and trunks were daily seen floating down and up with the tide.[12]

In all too many mission settings, wives and single women assumed no more than a mute, supportive role, but the Scottish ladies of Calabar quickly assumed roles of responsibility. The founder's wife Agnes Waddel wrote an account of how the tiny Euphemia Miller came out with her sister as a single woman and then, after being quickly widowed, made her name as the indestructible Mammy Sutherland. After teaching a school of eighty children through the morning, she would spend the afternoon visiting within the community, advising women on their children's health and giving smallpox vaccinations.[13] Even hard-boiled supercargoes, who disliked missionaries on principle, found her irresistible. Later in the century, independent-minded, and often eccentric, flame-haired Dundee mill girl Mary Slessor would work first in Calabar and then, single-handed, on an upriver station, ultimately becoming a missionary icon and sharing with David Livingstone the posthumous honour of having her portrait on a UK bank note.

Such women remained exceptions. While West Indians on the Oil Rivers certainly worked more comfortably alongside their Scottish colleagues than the Baptists did with Alfred Saker, none emerges from the record as a character to match the Scottish women, and the enterprise remained heavily dependant on the steady flow of Scottish money and personnel until well into the twentieth century. Ultimately, the problem of how a 'black to black' mission could be made to function had not been solved in either Victoria or Calabar.

The Anglicans
In his book *The Slave Trade and Its Remedy*, Thomas Fowell Buxton developed the argument passed down from the Philadelphia Quakers, Olaudah Equiano and the Clapham Sect, that civilisation and commerce must advance hand in hand into the 'dark places' of Africa. Calling in support from the Exeter Hall lobby, Buxton won government backing for a major expedition that was to bring the benefits of western civilisation by way of the river Niger.

Scientists and agriculturalists were among the 145 whites who sailed up the river in 1841, alongside commercial and government agents. They were armed with Hannah Kilham's phrase book of African languages as well as supplies of quinine to treat those who fell ill with fever. Henry Venn sent Basel linguist Frederick Schön and Fourah Bay graduate Samuel Crowther to take notes on suitable sites for CMS stations and, if possible, set up a self-governing black church.

When they stopped at a slave market, Schön addressed the people in faltering Hausa. 'I informed them, that the chief design of our expedition was to put an end to trade in human flesh and blood; and expatiated on the sinfulness of the practice, it being against the laws of God and the laws of the most enlightened kingdoms of the world, and productive of innumerable evils among themselves.'[14]

Although listeners were unclear why these foreigners had suddenly decided that slavery was evil, they did promise that the black men would surely stop selling their people provided that other white men would only stop buying. Like other African ventures, the expedition seemed to have made a promising start. Despite the high hopes, Buxton's venture quickly turned out to be a costly failure. By the time the crippled ships limped back into the delta, forty-eight Europeans had died, trading results were meagre and the Niger was closed behind it to whites for the next fifteen years. As a result, Buxton's credibility at home was fatally undermined, and Exeter Hall became identified with those 'telescopic philanthropists', like Charles Dickens's Mrs Jelleby, who expended their energies on savages, while neglecting more pressing needs of their people.

Meanwhile, re-captives from the Freetown villages had been finding their way back to their ancestral homes in the region. The largest distinct group were Yoruba-speaking Egba people from the south-west of modern Nigeria, who had long been a prime target of slaving raids by more powerful neighbours. In 1830, the Alake Sodeke, had gathered his people into a settlement that he named Abeokuta (refuge among the rocks). About a decade later, black Freetown traders recognised Badgary as the place where their personal *via dolorosa* out of Yoruba country had reached the sea and they soon returned to Freetown with heart-warming tales of homecoming. Bolder spirits uprooted their families to make Abeokuta their permanent home. They travelled as Christians, carrying Bibles and hymn-books, and once their community had built up to about 2,000, they petitioned the CMS to send them a resident missionary.

Home committee members remembered the long-held ambition to build a chain of stations that would stretch from the Atlantic Ocean to the interior, and with the Niger now closed to foreigners, it made sense to lay out the path across Yoruba country. It was agreed therefore that the headquarters would be established on the coast, at Badgary, and that stations would first be planted at Abeokuta and Ibadan – with more to follow, as far as the town of Lokoja, where the Benue tributary joined the Niger. According to mission strategy, future generations of missionaries would follow the main river into Hausa country and the northern grasslands or the Benue into unexplored pagan country of the region that would become known as the Middle Belt. Young, ambitious Henry Townsend was despatched on a fact-finding visit to Abeokuta and returned with an encouraging report that Sodeke had promised to supply the CMS with both ample land for its stations and more children than it would be able to teach.

Townsend was given charge of a strong party. Leaving Württemberger C.A. Gollmer in charge of the base camp at Badgary, he and Crowther were to travel to Abeokuta, with a party of Sierra Leonians – Mr Marsh, a catechist; Mr Phillips, a schoolmaster; Mr Willoughby, an interpreter; four carpenters; three labourers; and two servants. Crowther, Marsh and Willoughby also had their families with them. At Badgary, they received the unwelcome news that Sodoke had died and his son was less enthusiastic about welcoming missionaries, but after months of delay, the party did set off in 1843, and Townsend and Crowther set up separate stations in different parts of the Abeokuta. Home supporters were moved to read how Crowther joyfully discovered his aged mother and received her as the mission's first convert. They were later joined in Abeokuta by independent American Baptist missionary and old Indian fighter Thomas J. Bowen. Oblivious to the sensitivities of freed slaves who travelled with him, Bowen made no secret of how he detested the 'Guinea niggers … the hateful Popoes, the shrewd but thievish Fantees and others like them', who were surely close relations of the American slave population.[15] Some time earlier, Bowen had come upon a magazine article by DeGraft about the conversion of one Old Simeon in the northern Yoruba town of Igboho, which described the tall, thin-nosed and thin-lipped Fulani, who had reached that area in Uthman dan Fodio's *jihad*. Before setting eyes on a single Fulani, Bowen convinced himself that these people were descended from superior racial stock; once converted to Christianity, they would surely become missionaries to the rest of Africa. Working on this assumption, he, like others before him, planned for an ambitious chain of stations that would cross the grasslands to Lake Chad, the Nile and even distant Ethiopia.[16]

The three missionaries were in Abeokuta in 1851 when news arrived that the Dahomey army was approaching the city walls – with the king's ferocious Amazon warriors in the lead. As the Sierra Leonians and converts hurriedly formed a Christian brigade, Townsend demonstrated on how a bullet mould could be made out of clay, and the battle-hardened Indian fighter organised defences on the wall. The united effort was successful, and after the enemy had finally been beaten off, some townspeople were inclined to attribute their deliverance to the good offices of the white men's God.

Other missionaries might have been content to spend their lives saving souls behind the walls of a mission compound, but Townsend flourished in the wider political arena. For more than ten years he served as the Alake's secretary, and it was even rumoured that he had been inducted into the Yoruba freemasonry. He produced a newspaper in which Sierra Leonian merchants displayed the prices of a growing range of imported products available in their stores.[17] Townsend had now become used to getting his way and, after Bowen had finally left for Igboho, he was alarmed to discover that sermons against polygamy were being undermined by a copy of *The Book of Mormon* that circulated beyond his grasp. 'Ere long', he warned, 'we shall have another class of men to deal with; Free Blacks from America, full of bitterness against all white men',[18] and he did manage to frustrate a Baptist project to plant a freed-slave colony in Egba country. In home mission circles, it was Townsend's Abeokuta that now stood as harbinger for the future conversion of Africa, and when Townsend's influence was at its zenith in the mid-1860s, the British agent reported that he had 'been so long in the habit of directing the affairs of Abeokuta that he would not brook any interference'.[19] Back on the coast, Gollmer had never settled in Badgary. Apart from finding the spiritual soil exceptionally stony, the town was losing out to Lagos as the focus of coastal trade, and he determined that the mission headquarters must move to the more dynamic city. Capitalising on a dispute for the control of Lagos between rival slave traders Kosoko and Akitoye, he managed to convince Henry Venn that the CMS should take Akitoye's side. In a determined effort to influence government policy, Crowther was summoned to England, where he was granted an audience at Windsor Castle. He would later describe how he became so involved in demonstrating the mission's great strategy to Prince Albert on a large map that he hardly noticed a small woman enter the room and join the discussion. If he did not notice her, his zeal must have nevertheless won over the Queen. With the royal couple's approval, Prime Minister Palmerston ordered a British assault on Lagos, and Akitoye was installed as ruler of Lagos, under a British protectorate. Celebrating the victory as 'God's interposition for the good of Africa',[20] Gollmer moved onto land provided by Akitoye 'without any condition, free of expenses, and without limit of time'. It was of no concern to him that Liverpool traders – who had always supported Kosoko – protested bitterly that the British government had allowed its foreign policy to be driven by missionaries. 'The fact is, Akitoye was made a tool to carry out the ambitions of these two men, Messers Gollmer and Townsend.'[21]

With bases at Lagos and Abeokuta secure, Basel graduate David Hinderer was dispatched to establish the third station at Ibadan. His young wife Anna Maria, who had been raised as an orphan in an East Anglican vicarage, was at first overcome by a terrible yearning for home; her new country seemed to be regulated on an alien set of values, with violence a routine part of everyday existence. In time, she learned to take pride in the girls who sat at her feet as she sewed and in the lads who looked like real English schoolboys in smart blue shirts. Together the Hinderers worked to construct the nucleus of a future church, within which total abstinence from alcohol, sexual purity, Sunday observance and regular churchgoing were the key marks of grace. When a young woman described how her father had beaten her with a cutlass for the crime of going to church, Hinderer delivered with a lecture on the text, 'Whosoever shall confess me before men …'. She was then cut off from the fellowship for defiling the Sabbath after she had been spotted carrying water from the stream on a Sunday.[22]

Internecine conflict was to prove the Hinderers' downfall. After some ten years of barely productive work, they found themselves caught up in a war between their own Ibadan and Townsend's Abeokuta. When news arrived that their colleague was publicly and stridently supporting the Abeokuta cause, the Ibadan authorities issued an order that all contact between the town and the mission station should be severed. With no means of buying food, the Hunderers struggled for five long years to keep themselves and the mission children alive. While the German maintained a stoic silence, his emotional wife bombarded Townsend and Venn with ever more hysterical letters.[23] The couple survived the conflict only at the cost of Anna Maria's health.

An African Bishop on the Niger

Having risen out of poverty and surviving on the coast while others were
dying, Townsend believed that any ecclesiastical preferment on offer
would surely be offered first to him. Anglicans of high-church persuasion
had long argued – however improbably – that the American colonists
might not have broken away from the mother country if they had only
been allowed to have their own bishop. The Colonial Churches Bill
of 1853, which relaxed the rules for the creation of Anglican bishops
overseas, gave Venn the freedom to implement his vision, and Townsend
was outraged to hear that Crowther was to be elevated to the episcopate
over his head. Gollmer and Hinderer added their names to their
colleague's letter of protest. 'Native teachers of whatever grade have been
received and respected by the chiefs and people only as being the agents
and servants of white men.... This state of things is not the result of white
men's teaching but has existed for ages past. The superiority of the white
over the black man, the negro has been forward to acknowledge. The
correctness of this belief no white man can deny.'[24]

After being released from slavery by the British navy and then
converted and educated by CMS clergy, Crowther, for his part, was
bewildered at the preferment that was being thrust upon him. Years later,
he would write a sad letter to headquarters that revealed a deep and
lasting sense of inadequacy. 'I know my place as a negro, but I have ever
paid my respects to Europeans, whether old or young, missionaries
or those in secular occupations, as the race of our benefactors, to whom
we owe bodily freedom and the spiritual privileges of the glorious liberty
of the Christian religion.'[25]

According to Venn's long-held belief, the white missionary's only task
was to open up new territory and establish an indigenous church, before
moving on with the missionary frontier. The fact that progress in
planting that chain of stations across Yoruba country was slower than
anticipated could be put down to the fact that Townsend, Hinderer and
Gollmer had chosen to sink roots within their territories. In any case, the
Niger had now reopened, and Crowther joined Baikie's 1854 expedition,
which opened the lower and middle river to foreign trade. Ten years later,
Samuel Ajayi Crowther was consecrated 'Bishop of the United Church
of England and Ireland, in the said countries of West Africa beyond the
limits of our dominions'. The wording was significant – since the Yoruba
mission had its base in colonial Lagos, no white clergy would come

within his jurisdiction. The new bishop was charged with establishing Christianity and legitimate trade along the banks of the Niger, from the mangrove swamps of the delta to the confluence with its Benue tributary at Lokoja.

As Townsend became increasingly identified with British imperialism, his influence in Yoruba country waned. In 1867, while he was on home leave, an anti-white faction led by Sierra Leonian George 'Reversible' Johnson took power, and all whites were expelled from Yoruba country. With the American Baptists already gone (following the outbreak of the Civil War at home), the African Christians were left to manage as best they could. As an African, Samuel Crowther remained free to travel where he wished, and he would later make a pastoral tour of all Yoruba stations. What he found was encouraging. At American Baptist Ogbomosho, home of a group of twenty-one converts who were out of contact with other Christians, regular worship had been maintained: each Sunday literate younger men read from the Bible before their elders led the meeting in prayer. At Ibadan, the Hinderer's elderly cook was ministering to three city congregations and visiting outstations regularly. In Abeokuta, church members were providing the funds needed to support their own clergy and had recruited evangelists to open work in new areas. Venn's belief that Africans were capable of both running and expanding their operations at last appeared to be well vindicated.

Meanwhile, on the Niger, Crowther's main energies remained focused on delivering Buxton's civilising vision. Crowther's family set the model for others, dividing between traders and clergy: while both his older sons and a son-in-law earned their living as trading agents, Dandeson, the youngest, was ordained and became his father's archdeacon in the delta. The new prelate was most at ease with men of simple faith and comparatively little learning. In the early years, he recruited workers who were fluent in riverine dialects, but when the supply of first generation re-captives dried up, his Sierra Leonians became increasingly isolated. On the one side, church discipline and expatriate background set them apart from the indigenous African community, while, on the other, the European traders, who were arriving on the river in increasing numbers, roundly detested these African competitors.

Despite these problems, Venn's native church strategy was bearing fruit here, as it had done elsewhere. While father Samuel, son Dandeson and Lokoja-based archdeacon Henry 'Jerusalem' Johnson supervised progress, individual pastors were building up flourishing congregations, and when Henry Venn died in office in 1873, his Niger mission was being widely held up as a model for the conversion of Africa. Now unwelcome in their old cities, both Townsend and Hinderer finally accepted the principle of African leadership; while the German advised that Crowther's territory should be increased to include the whole of Yoruba country, Townsend preferred that a rising Sierra Leonian, known to all as James 'Holy' Johnson, should be consecrated bishop of a new diocese on the western side of the Niger. But even as the veterans in the field were being reconciled, younger men at home were laying plans to reverse the whole direction of CMS policy.

Chapter 4

A Crucifix and a Breviary

The Catholic Revival

Ultramontanes and Gallicians

In the summer of 1792, the Catholic Church faced a catastrophe in its own European heartland. As the Paris mob roamed free, the clergy could do little more than look to their own safety. Those parish priests who remained in post had lost authority in the community, and their superiors had to choose between compromise and exile. Over the next decades, French soldiers would export religious scepticism across the continent, destroying Catholic monarchies, occupying the Papal States and even holding the Pope prisoner. Only after Protestant armies defeated Napoleon at Waterloo did clerics become free to condemn both the enlightenment and the revolution. Even in defeat, the French Revolution left a legacy of bitter anti-clericalism, and the new Bourbon dynasty, which was closely allied to the church, fell after just fifteen years. In 1830, 1848 and 1871, a liberal bourgeois monarchy, a new Napoleonic empire and an anti-clerical republic emerged in turn from the cauldron of civil unrest.

As long as Napoleon I held power at home, the church was in no position to match the Protestant initiative in a wider world. Global mission policy was entrusted to the Sacred Congregation of Propaganda within the Roman curia, but after a century of inactivity, this body had little sense of direction and no access to expertise or significant resources. In the post-revolution years, most Catholic initiatives on the African continent therefore originated in France. But throughout much of the nineteenth century, the French clergy were themselves divided. 'Ultramontane' Catholics looked back to medieval times, before the perfect unity between church and state was broken – first by the Reformation and then by the enlightenment. Hard-line ultramontanes, who refused to recognise any government that claimed to draw authority from the public will rather than divine authority, gave their first loyalty to the Pope, who lived 'beyond the mountains' – and this left them vulnerable to the charge of treason. At the same time, smaller number of well-born and influential clergy became committed to closing the gap between church and state. These were the 'Gallicians', who looked even further back to the baptism of the Frankish chief Clovis in 496. From that time, they argued, the centre of Western Christendom had lain not in Rome but in France.

Just as most Protestant missionaries were recruited from the more 'fundamentalist' wings of their own denominations, so those Catholics who travelled to Africa – almost to a priest, sister and lay brother – held uncompromisingly ultramontane beliefs. One Catholic order did have a tradition of involvement in overseas mission work. During the slaving years, responsibility for the spiritual care of French overseas possessions lay with the Congregation of the Holy Ghost, whose missionaries were popularly known as Spiritians. Answering directly to the department within the Roman curia known as Propaganda, they took responsibility for ministering to the needs of expatriates and doing some work with native populations. The order had, however, emerged from the revolutionary years desperately short of both money and volunteers and, in the view of many, also lacking the 'odour of sanctity'. But in 1817, two years after the restored French government followed the British example by abolishing its national slave trade, a single Spiritian was sent to Senegal, carrying the prestigious, if empty, title of Vicar Apostolic of West Africa. Although little would result, this initiative did mark the start of a second phase of Catholic work in Africa.

The Sisters of Cluny

Meanwhile, a remarkable French lady was developing plans for the conversion of Africans. In common with their Protestant rivals, Catholic planners believed that Africa would not be converted by the learned but, in their case, by simple monks and nuns recruited from deprived communities. Well-born Burgundian nun Anne-Marie Javouhey – who had managed to survive the revolutionary years with both life and reputation intact – founded an order dedicated to St. Joseph of Cluny, patron saint of manual workers, and set about recruiting simple, often barely literate, peasant girls, whom she dressed in a habit that mimicked clothes worn by grape pickers, who were among the poorest people in France. Missionary operations began in the Caribbean, but soon the mother superior recruited her natural sister Rosalie to help set up a house on an abandoned slaving station on the island of Gorrée, off the Senegalese capital of Dakar.

After arriving in 1822, the Javouhey sisters discovered that the power struggle between the ultramontane clergy and anti-clerical officials was as acute in colonial Senegal as in the metropolitan homeland. As soon as the new Vicar Apostolic had set about imposing Catholic discipline on the expatriate community, the Governor used every known device to obstruct the plans until, finally losing patience, the furious cleric placed the whole territory under an interdict and sailed for home. Although the experience of being severed from the church and sacraments posed few problems to colonial Frenchmen, it was intolerable for the Sisters of Cluny. Laying blame on the priest who had failed to see his task through to the end, Mother Javouhey drew the conclusion that Africa could only be converted by African priests, who had been trained in Africa. Admittedly, the need for every priest to be celibate and fluent in Latin posed a problem, but, undismayed, she laid her plans before the Minister of Colonies:

> I am deeply concerned about Africa, and wish to use all means in
> my power to advance the present and future welfare of its people.
> I am asking His Excellency the Governor to facilitate the formation
> of two establishments for the training of young negroes.... I consider
> it one of the most efficient means of spreading civilisation in the
> Colony, and making a pastoral people more industrious, and, at the
> same time honest and good Christians.[1]

Her educational plans had to be put on hold when the great yellow fever epidemic struck neighbouring Sierra Leone, plunging the Sisters of Cluny into the urgent task of caring for the Protestant sick. Both Anne-Marie and Rosalie were invalided home, and their surviving nuns were unqualified to take the project forwards. Mother Javouhey now decided that the whole project for training African priests needed to be based in Europe. By 1825, some twenty children – most Senegalese boys – were under instruction in France, but like Macaulay's children, they soon fell victim to European diseases. About half of them died, and after others had been summoned home by anxious parents, just three remained to complete the sixteen-year course. Of these, David Boilat and Arsene Fridoil had European fathers, which meant Pierre Moussa was the only full-blooded African to achieve ordination. The hopes of the Sisters of Cluny depended on them. Indeed, their mission attracted the interest of French royalty, and before returning to Africa, they were

summoned to the palace of Fontainebleu, where Moussa said mass
before the king and queen.

In Senegal, Moussa was given temporary charge of the colonial
church, pending the arrival of a new Vicar Apostolic, while Boilat set
up a higher school, which was to be the equal of any in France. If this
was a promising start, it was not to last. Mother Javouhey's vision
for an African priesthood began to fade when a newly arrived party
of Ploërmel fathers set about orchestrating a 'shrill and implacable'
campaign against the very idea of providing higher education to Africans.
Soon a new prefect arrived to displace Moussa. Letting it be known that
he found the very idea of working with coloured priests highly distasteful,
he added his weight behind the Ploërmel campaign. Such pressure from
within the church was too much to bear, and the Paris ministry issued
instructions that, in any programme for African education, elementary
schools should always take priority over institutes of higher studies.
Boilat, Fridoil and Moussa were demoted to less-sensitive work, and
from that time, Senegal became known as a troublesome station that
was staffed by priests 'who too often leave something to be desired
in part of morality'.[2]

An American Bishop and an Alsatian Priest

At the same time, wealthy Irish-American priest Fr Edward Barron was
laying his plans for the conversion of Africa. The state of Maryland had
a long Catholic tradition, and when the Bishop of Charleston looked
for a chaplain to work at Cape Palmas, Barron offered to organise
an expedition at his own expense. After convincing Propaganda to give
him the grand title of Prefect Apostolic of Two Guineas, he assumed
responsibility for some 5,000 miles of coast between the Senegal and
the Orange Rivers and stretching as far inland as anyone would choose
to venture. However, on arriving in Liberia in 1842, with Irish-born
Fr Kelly and one lay assistant, Barron quickly discovered that, while
some settlers in Africa from Maryland did indeed have a Catholic
background, all had defected to the heretics and none had any intention
of returning to the fold. Seeing that they had their work cut out with the
colonists, Barron and his colleagues took immediate action to convert the
local Africans. On the first Sunday, both priests put on their vestments,
the layman took up the cross and the three men processed into the

nearest village, chanting the litany. The Grebo listened respectfully as an interpreter started translating Barron's sermon until the point when he began to expound on the doctrines of hell and the Trinity, when everyone broke out laughing. Nevertheless, Barron remained confident. He reported that 'my hopes for the conversion of the region rest on the character of the people shown to us in their friendly and docile disposition'.[3] And while Fr Kelly remained at Cape Palmas, Barron sailed for Rome to present Propaganda with a grand plan to mount a Catholic offensive along the whole western coast of Africa.

Now consecrated bishop, Barron travelled on to France to discuss his plans with a priest who was training young men for work in Africa. Born epileptic into an Alsatian-Jewish family, Francis Libermann had overcome more obstacles than most in achieving his ambition of ordination into the Catholic Church. After consulting Mother Javouhey, this determined man set up an order of missionary priests, which he named the Congregation of the Holy Heart of Mary. When Barron arrived there, Propaganda had still not allocated the order with any area of operation, and Libermann's young men were becoming restless. Barron had a challenge for these prospective missionaries. Assuring them that the high mortality rate among Protestant missionaries was a judgement on heresy, and that God would surely protect those who proclaimed the true faith, he described his vision for Africa. As a result, seven priests, along with three laymen from a foundling home, were assigned to join his Liberian venture.

Instructed by the bishop to prepare everything needed for the expedition, Fr Libermann assembled no less than 24 tons of luggage, to the great surprise and profound disgust of the departing missionaries, whose apostolic dream left room only for a crucifix and a breviary.[4] While Barron continued to search for more recruits, the ten young Frenchmen sailed for Liberia; none knew any Grebo, only one had a smattering of English and they would even find Fr Kelly's Americanised Latin incomprehensible. Despite Barron's previous reassurances, seven were soon laid low with malaria, and by the time the bishop finally arrived with two more lay recruits, three were dead and the disgusted Fr Kelly had sailed home.

Disasters continued after Barron decided to move operations to French colonies further down the coast – when his priests tried to land in the Ivory Coast, anti-clerical sailors tipped all their stores into the sea. Barron departed to deliver his resignation to Propaganda, leaving just two survivors clinging to life in the dense rain forest at the mouth of the

Gabon River. Back in France, Libermann was appalled to hear rumours of their fate – they had been shipwrecked, killed by natives or even burnt at the stake. Unable to reconcile himself with the idea of sending out young men to near certain death, he prohibited his seminarians from even discussing the idea of travelling out to take the place of those who had died. Another missionary initiative had come to an end. After Barron had returned to America, Libermann's Congregation of the Holy Heart of Mary inherited the poisoned chalice of his vast vicarate. Although Mother Javouhey's logic that Africa had to be converted by a native ministry appeared irresistible, Barron's experience could only question whether her ambition to train battalions of black priests could ever be a practical proposition.

From Propaganda in Rome, Libermann now received instructions to undertake a 'reverse take-over' of the unruly and much larger Congregation of the Holy Ghost. Over the protests of his workers and the bitter resentment of the Spiritians themselves, he managed to complete the task of bringing the two orders into one – in the process saving the tiny Gabon station from being overwhelmed by newly arrived and better-funded Protestants from the American Board.

Even more challenging was the task of bringing disgruntled Senegal Spiritians into some kind of order. Pragmatism was needed. Although theologically ultramontane, Libermann recognised that church and state did have interests in common. On the one side, colonial officials could help 'advancing the salvation of souls' and, on the other, priests should play their part in advancing French interests. 'It appears evident,' he declared, 'that the method by which we plan to civilise them is the most efficacious way to establish French rule in these lands.'[5] Following these pragmatic principles, he negotiated an agreement with the French navy, under which the mission fathers in Senegal would provide the colonial authorities with regular intelligence reports in return for free transport, medical care, basic rations and an annual grant.

Once in the field, however, the mission superior answered directly to Propaganda, not to Libermann, and the eccentric Spiritian Bishop Truffet repudiated the whole deal, with it sacrificing the mission's sole source of income and medical care. Even after all the clergy – himself included – became sick, he refused to let the government doctor into the compound, insisting that his clergy must rely only on divine intervention. He then decreed that they had to live on what he deemed to

be the local diet of 'canary seed, rice and fish', but, as soon as his back
was turned, half-starved priests rooted round for anything that looked
remotely edible. Finally, discovering that some priests had been briefly
held as hostages in a tribal war, Truffet confined every member of staff
inside the mission compound walls, leaving some half-dozen priests
trying to fill their time in a school with just seven pupils. It was not
a tenable situation, and, in fact, Truffet survived his own regime for just
seven months. After his death, Fr Arlabosse led a group of six priests and
brothers up the Senegal River on a quixotic search for the fabled city
of Timbuktu. Four hundred miles inland, surrounded by hostile people,
with their newly built mission buildings washed away in a flood, the
expedition came to an end. Arlabosse died, and his comrades returned
to the coast – only to be rewarded for their pains by a sharp personal
rebuke from Pope Pius IX, who insisted that individual acts of heroism
would not win Muslim souls.

Muslims were now high on the Catholic agenda. Libermann
understood clearly that the Catholic Church's main confrontation was
not with a handful of Protestant societies, which had, as yet, established
only the barest foothold along the coast, but with the great wave of
Islam spilling out of the interior grasslands. If it was impossible to train
enough black priests, then their progress would have to be halted by
a 'dam of catechists'; under his plan, white missionary priests would
gather ransomed boy slaves – known on the coast as *pawns* – into an
enclosed community that would form a small enclave of Christendom
(*chrétienté*) within the pagan environment. Isolated from the outside
world, his missionaries would turn their hands to the task of teaching
these boys everything that a catechist needed to know. He urged his
seminarians to approach this task with humility. 'Empty yourselves of
Europe, of its manners and mentality … make yourselves blacks with the
blacks … to form them as they should be, not in the way of Europe, but
leaving them what is their own; behave towards them as servants would
behave to their masters, adapting to the customs, attitudes and habits
of their masters.'[6] Only in this way, he thought, could they avoid the
arrogance that gripped every young priest as soon as he set foot in Africa;
'however pure his orthodoxy and great his zeal, the missionary has
a terrible tendency to be pope and king at one and the same time'.[7]
When his fathers insisted that they had been ordained as priests, not
schoolmasters, Libermann begged them to reconsider their position.

I understand that it would cost the missionaries very much to act
as teachers. Nevertheless, it is urgent to take this step in order
to consolidate their efforts and aim at the formation of a coloured
clergy, of teachers and of catechists. In my opinion to abandon the
schools is to destroy the future of the missions. Your reply that you
will start them again at a later time is a joke. Once badly started
a mission is difficult to bring to a successful conclusion. Just
because the work of schools is time-consuming and full of trouble,
it is important to undertake it from the very beginning.[8]

For more than a generation, the Spiritians would make little contribution
in West Africa. After his death in 1852, Libermann's Holy Ghost Fathers
were invited to start work on what was believed to be the healthier east
coast, and his successor funnelled available resources into building up
a large *chrétienté* opposite Zanzibar Island at Bagamoyo. When the
opportunity arose, the order was happy to hand over much of their
West African territory to a newly formed French society.

Devotees of the Black Virgin

Three years after Libermann died, the well-born Bishop Melchior
de Marion Brésillac landed at the West African port of Ouidah. After
quarrelling with fellow priests over their opposition to the ordination
of Indians, he had been travelling back to Rome to resign his bishopric.
At Ouidah, Brésillac was shocked to discover that the slave trade still
flourished half a century after Wilberforce's Abolition Bill – in fact,
it has been estimated that more slaves were being exported from West
Africa then than ever before. There was much about this part of West
Africa that remained unknown to Europeans like Brésillac. While the
coastal strip was familiar to sailors, just 70 miles inland lay Abomey,
the mysterious capital of warlike Dahomey. During the decade since
Protestant missionaries took their part in defeating that kingdom's
warriors under the walls of Abeokuta, it had continued to wage
war against neighbouring states. Brésillac was seized by the idea of
establishing an order that would be dedicated to the task of taking the
faith into areas that were still beyond any missionary influence. Once
back in France, he read every book that he could find on Africa. On the

one hand, travellers' accounts of human sacrifice suggested that Africans were possessed by diabolical spirits, while, on the other, he learnt how Europeans had treated them as worse than beasts. During church services, he scanned fine jewels worn by society ladies and wondered how many had been bought from the ill-gained profits of the slave trade.

In 1856, he led a small group of fellow priests into the church of Nôtre Dame de Fourvière in Lyons. Kneeling before an ancient shrine of a black virgin, they consecrated themselves in the words that would form the oath taken by members of his Society of African Missions – who would be simply known as the Lyons Fathers. 'Here and now I offer my life to God, accepting in advance and with joy, for his greater glory, the salvation of my soul and those of the peoples confided to me, the sufferings, the privations, the discomforts of the climate, the miseries of persecution and even martyrdom should God find me worthy to witness to the faith by my death.'[9]

Experienced Spiritians advised Brésillac that it would be foolhardy to start work in Dahomey, and he submitted (with ill grace) when Propaganda decreed that the order's first task should be to recapture Sierra Leone from the heretics: 'We shall have all the miseries of the European colonials as well as those of the Africans to cope with; whereas at Dahomey we should only have had the savages, who might have knocked off our heads soon enough, it is true, but who might also have been able to recognise the truth.'[10]

An advance party of two priests and a lay brother sailed in November 1858, and after delivering the home office into the charge of colleague Augustin Planque, Brésillac followed shortly after with reinforcements. By bad chance, both parties arrived in Sierra Leone just as the colony was in the grip of another yellow fever epidemic. All the Lyons Fathers died – Brésillac last of all, when no Catholic priest was left to say the office, though an Anglican, who was returning from burying his own bishop, did pause to say prayers over the coffins.

Now confirmed by Propaganda as superior of the order, Planque comforted the brethren with the assurance that all would work for good:

If we have lost our father and our elder brothers, yet I have the agreeable certainty of advocates in heaven, who will be able to pray for our cause all the more effectively now that they are near to God.[11]

Three Lyons Fathers finally sailed for Dahomey in 1861: thirty-two-year-old Italian, Francesco Borghero, designated 'superior ad interim' for a stretch of coast between the Niger and Volta rivers, and two younger men, Frenchman Louis Edde and Spaniard Francisco Fernandez. Eddie died almost immediately and was buried alongside Brésillac in Freetown. The two survivors settled in an old Portuguese fort in Ouidah. Although most of the building was crumbling to ruins, the chapel remained in good repair and they discovered with surprise that a congregation of about 100 Catholics met there every Sunday. The majority were local people, claiming descent from at least one Portuguese ancestor, but there were also ex-slaves, who had somehow found their way home from Brazil. Twice a year an African priest arrived from the Portuguese island of São Tomé to say mass; though, as chance would have it, just a few days before the Lyons priests arrived, he had been caught trying to smuggle the church's crucifix statues and other valuables out to his island.

The Lyons Fathers were keen to begin work on the coast while they waited for King Glele's permission to enter Dahomey, but discovered to their dismay that the French authorities prohibited any attempt to proselytise those who lived within the traditional tribal framework. When the king's invitation finally arrived, Borghero laid his three key mission objectives before the royal messengers: to prevent human sacrifice, to stop the slave trade and to persuade the king to abandon offensive campaigns against others. But when Borghero arrived in Dahomey, Glele took the first opportunity to make it clear that he would receive no lectures from foreigners. Just then his army was preparing for another assault on Abeokuta, and the priest could not rest for the sound of drumming and dancing. After Sunday mass, Borghero asked his guides to show him round the town of Abomey, and in the main square, he confronted grim reality: 'The whole army was there on foot. You could see on every side trophies of human victims displayed on posts built like triumphant arches. I turned my eyes away from the sight.... Flocks of vultures drawn by the smell of the victims were hovering all round. A little further on we were almost stifled by the horrible stink of bodies accumulated during several days' sacrifice.'[12] Having made his point, Glele was happy to see the 'white fetish man' retreat to the coast as quickly as he had come.

Since Planque's training course concentrated almost entirely on the devotional and sacramental aspect of missionary work, recruits continued to arrive in Ouida without any knowledge of foreign languages or of African culture. Since most communication between races was conducted in English or Portuguese, the Lyons Fathers could not even hold a conversation with anybody in the African, expatriate or mixed race communities. To make matters worse, the two mission founders were soon at odds over policy. While Fernandez argued that the mission's first priority must be to improve language skills, Borghero was only interested in exposing pawns to the full rigour of Catholic instruction – delivered only in French and Latin. But, for all the Lyons Fathers' divisions and shortcomings, most Protestants could only have envied the figures that Borghero sent home to Planque; within just three years of their arrival, his fathers had conducted 288 baptisms of children and 31 of adults, heard 400 confessions, given 100 communions and conducted 33 confirmations. A school, an orphanage and a dispensary functioned adequately, and a second station had been opened along the coast at Porto Novo. Most significantly for the future, Borghero had started work in British territory. On his first visit to Lagos, he discovered that an elderly catechist, known as Pa Antonio, had gathered repatriated slaves from Brazil and Cuba, and in a purpose-built church, they re-enacted the services that they remembered from the New World. Priest and catechist eyed each other with suspicion; while Pa Antonio feared that Borghero might be an impostor, the priest was concerned that this layman might have assumed priestly functions. After both had been reassured, Borghero said mass in front of some 400 people. He did, however, warn Planque that, whatever their apparent devotion, most Lagos Catholics had strayed far from the Christian path. 'I will tell you of the Christians who have come from Brazil. From their morals you would not think that they are Christians. Apart from polygamy, which all but a few practice, they follow many superstitious pagan practises.'[13] Whatever their moral shortcomings, Pa Antonio's flock did provide the Lyons Fathers with a ready-made congregation as a base for long-term development.

In 1865, Augustin Planque recalled Borghero to Lyons. Ostensibly, this was to allow Borghero to rebuild his fragile physical and mental health, but Planque was also determined to resolve the issue of divided command that had frustrated Libermann's plans. As superior of the whole society, Planque exercised control over recruitment, fund-raising and training, but day-to-day decisions in the field were left to the mission superior, who answered directly to Propaganda. After successful lobbying in the curia, Planque now managed to consolidate the two positions of Superior of the

Society and Superior of the Mission into his own hands. The new structure provided the Lyons Fathers with a coherent command structure, but it was bought at too high a price when all power now became concentrated in the hands of a man of limited vision and little compassion.

Catholic progress was brought to an abrupt halt when the Franco-Prussian war of 1870 severed the Lyons Fathers' crucial lifeline with home. For the next six years, the Catholics struggled to survive with little food and virtually no medical drugs – nursing 'their fevers literally sitting up in bed, crouched under umbrellas, while the rain streamed in through the miserable sheds they sheltered in'.[14] During those years, the death toll rose inexorably, and out of eleven priests who arrived in Lagos between March 1870 and May 1873, nine died.

> Protestant ministers launch bitter attacks against the poor little Catholic mission. Our poverty should not give offence to anyone. We only have two small schools and a chapel made out of bamboo, while around us, in the whole Lagos region, Anglicans, Methodists and Baptists live in fine houses, have large and beautiful schools and splendid places of worship.[15]

However, after the crisis was over, work recovered quickly; a cathedral, large enough to seat 2,000 people, opened in 1881, and even that was soon reported to be too small to accommodate the congregation. But the whole order remained short of funds, and Planque insisted that the West African mission must now become self-sufficient. Help came from an unexpected quarter, when Catholic convert Sir James Marshall – who was both colonial chief justice and a leading Lagos trader – prevailed on the colonial government to give the Lyons Fathers a large area of land between the lagoon and the ocean to the west of Lagos. The Topo settlement built on this site had the dual purpose of furnishing resources for the mission and receiving orphans and children purchased out of slavery. This grand scheme was based on the lowest assessment of the African character.

> One knows well enough that the adage working like a 'nègre' is not even true in America where the black is constantly under the whip of a planter who is avid for gain. In Africa, where he feels at home, he is, for many reasons, very inclined towards idleness. When left

to himself, or working under the benign hand of a missionary,
it is more true to describe him as 'doing nothing like a 'nègre'.[16]

Project director Fr Langlais – who was certainly no 'benign missionary' –
subjected a selection of pawns, orphans and young offenders referred
from Marshall's courts to a harsh and regimented life. Throughout
the hours of daylight, school classes were sandwiched between hours
of coconut cultivation and religious devotion. Before long, Topo had
acquired such a reputation for physical violence that Langlais' colleagues
refused to entrust their own mission children into his care.[17]

The Society of African Missions of Lyons remained a young person's
operation, fraught with hardship and danger. Expectation of life on the
coast for a male worker was just two years and ten months and even
those who survived long enough to be made bishop, rarely attained the
age of forty. When the sisters started to arrive, their expectation of life
at three years and eight months was rather better, but still alarmingly
low. Descended from generations of peasants, Planque had a reputation
for toughness. Pope Pius IX expressed delight at the 'cold-blooded
courage' of this man who could dispose his forces, like a general sending
men into battle. But he never set foot on African soil, even after sea travel
had become quick, safe and comparatively cheap. Nor, in more than half
a century, did his Lyons Fathers ordain an African priest. As he grew old,
Augustin Planque's day started with spiritual exercises and the writing
of fund-raising letters; then, in the afternoon, like any country curé,
he would knock on the door of a faithful household and settle for
sleep beside the fire. Despite growing protests over his ignorance and
incompetence from within his order, he never lost the confidence of
Propaganda, remaining superior of Society of African Missions until
he died in 1907 at the age of eighty-one. By this time – for all the
late start and high cost in missionary life – the Catholic Church had
established a secure presence in the French colonies and British Lagos.
The bridgehead in British territory would be consolidated and expanded
by Irish priests, nuns and lay brothers, who arrived in large numbers
during the early years of the twentieth century.

Chapter 5

Stolen Country

London Missionaries in South Africa

South African Society

In April 1797, an unusual job application arrived at the London Missionary Society (LMS) headquarters. Even by eighteenth-century standards, the early life of Dr Johannes van der Kemp had been a spectacular rake's progress: born into a wealthy Dutch family, he joined the dragoons, and set out on a ruthless quest to seduce women from the lower orders. In early middle age, he settled down with a new wife and a daughter born to one of his mistresses, studied medicine in Edinburgh and worked as an army doctor in the revolutionary wars. He turned to religion only when the two women in his life drowned in a boating accident.

The directors had formed a clear profile of those who were likely to volunteer for overseas work. 'We expect to receive the chief supply of missionaries from Brethren in the lower order of life, ingenious artificers of any sort – men of sound understanding – solidly acquainted with the truth … whose experience and examination shall give good evidence of their real conversion to God and whose hearts appear simply devoted to our Saviour, and to seeking to poor heathen.'[1] They sat across the table with a fifty-year-old man from a good family but dubious reputation, who expected to assume some kind of leadership role. In those years, the world seemed open to missionary work. The directors proposed that the Dutchman establish a base in India from where he could supervise all operations in the East. He countered with the suggestion that he could go to Persia or the Cape, with a preference for the latter on the grounds that, while he had no knowledge of Persian, he did speak 'a little Aethiopic'. They finally agreed that work should begin in South Africa, where both nations shared an interest. He landed at Cape Town in April 1799, supported by ordained young compatriot Johannes Kircherer and English artisans, John Edmonds and William Edwards.

In South Africa, perhaps more than anywhere else in Africa, missionaries had to navigate issues of race. A century and a half earlier, the Dutch government had planted a settlement of farmers – known in their own language as Boers – whose duty was to provide provisions for their East India Company ships on the long journey to and from the Spice Islands. Protestant colonists, mainly from the Netherlands, but also of French, German and Scandinavian origin, communicated in a form of Cape Dutch that would later develop into Afrikaans. Van der Kemp and his companions quickly discovered a complex situation of racial tension. The earliest Europeans had found the Cape populated by nomadic herdsmen, who called themselves the Khoisan but were known to the whites as Hottentots. Many died from imported diseases or had been killed by white settlers, and those who survived had no means of defending their territory against the land-hungry and often violent Boers, who were spreading from the Cape. Although Khoisan farm workers were technically free, in practice they were tied from birth, and an English sea captain compared their relationship with the Boers to that between a dog and his master: 'There is one or more of them belonging to every house. They do all sorts of servile work, and there take their Food and Grease. Three or four of their nearest relations sit at the doors or near the Dutch House, waiting for the scraps and fragments that come from the table.'[2]

White farmers exercised an unofficial *droit de seigneur* over Khoisan women, and a constantly shifting population of soldiers and sailors, along with other Africans and an international variety of slaves, contributed to the diverse gene pool of those who would later be known as the 'Cape Coloureds'. Although most Boers had some African inheritance intermingled with that of their European ancestors, in their everyday conversation the word 'black' was interchangeable with 'heathen', and 'white' with 'Christian'. Just four years before the missionaries arrived, the British had seized the Cape off the Dutch, and the Boers feared that these new rulers planned to undermine their traditional way of life. But whites did at least agree that Africans were a naturally lazy people, who would only work when compelled by stark necessity.

The Boers had also imported slaves from Madagascar, East Africa and the Far East, but while the Muslim slaves could practice their religion undisturbed, every possible barrier was erected by the Boers against the conversion of Africans to Christianity. Self-interest was compounded by a growing belief in the white superiority. 'Susanna's master ... was a deacon, and reputed one of the best-intentioned members of the reformed church, but he persisted in refusing to have his slave baptised. He said, that it was not so much the loss of his right to sell her that determined him to object to it, but his apprehension lest her pride should grow unsupportable by her admission among the Christians.'³

Van der Kemp lost no time in organising meetings where slaves were encouraged to voice their complaints. Although he was bound to explain that missionaries had no power to change the social order, he gave an assurance that every true believer would be baptised with the Holy Ghost. He visited the re-established Moravian settlement at Genadendal. Here pietists, who started from the assumption that persecution and injustice were part of the lot of man, endlessly drilled converts in the Christian duty of obedience to the civil powers. Even so, they were distrusted by the Boers – many of whom were themselves illiterate – who remained hostile to the fact that the Germans were teaching their servants to acquire the literacy and practical skills that would one day make them self-sufficient.

But the LMS directors had not charged their envoys to solve the racial problems of South African society – their task was to carry the Christian message beyond the colonial borders. Faced with this limitless challenge, Van der Kemp split his party into two; he and Edmonds would go east into Xhosa country, while Kircherer and Edwards travelled north to contact Africans of the interior. Before going their separate ways, the two Dutchmen ordained their artisan comrades.

The Eastern Party

When the missionaries' wagon drew into the garrison town Graaff Reinet, the locals gave grim accounts of frontier turmoil and urged them to turn back. Dismissing such talk as no more than 'the wrestlings of Satan', Van der Kemp urged the reluctant Edmonds forward to the Great Fish River which provided a border between the colony and Xhosa country. Beyond the river, Boers warned Paramount Chief Ngqika that these newcomers were 'spies and murderers', but Ngqika insisted on receiving them into his kraal, where Van der Kemp's first Christian service was attended by a bizarre collection of Khoisan carriers, renegade Boers, British army deserters and a handful of inquisitive Xhosa.

The two men reacted differently to their new environment. With both his physical and mental health collapsing, Edmonds lost little time in deciding that he detested all Africans and that God was calling him to distant Bengal. His leader, in contrast, took to the new life with relish, eating African food and walking barefoot through the bush, even when thorns cut his feet to ribbons. After a time, however, Van der Kemp had to accept that they would do no effective work as long as the frontier was in turmoil, and they crossed back into the colony together. Edmonds then set off for Cape Town, where he penned the directors a parting farewell. 'I was far from having that love and compassion for the poor inhabitants that I consider as absolutely necessary for the people among whom he is to labour',[4] and his solitary figure was last seen boarding a ship for Bengal. For his part, Van der Kemp refused to pass judgement on the Xhosa. Having worked as a military doctor in time of war, he had first-hand experience of his fellow Europeans' terrible capacity for violence. Certainly, many actions that were considered serious offences in Xhosa country would pass unnoticed in Europe. Local law was relaxed. Although 'committing a nuisance' in a river or near a cattle kraal was, in theory, a capital offence; in practice, justice was casually dispensed: 'Often a man condemned to death escapes by the indulgence of those who are charged with the execution; they lead him aside to a remote place, there they throw their assegais at him, but in such a manner that they leave him room to escape their hands, and to take his refuge in another country. The king seldom takes any notice of these evasions.'[5] He noted that Xhosa law had little concern with property. 'The Caffres seldom steal except from strangers, or from the king himself, whom they almost daily rob of cattle, and who rarely punishes the thefts if they are not extravagant.' Overall, the African way of life did not strike him as unusually violent.

While waiting for the border to settle down, Van der Kemp accepted the position of minister of the Dutch Reformed Church in Graaff Reinet, where he was later joined by artisan James Read. Their appointments had immediate consequences. When the two men began to bring Xhoisan converts to the church, Boer members of the congregation were outraged to discover that they were expected to worship alongside blacks. On 1 July 1801, when members of the two communities gathered for the monthly prayer meeting, the service descended into chaos. After the minister announced the singing of Psalm 134, the Khoisan Christians started to use the correct version

Come bless the Lord, all ye servants of the Lord,
Who stand by night in the house of the Lord

while the Boers struck up in competition with the words of Psalm 74:

> Remember thy congregation which thou hast gotten of old ...
> Thy foes have roared in the midst of thy holy place.
> They desecrated the dwelling place of thy name.

The Boers then marched out of church and dispatched a petition to the civil governor. They demanded that all traces of the Khoisan be purged from the church building – seats washed, flooring replaced and a wall built around the churchyard. In response, Van der Kemp made it clear that he would never preach before a congregation from which anyone was excluded on racial grounds, and Read pronounced a passionate anathema on the existing racist church: 'What clergyman ever introduced the subject of slavery or oppression of the hireling into the pulpit? Which even enquired into the bloodguiltiness of his members? Or where was a member ever excommunicated for having taken away the lives of Hottentots, Bushmen etc.? Blood lays at our door ... oh, what a day of retribution is yet to come?'[6]

The two LMS missionaries realised that they could not stay longer. Turning their backs on Graaff Reinet, they led their Khoisan followers to a site near Algoa Bay, where they set up a closed community on the Moravian pattern, which they called Bethelsdorp. Although Van der Kemp had chosen a poor site, where water lay stagnant and most of the soil was unfit for agriculture, he announced that the settlement would operate on the Biblical principle that 'if a man does not work, neither shall he eat'. But it was difficult to meet this demand. Early visitors reported that they saw only 'lean, ragged or naked figures, with indolent, sleepy countenances'.[7]

Whites found the way in which the Khoisan protected their bodies from flying insects with grease and cattle dung deeply offensive, and they were disgusted when Van der Kemp announced that, at Bethelsdorp, all races would live as one. When visitors found black and white living together in squalor, they insisted that, instead of allowing themselves to be dragged down into barbarian ways, missionaries ought to direct their energies towards raising the Khoisan to proper standards of Christian civilisation. Disapproval tipped over into scandal when news spread that both missionaries had taken Khoisan wives. With old age approaching, Van der Kemp married a fourteen-year-old girl, whom he bought out of slavery at a huge cost of £740 – enough to keep some twenty white missionaries in the field for a year. Old fires were still alight, for she bore him four children in his remaining years. Meanwhile, as his superior grew older, James Read assumed responsibility for practical affairs. Artisans were sent out to work alongside the Khoisan and together they produced goods, for trading with farmers and the military. The economy strengthened as enterprising Khoisan set up businesses in the carrying and timber trades. When Van der Kemp died in 1811, Read's reputation stood high at home and the directors felt that they needed to look no further for a general superintendent. Although this was the highest possible compliment to a man who had arrived as an artisan, Read rejected the offer on the grounds that he could not expect his Khoisan wife and coloured children to live within racist Cape Town society. Instead, he set about gathering examples of the brutality and injustice that was routinely inflicted on his wife's people and dispatched his findings to mission headquarters in London. After doing the rounds of Exeter Hall activists, the Cape government was instructed to carry out an investigation, which would become infamous in Boer mythology as the Black Circuit. As the Khoisan accused their masters in open court, the testimony of a person they categorised as a 'heathen' was for the first time given equal weight with that of a 'Christian'.

But Read's accusations lost credibility when the story broke that he had fathered a child by a second Khoisan woman. A fellow missionary wrote home the news that the sex life of the society's most prominent missionary had become the hottest item of colonial gossip: 'Tell it not in Gath, publish it not in the streets of Ascelon, lest the daughters of the Philistines rejoice, lest the daughters of the uncircumcised triumph! ... It is gone far and wide through the colony ... We don't know how to show our faces in the world.'[8] Read accepted the child as his own and set aside the second woman. While the society would put out that he had fallen once to a scheming girl, the accurate story was that its most senior worker had embraced polygamy. Previously, it had been accepted that a properly blessed inter-racial marriage was as legitimate as any other; then, Scottish minister George Thom (who had assumed the vacant title of LMS superintendent for southern Africa without any authorisation) announced that no mixed union could qualify as a Christian marriage, and he brought charges of immorality against four more LMS colleagues. One of them, a German, had been travelling on the frontier far from any Christian minister, when he called the members of his trek together to witness that he had married his housekeeper. From such events, LMS church members learned that the most efficient way of getting rid of an unpopular minister was to accuse him of adultery – preferably with the wife of a leading church member.[9]

In January 1817, Thom greeted five new recruits, three of whom were to have long careers with the society: twenty-one-year-old gardener Robert Moffat would live to be a legend on the northern frontier; pacifist and shoemaker James Kitchingman became Read's ally and successor at Bethelsdorp and John Brownlee would make his name as pioneer of the Xhosa frontier. After informing them that every one of the Society's stations was a hotbed of laziness and immorality, Thom advised them not to waste time on thankless Hottentots but to direct their efforts at improving the Boers. Thom himself left the mission to join the Dutch Reformed Church, recruiting ten fellow Scottish evangelical ministers to reinforce the depleted ranks of native Boer *dominees*. Prominent among them was James Murray, who would become patriarch to a huge clan of Scottish Boers.

Superintendent John Philip

Faced with a leadership vacuum, LMS directors scoured Britain for a new superintendent who could command the respect of his colleagues and of the Cape Town and London governments, and they finally settled on the minister of a flourishing Congregationalist church in Aberdeen. Like many successful Scots, John Philip came from a humble but serious and hard-working family, and after reading the works of Adam Smith, he had adopted key principles of the Scottish enlightenment. Before leaving for Cape Town, he established contact with the members of the Exeter Hall lobby and the sympathisers within the British government.

With the South African operation still engulfed in scandal, Philip's early task was to find suitable partners for mission workers, and he quickly won a reputation as an 'inveterate matchmaker' within the mission community. Many older LMS workers were raising huge families in the benign South African climate, but Philip was determined that lonely men on distant outstations should not import unacceptable attitudes onto their stations by marrying into the colonial community; Read had now been demoted to artisan status, with the younger Kitchingman promoted over his head, but the two men were good friends, and Philip found that Bethelsdorp ran happily enough. The superintendent and the artisan approached their work from very

different positions. Having rejected the trappings of western civilisation
in his own life, Read saw no reason to impose them on converts. Philip,
in contrast, argued the enlightenment case. Civilisation, he reasoned,
involves the accumulation of possessions, which have to be stored
somewhere. But cramped, traditional round huts offered no space for
a chest, no quiet place for children to study and afforded no privacy
in which to conduct sexual relations with propriety. He, therefore, drew
up a detailed plan for a reconstructed Bethelsdorp settlement, which
showed carefully laid out roads, rectangular houses and even a square
with a sundial in the centre. Whatever their differences, Philip and Read
shared a common concern that every person, black or white, should have
equal opportunity for personal advancement, access to an impartial
justice system and the same rights of land ownership. In Philip's opinion,
this was South Africa's 'great moral and religious topic', which must
draw the mission into colonial politics, and on this basis he concluded
a deal with the people of Bethelsdorp. Each month, Kitchingman would
send him a report on the progress made in pulling down the old buildings
and replacing them with new and, in return, he solemnly pledged that
he would never cease, by every lawful means, 'to secure their just rights
as subjects of the British government' for the Khoisan people.[10]

Further afield, LMS missionaries were less united behind their
superintendent. A few openly supported the Boers, while others argued
that a missionary's sole duty was to preach personal salvation and
he should never become involved in any kind of politics. Read,
Kitchingman and the Griqua Town minister, William Wright, formed the
core of Philip's party, while opponents grouped around Robert Moffat,
the young gardener who had been briefed by Thom in 1817. Feeling
himself to be surrounded by poisonous whispers, Philip appealed directly
to the British people in his two-volume book, *Researches in South Africa*.
Basing his case on the doctrines of Adam Smith, he argued that slavery
and oppression were, at the same time, morally wrong and economically
inefficient.[11] If the Khoisan were allowed to accumulate wealth, they
would consume British goods, to the profit of home manufacturers. The
leader of the parliamentary anti-slavery movement, Thomas Fowell
Buxton, took up his case, moving that a Parliamentary Select Committee
on Aborigines should examine the treatment of indigenous people in all
British possessions. Surely, he forecast, there would be much to uncover.
'Oh! We Englishmen are, by our own account, fine fellows at home!
Who among us doubts that we surpass the world in justice, knowledge,

refinement and practical honesty? But such a set of miscreants and ravening wolves as we prove when we escape from the range of laws, the earth does not contain.'[12]

The moment in 1835, when James Read, his son – James Read Jr – and the Xhosa chief Dyani Tshatshu travelled to London to present the African case before Buxton's committee, marked the high point in Philip's career. Thereafter it went into decline. Four years later, Robert Moffat returned to England on an extended leave, to find that his own best-selling autobiography had made him a celebrity. Philip's domestic position was more seriously undermined by the disastrous 1841 Niger expedition. In his last years, African land was alienated faster than ever before, while his LMS directors remembered that their first objective had been to use South Africa as a base for work in the north and began to distance themselves from the region's 'great moral and religious topic'. He died in 1851, believing that his own country had betrayed its civilising mission.

The Xhosa Frontier Wars

The civilising mission was fatally complicated by another factor: war. In 1819, the British parliament voted £50,000 to help emigrants travel to a newly occupied area of the Eastern Cape. Each settler family was promised 150 acres of land, and £100 was allocated for any clergyman who would make the voyage. The Methodists recruited the young minister William Shaw to represent the denomination, whereas lay preachers William Shepstone and John Ayliff travelled without official funding. Even as their ships dropped anchor in Algoa Bay in April 1820, Xhosa bands were plundering the colonial countryside. Nobody had explained to the settlers that their true role was to form a human shield for the Cape Colony. They had arrived in Africa towards the mid-point of an intermittent 100-year struggle over the possession of rich African-owned farming land. The decision to create 150-acre farms had been taken without any reference to the requirements of agriculture – the size was based on the density of population needed to create an effective barrier against raiders. Most of the new settlers were ill-equipped for the challenge ahead; many came from London, where they had never seen a cabbage growing on its stalk, and some followed trades that had little application in a pioneer community.

After William Shaw established his headquarters at the military outpost of Grahamstown, the settlement quickly became a flourishing community, clustered around his handsome Methodist church. Prominent among Shaw's congregation was Robert 'Moral Bob' Godlonton, editor of *The Graham's Town Journal*, which was the strident mouthpiece of the settler community, Shaw made it his personal priority to provide for the religious needs of his settler compatriots, but as superintendent, he was also responsible for missionary work, and he urged his society to focus on the great continent to the north, which was, he said, 'abounding with heathen inhabitants'. 'There is not a single Missionary Station between the place of my residence and the northern extremity of the Red Sea; nor any people professedly Christian, with the exception of those of Abyssinia. Here then is a wide field – the whole eastern coast of the continent of Africa.'[13]

In 1823, Shaw, Shepstone and their wives crossed the colonial frontier and gathered people in the nearest village, though the planned worship became impossible when 'a fit of cachinnation [laughter] spread itself around the circle'. Undaunted, Shaw set about delivering the message that the Xhosa had to stop all stealing from the colony. To his delight, the chiefs agreed to mount a watch at all the drifts where cattle could ford the river. For his side of the bargain, Shaw gave assurances that Methodist preachers would do everything possible to uphold the authority of chiefs: 'It is not only allowed, but *required* obedience to authority in everything not sinful; that this obedience was not a mere appendage to Christianity, but was interwoven with its spirit and laws.'[14]

The conversion of border chief Kama was recorded as the first Wesleyan success in southern Africa, and Shaw presented his society with a plan to establish a 400-mile-long mission chain from the colonial border to the British military base at Port Natal. In the event, only six stations were opened before the operation petered out in country that had been depopulated by warfare. Indeed, even as the British settled their new plots on the Xhosa's southern border, the armies of Zulu King Shaka were pounding the ninety-four tribes of Natal from the north, creating a mass cross-border migration into Xhosa territory. The unwilling hosts called these dispossessed folk the *mfengu*, or 'hungry people in search of work' – corrupted by European ears to Fingos. It was the first manifestation of a larger chain movement of peoples that would become known as the *lifaqane* (or *mfecane*) – 'the time of crushing'. Accounts of this terrible period are drawn largely from missionary reports, and

historians discuss the extent to which other migrations – particularly
of whites from the Cape and Mozambique – contributed to the
destruction.[15]

Shaw was in England at the time when Buxton's Select Committee was
gathering evidence of colonial abuse. While admitting that individual
instances of injustice might occur, he proposed that the indigenous people
should lose the fertile territory between the Great Fish and Keiskamma
Rivers and then be given long-term security on their land holdings within
the new frontier. 'If we deprive them of the soil, we deprive them of the
means of sustenance and we compel them to become robbers and thus
war must be perpetrated till we have extirpated them.'[16] Xhosa tribal
chiefs found evidence for their growing suspicion that, for all their talk
of peace, Methodist ministers were warmongers at heart. Pugnacious
Lieutenant Governor Sir Harry Smith did nothing to undermine this view
when he admired the authoritarian way in which missionary Boyce
handled the Africans in his charge.

> The man of the gospel is after all a worldly fellow … more full of
> dragooning our new subjects than a hundred soldiers.'[17] Ayliff was
> another robust advocate of the colonial cause, and Dugmore was
> perceived by Africans as 'a man who came to teach the truth to the
> Caffers: but he does not know the truth himself. Such men from
> the colony speak lightly of war; they delight in the grass and water
> of Caffaria and make strings of lies to secure it.[18]

In John Philip's eyes, Shaw and his Methodists served as puppets
of the colonial interest. 'I have viewed them for some years past', he
declared, 'as the eulogists of the commando system and the servile tools
of the men who are most deeply stained with the blood of the caffres.'[19]

Progress achieved in times of peace was easily lost in times of war.
After the Presbyterians built stations across Xhosa country, they were
happy to take credit for the fact that there was little cross-border theft
and that the whole territory was at peace. In 1824, John and Helen Ross
established the first Glasgow Missionary Society station on a site that
they called Lovedale in the honour of Society Secretary Dr Love.
Following Scottish practice, they installed a printing press and opened
the multiracial school that would make the station's international
reputation. Chief Maqoma then invited the missionary couple to set up
another station in the beautiful and fertile land around his own kraal,

in a countryside that had long been contested between the Khoisan
and Xhosa. Progress was encouraging, and before long, Ross was able
to report that the chief knew 'nearly the whole of the little catechism,
which the missionaries had prepared'.[20] The Scots then heard that
Maqoma's Xhosa were to be driven from their homes to make way for
a Khoisan resettlement project, to be known as the Kat River Settlement.
In 1829, the missionary husband and wife could only watch as Maqoma's
village and then their mission church and compound were burnt to the
ground. They followed Maqoma's people to their new home north of the
Keiskamma River, and when war erupted once again, Helen Ross took
the personal risk of hiding a fugitive chief under her kitchen table as
British soldiers ransacked the compound.

Now restored to favour, James Read became resident missionary
on the new Kat River Settlement and single-mindedly set about making
the project a success. In his devotion to the Khoisan cause, he failed
to recognise that his Khoisan wife's people were still being exploited – for
now it was their turn to provide the Cape with a 'hard frontier' against
the raiding Xhosa. While *The Graham's Town Journal* resisted any
suggestion that white settlers might be subject to conscription in their
own defence, the Kat River Khoisan could be impressed into the frontier
army, and in troubled times, it was not unusual for 70 percent of adult
males to be away from their farms and families on military duty. Any
who deserted were hanged without compunction by British officers.

* * *

By the middle of the century, it was said that more missionaries were
concentrated in Xhosa country than in any comparably sized region
in the world, with the possible exception of New Zealand. Their attempts
to provide Africans with a religious education were considerable. Mainly,
they used catechisms, in which the teacher asked a set question, and the
enquirer provided a prepared answer. The Xhosa proved to be an argu-
mentative people, however, who insisted on giving all the wrong answers.
William Shaw complained that he often found himself 'in the position of
a person to be catechised, rather than in that of a teacher'. Neither he nor
any missionary colleague could entertain the possibility that a Xhosa
might reject the Christian message as intellectually unsatisfying. Even
among Methodist colleagues, William Shrewsbury was known as a man
of rigid beliefs; he had finished his education at the age of ten and
interrogation taxed him sorely.

When speaking of the happiness of those who turned to God, in that
at death they were received into His kingdom, one said, 'How can
that be?' As kaffirs never bury their dead, he continued, 'We see and
know that the wolf eats them up, and how can he go to God?' …
He then asked a variety of frivolous questions concerning God,
as – What sort of being he was? Whether he had cattle? How many
and of what kind they were? When we reproved him for such idle
questions, he replied that he had too much wisdom to ask idly, but,
being ignorant, he wished to learn.[21]

Africans who lived within traditional society had difficulty in reconciling
the core Christian doctrines that God was both loving and all powerful;
if he caused the sun to shine, they asked, did he not also make it bring
famine by burning the crops? Also, if he caused the rain to fall, did he not
also withhold it in times of drought? The people whose lives depended
on these natural phenomena appeared to confirm their traditional belief
that gods were fickle beings, who demanded propitiation from their
adherents. And so, after many years of work, there remained little
to show for this concentration of educational efforts in Xhosa country.
The missionaries emphasised modest successes, such as when the
convert Dyani Tshatshu succeeded to his father's chiefdom, or when
one of Magoma's councillors, known as Old Soga, was reported to
be sympathetic, but the mass of Xhosa people remained stubbornly
indifferent. The displaced *mfengu*, however, proved to be more receptive
to the white man's message.

In the two decades between 1834 and 1853, the region was
convulsed by three frontier struggles – Hintsa's War, the War of the
Axe and Mlanjeni's War. They were to prove disastrous. Shaw's pledge
of allegiance to local chiefs was long forgotten as Methodists and many
other denominations sought to deliver their converts' allegiance to the
colonial cause. On the outbreak of Hintsa's War, for example, John Ayliff
drew up a compact with his Mfengu converts:

No Fingo shall in any way take part in the invasion of the Colony.

That as far as possible the Fingoes shall protect the English
missionaries and traders.

That the Fingoes shall be nightly bearers of letters from Mr Ayliff
to the commander of the British forces, giving him information
on the state of Kaffirland.[22]

Thousands fought on the colonists' side in return for empty promises of land when the conflict was over. At the end of the war, Ayliff led a mass exodus out of Xhosa country as a huge column of *mfengu* – reportedly some 17,000 strong, complete with animals – followed their missionary's wagon. An observer declared, 'Nothing like this flight has been seen, perhaps, since the days of Moses.'

When the Cape governor decided to take sovereignty over Xhosa country, he delegated the task of informing the local chiefs of the loss of their lands to loyal Methodist ministers. However, belatedly, John Philip came to the Xhosa's aid and denounced the peace terms to Secretary of State for the Colonies Lord Glenelg, who had himself grown up within the Clapham Sect, and he reversed the colonial governor's decision. Predictably, *The Graham's Town Journal* heaped derision on 'ignorant sentimentalists' who interfered with the decisions of hard-headed colonial administrators, who knew the ways of savages. Across the ecclesiastical divide, Catholic Bishop Ricards attributed later conflict to the blundering of the Home Government, urged on to this course by the fatal policy of Lord Glenelg, who had given too willing an ear to the representations of a small party in Cape Town. 'The chief work of this party seemed to consist in misrepresenting, as barbarous outrages on the Kaffirs, the spirited defensive struggles of the frontier colonists, and coddling the morbid sensibilities of so-called philanthropists in the mother country.'[23]

As war followed war, home supporters read graphic accounts of missionary 'perils and adventures' in which stations were burnt and property plundered, and intrepid white men and women faced warlike barbarians, escaping through hostile territory at dead of night. What home supporters never learned was that missionaries were rarely in danger. Xhosa armies operated under different rules from their own. Under Bantu tradition, warfare was seen not only as a means of obtaining enemy land but also as a device for supplementing the breeding stock of the victorious people. Men and older boys of fighting age were killed without compunction, but women and younger children were spared and absorbed into the victorious tribe. While missionary 'teachers' shared the women's immunity, artisans were theoretically vulnerable; but in practice, none were harmed. An army officer recorded that the 'forces of civilisation' behaved differently.

I have heard and seen many horrible things, but this I must say, that the most atrocious villains and the most loveable on the face of the

earth, are to be found among the white men. A more kind hearted
soul than Sgt Shelley could never be conceived; and another man
in my corps used to carry about, concealed in his jacket, a broken
reaping-hook, to cut the throats of the women and children we had
taken prisoner on our night expeditions.[24]

The officer failed to explain why he turned a blind eye to his men's
barbarities.

Ordained clergy added to the chorus of hatred against the Xhosa.
LMS recruit Henry Calderwood developed his doctrine of the 'manifest
destiny' of the white races. Since the Xhosa had 'too much room
to roam about and live in idleness', the acquisition of land by the settler
community was no more than 'the following out of one of the grand
designs of a Gracious Providence to bless the world'.[25] Scottish
warmonger George Brown, who had won an unwholesome reputation
as a womanizer in both black and white communities, explained his
rejoicing at the death of a chief.

> People at home think it inconsistent with the genius of Christianity,
> to give God thanks for the destruction or slaughter of a fellow man.
> It is at small expense they nourish this kind of vapid, or rather
> unnatural sentimentality. At one time I was not without a share of
> it myself. But more assuredly I have given hearty thanks this day for
> the death of that man, and the discomfiture of his party, as ever I did
> for any mercy received at the hand of God.[26]

Caught up within this toxic environment, African converts reverted
to old loyalties. LMS workers were devastated to hear that Dyani
Tshatshu had thrown off his European clothes and taken up arms
with his own people. Spear in hand, Old Soga confronted his Scottish
dominee. 'My kraal was a school – my house was the house of God.
I prayed to God and sang praises to God every day, and why do you
permit my house to be burned? … You must now take care of yourself.'[27]

Although the elderly James Read was becoming increasingly
bewildered by this new world, he still tried ever harder to prove that his
Khoisan were loyal servants of the British crown. From Bethelsdorp,
pacifist James Kitchingman noted sadly that his old friend had deserted
the principles of a lifetime and followed other 'Caffre brethren' into the
war camp. Read's lifetime work fell to pieces when a Khoisan spokesman

declared that the Kat River settlers had declared independence from their missionaries and planned to make common cause with the Xhosa. The British governor expressed his astonishment at an event 'unparalleled, I believe, in the history of the world … [when] … a mass of civilised men, the greater part born in the Christian faith and the rest converted and improving Christians, for years assembled in villages and societies under excellent clergymen, suddenly, and without any cause whatever, rush back into barbarism and savage life'. At the very end, James Read came to question the settlement's whole moral foundation. 'The undertaking here was very dark. The country has been taken from the Caffres in a very unsatisfactory way and it was like occupying stolen country.'[28]

The Cattle Killing

When a people has been defeated in war, the traditional means of livelihood lie devastated and the whole culture is on the verge of collapse, survivors may turn to exotic religion. In April 1856, two Xhosa girls, Nongqawuse and Nombanda, set out from their homes to scare birds from the crops. Nongqawuse told how she heard a voice call her name as they stood in the field:

> Tell that the whole community will rise from the dead; and that all the cattle now living must be slaughtered, for they have been reared by contaminated hands because there are people about who deal in witchcraft. There should be no cultivation, but great new grain pits must be dug, new houses must be built, and great strong cattle enclosures must be erected.[29]

The voice promised that strong chiefs would return from the dead to drive the white men out of the land. As that desperate hope took root, believers began to kill their animals, destroy the crops and dig pits where they planned to store the abundant supplies that ancestors would bring from the grave. Unbelievers tried to protect their property against the craze of destruction, but Paramount Chief Sandili and the aged Maqoma announced their support. At first, famine spread slowly; then, when children began to die, believers announced that the young had gone ahead to summon the dead. At last, Nongqawuse set a date for the millennial event. On 16 February 1857, she declared, the sun would rise late and it would be blood red in colour. Then, before anybody needed to eat again, the grain pits would fill, and fine new cattle would rise from the earth. Some of her followers climbed into the hills to get first sight of the great event, while others lit fires beside their homes to ensure that the resurrected ones did not pass them by.[30] From his mission station, Charles Brownlee witnessed what became known as the Great Disappointment:

> And now that the final step was taken, a dreadful pause ensued. All intercourse between the two sets of people ceased, the believers being afraid of mixing with the unbelievers and exposing themselves to being swept into the sea. Those who had destroyed their property, sat at their villages with the silence of a desperate hope, waiting for the fulfilment of the prophesy. Every morning the kraals and the corn pits were eagerly inspected, and hope sickened, but was not quenched. The moon was anxiously watched by night and the sun by day by hunger-stricken hosts. The bones they had cast away in the days of feasting were gathered and gnawed. Women and children wandered through the fields to dig for roots.[31]

The response to such a humanitarian crisis needed to be immediate and decisive; but Cape Governor Sir George Grey was a committed member of that group of economic liberal politicians, led by Zacharay Macaulay's son-in-law Charles Trevelyan, who, twelve years earlier, had orchestrated the implacable British government response to the Irish potato famine. Following Trevelyan's ideology, Grey believed that industrial society must be grounded in sound education and health care, and he brought a distinguished reforming record in those two areas from earlier work in New Zealand and Australia. According to this doctrine, however, lasting progress would never be achieved without the creation of a mobile body of wage-earning labourers. Realising that the cattle killing had created a unique opportunity to make a 'clear sweep' of tribal society, he decreed that famine relief would be delivered at the lowest possible level to sustain life – and then only to the very old, the chronically sick and the disabled.[32] Anyone with the strength to walk out of Xhosa country had to leave homes and farms to accept work within the colony, on the government's terms.

The Anglicans had opened four stations on the Xhosa frontier, named after the Evangelists, and now they stood in the line of exodus from the stricken area. On 2 May 1857, one of the priests in charge placed an advertisement in the *King William's Town Gazette*.

DESTITUTE KAFFIR CHILDREN

The missionary with Unhala is constrained to appeal earnestly
to the benevolent throughout the colony for assistance to enable
him to feed STARVING CHILDREN of the T'Slambie Tribe. Great
numbers are reduced (by no fault of their own, but the errors
of their parents) to a wretched existence on GUM and ROOTS,
and even these resources are now failing them. This appeal is made
in the confident hope that good Christians will help these poor
people in the time of their need.[33]

The editor saw fit to distance his paper from the request. Such relief,
he suggested, 'would be a premium on idleness, and prevent [the Xhosa]
from becoming what we would find it so much to our and their interest for
them to be – labourers'. Newly arrived Anglican Bishop Henry Cotterill –
who, to everybody's surprise, turned out to be a hard-line evangelical –
was at first inclined to add his support to the relief effort, but after he had
been won round by the governor's arguments, all pleas for help fell on deaf
ears: 'The missionary comes here to preach the word of God, not to give
food; it is your duty to provide food for yourselves.... We are Christians
and love you, and wish to do you good; but when you bring God's
judgement on your sins, we do not know what is best to do for you.'
Cotterill closed the St. Luke mission and removed the over-sympathetic
priest who had placed the original advert on the grounds that he did not
have 'rigour of mind enough to deal with kaffirs'.

Anglo-Catholic Archbishop Gray, who had never been comfortable
with his near namesake Governor Grey's policy, announced that help
must be provided for the children of chiefs who now languished in
detention on Robben Island, and he accordingly set up a school within
his palace. During those hard years, Old Soga's son, Tio Soga, had been
receiving higher education in Scotland, and his return with a Scottish
wife as a fully accredited Presbyterian minister created a sensation. Faced
with this model of regeneration, Paramount Chief Sandili agreed to send
his eldest son and daughter to the bishop's school, and others followed
his example. Gray's schoolmaster approached his task with trepidation;
he anticipated entering 'a compound of the wild beast, with passions
uncontrolled, and full of the mixture of duplicity and cruelty which
is generally considered the characteristic of those who for long ages
have sat in dankness' – but instead he found that he had assumed
responsibility for well-ordered children of 'exceeding promise'.[34] But

the bishop's lady, Sophie Gray, wanted this kaffir school out of her house, and forty-four boys, three girls, a clergyman, teacher, music teacher, shoemaker and carpenter were moved to the cold Zonnenbloem (Sunflower) site that was blasted by prevalent south-easterly winds.[35]

It has been estimated that some 40,000 people died in the great starvation. After many years of bonded labour in the Cape, survivors were resettled in satellite villages, sited conveniently close to the white men's lands that could now be found across Xhosa country. Henry Callaway, first Anglican bishop of Kaffaria, laid out the huge task that faced his clergy:

> To teach them to plough instead of to hoe; to enclose their land
> instead of keeping people to watch it; to get men to work and
> to learn that women were not made to be slaves, but companions;
> to teach them to sit on chairs and eat off plates, instead of squatting
> on the ground and eating with a chip out of a pot; to teach them
> to build square houses instead of round hovels.[36]

Many years later, Archbishop Desmond Tutu would enjoy repeating the parable that had passed among his own Xhosa people. 'When the white man first came here, he had the Bible and we had the land. Then the white man said to us, "Come let us kneel and pray together". So we knelt and closed our eyes and prayed, and when we opened our eyes again, lo! – we had the Bible and he had the land.'

Chapter 6

The Cheapest and Best Military Posts

The London Missionary Society Northern Party

While still in Cape Town, the LMS pioneers were introduced to three
men, Vigilant, Slapcorm and Orclam, who wanted to tell the story
of their people, whom the whites called Bushmen and the Khoisan called
the San.[1] They told how their families had been free to hunt game on the
northern veld until intruders encroached on their territory. First came
nomadic bands of mixed race people, known as 'baastards', who stole
animals off the white men's farms to the south and from African villages
in the north. Behind them came the Boers; by their tradition, the youngest
son remained on the family farm to look after the parents and eventually
inherit the property, while elder sons travelled out in search of land.
Between them, these intruders were destroying the fragile veld ecosystem
that had sustained the San lifestyle, killing wildlife and trampling down
vegetation beneath the hooves of countless cattle. Both baastards and
Boers described the San as baboons, even speculating whether these
surviving hunter-gatherers could be members of the human race. Year
by year, the San were driven ever further back into barren desert.
Vigilant, Slapcorm and Orclam's people fought back as best they could,
moving across the country like shadows and attacking the intruders
and their animals with poisoned arrows, but in this unequal contest,
baastards and Boers showed no mercy as they hunted down and shot
thousands of San men, women and children.

After separating from Van der Kemp's eastern party, Kircherer and
Edwards followed the northbound wagon trail into an arid country. They
travelled with two young Boers. Adrian Kramer was anxious to have
a part in the task of converting the people of Africa, and Edwards found
himself a wife in Cape Town. When they finally made contact with the
San, Kircherer quickly decided that a people with no chief or tribal
structure could hardly be suitable targets for conversion.[2] In common
with many artisans, Edwards had volunteered for missionary work in the
hope of improving his fortunes in life, and the young couple journeyed
on with plans to contact the baastards and trade in ivory. Fortunately,
his replacement, William Anderson, proved to be 'strung with the fibre

required of pioneer missionaries', and the strengthened party moved forwards into a country occupied by the Nama people.

Whites called the land to the south of the Orange River (now in modern South Africa) Little Namaqualand and that to the north (in modern Namibia), Great Namaqualand. As they came under pressure from baastards and Boers on both sides of the river, the Nama learnt the bitter lesson that they would remain victims to both baastards and Boers until they possessed firearms and knew how to use and maintain them. The little LMS party did not have the resources to trade in guns, even if they wished to do so, but they did travel with hunting weapons. Kircherer's party therefore faced a dilemma that would haunt missionaries in southern and central Africa. On the one hand, home supporters would be shocked if news broke that their representatives were cleaning and repairing guns and showing 'savages' how to point them at the enemy instead of firing over their heads as if they were using spears; on the other hand, they were reluctant to abandon the continent's indigenous people to the mercy of the armed and mounted enemies, who planned to kill their men-folk, steal their land and take their women and children into slavery. The issue rarely features in correspondence; it can be said, however, that the Nama did welcome Kircherer's party, and it is likely that the missionaries gave practical assistance in exchange.

Back in London, expectation grew that Kircherer's party was opening a route into the heart of the continent, and even more excitingly, it seemed possible that the work of conversion could be undertaken at little cost to the society. According to the received wisdom, pre-industrial man had passed through three phases of development. The San, who followed the ancient hunter-gatherer way of life, were locked into the most primitive stage, while the Nama had taken the upwards step into the second stage of nomadic pastoralism. But wandering people did not stay in one place long enough to practice the 'industrial arts' or learn to read the Bible. It followed therefore that the missionary's first task was to help them take the third step and become settled farmers. LMS workers were therefore expected to set up model farms to attract pastoralists into satellite villages. As they started to grow cash crops, mission stations would become self-supporting, and the potential for expansion would be endless. To provide the necessary motivation to achieve this end, British, German and Dutch LMS recruits on the north-western frontier were kept desperately short of funds. But the whole project was built on a catastrophic error. The land was unsuitable for arable cultivation.

It is no coincidence that the Great Wall of China runs approximately along the line where annual precipitation drops below 20 inches, which is the amount required to sustain settled farming. As missionaries moved north in southern Africa, they first passed the 20- and then the 10-inch lines. Europeans might have an unshakable confidence in the potential of irrigation to conquer drought, but on this northern frontier the rain that did fall was erratic and irrigation ditches quickly dried up. Driven to desperation by shortages of money and supplies, LMS workers dispatched a joint letter to the headquarters. 'Much as we study economy, experience teaches us that the needful provision for each person will amount to no less than 300 Dutch florins (about £30) annually.'[3]

In 1813, John Campbell, director of the LMS, visited South Africa to make a tour of the society's stations to see for himself. Inseparable from his huge umbrella, this tiny Londoner might have been an easy figure of ridicule, but he was also a careful listener and close observer. His long-term task was to identify the course for a 'missionary road' that future generations would follow into the continental heartland. He confirmed that the two coastal routes were impractical; on the western side, travellers would need to survive many hundred miles of Namaqualand desert – only to finish their journey in Catholic Angola, and on the other side of the continent, the eastern way was blocked by endemic warfare in Xhosa and Zulu countries. Therefore, Campbell travelled into the territory in the centre that was occupied by various branches of the Tswana (Bechuana) people, who belonged to the larger Sotho language group. Till his arrival, missionary William Anderson had been working this huge area single-handedly. After following nomadic baastard bands for many years, he had managed to establish a station, where a number of the wanderers were beginning to put down roots. On arrival at Anderson's station, Campbell called a meeting and suggested that the name baastard was unsuited to a Christian people; someone remembered that his own clan was descended from an ancestor called Griqua, and from that time, Anderson's baastards became known as Griquas and his station, Griquatown.

After travelling a further 100 miles north to the Tswana settlement of Lattakoo, Campbell learnt that beyond the dry and forbidding Kalahari desert (sparsely occupied by northern Tswana pastoralists) lay a fertile and heavily populated countryside watered by a great river. Local people warned him that, although Africans did make the journey across the dry country, the desert road was unsuited to the white men's wagons. Ignoring them, Campbell decreed that his missionary road

would start from Lattakoo. The young Robert Moffat was chosen
to found a station which would serve as the road's base at nearby
Kuruman. More than once in his lifetime, this imposing and powerful
man had to cross 500 miles of desert to reach the fertile Zambezi Basin
that lay on the other side. There were hopes that the great missionary
road that the LMS dreamed of would open Central Africa to the Gospel.

John Philip's Strategy

During this period, missionaries who lived in isolated stations on the
northern frontier were first-hand witnesses of the *lifaqane* – migrating
war parties of different Bantu peoples caught between their turbulent
homeland and advancing whites. As one displaced people moved
into a new territory, they violently displaced another that lay in their
path. After 1820, Northern Nguni war parties began to emerge out
of Zululand onto the high veld, and of these, the most fearsome were the
Ndebele – who became known to the world as the Matabele – followers
of Shaka's former army officer Mzilikazi.[4] After Ndebele warriors had
driven Shona farmers from their lands, the Shona, in their turn, preyed
on people who lay in the path of their flight. As Methodist minister
to the Borolong, Samuel Broadbent, watched the 'forlorn, haggard and
wretched' flotsam' pass by his station, he was reminded of the Gibeonites
in the days of Joshua; while the Bible told of events long gone, this
distress was 'painful reality'.[5] Hearing that a huge band, the Manatee
army, was approaching Kuruman, Moffat hurried to Griquatown,
to return with a mounted commando, but the local Tswana set on the
disorganised and starving Manatees, without respect for age or sex.

> The Bechuanas, like voracious wolves, with their spears and axes
> began despatching the wounded men and butchering the women
> and children.... It was truly affecting to see the mother and infant
> rolled in blood, and I more than once saw the living infant in the
> arms of a dead mother. All ages and sexes were lying prostrate
> on the ground. Shortly after the enemy began their retreat, many
> of the women, seeing that mercy was shown to them, instead
> of flying, generally sat down, baring their bosoms exclaiming,
> 'I am a woman', 'we are women'.[6]

After the killing was over, Moffat could only offer thanks that, in the providence of God, not a single member of the mission staff or the Griqua commando had died. His report concluded with the Old Testament resonance: 'The slain of the enemy was between 400 and 500.' But the tide of the *lifaqane* continued to flow northwards towards the Kalahari, leaving wide swathes of depopulated country; in Moffat's memorable metaphor, the traditional inhabitants had been left 'scattered and peeled'.

* * *

By 1830, stability seemed to be returning. The once-feared baastard raiders had abandoned old ways to become middlemen in the trade between the colony and the interior, and social life revolved around their churches. John Philip could announce that his missionaries had secured the whole northern frontier without the expenditure of one drop of colonial blood or one ounce of government powder: 'Missionary stations are the most efficient agents which can be employed to promote the internal strength of our colonies, and the cheapest and best military posts that a wise government can employ to defend its frontiers against the predatory incursions of savage tribes.'[7]

Philip planned to plant missionaries in all key centres beyond the northern frontier, with the Zulu and Ndebele as prime targets for conversion; but LMS resources were stretched, and Philip persisted in treating the Methodists as enemies of the great project. Instead, he sought new associates, and, while on leave in Europe, he contacted two newly formed societies that were looking for fields of operation. A Lutheran congregation in the town of Barmen – now a suburb in the Rhineland conurbation – had long provided the LMS with recruits for work in Namaqualand, and on Philip's advice, it now formed itself as an independent society, with full responsibility for the punishing work north of the Orange River. The Paris Evangelical Missionary Society, which drew support from both French and Swiss Calvinists, also agreed to send a party to make contact with the Ndebele. Philip returned to Cape Town in 1833 with four young Frenchmen – missionaries Jean Pierre Pellissier, Thomas Arbousset, Eugène Casalis and artisan Constant Gosselin. Philip had also kept in touch with American Board secretary Rufus Anderson, and waiting in his mail, he found a letter from a student at Princeton Theological College. The writer explained that between twenty and thirty fellow students were interested in missionary work, but they had no idea where to start, and he requested Philip to send the same advice that he would give if he were writing to his own son. In a long, careful reply, Philip encouraged the Americans to join him, assuring them that Africans were not intrinsically inferior to people of European inheritance: 'The civilisation of the people among whom we labour in Africa is not our highest object; but that object can never be secured and rendered permanent among them without their civilisation. Civilisation is to the Christian religion what the body is to the soul.'[8]

Two years later, the *American Missionary Herald* announced a departure for southern Africa. Members were divided into two parties according to whether they came from the southern or the northern states. From the south were 'Rev Daniel Lindley, Missionary; Rev Alex E. Wilson, Missionary and Physician; Rev H.L. Venable', and from the north, 'Rev Aldin Grout, Missionary; Rev G. Champion, Missionary; and Dr Newton Adams, Physician'. Although Lindley was born in the north and had married a northern woman, the couple had been living in the south. All the members were married, and the fact that they travelled with their unnamed wives was acknowledged only in parentheses.[9]

Ndebele, Zulu and Boer

Meanwhile, the four young Frenchmen had set off on a long journey to the kraal of Ndebele King Mzilikazi (on the site where the City of Pretoria stands today). When they drew close, the main party pitched camp, leaving Pellissier to finish the journey alone. He returned several days later with a dispiriting story; instead of welcoming his new missionary, the Ndebele king had him sit alone in a hut to clean piles of captured firearms. Mzilikazi had ways of testing a man's mettle and he made Pellissier watch an execution before letting him rejoin his companions. Abandoning any attempt to convert his people, the young Frenchmen turned back to look for a more promising field of operation.

The newly arrived Americans were then despatched to try where the French had failed. On the long journey to Kuruman, Lindley struggled to adjust to the pace of the trek: 'monotony, monotony, wearisome monotony. A clumsy dead wagon drawn by jaded, creeping oxen, panting under an almost vertical sun'.[10] A whole year would pass, in fact, before Moffat finally led them into the royal kraal. At that time, the women in the party had fared differently from each other. While Mary Jane Wilson would be remembered as the first white woman to be buried north of the Orange River, Lindley's young wife, Lucy Allen, flourished; darkened by the sun and toughened by fresh air and exercise, she was easily mistaken for a 'Dutch *vrouw*'.

Even as the American wagon was making its slow journey north, some 10,000 Voortrekkers were also leaving the Cape Colony in search of a homeland, where they would be beyond the reach of interfering officials and missionaries. The 'Great Trek' was made up of three main parties, led by the narrowly religious Andries Hendrik Potgeiter, frontier farmer Piet Retief and the irascible Gert Maritz. All twelve ordained ministers of the Cape Synod – eleven Scots and one Dutch – decided to stay at the Cape, so spiritual guidance for the trekkers was provided by sixty-year-old LMS artisan Erasmus Smit. Born in a Rotterdam orphanage, he was desperately poor, pathologically nervous and given to drink, but twenty-five years earlier, he had married Maritz's thirteen-year-old sister, and as she grew to be a tall, courageous woman.' Smit identified with the only family that he had ever known and was finally accepted as official minister to the trek. Perhaps he had not realised how dangerous it would be. In October 1836, Mzilikazi's warriors closed in on the Boer camp at a place that would become known as Vechtkop, and while the men, women and children pulled their wagons into a circle and stuffed thorn branches into the wheels, their terrified minister tried to pray as best he could. Although the laager was never broken, the Boers lost most of their cattle. On the other side, a third of Ndebele warriors died, and when news of the battle reached Mzilikazi's kraal, the Americans heard sounds of mourning rise from every home. For their part, the Boers were determined to exact revenge for the loss of their cattle, and later, the Americans recorded their assault on the Ndebele encampment. 'In a few minutes we were in the midst of slaughter. The people fled towards our house, some of them that they might find protection in it, and others that they might hide themselves in the reeds growing in a small stream near it. Those who fled were pursued by the Boers with a determination to avenge themselves for the injury they had received. This brought us in the midst of the carnage.'[11] Another 400 Ndebele died in the assault, and both kraal and mission station were reduced to ruins.

Now the Americans, like the French before them, decided that they had seen enough. Those from the slave-owning states left with the Boers,

while the New Englanders set off separately on a roundabout journey
to Zululand. John Philip and Robert Moffat, who otherwise agreed on
so little, were united in fury that two parties of young missionaries could
reach the Ndebele headquarters and then turn tail at the first sign of
trouble. Even Mzilikazi had hoped that the Americans would stay with
his people as they began a new migration that would take them into
modern Zimbabwe. Later, the indefatigable Robert Moffat earned
Mzilikazi's respect by making that journey. But he was an exception.
No other missionary could win Mzilikazi's trust.

* * *

It was said that, even as Shaka was being struck down by his half-brother
Dingaan, he looked up and delivered a warning: 'It will not be you but
the white man who will rule over the land.' A Xhosa prophet later
warned Dingaan not to allow missionaries into his country: 'First
the white people came and took part of the [Xhosa] land, then they
encroached and drove them further back, and have repeatedly taken
more land as well as cattle. Then they built houses [mission stations]
among them for the purpose of subduing them by witchcraft.'[12] But
Dingaan was fascinated by the new industrial civilisation, and when
the three American Board northerners, Grout, Champion and Adams,
finally arrived at his kraal, they were given permission to work at a
safe distance, near the Natal border. First impressions were promising;
Adams reported that 'both adults and children evince a capacity for
learning equal to that of Europeans or Americans'. But the king only
showed interest in practical things. 'He has a very inquisitive mind',
recorded Champion, 'and often starts questions which show him
to be superior to the generality of his people. Every part of the lathe
underwent the strictest scrutiny, and nothing was left unexplained.'[13]

The Americans did not know that, two years before their arrival,
English sea captain Allen Gardiner had convinced Dingaan to allow
the CMS to work within his kraal. They were therefore surprised when
Cambridge graduate and CMS missionary Francis Owen arrived with his
sister and a servant girl to set up a station in this favoured site, and they
concluded, reasonably enough, that John Philip had betrayed them.
In an act typical of the imperialist British, he had promised them sole
possession of the Zulu mission, only to hand the key station to one of his
own countrymen. 'Mr Owen has arrived – his plans are, I can't say what.
This, I know, they are mutable. He is a well informed, truly estimable

English clergyman, who knows nothing of this world and is determined to have as little to do with it as possible.'[14]

Owen made his first Sunday presentation to some 2,000 Zulu warriors, who sat in a great semicircle around their king. Dingaan opened the proceedings as beer pots circulated: 'Now, my men, there is something to quench your thirst while the white man is talking.' Owen launched into a methodical overview of Christian doctrine, until Dingaan ordered him to stop.

> 'I have a few questions to ask you that I may not misunderstand. First, do you say there is a God and but one God?' The Minister replied, 'Yes.'
>
> 'Second, do you say there is a heaven for good people and only one?' Reply: 'Yes.'
>
> 'Third, do you say there is a devil?' Reply: 'Yes'
>
> 'Fourth, do you say there is a hell for wicked people?' The Minister replied, 'Yes'
>
> Said the King, 'If that is your belief you are no use to me or to my people; we knew all that before you came to preach to us. I and my people believe there is only one God. I am that God.'

The king ended with the announcement that, while the Owens could stay, he wanted no more of the white men's fictions.[15]

Two months later, a small advance party of the Great Trek Boers, led by Piet Retief, arrived to ask permission for the trekkers to settle across the border in the empty territory of Natal. Dingaan agreed on the sole condition that Retief must first recover some cattle stolen by the Sotho chief, Sekonyela, who lived beyond the Drakensberg Mountains. After Retief's men had left to carry out the task, however, Dingaan received news that Mzilikazi's hitherto invincible army was in full retreat towards the north, and his spies also told him that hundreds of Boer wagons were descending the Drakensberg. Now his thoughts turned to revenge against Piet Retief's party. On his mission station, Champion felt a sense of growing mistrust, and when Retief passed by with the recovered cattle, he urged him to turn back or 'God would hold him responsible for the lives of all the men Mr Retief intended to sacrifice so uselessly', but all warnings were brushed aside and the Boer party continued on its way.

Owen described 6 February 1838 as 'a dreadful day in the annals of the mission'. Early in the morning, Dingaan sent him a message that

he planned to kill the Boers but reassured them that they had no reason
to be alarmed. Huddled together, missionary, wife and maidservant
began to sing the Psalm 91: 'A thousand may fall at your side, ten
thousand at your right hand but it will not come near you.' 'They
are killing the Boers *now*. I turned my eyes and behold! an immense
multitude on the hill. About nine or ten Zoolus to each Boer were
dragging their helpless unarmed victims to the fatal spot, where those
eyes which awakened to see the cheerful light of day for the last time, are
now closed in death.'[16]
Despite Dingaan's repeated assurance that he had no quarrel with
teachers who came to his country 'by few and few', the Owens set off for
home with all possible speed. The Americans too retreated into Natal,
with Susan Champion in a state of nervous collapse, though her husband
would later accuse himself of being faithless and unbelieving: 'the
question with me has been ever since our arrival here, "Shall we give
up Africa?"'

The main body of trekkers knew nothing of their companions' fate
when they made camp at the foot of the Drakensberg Mountains. Zulu
warriors struck without warning. Erasmus Smit's party was spared
the main assault, and he did his best to comfort survivors who arrived
in blood-stained wagons.[17] It was now the Boers' turn to feel betrayed.
First, Dingaan had promised them a home in Natal, then he had gone
back on his word. In December 1838, they prepared for battle at the
place that would become known as Blood River, with full confidence
that God was on their side. Zulu soldiers were trained to fight in tight
formation, and while this had served them well in battles against
traditionally armed enemies, it left them desperately exposed to firearms.
Dingaan's army was summarily destroyed, and the Boers offered thanks
to the Almighty for their victory.

* * *

It was while this drama was being played out that the Americans from
the northern states arrived in Natal. Reunited, the six families were
discouraged to discover that none had made any progress in the main
evangelical task. Wilson at once requested a transfer to Liberia, and
Venable left to work with freed slaves in America, while both Grout and
Champion took leave in America – where Champion died at the age
of thirty-one. At the lowest point, only the Adams and Lindley families
remained in Natal.

Daniel Lindley was convinced that the British would not sacrifice
Natal to the Boers. Trapped without firearms between warring whites,
African tribes could pose no greater threat to either Boer or Briton
than native Americans did to settlers in his homeland.[18] According
to Lindley's logic, it followed that he should work among the Boers –
with whom he and Lucy Allen had so much in common – and try to tame
their ferocity towards the Africans. After succeeding the aged Smit
as official minister to the trek, Lindley followed his congregation across
the Drakensberg Range as they set off in another search for a purer land
of their own.

Now, of all the American Board pioneers, only Dr Newton Adams
seemed on course to fulfil early expectations. As displaced *mfengu*
returned to Natal to find their land occupied by white settlers, some
12,000 settled around his station, and the sick travelled long distances
to Newton's busy clinic. He also founded a school that later became
famous as Adams College, alma mater to Chief Buthelezi, Joshua
Nkomo and other African leaders of later generations. His evangelical
efforts were not, however, so effective. Even after Aldin Grout had
returned to his old station, not a single African had been accepted into
church membership.

At home in Boston, the commissioners were not impressed. They
remained clear that they did not send missionaries out as social workers
but to save souls, and accordingly they took the decision to withdraw
from South Africa. While Adams stayed and earned his living as a
doctor, the Grout family set off for Cape Town on the first leg of the
journey home. Governor Sir George Grey, who had other notions of a
missionary's work, was furious at the Board's decision and announced
'I think more of missionaries than of soldiers to keep savages quiet.'[19]
In Cape Town, he concluded a deal with Grout, under which his family
would return to the Zulu border as fully funded government missionaries,
where they would use influence to stop cattle stealing, discourage Zulu
emigration into Natal and report 'all hostile aggressions of any parties
whereby the condition of the natives is affected'.[20] Anti-British feeling
ran high in Boston, and the commissioners could not contemplate the idea
that any American station should be converted into an outpost of British
imperialism, and they hurriedly reversed the decision to withdraw. The
Lindleys came back onto mission staff and recruits, including an apparently
unrelated Lewis Grout and a number of unmarried women began to arrive
from America for a new missionary assault on South Africa.

A Mathematical Bishop

In 1854, Cambridge scholar John Colenso, newly appointed bishop
of Natal, made a fraternal tour of the American Board stations.
On Lindley's reserve, he found little contact between black and white,
and while the eleven missionary children spoke acceptable Nguni, their
parents took care that they had no 'free intercourse' with the blacks
because 'the conversation of the latter is said to be so impure and
disgusting, that a Christian parent cannot commit his children to its
contamination'.[21] Lewis Grout admitted that he could not bear to look
at the smiling faces of the Africans around his station, and he shielded his
daughter against any contamination from local languages. On leaving
his station, Colenso was given sandwiches, wrapped in a copy of the
American Board's *Missionary Intelligencer*, and when he stopped for
lunch, he idly started to read. All those who were careless of divine
things, announced one article, would perish, and their children 'would
twine about them, like creepers on a gnarled oak, and they would burn –
burn – burn on for ever'. The conclusion Colenso unsurprisingly reached
was that missionary colleagues were alienated from the people around
them. Alarmingly, it seemed to him that the core problem lay not
in cultural attitudes but in the message itself. Meaningful dialogue,
he decided, would remain impossible until missionaries had the courage
to give serious answers to honest questions. With these bold deductions,
he set himself on course for a collision with both religious and secular
authorities that would make him one of the most notorious figures
in Africa.

After his visit to the American Board stations, Colenso devoted himself
to a study of the problems arising from a literal reading of the scriptures.
With his Zulu friend and interpreter, William Ngidi, who knew his
Bible well, he threw himself into the task – later recalling hours of
wretchedness when doubt arrived like artillery shell that had to be flung
from the fortress of his own soul. After learning German, so that he
could read works of biblical criticism that had not yet been translated
into English, he finally set his lance at the whole structure of biblical
literalism. Colenso was a distinguished mathematician, and to a modern
reader, his computations of the number of people, tents and oxen
involved in the Exodus, contained in his book *The Pentateuch and Book
of Joshua Critically Examined*, would seem alien to debate. But such
minute analysis was dictated by his conviction that if a single statement

in the biblical narrative could be proved erroneous, the whole literalist structure of belief must immediately fall apart. His first volume was published in 1862, at a time when defenders of the old order were still reeling under the impact of Charles Darwin's 1859 *Origin of Species*. A limerick went the rounds of London clubs:

A bishop there was of Natal
Who took a Zulu for a pal,
Said the Native 'Look 'ere,
Ain't the Pentateuch queer?'
Which converted my Lord of Natal.

Now at odds with the whole missionary community, Colenso directed his polemic at both the evangelical and the Catholic doctrine of atonement. The resulting clash with Archbishop Gray plunged them both in a heresy trial, schism and bitter civil litigation. Colenso courted controversy in a way that his contemporaries Zimmerman and Christaller did not; but the new German school of biblical criticism in which he had become immersed had pietist roots and, in their widely separated parts of Africa, the German pietists and the English bishop drew similar conclusions about the interaction of Christianity with African society.

On the political level, the whole Colenso family became isolated – even hated – defenders of the human and property rights of indigenous people and, in particular, of the Zulus. They refused to let atrocities pass unchallenged. In 1873, the papers carried news of how British troops suppressed 'a rebellion' by Chief Langalibalele. Through his Zulu sources, Colenso heard an accurate account of how the colonial authorities had exploited a trivial incident to expropriate the chief's land and expel his people from their homes. The deeper the bishop dug, the more injustice he unearthed. Two years later, new Commissioner Sir Garnet Wolseley described his reception at the bishop's palace:

I was attacked by the whole family about the native policy in very bad taste, the Bishop losing his temper and in fact becoming so excited that his voice quavered so that he could barely utter.... Mrs Colenso seems to be a drivelling idiot and to be tolerated by her family as such: all the lot have kaffir on the brain and to be really mad on the subject viewing everything from one side alone and

being incapable of taking a broad view on any matter where the
interests of the Kaffirs are in any way concerned.[22]

Wolseley's response was to recruit other clerical allies. Late in 1878, the
'Zululand brethren' – British, German and Norwegian – combined to issue
a statement urging Britain to annex Cetshwayo's kingdom – before leaving
Zululand in a united body. In the home newspapers, this was reported
as an 'expulsion of missionaries', requiring an armed response from the
British. The Exeter Hall lobby was silent when British troops crossed the
border in January the following year. But Colenso's bitterest theological
opponent within the divided Natal church later confirmed that the Zulu
brethren had been in no danger: 'it was undoubtedly the English, not the
Zulu, army that first desecrated mission stations'.[23] For his part, Colenso
thundered that Christians had come into Zululand equipped with 'terrible
engines, horribly destructive of human life … as Gattling-guns, shells,
rockets &c., have swept away the legs, arms and heads or cruelly smashed
the bodies, of thousands of brave, but helpless, Zulus'.[24] White sentiment
was not on his side. After the war, aspiring writer Rider Haggard directed
a vicious attack on the 'lady advocates' for Zulu rights, the bishop's
daughters Harriette and Frances Ellen Colenso; their writings, he declared,
bore the same resemblance to the truth 'that a speech to the jury by the
counsel for the defence in a hopeless murder case does to the summing up
of the judge'.[25] In 1883, the embattled family was too preoccupied with
Zulu affairs to notice the bishop's failing health. He quietly died within
a few days. 'What did he want with death bed scenes?' asked his ageing
wife; 'rest was his greatest need'.

The Sotho

When the young Frenchmen turned their backs on Mzilikazi's kraal,
Pellissier set off alone to establish his Bethulie station in Tswana country.
As the other members of the party travelled through empty land, towards
what is today the state of Lesotho, they crossed battlefields that were
strewn with bones from the time, ten years before, when the *lifaqane*
had passed that way. After the Ndebele had moved on, survivors from
a variety of tribes gathered round Basuto leader Moshoeshoe in his
impregnable rock fortress of Thaba Bosiu. The young Frenchmen found
the leader to be a strongly built man in his mid-forties, with weary eyes

'but full of intelligence and softness'.[26] Concerned that Thaba Bosiu's defensive virtues made it unsuited to 'civilised living', Eugène Casalis tried to convince Moshoeshoe to move his capital onto the plain. 'This mountain is my mother,' he replied. 'Had it not been for her, you would have found this country entirely without inhabitants. You think that the war is at an end; I do not believe it: this is a rod that God has not yet broken.'[27] The Frenchmen decided to settle on a nearby lowland site and wait for Moshoeshoe's people to join them. It was the beginning of the struggle for souls in Lesotho.

At first, the missionaries had to rely on an interpreter, who was later found to have unfortunate habits – most notably of omitting negatives from the Ten Commandments – but Casalis and Arbrousset proved to be talented linguists, and Moshoeshoe came to value Casalis as a wise political adviser, talented translator and good friend. However, although the king found the white men's philosophy fascinating, the missionaries had to reconcile themselves with certain facts. Moshoeshoe's state was bound together by ties of marriage: the whole structure would fall apart if he were to renounce all his 150 wives but 1. Nevertheless, Moshoeshoe did not object if his subjects chose to find consolation in the white man's faith – a tolerance (unusual among African rulers) of great significance to the missionaries' efforts. Others could work for decades without enrolling a single convert; in Basutoland, the young Frenchmen were soon accepting councillors and members of the royal family into their Calvinist church. 'Circumcision falls into disuse; polygamy is no longer so strong. People hardly believe any more in sorcerers and rainmakers, and the cult of the false gods is abandoned more and more.'[28]

When John Philip came on a visit, he was astonished to see what the French had achieved in less than a decade. By this time, Pellissier was also reporting success at Bethulie, and a later recruit, Samuel Rolland, was building a major station at Beersheba. By the mid-1840s, the Paris Evangelicals boasted over 1,000 full members and a further 2,000 enquirers who attended services regularly.[29] Philip could now claim that his great frontier strategy was at last taking shape. With the Americans established on the east coast and the Germans on the Atlantic, and his own LMS and Paris Evangelicals in the centre, the defensive arch was essentially in place. His main concern was that the Methodists were filling spaces in between, and he saw these as vulnerable points in the structure.

In this pastoral environment, no defined frontier separated Moshoeshoe's people from those of his neighbour Sekonyela, and while

Moshoeshoe's capital of Thaba Bosiu offered shelter to the French Protestants, Sekonyela's Thaba Nemu provided the headquarters for Methodist operations. Cattle raiding existed on both sides, as it always had, and at this period it was getting worse. But the missionary response to it was unhelpful. Methodist Jeremiah Hartley developed a 'hysteric conviction' that the Basuto king was planning the murder of all Wesleyans – before he died of a 'bursting of the blood vessels near the heart, occasioned by the unnatural excitement of his mind'.[30] As the Moshoeshoe's Basuto got the better of the cross-border conflict, Sekonyela's country became virtually stripped of animals, and Moshoeshoe followed the Sotho custom of distributing the booty among his followers. At this time of crisis, Casalis was in Europe, and local policy was driven by a new wave of inflexibly Calvinist recruits from the Vaud. Considering the cross-border raids, they announced that Sekonyela's cattle were stolen goods which must be returned on pain of excommunication. As a result, the outraged Sotho Christians abandoned the church in droves, and Casalis returned to find his station's old tranquillity shattered: 'We were suddenly awakened from our slumbers by a terrible noise. Thousands of heathens had gathered … to celebrate their festival. I thought I was dreaming. The yelling of the multitude, the dismal echoes of those dances awakened in my mind heart-rending reminiscences. It was like a frightful anachronism.'[31]

While the Sotho were busy fighting among themselves, Boer farmers were increasingly grazing cattle in the southern part of their country. In the face of this new pressure, John Philip's 'cheapest and best military posts' could offer no protection to vulnerable people, and Moshoeshoe was driven to seek protection from the British army. Boer Andries Pretorius issued him with a solemn warning: 'You don't know the English. They are odd people. Remember my words. You will repent for having joined them.'[32] Indeed, as political power changed at Westminster, frontier policy became erratic, until Sotho country was effectively abandoned to the Boers at the Sand River Convention of 1852. Jean Pierre Pellissier surveyed a disaster of cataclysmic proportions from his station at Bethulie: 'We are on the eve of great events for our mission. We are anxious with regard to the future. A terrible storm is brewing in the distance.... The antipathy which the farmers feel towards the natives and the missionaries is so great, that they will not be satisfied until they have ruined our enterprise and expelled the messengers of the Gospel.'[33]

After Bethulie and Beersheba were destroyed by the Boers, with considerable loss of life, and Morija had been sacked for the seventh time, the Paris Evangelicals withdrew from Basutoland. Although Thaba Bosiu never fell to the Boers, the rest of Moshoeshoe's country – including all the fertile land – was lost. When the job of conquest was done, President Brandt of the Orange Free State stood on a wagon at the foot of the king's mountain, holding aloft a Bible to thank God for victory.

The situation was even more desperate in Sekonyela's territory. Weslean James Cameron could offer no comfort to Methodist chiefs when they gathered to debate the growing Boer threat:

> I could give them no advice for had I said that they must remain, they would have been slaughtered. I said there are three deaths choose the one you will die.
>   1st Take some cattle and go to the Boers and pray to have peace and give up your guns, pay taxes, become their slaves, or
>   2nd Look without delay for a hiding place but look to the consequence, no water and burning sun.
>   3rd Stand and fight like men for your life, property and freedom.
>   As for me I cannot say which will be best for you. God give you wisdom, make him your hiding place, the shield of your security.[34]

Seven years later, a new generation of Paris Evangelicals returned to Thaba Bosiu to discover that – as before in Yoruba country – African Christians had proved that they could carry the work on while their white missionaries were out of the country and the churches had actually gained in strength while they had been away. The Morija station had been restored, and 436 candidates were waiting for admission – of whom over 100 were presented by a single schoolmaster. At Leribé, the congregation was twice the size of the one that they had left, and Sotho Christians started pressing their reluctant white clergy for assistance in opening a Sotho mission in the pagan north. When Catholics arrived to work in competition, Moshoeshoe was shocked to see the intensity with which two groups of Christians could hate one another.[35] Catholic superior Fr Gerard was quick to spot that, despite their long time lead, the Protestants had failed to establish any meaningful school system, and his priests quickly established an educational advantage that they would never lose. Calvinist fury overflowed when Gerard announced that the Sotho were a naturally religious people: 'Though God is unknown to you, your fables contain a germ of the truth which Christianity reveals. If you listen to my explanations you will see that you are not so far from Christianity as you suppose.' Such words confirmed every Calvinist's worst suspicion that Catholicism was no better than paganism in disguise. As Moshoeshoe neared death, Protestants and Catholics competed to win the old man's soul, but he died as he had lived. 'My great sin', he confessed, 'is that I possessed a good and fertile country.'

The Tswana

When a young working man from Blantyre first developed an ambition to become a missionary, he adopted fellow Scot Robert Moffat as a role model. David Livingstone – later to become the most famous missionary of all – heard Moffat speak about the work at Kuruman, and as they talked after the meeting, he learned from Moffat the true state of missionary affairs. Giving vent to long pent-up anger, the older man bluntly asserted that John Philip was senile and autocratic and had lost interest in the conversion of the heathen. On arrival in Cape Town, Livingstone discovered that the whole LMS operation was riven by internal feuds: 'Mr Moffat is not on speaking terms with the Griqua missionaries and takes another route when visiting the colony to avoid seeing them. They in their turn *hate* their brethren in the colony.'[36] While mission propaganda presented Kuruman as an oasis of civilisation, Livingstone found reality very different; after a generation, the station had no school, no outstations and only a handful of converts. Most significantly, those Tswana who lived outside the compound walls showed not the smallest interest in the faith. From the beginning, Livingstone found it hard to work within the boundaries of station life. 'Missionaries', he declared, 'should be riding the world's backbone and snuffling like zebras the pure delightful air of the great western desert.'[37] His – surely bipolar – moods swung between elation to the deepest depression, and throughout his life he could be a temperamental, irrational and unforgiving colleague, always appearing comfortable in the company of Africans, who seemed to understand the loneliness at the core of his being. He also lived with pain resulting from injuries received when he was savaged by a lion. In the desperate hope that a family life might ease his terrible isolation, he proposed to Moffat's oldest daughter Mary, and together they travelled north to start a new work.

Most of Livingstone's colleagues detested the semi-westernised Sechele, chief of the Bakwain, who had abandoned the traditional karos for a bizarre assortment of western clothes – military boots, moleskin trousers, duffel jacket and wide-awake hat. Nevertheless, he and Livingstone established a relationship that came close to friendship. In that dry land, a chief's authority was based on his standing as a rainmaker, and Livingstone worked hard to convince Sechele that the problems of surviving in an arid country were better addressed by logic than ancient superstition. 'I pointed out to him that the only feasible way of watering gardens was to select some good never-failing river, make a canal and irrigate the adjacent lands.'[38] Sechele agreed to move his people to a riverside site at Kolombeng, where his missionary would supervise the construction of an irrigation system. But after one season of plenty, there followed the longest and deepest drought in living memory. In that land, there was no such thing as a 'never-failing' river and the irrigation system failed. Sechele's people found no difficulty in allocating blame for the disaster. It is our bellies that make us hungry, they said. 'We want rain, and if you argue about the means, we think you don't want it, and our throats make us angry.'[39] It was a bad time for Sechele to announce that he planned to accept baptism, and his people listened in disbelief as he announced that his junior wives must leave their children in his kraal and return to their fathers' homes. One distraught young wife thrust her Bible into the missionary's face and begged him to take her into his own home; with tears streaming down her face, she explained that she was still breastfeeding and both her parents were dead. Livingstone did find it difficult to reconcile his duty as a missionary with a growing understanding of African society, but Sechele was immovable and the wives were dismissed. All the pain proved futile when Livingstone excommunicated the only convert he would ever make on the grounds that he had resumed sexual relations with a favoured ex-wife.

As the traveller moves west across the continent, so the country becomes more arid. While few Boers had any ambition to settle in Tswana country, they did see it as a strategically important region. They were worried that once the British had consolidated their hold there, residents of the fledgling Transvaal and Orange Free State republics would find themselves cut off from the interior. On the other hand, if they, in collaboration with the Germans in Great Namaqualand, could control the area, then it would be the British colonies that would become severed from the larger continent. The Tswana could also serve as a reservoir of cheap labour. Whenever a Boer commando raided a village, they separated children from their mothers with no more compunction than when a farmer took calves from the cow; while the adults were destined for a life of forced labour, the children were to be sold as 'apprentices', to work without pay for up to twenty years.

Neither David nor Mary Livingstone had any doubt where their allegiance lay.

> We have witnessed the entire female population of a town turned out to weed one of these slaveholder's fields. We have seen the scars inflicted by a whip made of the untanned hide of the rhinoceros; and these scars may be seen by anyone who visits the country on the bare backs of even chiefs and principal men in the tribes. We have seen women carrying food on their heads, because they know that, though they went several miles from their homes to perform these unrequited tasks under a burning sun, not a morsel would be bestowed.[40]

To maintain control over this workforce, the Boers needed to ensure that firearms never fell into African hands. When rumours reached England that some LMS workers had a part in their supply and maintenance, the directors wrote to Philip, asking whether this could be true. Under the congregational system of government, the mission superintendent exercised no disciplinary control over missionaries in the field, and a secretary, writing on Philip's behalf, replied that it was not likely to have happened 'at least to any extent'. He identified David Livingstone as a possible exception. 'Mr Livingston was of the opinion, that the natives *ought* to have firearms and ammunition for their own defence; in that Mr L will readily admit the fact and explain the course that he has taken in the matter.... Dr Philip thinks that if it shall be found that Mr Livingston obtained for the people any guns etc. it was not as a matter of *trade*.'[41]

The Boers waited until Livingstone was away at the Cape before sending Sechele an ultimatum that his people must surrender all their arms and close the country to traders and hunters. Then, when the chief refused these terms, they duly dispatched a punitive commando raid.

Casualties in battles between black and white were generally wildly unequal, but in this case, thirty-nine Boers died at Kolombeng, against sixty Tswana warriors. In Livingstone's workshop, the Boers found clear evidence that this missionary had been mending weapons and making shots. After the commando had driven off some 200 women and children and 3,000 cattle, Sechele set off on a long journey to lodge a complaint, face-to-face, with Queen Victoria, but lost heart when he could not even get a hearing in Cape Town. Meanwhile, his pagan brother Kgosidintsi raged at Moffat about missionaries who brought the Bible but neglected the duty of care.

> Where are our children? When fathers and mothers lie down at night and ask, 'Where are our children?' and when they rise in the morning and ask 'Where are our sons and daughters?' And because there is none to answer they weep. Are the Boers to be permitted to kill us, that our children may become their slaves? Is it because we have not white skins that we are to be killed like beasts of prey?[42]

For all his commitment to the Tswana cause, Livingstone could not resist employing the time-honoured Scottish rhetoric, traditionally reserved for times of disaster: 'God has dealt graciously with them for some years and now suffers them to feel the rod of his anger.'[43] Returning to the Kolombeng settlement, he found it deserted, his compound, house and workshop destroyed, and skeletons scattered all around. The restless missionary interpreted these events as a sign that God was beckoning him forward. In 1852, he put his wife and children on board a ship for England but failed to confirm that the mission would take responsibility for their daily needs. As Mary Livingstone struggled to maintain her family on the charity of friends, she slid into obesity, alcoholism and bitter resentment, and it was even said that, occasionally, pious folk heard her roundly abusing the whole race of missionaries.

Chapter 7

The Rewards of Great Sanctity

The Blue Nile

Catholics could never forget that, in ancient times, North Africa had been a centre of Christianity and home to church fathers. Even after the Muslim *jihad* had swept across the region, Coptic Christians continued to form a significant and influential minority within Egypt. When Napoleon entered Egypt in 1798, scholars, men of letters and priests followed close behind, and Alexandria soon became a thriving and cosmopolitan port of wide religious diversity. Within this mixed society, a community of some 20,000 Roman Catholics sustained a huge Franciscan compound, with a church, bishop's palace, monastery, brothers' college and boys' school, while Sisters of Charity offered western education to Muslim women.

Europeans had long heard stories of a Christian civilisation that flourished in the highlands that supplied water for the Blue Nile, but, for many centuries, information could only be gleaned from an assembly of fables and travellers' tales. In the mid-sixteenth century, Pope Paul III had despatched Jesuits with instructions to bring these isolated Christians back into communion with Rome. According to the letter of canon law, the Ethiopians had no need to sacrifice their sacred Ge'ez church language and well-loved rituals – they simply needed to renounce their allegiance to the Patriarch of Alexandria and submit to the authority of the Pope. But the Jesuits demanded more. After dividing the rulers from their people and plunging wide areas into bloody warfare, the whole enterprise ended in disaster. Common people sang a chant of rejoicing as news spread that the last foreign priest was dead.

> At length the sheep of Ethiopia freed
> From the bad lions of the West
> Securely in their pastures feed
> St. Mark and St. Cyril's doctrine have overcome
> The follies of the Church of Rome.[1]

The task of summoning schismatic Christians back to their proper obedience would continue to be the first objective of Catholic missionaries. Protestants, in contrast, looked to the day when a reformed Ethiopian church would take its place as a partner in the conversion of Africa.

In 1819, the British and Foreign Bible Society were keen to send a translation of the Psalter into the highlands of Ethiopia. To carry it there, they recruited a somewhat shady character, a sailor called Nathaniel Pearce, who had jumped ship at Red Sea port of Massawa to avoid standing trial on a charge of killing an Indian sepoy. Pearce's mission could not be described as a total success. On his arrival in the highlands, he was surprised to discover that Ethiopian clerics had never seen a printed book. They pored over his wares, trying to work out how many scribes would have been employed in producing so many identical copies and judging the product by manuscript standards, expressing concern that established conventions had been overlooked: 'the ink not black enough, the strokes too thin, the letters too much crowded together, no red ink at the name of God ... so that they cannot be considered as church books'.[2] On his side, Pearce described the higher clergy in distinctly unflattering terms: They were, he wrote, 'more like ravening beasts than human beings'. Besides being the greatest drinkers in the country, they were 'addicted to fighting, quarrelling, lying, swearing, cheating and adultery'.[3]

Next it was the turn of the CMS. Five years later, they dispatched Basel pietist Samuel Gobat with instructions to travel up the Blue Nile into Ethiopia. As a native of Alsace, Gobat's first language was French, but he was also proficient in German, English, Latin, Greek, Hebrew and Arabic, and – while waiting in Alexandria – he added living Amharic and ritual Ge'ez to his repertoire. Once in Ethiopia, he set about his task with unusual cultural sensitivity. Ancient controversies over the natures of Christ still raged fiercely, and he debated these recondite issues with courtesy, wearing local dress and speaking in a language that others could understand. When Gobat returned home on leave, replacement C. W. Isenberg set about undoing all his work. Mission staff were ordered to wear western clothes, to promote 'civilised standards' and to keep the Ethiopians at a respectful distance. Most seriously, Isenberg replaced his predecessor's patient conversation with intemperate assaults on the cult of the Virgin.

Isenberg and his German colleagues were in the Tigrean capital of Aduwa in 1838 when two Catholics, French layman Arnauld d'Abbadie and Italian Lazarist priest Guiseppe Sapeto, presented

themselves at court. Just days later, the Protestants were expelled on
a charge of insulting the Virgin Mary – an event which would pass down
in CMS mythology as an early example of popish treachery. While
Isenberg led the main party back to Alexandria, his colleague Ludwig
Krapf stayed behind to take up an invitation for a missionary to visit the
central highland kingdom of Shoa. Disillusioned by the discovery that
ruler Sehala Selasse only wanted to pump any white man he could lay
his hands on for information about western technology, Krapf quickly
decided that the whole Ethiopian church was corrupt beyond redemption.
But, by chance, he discovered a tall 'fine featured' people, who had recently
been driven off their land by Sehala's army and reduced to menial labour.
(Known to themselves as the Oromo, Krapf used the Ethiopian abusive
name of Galla, and it was as Galla that they would become famous
within missionary circles.) He appointed one of them as his servant and
from him learned some tantalising information: 'My Galla servant told
me, that his people paid great reverence to the Lord's Day; that they did
not work on that day, nor sleep with their wives; that they rose up early
before day break, to pray to the Wake.'[4] On this flimsy evidence, Krapf
reached the conclusion that this people had retained some memory of the
Mosaic law and must therefore be of Mediterranean – and probably
Semitic – origins: 'I consider them destined by Providence after their
conversion to Christianity to attain the importance and fulfil the mission
which heaven has pointed out to the Germans in Europe.... It may seem
providentially ordained by this migration of the Gallas to oppose a
barrier to the onward rush of the Mohammedans from Arabia, and so at
the same time to punish the abominable heresies of Christian Abyssinia.'[5]

Krapf was, in his turn, expelled from Shoa, and Ethiopia remained
closed to Protestant missions for the next twenty-five years. To keep in
some kind of touch with his chosen Galla people, however, he set up
a station in Mombassa, some 800 miles to the south, where he waited,
consumed by anxiety, lest news of his great discovery reach the curia and
the whole continent be lost to the reformed faith.

* * *

Catholic hopes rose high when Guiseppe Sapeto reported from Tigre
that a number of local clergy were minded to accept papal supremacy.
But policy makers in Propaganda faced a problem: Sapeto had already
acquired a reputation as a rebellious priest, and there was concern that
he could repeat the mistakes that had undermined the early Jesuit initiative.

Accordingly, they appointed fellow Lazarist Justin de Jacobis with the title of Prefect Apostolic of Ethiopia. When he arrived in Tigre, Sapeto angrily left the highlands to set up his own operation beside the Red Sea.

De Jacobis had been cautioned against making any attempt to impose the Latin rite on a reluctant Ethiopian church, and he took the lesson to heart. Self-deprecating by nature, he grieved that his unworthiness deprived him of any hope of the martyr's crown that can only be 'the reward of great sanctity'.[6] At a meeting of the local clergy he spoke of his long-held ambition to meet the people of Abyssinia.

> Now I am here, and have seen you, and I am content.... I have
> nothing left on earth – neither father, nor mother, nor home,
> nor country. There only remains to me God and my brothers in
> Abyssinia.... Therefore I will do what you will. If you wish me to
> stay with you, I will stay; to go away from you, I will go; to speak
> in your churches, I will speak; to be silent, I will be mute.[7]

He asked only for an act of obedience to the Pope.

Meanwhile, Krapf's fears were not without foundation, for news of his chosen people had reached an interested curia, and in 1846, Propaganda dispatched Bishop Guglielmo Massaja and a party of Italian Capuchins to forestall any Protestant initiative to the Galla. Massaja had been advised that de Jacobis would meet his party at the Red Sea Port and, from board ship, he could see a bizarre group of Catholics on the quayside, who wore turbans and carried identical parasols, but, however hard he looked, he could make out no European priest among them.

> 'Where is Mr de Jacobis?' I exclaimed. Hardly had the words
> escaped me, when the smallest and most poorly clad of the party ...
> made his way through the crowd of Arabs on the quay, and
> threw himself at my feet, which he pressed and kissed. This was
> M. de Jacobis.... I said to him, in our own language, how distressed
> I was at this conduct on his part, and implored him to remember
> that he was a European like myself, besides being Vicar-Apostolic,
> and, as such, entitled to the same respect.[8]

The division that had existed between Gobat and Isemberg was now replicated in a growing rift between de Jacobis and Massaja. The Lazarist's love of all things Ethiopian found expression in his use of Ethiopian

vestments and devotion to the Ge'ez rite, while the Capuchin's loyalty
to Rome left him determined to impose the Latin order. 'The levantines
will never be Catholics in their hearts', he declared, 'until they are
Latins, and sons of Latins born and educated in the Latin rite.'[9] Despite
their disagreements, Massaja's Capuchins managed, after a fearsome
journey, to reach Galla country – only to find Islam already well
entrenched. A chief apologised, 'had you come thirty years ago, not only
I but all my countrymen might have embraced your religion, but now
it is impossible'.[10] Though they did retain a base in that remote area
for a while, the Capuchins were eventually expelled in 1879.

For his part, Krapf continued to promote his Galla mission to the end
of his life. Since eastern Africa was designated to fall within the British
Indian sphere of influence, he bombarded the sceptical Viceroy with
demands that their homeland must be annexed to the Empire. He even
created the fiction that, somewhere in the borderlands of Ethiopia and
modern Kenya, a Galla chief held court in a magnificent capital city
called Ganda. After Johannes Rebmann joined him in Mombassa, the
two men pursued an obsessive search for the Galla. Sometimes travelling
in quite the wrong direction, the two men separately became the first
Europeans to see the snow-capped peaks of mountains on the equator –
Rebmann climbed to the snowline of Mount Kilimanjaro in 1848, and
Krapf reached the foot of Mount Kenya in the following year. More than
a generation would pass before a party of British Methodists finally
found their way to Krapf's city of dreams. 'Behold! Ganda in all its glory
lay directly before us.... "Cloud-capped towers; gorgeous palaces" –
nothing of the kind! Three or four little bee-hive huts, half surrounded
by a dry-thorn hedge, is all that belongs to the city we have been seeking
at so much pain and trouble! Yes, that is Ganda, the abode of Mara
Barowat, chief of the Gallas!'[11]

* * *

As with the efforts of the Jesuits of old, the nineteenth-century Christian
initiatives to Ethiopia only ended in bloodshed and failure. In 1855,
Kassa Hailu overcame rival warlords to assume the title of Emperor
Tewodros II of all Ethiopia, and after forming an alliance with orthodox
clerics, he first imprisoned and then expelled de Jacobis and his foreign
priests. From his exile in Eritrea, the Lazarist received news of the faithful
few Ethiopians left behind in Tigre. 'To our dear and venerable father
and Bishop, from his children, who have remained faithful and constant

to his teaching … From the salt and bitter ocean arise the mists which irrigate our land; and so, from the depths of our dark dungeon, our holy faith shines brighter than it ever did before.'[12]

Now consecrated Anglican bishop of Jerusalem, Samuel Gobat interpreted Catholic misfortune as a window of opportunity for his Protestants. Remembering that Ethiopian rulers were more interested in technicians than preachers, he recruited German artisans to start a work that he believed was destined to take Christianity 'far beyond Abyssinia, to the Galla and into the heart of the devil's African kingdom'. After five productive years spent on constructing roads and other civil projects, the Germans noticed that Tewodros was developing a mental disorder that showed itself in increasing cruelty to his people and suspicion of foreigners. Disaster struck when one of the Emperor's spies intercepted a mission report: 'King Tewodros is not a descendant of the Royal Dynasty, but only the son of a poor woman.… He is a cruel bloodthirsty man, like a wild animal.' In his fury, Tewodros chained the mission artisans in his Magdala fortress, along with the British consul, who had also offended him. After they had been forced to watch the execution of their local servants, these most practical of missionaries saved their lives by promising to build a 'supergun' that would be capable of firing missiles weighing 1,000 pounds. They did indeed build such a gun, but the men of God took comfort in the fact that the emperor had no shot of equivalent size, and the weapon was never used. While the British government accepted no responsibility for German missionaries – even if they were employed by an Anglican society – it could not ignore the fact that Her Majesty's consul was being held in chains, and Magdala fell to a punitive expedition on Easter Monday 1868. After fighting furiously in defence of his capital city, Tewodros committed suicide. The consul and missionaries were released unharmed, and the forces of civilisation righteously ransacked Magdala, taking off some 350 of the Ethiopian church's most venerated manuscripts, which remain on display in museums across Europe.

The White Nile

Meanwhile, the Catholics had also turned their attention to the lands around the White Nile. Towards the end of 1847, a group of priests crossed the boundary from Egypt into the land known in antiquity

as Nubia and later the Sudan. To mark the event, Maltese bishop Annetto
Cassolini celebrated mass in the ruins of an ancient temple of Isis,
which long ago had also served as a church. One member of the party
supposedly knew enough Arabic to talk with bystanders, and he reported
an encouraging message: 'Our fathers were once Christian. Then they
were happy people, they built stone churches and stone houses; but as for
us, ill fated that we are, we live in huts of mud and wattle.'[13] From this
the priests drew the improbable conclusion that some memory of a happy
Christian past had survived more than a millennium of Islamic rule.

Pope Gregory XVI had given Cassolini responsibility for the largest
ecclesiastical territory in the world. From north to south, his newly
created Vicarate of Central Africa stretched from the Sudan to the
Zambezi River; from east to west, only omitting Eritrea and Ethiopia,
it reached from the Indian Ocean to a notional frontier with the Vicarate
of the Two Guineas at some undefined place to the west of Lake Chad.
The little group of priests were charged with the provision of religious
services for the motley array of Christians now entering the region, as
well as with the formidable tasks of mounting an assault on the region's
slave trade and taking the faith to the unconverted masses of their vast
region. Such tasks called for superhuman efforts. Feeling unequal to such
a challenge, Cassolini returned home and his position passed to the
unusually determined Slovene priest Ignaz Knoblehar. Taking advantage
of the fact that his homeland lay within the Austro-Hungarian Empire,
he made an agreement with the Hapsburg emperor, under which his
priests would receive financial support in return for establishing an
Austrian presence on the Nile. Backed by imperial money, Knoblehar's
'Austrian mission' built a model compound in the heart of Muslim
Khartoum. As reported by a passing traveller, 'The only stone edifice is
that occupied by a Roman Catholic mission for the intended conversion
of negroes.... It is handsomely constructed, and contains a neat church
and schoolrooms.... Situated at about 500 yards from the river, the space
between it and the stream is laid out into a fine garden, containing
delicious fruit trees and luxuriant shrubberies.'[14]

After 1858, when British explorer John Hanning Speke reached the
place where the White Nile flowed out of Lake Nyanza (to be renamed
Lake Victoria), the Khedive of Egypt lost no time in claiming both banks
of the White Nile on behalf of his overlord, the Ottoman Emperor. From
that time, the riverine tribes were endlessly harried by slaving parties,
often led by Egyptian army officers, which were followed by freebooting

traders and a steady flow of Catholic missionaries. Propaganda had
issued instructions that – on this river at least – their Catholics must stay
ahead of the heretics, and Knoblehar drew up plans to establish stations
along the length of the river. It was a tall order. From the beginning,
priests, brothers and sisters fell ill and died within weeks of arrival. The
territory was, to say the least, hostile. As Daniele Comboni – straight out
of seminary – travelled south on a ten-gun vessel, he was astonished at
the sight of the wild people who caked their hair in mud, so that it stuck
straight up into the air. On one bank lived the Dinka, who had recently
killed the entire crew of a trading ship; on the opposite bank were the
Schillak, who were reputed to be 'the most powerful and ferocious tribe
of all in central Africa'. Comboni comforted himself with the fact that,
alongside the guns, his vessel also carried a picture of the Virgin Mary.
'How could this good mother see us suffering', he asked, 'and not
come to our help?'[15] He reminded himself that 'missionaries prefer to
be murdered a hundred times than defend themselves.... If the Schillaks
attack, we will become their slaves and with the grace of God will preach
to them Christ crucified.'

Egyptian soldiers and European freebooters took every opportunity
to spread the rumour that the priests were evil sorcerers who planned
to stop the rain, dry up the pastures, deprive the people of food and
drink and even 'feed on the flesh of children'.[16] In response, the priests
presented a Christian God, customised to local needs: 'This is the
God who makes the rains fall, thus preventing your fields from being
scorched; He keeps you in good health; He multiplies your cattle;
He gives you strength to overcome your enemies.'[17]

Those who heard these assurances must have been perplexed at the
way in which that same Christian God treated his missionaries. Clothes,
food and documents turned mouldy during the rainy season; termites,
snakes, scorpions and countless mosquitoes plagued the stations, while
sickness and death became 'inseparable companions' to both the fathers
and sisters. When the Franciscans sent out a party of fifty-eight friars and
lay helpers to bolster the flagging enterprise, the majority were struck
down within weeks of arriving on the river. In just four catastrophic
months of 1862, twenty-two Catholic missionaries died on the White
Nile. To make matters worse, nationalist tensions between German and
Italian speakers, which were tearing the Austro-Hungarian empire apart
at home, were being imported into Africa – to the extent that, when
Austrian monks found they had been posted to an Italian station, they

promptly turned round their vessels and sailed back to Alexandria. By the mid-1860s, Daniele Comboni was virtually alone on the river. When he too was invalided home, Pius IX ordered the whole enterprise to be abandoned.

Like others before him, Comboni had now reached the conclusion that Africa would never be converted by foreign priests. After publishing an essay *Plan for the Regeneration of Africa by Means of Africans*, he toured Europe, arguing that Africans, working as craftsmen, teachers, lawyers, priests, nuns and even bishops, should take responsibility for their continent.[18] He succeeded in raising enough money to set up two training schools – one in his home city of Verona and the other in Egypt. With souls perishing every day, however, he found it impossible to wait for his project to mature and he returned to the river with a party of Verona fathers and sisters. The passage of years had not made the region any healthier, and it was said that some half of the African population of the Upper Nile died in the great famine that followed the failure of the rains in 1887 and 1888. Comboni's Catholics shared in the general misery, as the Verona sisters walked long miles to jostle for blackened water at the few remaining wells: 'Every day either a sister, a brother, catechists or catechumens are taken to their eternal resting place by our bishop or one of the fathers, who are themselves ill with the fever. After dusk, after a day of exhausting fatigue, and accompanied by some of our converts, I take the last of the dead to the cemetery. I come back late at night and think that perhaps tomorrow somebody else will take me there.'[19]

In the end, the whole Catholic investment of money and human life on the White Nile left a legacy of some thirty Christian families, while Comboni's schools produced just two priests and one nun. The misery culminated with old disputes resurfacing, as members of Comboni's staff despatched letters to Propaganda which contained 'nothing but vomit and fire'. Recalled to Rome, he continued to insist that one last great effort could change everything – if the Lord of the harvest would only provide both workers and resources, 'the negroes will soon become members of the great Catholic society'.[20] Returning to the river for the last time, he died in Khartoum in 1881 – the same year in which Muhammad Ahmed proclaimed himself the promised Mahdi and began to gather followers for a new Muslim *jihad*, which drove missionaries back, first to Khartoum and then to Cairo. As all communications on the Nile were cut, geographers lost hope that – at least for the foreseeable future – the White Nile could provide a highway into Africa's heartland.

The White Fathers

In 1860, a thirty-five-year-old teacher was making his name in the faculty of Theology at the Sorbonne. As a theologian, Charles Lavigerie veered first to one side and then to the other in the great clerical debate. On one day his ultramontane emotions made him defend the doctrine of papal infallibility, while on the next, his Gallician intellect would insist that church people had to stop pining for some rosy medieval past. Any hope that these two positions could be reconciled were shattered when Pius IX set his face against the modern world in his 1864 *Syllabus of Errors*, which concluded, 'It is an error to teach that the Roman Pontiff can or ought to reconcile himself to or agree with progress, liberalism and modern civilisation.' Splashed across the anti-clerical press, the pronouncement seemed to provide a final proof that Catholics could no longer live as loyal citizens of France.

But he would find an outlet for his deepest convictions when he accepted the Archbishopric of Algiers in 1867. As a result of his previous travels in the Middle East distributing relief aid for Lebanese Catholics who had survived bloody Druse massacres, he had developed a deep hostility to Islam. On arrival in North Africa, he was outraged to discover that the French administration operated a system of religious segregation – 'the gospel for the settlers; the Koran for the natives'. The archbishop had other ideas, 'in his providence', he declared, 'God has chosen France to make Algeria the cradle of a great and Christian nation, a nation like unto herself.'[21] He therefore put forward a radical programme of conversion and assimilation, under which any Algerian who adopted civilised ways and rediscovered the region's ancient faith would be accepted as a full French citizen. Just a few months after Lavigerie's arrival, the city of Algiers was struck by a terrible cholera epidemic, and he took the opportunity to build orphanages where thousands of children would be protected against starvation and disease. Here Muslim children were baptised on the grounds that they were in danger of death, and it was reported that some even received the sacrament unawares. While many of these children would later be reunited with their Muslim families, others grew up within these institutions, under training as the first generation of native Christian workers. As Lavigerie supervised the famine project with military precision, word spread that this churchman must wear 'a suit of mail under his surplice'. But he could also display human emotions. When one mother superior used blankets as shrouds for burying dead children, he, first of all, furiously accused her of misappropriating church property, and then, after the wretched woman had taken to her bed in a state of collapse, kept knocking at her door to beg for forgiveness.

When the work with Muslims failed to make progress, the archbishop began to direct his volatile energies towards lands south of the Sahara. 'Algeria is but a door opened by Providence on a backward continent of two hundred million souls. That is the vast perspective that draws me on.... What motives could I have in the presence of God for refusing so great a call?'²² He asked Propaganda for the title of Vicar Apostolic, with responsibility for the Sahara desert and the savannah country to its south, but since all this virgin territory was already split between the vicarates of Central Africa in the east and the Two Guineas in the west, he had to make do with the less-prestigious title of Apostolic Delegate to the Sahara and the Sudan. Thus authorised, he set about forming the new *Société de Notre Dame d'Afrique*. Dressed in Arab *disdashas*, with a rosary in the place of Muslim prayer beads, his recruits soon became known to all as the White Fathers.

Arab traders and Tuareg nomads became understandably alarmed when they learned that the Christians, who had already taken possession of Algeria, were now laying plans to cross the Sahara. In 1875, Fathers Pallier, Bouchard and Mainyard set off to find the fabled city of Timbuktu, 'or lay down their lives in the attempt'. Four years later, some half-burned books, a broken altar stone, two boxes, some charred bones and two skulls were discovered in the desert.²³ With the desert route closed, Lavigerie comforted himself by remembering that, for all their half-century start, the Protestants still had no inland stations north of the Zambezi Basin; they had also comprehensively failed to penetrate traditional African society. Never doubting that he could succeed where others had failed, Lavigerie seethed with anger at the ignorant ecclesiastical placemen of Propaganda who had no better occupation than to block his efforts. At heart, he was an armchair explorer. His personal library was full of carefully annotated works of exploration, which he studied in pondering the best route to the interior. With the Suez Canal now open, he concluded that it lay along those overland routes from the East African ports that had been well-trodden by slaving caravans.

Lavigerie had no time for those who courted adventure for its own sake; these he christened 'Robinsons' – a word borrowed from the English adventure book *The Swiss Family Robinson*. His missionaries took no vow of poverty and were expected to eat well and take good care of their and their colleagues' health. He devoted his formidable administrative talents to taking care of them, emphasising the value of quinine in a malarial continent (though he mistakenly still recommended its use as a cure, rather than as a prophylactic). When his fathers arrived in a new field, their first duty was to learn the local language; indeed, once they became fluent, they were expected to speak it among themselves. The archbishop always stressed the virtue of companionship: 'Never, under any circumstances, and under no pretext whatever, will the missionaries, Fathers and Brothers, be less than three together, when they go to the Mission. Rather than relax this rule, we will refuse any offer, however advantageous, or urgent, or useful and we would rather see the Society disappear altogether than give way on this capital point.'[24] Although discipline within the community was maintained by a system of 'fraternal correction' he did recognise that missionaries were as subject to depression and temptation as anybody else, and he took prompt action to defuse difficult situations.

Throughout his life, Lavigerie pursued three clear objectives – the promotion of the Catholic mission, the advancement of French interest and the achievement of personal ambition – and he recognised no tension within that agenda. Although authoritarian by temperament, he could show considerable flexibility of practice. Most strikingly, he abandoned his early conviction that missionaries should behave as ambassadors of European culture. While Protestants were insisting that converts must adopt western table manners, he reminded his fathers that 'fingers were invented before forks' and urged them to sit on the ground and share the people's food. Similarly, while opponents continued to excommunicate all who 'deviated from the way', he advised his workers that deeply rooted customs could never vanish overnight.

> The Africans must never be refused absolution for sins which are sins of weakness and not committed with the deliberate notion of making evil a rule of life. They must be pitied, not bullied.... Heroic virtues, angelic purity, faith strong and untarnished, have never existed in neophytes unless by way of exception. To wish to make them a general rule would be to lay oneself open to bitter disillusionment and to take day-dreams for reality.[25]

In 1875, Leopold II, King of the Belgians, summoned African experts to an international geographical conference in Brussels. While in private he would admit his ambition to secure 'a slice of this magnificent African cake', for the present he concealed his greed within the verbiage of mission and philanthropy, assuring delegates that he planned

> to open to civilisation the only part of our globe where it has yet to penetrate, to pierce the darkness which envelops whole populations; it is, I dare say, a crusade worthy of a century of progress.... Needless to say, in bringing you to Brussels I was in no way motivated by selfish designs. No, gentlemen, if Belgium is small, she is happy and satisfied with her lot. My only ambition is to serve her.[26]

It was agreed that, acting in his personal capacity and not as King of the Belgians, Leopold should become president of a new International African Association (AIA), pledged to uphold freedom of trade and religion on the River Congo. Lacking Lavigerie's ingrained suspicion of other men's motives, delegates greeted the Belgian king as the 'dark continent's' saviour and Protestant magazines lavished praise on his 'society which would never sanction cruelty, oppression or deeds of blood and violence'.[27]

Although Leopold was a Catholic monarch, most of the delegates at Brussels were either Protestants or free thinkers, and when news of the conference reached the curia, Propaganda asked the four orders already involved in Africa to submit proposals for a Catholic reaction. Comboni reported on his project for setting up training centres, Planque offered no strategic plan, noting only that tropical Africa territory was already divided between the two vicarates, and the Holy Ghost Fathers apparently ignored the circular altogether.[28] Lavigerie alone grasped the opportunity to put forward a vision for Africa. His fifty-page document was constructed on the assumption that nobody in the curia had even the most elementary knowledge of geography; maps showed that heretics were already entrenched in South and West Africa, and he described how – even as he wrote – they were busy establishing bases along the East African coast. By his analysis, the Protestant weakness lay in the fact that their societies lacked centralised control and unity of purpose. He concluded that the church stood at a turning point of history and that the Catholic counter-attack needed to be brought under unified (by implication Lavigerie's own) control, and that it should have a strong public relations focus. Despite the fact that David Livingstone was both a Protestant and the ultimate 'Robinson', Lavigerie greatly admired his

work in the anti-slavery cause. He concluded, however, that the
Protestants were at their most vulnerable on that very issue: 'delegates
hardly mentioned slavery, or if they did speak of it, it was only as an
objective that might "ultimately" be achieved'.²⁹ The White Fathers'
submission concluded that the Catholic Church could only seize the
initiative if it went forward with the anti-slavery standard raised high:

> It is a piece of good fortune that the Holy See, under attack from
> all sides, has now a great opportunity. We can see Pius IX crowning
> his immortal Pontificate with such an act, or his successor similarly
> inaugurating his. What profound emotion would grip the world
> when it witnessed such a sign of power and moral grandeur.
> A Pontifical Bull, announcing this great crusade of humanity
> and faith ... to save life and restore liberty to the poor children
> of Ham ... would be one of the greatest events of the century
> and indeed of the whole history of the church.³⁰

The three Catholic missionaries' responses (Comboni's, Planque's and
Lavigerie's) 'sat on the table' through the declining months of Pius IX's
pontificate. Then, in one of the earliest acts of his pontificate, successor
Leo XIII transferred the greater part of Comboni's Vicarate of Central
Africa to the Archbishop of Algiers – a decision which provoked
venomous infighting within the Catholic missionary orders. Holy Ghost
and Lyons Fathers now denounced the archbishop as an empire builder
whose main objective was to scoop up as much territory as possible.
But, in June of the same year, the first party of White Fathers was ready
to start the order's assault on the interior.

* * *

Even as the White Fathers were advancing in sub-Saharan Africa,
the lack of evangelical success in Muslim lands remained profoundly
depressing. 'One is perhaps surprised at the meagre results of the
work of missionaries between 1873 and 1892,' Lavigerie wrote.
'Fifty missionaries working almost thirty years to obtain four or five
converts.'³¹ In the end, Lavigerie came to share the colonial government's
concern that direct evangelism within the Muslim community could
create a threat to public order. Without ever abandoning his dream
of ultimate mass conversion, he now forecast that the process could take
a full century to complete, and he prohibited priests from baptising any

adult without his personal authorisation. Now appointed cardinal, he argued that the church's first task was to raise the whole level of Islamic society, and that Christian teachers should properly confine themselves to imparting 'the grand divine truths that are the natural object of the human mind'. For their part, his clergy found these restrictions intolerable: 'No crucifix in the classroom. No prayers or sign of the cross at the beginning and end of the lessons. No medals or scapulars round the necks of the children. No catechism in their hands, no public or private prayers ... We have none of those consolations for which missionaries are happy to live and die.'[32]

In later life, Lavigerie's schemes became ever more unrealistic. As French soldiers fought to gain control of the Saharan oases, he proposed a new order of chivalry, named the Armed Brothers of the Sahara. With a red crusading cross on their breast and a gold cross on their red plumed helmet, these modern knights of the church would man fortified stations to provide sanctuary for slaves and bases for the spread of Christianity. While the French republican press was pouring scorn on a project, declaring that it would inevitably draw the French into destructive religious conflict, Lavigerie managed to gather ninety-five modern crusaders into a desert training camp, but the project collapsed when two thirds of his recruits deserted.

After Lavigerie died in 1894, the order's General Council debated the reasons for the sharp contrast between the White Fathers' sub-Saharan success and their abysmal failure in the Islamic lands. As a result, they decided that the ban on direct evangelism should be lifted. The catechism was translated into Berber, Catholic schools were permitted to take boarding pupils and converts were encouraged to settle on church land. A small army of White Sisters was also recruited to staff hospitals and schools and start a programme of medical home visiting. Even so, the initiatives met only failure, as White Sisters encountered a wall of hostility in the villages and the few families that did choose to settle on church land found themselves shunned as apostate by their own people.

Both Justin de Jacobis and Daniele Comboni would become canonised saints of the Catholic Church and a process was also begun on behalf of Guglielmo Massaja. Nobody seems to have considered the idiosyncratic and self-seeking Archbishop of Algiers as a candidate for beatification, though it was due to him more than any other individual that by the year 2000 almost half of all African Christians would – for better or worse – profess themselves Catholic.

Chapter 8
Pitching Tents in the Interior

The Zambezi Basin

The London Missionaries
Forty years after John Campbell identified the starting point for the missionary road into central Africa, it finally seemed that the LMS's long-term strategy could bear fruit. First, Robert Moffat crossed the desert to make contact with Mizikali in his kraal, sited where the city of Bulawayo stands today. Then, in 1856, Moffat's son-in-law, David Livingstone, announced that he had found and successfully followed the path taken by the Manatees after their defeat at Kuruman. Under the vigorous leadership of Chief Sebitwane, this one-time band of refugees – renamed the Kololo – had crossed the Kalahari desert, subdued the Lozi people of the upper Zambezi and settled in mosquito-infested marshland that provided some protection against persistent Ndebele raids. Both rulers had assured their respective visitors that they were prepared to welcome missionaries. Mzilikazi remained alive and well to make good his promise, and although Sebitwane had died, Livingstone did not doubt that his son Sekeletu would honour his father's promise. Now, at last, the LMS could mount a double-pronged mission to both the Kololo and the Ndebele.

Since Livingstone was already committed to a government expedition to the lower Zambezi, leadership of the Kololo party fell to the experienced James Helmore, supported by younger missionaries David and Isabella Price. Helmore also chose to take his wife and two of his children on the journey – risky, but no more than what Livingstone had done without disaster on several occasions. Sixty-four-year-old Robert Moffat also agreed to lead his younger colleagues William Sykes and the Welsh couple Thomas and Annie Thomas to the Ndebele and stay with them until they were settled in their new home. His son John, who had resigned from the LMS, also joined the party as an independent missionary, along with his new wife Emily. Strengthened by Tswana evangelists and teachers, the two parties set off together in 1859, before parting to go their different ways.

For six fearsome months, the Helmore children cried from thirst
as the oxen struggled, from one waterhole to the next, across the
Kalahari desert. And when they arrived at their destination, despite all
Livingstone's assurances, they received a poor welcome from the Kololo.
Swiftly discounting the very idea that this bedraggled missionary band
could offer any kind of protection from Ndebele raiding bands, the tribal
elders made it clear that their people would remain in their marshes.
The missionaries, on the other hand, were left to their fate. Suggestions
would later be made that they were poisoned, and certainly both black
and white members of the party were soon being struck down – but most
probably by malaria. Little Lizzie Helmore told the story in a letter to
a sister who had stayed behind: 'On the first Sonday Papa held service
at the waggon on the second Sonday he held service in the town he came
home with a headache he was very poorly for a few days. We all got ill
one after the other the first one that died was Mabutsi the second Henry
the third Mrs Price's baby the fourth Selina the fifth Thabi the sixth
Mama the seventh Setloke in one month.'[1]

When Papa Helmore died, Sekeletu announced that, according to
Kololo custom, all the party's goods were forfeit to him. Now destitute,
David and Isabella Price had little choice but to set off for home with the
two Helmore children. Isabella did not survive the journey, but, by good
chance, the three others were rescued by their young colleague John
Mackenzie, who had been led to them by San tribespeople.

Meanwhile, the expedition to the Ndebele was faring little better. For
one thing, the culture shock experienced by the young missionaries was
terrific. Nothing in Emily Moffat's middle-class, sheltered childhood
had prepared her to witness the warriors' welcome to Mzilikazi's kraal:
dancing men 'struck their spears on the ground, some only once or twice,
and others eight or nine times corresponding to the number of men killed
by the actor, and each received his merited shouts of applause from the
onlookers'.[2] Soon after he had settled his young colleagues on a site
outside the royal kraal, Grandpapa Moffat returned to Kuruman – along
with all the Tswana Christians who chose to return with him – leaving
behind a demoralised and inexperienced group of young people, who
were rarely on speaking terms with one another. After losing his wife
and child to fever, Thomas was sent home under the accusation of
becoming involved in tribal politics and trading in arms – though he
returned later with the support of independent Welsh chapels. The
longest survivor, William Sykes, remained for twenty-eight years without

seeing the smallest return for a lifetime's work. Visiting French Protestant François Coillard recorded his astonishment; 'You will ask me what influence the Gospel has had on this savage nation? Alas! apparently none whatever! I confess it is the most perplexing problem of modern missions.... In spite of all these efforts and sacrifices, there is no school, no church, not a single convert – *not one*!'3

Catholics fared no better. Mzilikazi's son Lobengula allowed eighteen Jesuit priests and lay brothers to settle within the royal kraal, where, for eight tedious years, they plied sewing machines to mend the royal wagons, while little Brother Nigg entertained the king with his accordion – again without making a single convert. 'Our failure', they recorded, 'was not owing to the unwillingness of the natives to learn, and even become Christians, but was due to the overwhelming terror, engaged by the system of government.'4 As he had feared, Mzilikazi lived to regret that he had ever allowed missionaries to settle in the country, but his son continued to hope that these men would one day be of value. For one thing, none of the other white men who came and went in Ndebele country could interpret the messages that came from Boers and British. For all their alien and abrasive ways, Lobengula still believed missionaries to be men of honour, whose word could be trusted.

They were not to remain the only white men in the region. When the rumour spread that gold had been discovered in Matabeleland, long-serving missionaries found their influence undermined by 'degraded loafers' who swore freely, drank copiously and took no account of the Sabbath. For their part, however, prospectors were astonished at the venom with which men of God argued that the British should take violent action against the Ndebele. 'It is amusing to hear the missionaries talk. Regular fire-brands, they admit that the sword alone will Christianise the natives.'5

The Anglo-Catholics

In 1857, and again in 1860, David Livingstone toured Britain, lecturing about his expeditions on the Zambezi River. A messianic aura enveloped the introverted Scotsman as he painted a harrowing picture of the human suffering that was inflicted by a trade in slaves that flourished across the interior. The slavers were Africans, but – being Muslims who wore the *disdasha* – they were generally called Arabs. Like Buxton before him, Livingstone argued that 'legitimate trade' offered the only solution to Africa's problems. 'The natives of Central Africa are very desirous of trading, but their only traffic is at present in slaves, of which the poorer people have an unmitigated horror: it is therefore most desirable to … open the way for the consumption of free productions, and the introduction of Christianity and commerce.'6

He assured listeners that the climate was suitable for European settlement and described how he had seen both wheat and cotton growing wild on plains north of the Zambezi. 'The highlands generally are cool and salubrious and fit for European residence. The Zambezi was full when I passed it, but even at low water it was as deep as the Thames at London.' While admitting that travellers would need to negotiate rapids, he left no doubt that the Zambezi and its tributary, the Shire, could provide a viable highway into the heart of the continent.

At Oxford and Cambridge, Livingstone urged that university men must delay no longer in engaging with Africa. Picking up the challenge, confident Anglo-Catholics from the two universities joined with colleagues in Dublin and Durham to establish the Universities' Mission to Central Africa (UMCA). Charles Mackenzie, who was on leave from his mission station in Natal, agreed to lead a party to the Zambezi, and accordingly, six clergy and several medical, agricultural and industrial experts sailed for South Africa in 1860 in the full glare of publicity (and under the close scrutiny of the clerical establishment). Seated around Archbishop Gray's table in Cape Town, they discussed how they should behave if they had to confront the slavers, and – in that safe environment – all agreed that ordained clergy must never become involved in violence. Archbishop Gray had been a leading advocate of the Colonial Churches Bill. In the early church, he argued, bishops did not enjoy wealth and live in mansions; they took risks with their lives, leading parties of missionaries into heathen lands. As he consecrated Mackenzie to be Bishop of Central Africa, he provided the Anglican communion with a model for the modern missionary bishop, which would be so quickly copied by the evangelical Henry Venn when he sought consecration for Samuel Crowther.

In Africa, Mackenzie's high churchmen discovered that the task of navigating the Zambezi and the Shire was a considerably more challenging task than Livingstone had led them to expect:

Swamp, swamp – reeking festering rotting, malaria-pregnant swamp – where poisonous vapours for several months in the year are ever bulging up and out into the air, lies before you as far as the

eye can reach and further.… If you are detained any great length
of time in the neighbourhood of these pestiferous localities … then
the chances are you will take the worst type of fever, which will be
again and again repeated.[7]

Mackenzie led the way onto the plateau that would be known as the Shire
Highlands, in one hand his bishop's crozier (which Africans assumed was
some unknown weapon) and in the other a rifle. His companions also had
firearms for hunting the game that they expected to find teeming on the
African plain, and in the porters' loads was a dismantled cotton mill,
designed to produce the first fruits of legitimate industry. But, to their
surprise and horror, they emerged into an environment different from that
described in Livingstone's lectures. The *lifaqane* had passed by during
the years since Livingstone came that way, and the university men now
arrived in a land whose inhabitants had been 'scattered and peeled'.

> There was war on the plateau. The Ajawa had invaded the
> Manganja (Nyanja) territory, occupied villages around Mount
> Zomba and were destroying and taking captives. The hill Manganja
> were in a state of greatest excitement and terror and were quite
> unable to withstand the invaders, many of whom, it was said, were
> armed with guns, while the Manganja had but bows and arrows.[8]

Livingstone had warned that the Ajawa – properly called the Yao – were
a depraved race, and the newcomers were duly shocked to be confronted
by men with filed front teeth and women who disfigured their lips with
enormous rings. When they came face-to-face with slave caravans, these
young men decided that they did, after all, have a moral duty 'to set
captives free' – by force, if necessary. The ordained clergy later claimed
that they fired over the heads of the enemy. True or false, their presence
decided the outcome of what Mackenzie would call the First Ajawi War.
Flushed with victory, they led the women and children back to the
mission station, where everybody remembered the image of their heroic
bishop carrying the girl child Dauma on his shoulders. After the Second
Ajawi War, however, they looked closely at those who had been released
and made an embarrassing discovery. 'We found that three-fourths were
Ajawa, for most of those that had been released from the slavers to our
astonishment, proved to be Ajawa that had been sold by the Manganja,
instead of Manganja that had been sold by the Ajawa.'[9]

The young men of the expedition were followed by five women
who had taken Livingstone's advice that Christian ladies could provide
a model of civilisation in a savage world. News of their progress up the
Zambezi went before them. The explorer's wife Mary Livingstone was
accompanied by the bishop's older sister Anne and Mrs Burrup, who
was newly married to one of the younger clergy. Both Anglican wives
travelled with maids – one unnamed, the other only known to posterity
as Lizzie. Mary Livingstone was in an emotional state, having fallen
heavily for a young Scottish clergyman, James Stewart, who had joined
the party out of a sense of devotion to Livingstone, whom he had idolised
since he was a child. Anne Mackenzie was also emotional, anxious to be
reunited with her brother on the route ahead of them. Her diary entry for
6 March 1863 told a story of personal disaster: 'We landed at the Rua
where we hoped to be met by the Bishop, or find a letter waiting for us.
The natives denied having seen or heard anything of white men. They
lied. My darling brother was in his grave there. He died towards the end
of January.'[10]

When news reached David Livingstone that his wife Mary had also
died of malaria, he sincerely mourned the woman who, by normal
marital standards, he had so long neglected. James Stewart, on the other
hand, was furious. Thoroughly disillusioned, he recorded the moment
he decided that his lifetime model had feet of clay.

> In the afternoon I went down to the river-bank a short way and
> threw with all my strength into the turbid muddy weed covered
> Zambezi my copy of a certain 'Missionary Travels in South
> Africa'.[11] The volume was fragrant with odours of and memories
> of the earnestness with which I studied the book in days gone by.
> How different it appeared now! It was nothing short of an eyesore,
> the sight of its brown covers. I do not think of it as the Rev R[obert]
> M[offat] is said to have called it, 'a pack of lies', but it would need
> a great many additions to make it the truth. Thus I disliked the
> book and sent it to sink or swim into the vaunted Zambezi.[12]

According to Stewart's analysis, 'the fallacy of Livingstone's method' was
that, having overcome obstacles by a huge moral and physical effort that
even the strongest human can only deliver once or twice in a lifetime, he
had returned home to announce blithely that the road into central Africa
was open. It was not.

Reports of the Ajawi wars raised an outcry among home supporters.
Dublin and Durham universities withdrew support when the patriarch
of the Oxford Movement, Edward Pusey, publicly repudiated the
missionaries' resort to force.[13] With the operation reeling under loss
of life in the field and criticism at home, a new bishop was sent out with
instructions to withdraw all staff from the Zambezi basin. Survivors
of Mackenzie's party were distressed to abandon freed slaves their fate,
though the party took modest comfort from the fact that little Dauma
was settled in a Christian home in South Africa. To Livingstone's disgust,
the Universities' Mission to Central Africa set up its new headquarters at
the epicentre of the Arab slave trade – on Zanzibar Island. The sustained
efforts of the Scots to establish a missionary presence in the Zambesi
basin were yet to come, but Livingstone would not live to see them. They
were, in fact, inspired by his death.

The Scots

In 1874, a mood of awe settled over Britain as the country prepared
to honour the passage of David Livingstone's heart. Crowds lined the
streets between Southampton and London as the *cortège* passed by,
and Westminster Abbey pews were filled with the great and the good for
the missionary hero's funeral. After carrying the coffin alongside other
companions of Livingstone's travels, James Stewart, now renowned
headmaster of Lovedale College, stood over the open grave and resolved
that his countrymen would establish a permanent mission on Lake
Nyassa (Malawi). Newly ordained medical doctor Robert Laws was
selected to lead the Free Church contingent. Members of the established
Church of Scotland insisted that their church must also take part, but
since no ordained minister could be recruited, layman Henry Henderson
was charged with finding a site for their 'Auld Kirk' mission. English
gunnery officer E. D. Young, who had already sailed the Zambezi, had
overall command of the expedition. Since Livingstone had recommended
that the lakes and rivers of the interior were best travelled by steam
vessel, the Scots ordered a boat that could be dismantled below the
Lower Zambesi rapids and reassembled for use on the continental
plateau. It was a successful operation, for which Young gave credit to the
porters: 'we had everything delivered to us unmolested, untampered with
and unhurt, and every man content with his well-earned wages.'[14]

Lest hopes were raised too high, home supporter Professor Henry
Drummond asked the public to consider the scale of the task ahead.

Supposing one day a small boat of strange build and propelled
by means unknown to civilisation came up the river Thames
containing half a dozen Esquimaux; supposing these men pitched
their tents in Battersea Park and gave out that they had come to
regenerate London society; supposing they took England generally
in hand and tried to reform its abuses, and then above all tried to
convert every subject of the country to the god of the Esquimaux –
that is very much the problem which our missionaries have to face
in Africa.[15]

A generation earlier, Ngoni warriors of the *lifaqane* had passed that
way, travelling 800 miles north to the shores of Lake Nyanza/Victoria,
before returning to settle on both shores of Lake Nyassa. In time, the
Scots would develop considerable respect for this violent but well-
ordered people. Their deepest loathing was reserved for those Swahili-
Arabs, who spread Islam while fishing for slaves in the region's troubled
waters. While Henderson settled the Auld Kirk operation at a site that
he called Blantyre, situated in the comparatively healthy Shire Highlands,
Laws placed his Livingstonia headquarters on the lake's fever-ridden
west bank, and despite a growing number of Free Church deaths from
malaria, both operations were publicised at home as a huge success.

The ethos of any missionary operation would often reflect the
founders' attitudes. In Calabar, the Wadells allowed capable Scottish
women to contribute fully to the effort. In Nyasaland, by contrast,
Stewart and the unbendingly authoritarian Laws created a mission
dominated by white males, where, throughout the century, Scottish
women appear in the record only when pouring visitors' tea from silver
pots or sewing flags to greet approaching colonists. African evangelists,
brought by Stewart from Lovedale, also found it difficult to integrate
into the missionary body. One of them, Isaac Williams Wauchope,
developed erratic and violent behaviour, which the missionaries
diagnosed as possession by the devil – though when he was sent home
to South Africa, he resumed a blameless Christian life. Cattle-killing
survivor William Koyi began life at the mission with low self-esteem:
'I have only half a talent, but I am willing to go and be a hewer of wood
and drawer of water'. Koyi had the advantage, however, of speaking
fluent Zulu, which was still the mother tongue of the Ngoni tribes. He
was also physically brave, climbing into the hills to settle beside the chief's
kraal. He named his station *Sibehleli* (we are settled) but the Ngoni called

it *Ekusinda Nyeriweni* (the place where shit is spread around).[16] During
Koyi's brief working life as a missionary, his superior, Walter Elmslie,
complained bitterly that he had become too familiar with the natives
and, as a result, degraded his missionary status. 'There is not that
respect shown to him which should be and which is a factor in raising
the people from their low condition.'[17] At his funeral, however, he
delivered a flattering oration. 'A common Kafir – a Mission Kafir – to
be sneered at by men not possessing a tithe of his manliness and good
character, he was one with whom it was a privilege to associate.
I acknowledge with pleasure, I received unmeasured help from him;
to his achievements in those early days the after-success of the work
was in large measure due.'[18]

Following the example set by other societies, the Auld Kirk committee
established the African Lakes Company to act as trading arm of their
operation and despatched the Moir brothers – whose undoubted piety
was balanced by an alarming appetite for reckless behaviour – to take
charge of the Blantyre side of the operation. Employees were expected
to run the business at a profit, while, at the same time, acting as befitted
agents of the gospel, and travellers were astonished to meet company
agents who maintained the strictest sabbatarian discipline in the
remotest bush and survived with no greater stimulant than soft drinks.
As employees travelled the caravan routes, they passed the bodies of dead
slaves that littered trade routes. In the light of this harsh reality, the Scots
concluded that Livingstone's great plan would remain no more than
a pious aspiration. 'What we need', declared Robert Laws, 'is a small
British gunboat and a score of trained men – that would stop the trade.'[19]

Relations between the two mission leaders were never easy, and each
had different visions for the future. While Laws planned to build a
centre of civilisation on the shores of Lake Nyasa. Stewart was equally
determined that the whole operation should remain a satellite of
Lovedale College. According to his plan, Livingstonia would have no
printing press and offer no education above primary grades. Six years on,
the Auld Kirk still had no ordained minister to take charge at Blantyre,
and Laws and Stewart were supervising operations on two sites that were
more than a 100 miles apart. Dividing his time between Xhosa country
and the Nyasaland, James Stewart confessed to 'a slow burning anger …
that I should be kept toiling away at rough work which suited me twenty
years ago but does not suit me at all now'. It might then have been
recognised that serious trouble was brewing.

The Evangelical Awakening

For more than half a century, preachers carried wave after wave
of religious revival across the eastern United States. In the second Great
Awakening of the 1830s, evangelist Charles Grandeson Finney had
presented a gospel of purification, declaring that nothing would be
impossible for those who purged themselves of all half-heartedness and
lived only by the light of the gospel. In 1875, evangelist Dwight Moody
and singer Ira Sankey took London by storm, and detached observers
were astonished to see the impact of the evangelists' zeal on the
supposedly secularised English. Britain also produced home-grown
evangelists. Anglican curate Thomas Harford Battersby established
a convention in his Lake District parish of Keswick, where the fires
of revival would be annually rekindled. At this time, the challenge to
conquer 'the World for Christ in Our Generation' was spreading out
from American campuses, with evangelists proclaiming the millennial
message that Christ would surely be true to his word and come again and
that the great event was delayed only because the church was still failing
to obey his missionary commandment. Until now, most evangelical
missionaries to Africa had been drawn from the lower orders of society,
but these new appeals were particularly directed at educated and well-
born young people. At a time of fervour, a new model of mission was
also gaining wide attention. James Hudson Taylor founded the China
Inland Mission in 1865 on the principle that dedicated men and women
needed to throw themselves on the pagan world, without salary or
security, in confidence that God would provide for their material needs.
Home supporters should not attend endless committees to discuss high
strategy, it was argued, but simply back those in the field with money and
prayers.

Nobody followed events in Africa more carefully than an eccentric
recluse who lived in the Leeds suburb of Headingley. Robert Arthington
inherited a fortune from a family brewing business; spending next to
nothing on himself, he lost count of the burgeoning value of his stock
as he concentrated on his single-minded aim to hasten the second coming
of Christ. In common with many 'end-timers' who would come after
him, he showed little concern for the fate of the perishing heathen. 'God's
plan as revealed to us in Holy Writ has ever been from the beginning of
Time – to take out of the human race a People for his name.... Millions
of the wicked have been massacred, murdered, and slain – in Asia, Africa

and America, and the saved have been "brands plucked from the burning".[20]

Since few would be saved, it followed that building expensive mission stations, schools and clinics was a waste of resources. Missionaries needed to operate as migrant preachers, proclaiming the gospel, before passing on, leaving behind key sections of the Bible translated into local languages.

As Lavigerie poured over his maps in Algiers, so did Arthington in Leeds. Thanks to the ocean liner and the Suez Canal, once-remote East Africa now stood on the great shipping route to India. Archbishop and miser were at least in agreement that the lakes and rivers of the Rift Valley held the key to the opening of Africa – the problem lay in how to reach those waterways. The northern and southern routes by way of, respectively, the White Nile and the Zambezi were proving more difficult than anybody had anticipated, and the two men's maps showed no navigable rivers in between. That country was, however, criss-crossed by the tracks left by slavers' caravans. On the western side of the Rift Valley, Arthington was inclined to accept the theory, most favoured by geographers, that the river known to Africans as the Lualaba was the true headwater of the River Congo. With slaving tracks to the east and the Congo river to the west, all the pieces of his grand plan were in place. Arthington planned to use his worldly wealth to put steamboats on all the waterways of the continental interior.

Towards the Rift Valley

On 15 November 1875, the *Daily Telegraph* published Stanley's description of Lake Nyanza (later Victoria), along with his account of a visit to the court of kabaka Mutesa at Mengo in Uganda. Just two days later, the CMS received an anonymous letter, which had surely come from Arthington.[21]

> The appeal of the energetic explorer Stanley to the Christian Church from Mutesa's capital, Uganda … seems to me to indicate that the time has come for the soldiers of the Cross to make an advance into this region. If the Committee of the Church Missionary society are prepared at once and with energy to organise a Mission to the Victoria Nyanza, I shall account it a high privilege to place £5,000 at their disposal for the expenses of the undertaking.[22]

Military men shook their heads over maps of the interior; in normal circumstances, they would recommend a staged approach, involving the construction of a chain of re-provisioning stations between the coast and the inland lakes, but the anonymous donor was demanding that they despatch men immediately on a 1,000 mile journey, and in the end, all agreed that the Society must respond to what was surely a divine call. So, in March 1876, a tiny steamer set sail for the Suez Canal under the command of Lieutenant George Shergold Smith and eight missionaries, led by a young Australian-born clergyman Charles Wilson. Some died on the overland journey, others were invalided home and a full year would pass before Smith and Wilson finally managed to launch Arthington's boat off the lake's southern shore. Even then, they had no engineer to start the engine and they crossed to Uganda under sail.

At last, the two men arrived at the kabaka's rambling court, where they were well-received by red-coated pages. They owed this gracious reception to Stanley. Before departing, Stanley had installed a Christian from Zanzibar called Scorpion Mufta with Mutesa, and Mufta had spent his time translating the Bible into Swahili and teaching the kabaka and his courtiers how they should properly behave when the white missionaries arrived. Wilson described the first Sunday service.

> The king, chief men, and others, about 100 in all, were present, I read a chapter from the Old and New Testament, Mufta translating, and explained a few things which the king asked. We then had a few prayers, all kneeling, and to my surprise and pleasure, a hearty 'Amen' followed each prayer. The king had told them to do so. I next gave a short address on the Fall, and our consequent need of a Saviour, telling them of Christ. Mufta translated. All listened with great attention and the king afterwards asked many questions. It was very encouraging indeed.[23]

As so often in Africa, encouragement was short-lived. It was decided that Shergold Smith should return to the lake's southern shore to collect an artisan, who would tend the boat and build a permanent station. The lake, however, was a dangerous place. On the return journey, the two men pitched camp on an island, where slavers had been routed by their intended victims and both Englishmen were killed while trying to shelter a fleeing slaver. Wilson remained in Uganda alone for many months until the arrival of Scottish engineer Alexander Mackay.

Even before the first CMS party left for Uganda, Arthington dispatched a second letter, this time challenging the LMS to place a vessel on Lake Tanganyika. Once again, the directors could not doubt that the call was inspired by God, and it was agreed that the task be undertaken, this time committed into the hands of seasoned campaigners. Eighteen years after surviving Helmore's Kololo venture, Roger Price was brought from South Africa to lead the party, with Matabeleland veteran J.B. Thompson as his second in command and sea captain Edward Hore to supervise transport of the steam boat and later take command of it on the lake. Price was determined to travel in the South African way, by wagons drawn by ninety oxen, but this was tsetse country, and after just two months, most of the animals were dead. With terrible memories of the Kololo disaster now flooding back, Price became convinced that the whole strategy was wrong-headed and left for home to argue that the society needed to install the traditional chain of support stations before any attempt was made to reach the lake. He never returned. With Thompson now in charge, the LMS party took more than a year to cover the 800 miles to Ujiji, at an average rate of barely 2 miles a day, while the baggage train at the rear took a further eight months. Thompson then died of fever, leaving the irascible Hore and just one colleague to start Arthington's great venture as best they could. Somehow they managed to survive until relief parties got through (at high cost in life and resources), and the mission at last put down roots on the eastern shore of Lake Tanganyika. To protect themselves and their converts from the region's all-pervasive violence, they converted their stations into fortified 'villages', where the missionary would be the sole arbiter of law and order.

* * *

Meanwhile, the Archbishop of Algiers impatiently kept abreast of these events. By the time that his first party of White Fathers left the east coast in June 1878, Protestant societies were – however tenuously – already established on Lakes Tanganyika and Victoria. Leo XIII issued clear instructions. Catholic priests were charged with confronting the twin evils of paganism and heresy – and between these two the priority was clear: Africans who had never heard the Gospel had some hope of divine mercy, but those who had embraced Protestantism were surely hell-bound. So the battle lines were drawn up. Lavigerie divided his White Fathers into two parties; Fr Livinhac, who was in overall command, would take the northern group to Uganda, while Fr Pascal led the southern to Lake Tanganyika. Ten priests set off, supported by armed askari and a massive team of 450 carriers. The fathers recorded pride in both nation and faith – and, unexpectedly, a sense of brotherhood with the Protestant pioneers.

> Other thoughts mingle in our hearts with those of faith: thoughts of France, our homeland and all those we have known and loved.... We will be working for France as well. Sent off by our bishop, who, like us, is French, we are the first Frenchmen who will carry our country's language and influence into deepest Africa. One day we will be followed along this peaceful road, where we will perhaps leave our graves, by peace loving explorers from our own France. Englishmen, Americans and Germans have gone ahead of us. Surely before long we will come together in a great *rendezvous* of humanity and civilisation.[24]

The two parties went their separate ways at Tabora where Pascal's group continued travelling westwards, and Livignac's turned north towards Lake Victoria. When Pascal reached Lake Tanganyika, he was happy to report that the LMS missionaries posed no threat; instead of getting on with the business of conversion, like all good Robinsons, they were wasting their energies in exploration. Pascal chose to set up his base on the western side of the Lake, where slavers were less active and his priests could operate at a good distance from Protestant competition. The situation was different on Lake Victoria. Here, Livignac immediately led his White Fathers into confrontation with both Protestants and Muslims at the court of Mutesa, black prince of Uganda.

The kabaka had once been attracted by a comparatively relaxed form of Islam imported by traders and slavers from the east coast, but his attitude changed when a more intransigent form of the faith began to infiltrate into his land from the White Nile. Royal anger exploded when his own pages refused to eat non-halal meat at the royal table; after shouting 'Is my meat only fit for dogs?', he told his executioners to kill every circumcised male in the land. 'The order was promptly obeyed and that same night two hundred Muslim youths were burnt to death.'[25] After hearing news of European advances across other parts of Africa, the volatile Mutesa changed his mind and decided that Christians might pose a greater threat to his kingdom than Muslims, but he was bewildered that Protestant and Catholics offered two sharply contrasting patterns of the same faith. Following Bugandan tradition, he invited the two groups of missionaries to debate their differences in the royal presence. Wilson opened proceedings by comparing Islam to the light of a pale moon, which had broken through the dark night of paganism until the bright sunshine of evangelical truth in turn arose to obliterate it. He then called everybody to prayer but, as courtiers dropped to their knees, Mutesa noticed that 'the gentlemen of the French mission sat on their chairs' and talked quietly among themselves. When challenged, Fr Siméon Lourdel explained that the Protestants were rebels against the one great ruler of the Christian world. Now warming to the controversy, Wilson responded by telling the king how Frenchmen had quite recently cut off their own king's head. However puzzling the history and theology, Mutesa and his courtiers found the whole controversy hugely enjoyable. Pages even began to group themselves into Muslim, Protestant and Catholic parties – though this was a dangerous game. From the time that a boy arrived at court, he was inducted into a culture of absolute and unquestioning loyalty, in which the most trivial breach of etiquette might be punished by imprisonment or even execution.

Malaria took an equal toll on both Catholics and Protestants, and for some time, Alexander Mackay and Siméon Lourdel survived alone on their stations. Religious orientation apart, they were, in fact, strikingly similar men. Both had been raised in small village communities, one near Aberdeen and the other outside Arras; both were physically impressive, rough-hewn, practical and intolerant characters. After two years' training as an engineer in Germany, Mackay could manufacture an impressive fountain that threw water far into the air, but Lourdel gained the reputation of being the better doctor. Stories spread that both possessed magical powers, and in time, each began to behave like a tribal chief, with his own band of followers. As Lourdel treated Mutesa for what proved to be a terminal illness, he nursed the hope that the kabaka would finally accept the true faith but, after one final orgy of bloodletting, Mutesa died a pagan.

Even after the new kabaka Mwanga had prohibited his pages from having any contact with white teachers, some boys and girls continued to find their way to the mission stations at night, and the competition between Protestants and Catholics for converts continued. Mackay urged his Protestants to stand firm; 'our beloved brethren, do not deny our Lord Jesus, and He will not deny you on that great day when he will come with glory.'[26] For his part, Lourdel held crash catechism classes (in defiance of Lavigerie's rule book) and baptised over 100 young people in just one session. Pages, who had been drawn to the white man's religions for a variety of motives, now became caught up in a frenzy of piety. It was an unstable situation. Missionaries on both sides would later spread the story that the 'fickle, nervous, sensuous and unstable' ruler had a predilection for 'unmentionable abomination' and that his control snapped when Christian pages managed to convert one of his favourites.[27] Others reported that his anger exploded when a fire broke out in the royal arsenal at a time when the pages were at their prayers. Whether or not either is true, Mwanga had become convinced that he no longer commanded the loyalty of his most intimate servants. 'Where are all my men? Have they not gone to the white men to read? ... Am I your king, or does Buganda belong to the white man?'[28] This time he ordered the death of all Christians in the country.

For the most part, this purge was carried out in a half-hearted manner; officials were generally left in peace and chiefs succeeded in protecting family members, but many did die and others were castrated and maimed. The world's attention focused on an *auto-da-fé* of pages, in which thirty-one youngsters were burnt to death, of which thirteen are thought to have been Catholic, eleven Protestant and seven may have been pagans, delivered by chiefs as substitutes for their own children. Mwanga expected that the boys would plead for mercy; in the awesome event, the only wailing came from executioner Mukanjaga as he put his son to death. As newspapers carried accounts of the outrage, Lavigerie opened proceedings for the beatification of these modern Catholic martyrs, while the story was told and retold in countless Protestant churches, chapels and Sunday schools. As Mwanga came to realise that he dared not alienate the whole Christian world, he reversed his policies, even allowing both Catholics and Protestants to form their own regiments – known as the *Wa-Fransa* and the *Wa-Ingleza* – with licence to harass non-Christians and enrich themselves at the people's expense. The instability grew worse. First, as public anger grew, the Muslim faction drove the kabaka and missionaries of both persuasions into exile; then, the Muslim rulers managed to alienate every male Ugandan by issuing an order that compelled universal circumcision and Mwanga was able to return at the head of both Christian regiments.

Soon the tension between the *Wa-Fransa* and the *Wa-Ingleza* had reached fever pitch, and when missionary-turned-trader Charles Stokes

arrived to supply the Protestant forces with arms, he could only liken
the situation with the sectarian bitterness that he had experienced in his
native Ulster. Under the vigorous leadership of Mgr Jean-Joseph Hirth,
the Catholics were now establishing an increasingly dominant position;
besides having more white missionaries than the Anglicans, they were
building a large following within the population, and – for all his errant
morality – they could even count Mwanga as an adherent. But in the
great carve-up of Africa, far away in Berlin, it had now been decided that
Uganda would be British territory, and late in 1890, British Imperial East
African company representative Captain Frederick Lugard arrived with
an armed force to negotiate a treaty with the kabaka. This secular man
was astonished to discover that, here in Uganda, 'Mohammedan,
Catholic and Protestant alike were seized by a *mania religiosa*'.[29] Tension
boiled over when the soldier decided to force his way into the royal
palace to negotiate his treaty.

> The day before Christmas the question of a treaty was introduced
> before the king in open court, where a dangerous and excited
> crowd of chiefs had collected. All came armed with loaded rifles,
> the Roman Catholics to support the king against the English and
> the Protestants to defend Captain Lugard…. The king was terrified
> and greatly excited as the strange Englishman, heedless of his
> evident disinclination, insisted that he should sign the treaty.
> Next day, however, a wonder happened, for the treaty was signed
> by the recalcitrant Catholics and the king, and the storm was
> stilled…. He need not have been astonished, for the explanation
> of the great change was simple enough. The French fathers bade
> their faction sign the treaty, an order which was immediately
> obeyed.[30]

But it was not over. Although the Catholics had accepted British
occupation as a *fait accompli*, they did not intend to hand the Ugandans
over to infidels. By the end of 1891, both Christian parties were
consolidating into armed camps. Swept up into millenarian hysteria, one
Anglican burst into the royal presence, where 'he loaded Mwanga with
maledictions and threatened him with the terrors of judgement: "The end
of the world is coming in just three years time"', he declared.[31] 'Poor
Uganda!' declared Bishop Hirth, 'when will these sorrows cease? This
year plague and famine have harvested a third of the population and

now a new war, war to the death, threatens to carry off half of those who remain.'[32]

Catholic mass on New Year's Day 1892 was hailed as a *vrai triomphe*. The moment that Mwanga entered the cathedral, 'ten thousand men' jostled for the honour to stand near him. Still, factional hostility spiralled to new heights, and less than a month later, two armies – the *Wa-Fransa* and the *Wa-Ingleza* – lined up for battle on low ground below Kampala. As the Protestant missionaries took shelter in the company fort, Lugard despatched soldiers to round up the White Fathers. He claimed that they were lodged in the fort for their protection, but by their own perspective, they were being taken prisoner. For years, Charles Stokes had been supplying Mwanga with old-fashioned, muzzle-loading guns; while the *Wa-Ingleza* and Lugard's company forces had modern rifles and maxim guns. As in so many colonial wars, the advanced weapons proved decisive and a Protestant missionary surveyed the devastation at the end of the day. 'Every RC house and garden is a mass of ashes and charred bananas and some Protestant places too.' The whole scene reminded him of entering Birmingham from Wolverhampton by night![33] When the fighting was finally over, Bishop Hirth warned Lugard that the world would hear how his Imperial British East Africa Company (IBEACo) had used brute force to suppress the Catholic Church, and from his death bed, Lavigerie sent out letters and pamphlets designed to whip up Catholic opinion across Europe and America.

When Lugard tried to calm emotions by sharing out offices of state between the three major factions, missionaries advised native Protestant chiefs on how they should draft an ultimatum demanding that every position of power must go to the victors. Missionary interference in secular affairs had now brought Lugard to his wits' end. 'It appears to me', he recorded, 'that if a missionary is consulted on political matters by the chiefs, it would be his first duty to ascertain what was the real attitude of the administration.'[34] In reality, both Protestants and Catholics were plotting to realise their own very different visions of a theocratic Christian state. 'Are we to settle down content with the miserable parody of Christianity which all too often passes muster in Christian England?'[35] one young CMS wife asked. Without wasting time with elaborate training, her male colleagues rose to the challenge by ordaining a number of Protestant chiefs as Anglican clergymen and started to recruit evangelists, who would be charged to take the faith into new areas. Nursing similar plans, Bishop Hirth surrendered the work in Kampala to English Mill Hill Fathers and led his White Fathers westwards to create his own Catholic state, beyond Lugard's reach, near the Ruwandan border. So the struggle between Protestants and Catholics for the souls of Africans did not end but merely relocated. In the coming decades, young armies of Protestant evangelists and Catholic catechists would compete for the allegiance of chiefs and people within the forests and across the grasslands of the great continental divide.

The Congo Basin

Back in 1876, Robert Arthington had been reserving the greatest challenge for his favourite society for the last, but he could wait no longer. Even before Stanley settled all controversy about the course of the River Congo, a letter arrived at the BMS's London office offering to fund a Christian thrust into the interior by the western gateway. Secretary Alfred Baines found the proposal attractive; results in Cameroon had been disappointing and he was already looking for a higher-profile field of operations. Accordingly, he released Thomas Comber and George Grenfell from their duties in Cameroon to conduct a pilot study, and although the party returned with little achieved after lower Congo chiefs had blocked their way upriver, committee members unanimously decided to take the project forwards. Grenfell, incidentally, had fallen from grace. Though supporters were informed that he had retired 'to study African trade questions', in truth he was no longer deemed fit to be a missionary because his West Indian housekeeper Rose was carrying his child.[36]

The society's directors anticipated that Belgian employees of the AIA would be at work in the region before their missionaries arrived. They were, however, upset to discover that one of their colleagues, Rev Tilly of Cardiff, had gone into partnership with the husband and wife team of Henry and Fanny Guinness to set up the Livingstone Interior Mission (LIM) for work on the river. LIM missionaries, recruited from fringe Baptist congregations, needed to accept challenging terms and conditions: 'As it is the aim of this mission to introduce into the Congo Valley as many Christian evangelists as possible, and as it is believed that land and native labour can be secured at small cost, the agents of the mission shall be men willing to avail themselves of these advantages, and resolved to be as little burdensome as possible to the funds of the mission. No salaries are guaranteed.'[37]

For both the Belgian and British missionaries, the first objective was to reach a lake, later known as Stanley Pool, where the upper river became navigable. Before this could be achieved, however, they had to negotiate some 250 miles of tropical rain forest and rapids, and this was made near impossible by the implacable hostility of the local chiefs and people. BMS worker Holman Bentley understood the fears of the native people: 'In vain did the party explain that they did not want to buy ivory; the natives felt that once the path was open, traders would not be kept out. It is a very real trouble, for by the sale of their ivory, some palm oil and India rubber, these people obtain their salt, cloth, hoop-iron, powder and other commodities.'[38]

Most chiefs recognised that violence only invited retribution, and the same end could be achieved by non-cooperation. Villagers, therefore, refused to build trading and mission stations, to disclose forest trade routes or – most important – to carry loads. Stanley had now been recruited to lead the AIA operation and he solved this labour problem in the only way he knew – by holding women and children prisoner while the men did forced labour. A race to the Pool developed between Baptists missionaries and Stanley's officers: 'It will be a lasting disgrace if the Belgian expedition, hunting for ivory and rubber, gets ahead of the Baptist Missionary Society, seeking to win jewels for the Saviour's crown', declared Bentley. 'It would be strange if missionaries fresh from religious colleges could do more than Belgian officers from their military schools', wrote Stanley.

In fact, unknown to the competitors, the race's outcome was being influenced by events outside the control of either. Towards the end of 1880, French explorer Pierre Savorgnan de Brazza had appeared out of the jungle to reveal that, in a spectacular journey, he had travelled from the French colony of Gabon, up the Ogowe River and across the watershed to the north shore of Stanley Pool. In the course of setting up treaties with local chiefs, he had made a deal that none would receive any white man who did not wear a cock's feather in his hat. Retracing Brazza's route in reverse, Bentley and Crudington reached Stanley Pool in January 1881, but, having no cock's feather in their hats, they were coldly received. Six months later, 'Belgian officers from military schools' arrived to establish Leopold's headquarters on the river's southern bank, and both missionary societies were given generous grants of land on the site that would grow to become the modern city of Kinshasa.

Now legally married and restored to favour, William Grenfell was given command of Arthington's steamer *Peace*, with instructions to sail the upper river to report on suitable sites for mission stations. In a series of huge journeys, he followed the main river east to the head of navigation, upstream of modern Kisangani, where he found wide areas devastated by slavers. On the major tributaries, he opened up the Kasai, which flowed out of mineral rich Katanga in the south, the Oubangui, which pointed north towards Lake Chad, and the Aruwimi, which rose in mountains that flanked the Ugandan border. However, to his lasting frustration, he never succeeded in fulfilling Arthington's dream by contacting those Protestants who were now settled within the Rift Valley.

The Miser of Headingley's plans were still not exhausted. In January 1878, a retired South African army officer working for Arthington made a presentation to the American Board of Commissioners in Boston. Unrolling a map, he proposed that they should take responsibility for a stretch of the river upstream from Stanley Pool, from which point they could build convergent chains of stations that would link the Congo with distant Natal. The commissioners found the incentive of a £3,000 donation less than compelling; their society dealt in large sums and they had just banked a bequest for a million dollars. At a time when Bentley and Crudington had still not reached Stanley Pool, they also questioned whether the project was practical. The officer's visit did, however, stimulate the commissioners to conduct investigations, which led in due course to the opening of American Board stations on the Bié plateau in Angola. Besides being a 'healthy, fertile and populous' area, this appeared to offer more realistic opportunities for the creation of some kind of evangelical connection across the centre of Africa.[39]

Meanwhile, in the face of continued losses from malaria, Henry and Fanny Guinness were forced to the conclusion that missionaries who worked in such a harsh environment needed better financial support than their little operation could provide. To the Rev Tilly's disgust, they handed their Congo work over to the northern branch of the American Baptist Union. The Americans brought new thinking to mission strategy. Finding most LIM stations in appalling condition, they imposed tight central control of a kind that was alien to any faith mission philosophy. They also challenged the received wisdom that stations should be built in chains because it was inefficient for any society to work across language frontiers.

By this time, the English Baptists had to accept the unpalatable fact that Britain had sacrificed all colonial ambitions in the Congo Basin. While the major colonial powers were still debating the matter, Leopold

was establishing effective control on the ground. If the work was
to continue, the Baptists needed to convince Leopold that he had the
unqualified allegiance of all BMS missionaries. Bentley insisted that every
new recruit must arrive on the river with a working knowledge of French;
he even advised his subordinates that they should speak the language at
their meal tables. After this, it came as a shock when the British Foreign
Secretary formally accepted Portuguese claims to sovereignty over
the delta area. In a letter to the *Times*, Baynes asked why the British
government was 'trying to stop the development, to which the benevolent
King Leopold of the Belgians has given so royally hundreds and
thousands of pounds'.[40] Stanley also argued Leopold's case before
packed meetings in the industrial north, reminding manufacturers that
'if every negro in the Congo bought one Sunday dress and four everyday
dresses, it would require 3,840 million yards of Manchester cotton,
worth £16 million – and this did not include cloth for winding sheets'.[41]

Baynes and Bentley travelled to Berlin in 1885 to be on hand in case
mission advice was needed when the European powers gathered to
discuss the partition of Africa. The General Act that emerged from
debate only set the ground rules for the new imperial age – firm territorial
deals were completed in private discussions either during or after
the official congress – but the Baptists were delighted when a broad
agreement finally emerged that Leopold would receive the southern side
of the lower Congo, mineral-rich Katanga and a huge stretch of central
Africa beyond Stanley Pool. Better still, he had been forced to concede
that religion and trade would be free in his African dominions. Baynes
could be confident that, in the world of real politics, Leopold dared not
alienate his powerful British and American allies by expelling Protestants
from the Congo, and there were not enough reformed Belgians to replace
the established missionaries.

As Leopold recruited Scheldt fathers to co-ordinate Catholics'
operations in his new territory, foreign Catholic orders quickly discovered
that they operated on less-secure ground. Belgian missionaries held the
upper hand. 'The Catholic work in the Congo will be founded on a firm
base. No more … letting in foreign missions: the new state will become
as Belgian in its religion as it already is in its politics and I hope that an
army of missionaries will come to help establish a new Belgium in this
distant land.'[42] When Planque tried to secure sites for his Lyons Fathers
on the lower river, his ambitions were quickly dashed, and the Spiritians
were instructed to withdraw all their catechists operating within the Free

State boundaries. Leopold also tried to expel Lavigerie's priests from their eastern stations, though Leo XIII ruled that the French could stay until Leopold proved that he could recruit Belgian White Fathers to take their place.

The king's missionary enterprise rode a wave of national enthusiasm and the Society of St. Augustine extolled the new collaboration between church and state:

> Hail noble Belgium,
> Glory to your sons, glory to your king.
> The black inhabitants of Africa
> Have been delivered from a long terror.
> Saved at last from the evil yoke,
> They now work peacefully
> By the light of a new faith …
> Priests and soldiers go hand in hand,
> With a single purpose,
> Fertilising the barren ground
> Where tomorrow there will be reaping.
> The cross shines beside the flags
> To guide them on their way.
> Your name, Oh Belgium
> Has long been blessed on this river,
> Hateful slavery has everywhere
> Been beaten, defeated, banished,
> And your courageous soldiers
> Always turn to face the enemy.[43]

Jesuits and Trappists provided recruits for the great venture, and the Antwerp quays were jammed with well-wishers as the first Sisters of Charity sailed for the Congo. In the reverse direction, African boys and girls were soon arriving to study in religious houses. In this new world, Catholics and Protestants could at least expect that Leopold II's enlightened rule would bring a new dawn of civilisation to the Africans living in the Congo basin.

Chapter 9

Losing It or Ruling It

Race

Throughout the first half of the nineteenth century, clergymen 'of colour'
could generally expect to be treated with respect by white colleagues,
and according to the stereotypical image, stations were full of black
children, with girls learning to sew and boys to read at the knees of their
white teachers. In those earlier years, white missionaries were not
inclined to look on Africans as fundamentally different from themselves,
but, paternalistically, as children, who were late starters in the great
upwards march of humanity. This comparatively relaxed approach
to race relations was challenged in 1850 with the publication of *The
Races of Men* by Scottish surgeon and body-snatcher Robert Knox. He
presented history as a tale of relentless struggle: 'the fair races against
the dark races; the strong against the feeble; the united against those
who could not or would not progress'. Nine years later, Charles Darwin
produced *The Origin of Species*, and in the hands of 'Social Darwinians',
his thesis of the survival of the fittest became a model for understanding
human as well as animal behaviour. Since the world's coloured races
were adjudged to be poorly adapted to the struggle for survival, it was
an inexorable law of nature that they must give way for the whites.
Converts to this new racism rejoiced that this process was already well
advanced in the outback of Australia and on the plains of North America.

Racial prejudice adopted contrasting disguises in different European
countries. While the French were inclined to admire non-Europeans who
assumed the manners of sophisticated Frenchmen, the British reserved
their greatest contempt for those 'natives' who attempted to copy
western ways. James Whitford, trader on the Gold Coast and fellow
of the Royal Geographical Society charted the chain of events proceeding
from any African's purchase of a pocket-knife:

The savage scratches his wool to consider, then rushes off into his
luxuriant country, collects cotton-pods, cleans the cotton of its
seeds, and produces the beautiful pillowy article of trade which all
people appreciate and, with one or other of these articles, he satisfies

the trader and becomes possessor of the coveted knife. He hugs
it and sleeps with it at night as little girls do with their dolls. Then
the difficulty arises; the knife requires a pocket. White men wear
pockets, and our savage must do the same; so he abandons his
fig-leaf, and organises a pocket, in which the Sheffield instrument
finds a home.... If endowed with intellect above his asserted
consanguineous friend, the monkey, he is eager to find out all about
the white man's 'God palaverman'; by this he means the missionary;
and then the savage begins to reflect in earnest.... He will decide
(and wisely) to be converted to Christianity; it is the best thing he
can do; so, presently, he appears 'sitting and clothed in his right
mind', partaking of Christian meat and drink, and by the next mail
will be reported at Exeter Hall as 'one more brand saved from the
burning.'[1]

Even though such outbursts challenged the whole foundation of their
enterprise, many missionaries were influenced by the new 'scientific
racism'. Firstly, the very idea of mixed partnerships – now branded
miscegenation – became physically distasteful; then, as black and white
residents led ever more separate lives, mission stations adapted to a more
segregated style of living. In this new environment, white workers also
became increasingly reluctant to give black colleagues full and equal
access to mission committees. Individual attitudes varied. David
Livingstone spoke for more enlightened colleagues when he rejected this
new racial 'science' outright: 'we must smile at the heaps of nonsense
which have been written about the negro intellect.... I do not believe in
any incapacity of the African either in mind or heart.'[2] At the opposite
end of the spectrum, a few 'men of God' embraced the full racist
vocabulary, while more measured racist vocabulary became common
currency in clerical meetings. Only Arthur Shearly Cripps raised a lone
voice of dissent as the following resolution passed through the Anglican
diocesan synod in Rhodesia: 'We believe that the Christian faith, while
accepting loyally the consequences of Christ's identification with
universal humanity, recognises the inequalities existing in individuals and
races, arising from the fact that neither individuals nor races are born
with equal faculties or opportunities.'[3]

Between the extremes, older paternalistic attitudes did persist: 'Why
should a white man be allowed to kill himself with drink', asked one
Anglican bishop, 'and why should not a native be allowed to do the

same? Our answer would be "Because he is a poor baby and ought to be protected"'.[4] The crucial dividing line lay between those who held that Africans might on some – however far distant – day rise to match the white races and their colleagues who were inclined to the view that they would always remain 'hewers of wood and drawers of water'.

While the multiracial Lovedale Academy was being held up to the world as a model of racial harmony, within his community, its headmaster James Stewart refused to acknowledge that Africans could ever achieve European standards of intellect and civilisation. With the full support of the home board, but to the outrage of black students (and to the dismay of many white colleagues), he removed academic subjects from their syllabus and set them to a programme of 'manual labour including sweeping yards, repairing roads, cracking stones and so on … enforced by a time-keeper and under the threat of punishment'.[5] 'Knowledge merely puffeth up', he announced, 'but manual labour taught with charity certainly edifieth the individual.' Photographs show white and black together at physical exercise and in the school band, but no white faces can be seen among students gathered for manual labour.

Violence

Before sailing for the new mission fields of East and Central Africa, recruits were given advice on how they should demonstrate the Christ-like qualities of gentleness, patience, meekness and forbearance. With memories of Bishop Mackenzie's Ajawi wars still fresh, it was 'to be considered absolute and to be scrupulously observed … that active interference by force initiated on your side is in no case and on no account whatsoever to be resorted to'.[6] Once in Africa, however, old hands delivered a very different message. 'Sentimental philanthropists', they declared, were sadly out of touch, and no African would respect a white man who failed to support threats with physical punishment.

The long caravan journey into the interior served as a newcomer's right of passage. Sixty porters were needed for the full ton of consumable supplies assigned to each missionary, and yet more porters to carry cloth for barter and perhaps a printing press, cotton gin and collapsible steam boat. Since few malnourished villagers would volunteer for such back-breaking work, most labour was conscripted by cash deals with tribal chiefs. Men who had lived by the rhythms of the sun now had to adapt to the white man's clock. After working unrelentingly hard for low rewards and facing a high probability of never returning home, it can be no surprise that many looked only for the first opportunity to abscond. LMS director Dr Mullins' sympathies lay only with his fellow whites: 'The trouble they have caused by their fickleness, their dishonesty, their bodily weakness, their indolence, their diseases and numerous deaths, has been indescribable. No one can read the experiences recorded in the travellers' books without feeling the deepest indignation against these fickle men, and the profoundest sympathy for the travellers whose patience was so tried.'[7]

Violence was part of the daily routine of caravan life. Huge lines of carriers were patrolled by armed askari, and those who fell out of the column were left to die by the roadside, where even the most compassionate traveller dared not linger for fear of being picked off by local warriors. Missionaries did their share of controlling the line: Alexander Mackay and a colleague opened fire and wounded four men who were threatening to defect, Anglo-Catholic Bishop Steere had a carrier thrashed at a wagon wheel and his evangelical colleague Bishop Hannington (who would later himself be killed on the journey) reportedly hurled firebrands at his own men.[8] In time, the use of physical force even became sanctioned in LMS advice to recruits.

When we were entering Equatorial Africa, over a quarter of a century ago, there was put into our hands by the Society, under whose auspices we were about to work, a printed leaflet of recommendations to Missionaries as to how to act towards the natives under various circumstances. Under the heading of 'Punishments', the leaflet stated, 'Stopping men's pay is not much good, as the negro does not look forward. Stopping their *'posho'* (or rations) when not actually on the march, and flogging in extreme cases are best.'[9]

There were exceptions: Plymouth Brother Frederick Arnot repudiated use of force and later colleagues appear to have followed his example. The CMS also discovered that the layman Charles Stokes, who possessed no other marked missionary ability, did have a unique talent for controlling large numbers of carriers without resorting to brutality. After being dismissed on account of his unorthodox sex life, this expansive Ulsterman branched out into the carrying trade on his own account,

organising vast caravans to transport missionary baggage, as well
as firearms for trade with the interior.

Missionaries, who found it hard to accept that they lived under the
jurisdiction of a local chief, were always tempted to set up a legal system
on their own station. In another Plymouth Brother's words, 'many a little
Protestant Pope in the lonely bush is forced by his self-imposed isolation
to be prophet, priest and king rolled into one – really a very big duck, he,
in his own private pond'.[10] Catholic superiors also complained that every
one of their priests believed that he carried a marshal's baton in his
knapsack. Working within this wider environment, members of the
clergy could become involved in levels of violence that were unacceptable
even by the relaxed standards of the day.

* * *

Following a spate of thefts, Auld Kirk missionaries at Blantyre decided
that their African Lakes Company would make no progress until
Africans learned the meaning of private ownership. Before leaving for
Lovedale, James Stewart recruited his engineer cousin James C.E. Stewart
as a manager, with instructions to implement a 'man o' war' regime
of punishment.[11] On this Scottish mission station, floggings of 100 lashes
became routine; suspected thieves were beaten to elicit a confession and
then beaten again in retribution for the crime. Two men are known
to have died from their injuries – one claimed to have laid down a case
of tea after falling ill and then returned to find that it had gone; the other
was punished for stealing beads out of the company store, although
it was later discovered that the Moirs had taken them without leaving
any record.

Soon after minister Duff McDonald arrived to take up the position
of Blantyre's first ordained superintendent, a woman was found dead,
and suspicion fell on two men who had been involved in a previous
incident. Although there was no clear evidence of guilt, McDonald
convened a court and pronounced a death sentence on both men. One
did manage to escape, but his companion was less fortunate. After
a passing Australian hunter had forwarded the gruesome story of the
execution to the British press, home supporters were outraged to learn
that such a brutal punishment could be carried out in the church's
name.[12] MacDonald was called home, but artisans who had been
involved in the case were left to prosper on their burgeoning estates. Free
Church clergy succeeded in distancing themselves from the Auld Kirk

atrocities, and it never became widely known that their own admired James Stewart had personally initiated the man o' war system of punishments. Although Laws had visited Blantyre just four days after the execution and knew the whole story, he registered no concern until events became public. From that time, Scottish missionaries were forbidden to inflict any corporal punishment on adults, but Laws later recorded that these instructions were commonly ignored on remote outstations.

Even after British consul John Kirk issued orders that British missionaries must never set up their legal system beyond the Queen's territories, these instructions were often flouted. In 1881, Kirk received news of trouble further up the Kenyan coast, in Freretown. As its name suggested, this CMS station was intended to replicate the success that the society had achieved in reintegrating liberated slaves into society at Freetown on the continent's western coast. Slaves freed by British ships on the Indian Ocean were taken to Bombay (Mumbai) for education and religious training before returning to Africa to take their part in the great missionary enterprise. Kirk now received information that both the 'Bombay Africans' and the local people were being abused by their white missionaries. His deputy and a sea captain, sent to investigate, discovered the appalling truth. The lay superintendent, clergyman and schoolmaster in Freretown had together established a savage regime of punishment based on indiscriminate use of the whip and stocks. Kirk's investigators were 'greatly astonished and shocked' by 'the ocular proofs as to the severity of these floggings'. 'Since I have been on the East Indian Station', wrote the captain, 'I have been the means of freeing several fugitive slaves on account of ill-treatment by their masters, but none of them has been beaten as severely as the two men I saw at the Mission.'[13] To make matters worse, the Freretown officials worked a double standard: even as Africans were being punished for sexual misconduct, the schoolmaster made no attempt to conceal his own visits to a black mistress in Mombasa. The findings were not made public and, on this occasion, the incident passed without public scandal.

The LMS village system on the shores of Lake Tanganyika also proved open to abuse. Security against slavers was only provided at a price, regular attendance at church and school was a condition of residence and the senior station minister held the right to give or withhold paid work. Missionaries converted their verandas into court-houses, where corporal punishment was freely administered. One issue of the Society's magazine carried an article by artisan Adam Purves, in which he described the

many uses of hippo-hide – one of which was 'the making of switches'.
Dr James Mackay, who had been newly posted to the lake from
Madagascar, enlightened home supporters on the meaning of the word
'switch': 'In one of our stations at this moment there are half a dozen
long strips of thick hippo-hide hanging from a tree, with heavy weights
being cured for the abominable practice, in the *hands of the missionaries
of the L.M. Society* of horsewhipping the natives.'[14]

Mackay argued that Purves should be dismissed and the village system
abandoned, but the directors chose to ignore his arguments. Instead,
Purves was promoted from artisan to the position of full missionary in
charge of a station, and the directors took the opportunity to reaffirm
their faith in the system. Predictably, complaints about Purves's
behaviour continued to arrive at mission headquarters. His ferocious
discipline was reported to have cost the life of a six-year-old; he had
thrown a child into a crocodile infested river 'to see if he could swim' and
beaten another boy with a cricket bat for the sin of dropping a catch.[15]
Across his station lands, many adults also carried scars of his floggings.
It is a measure of the directors' priorities that charges of swearing and
drunkenness – of which Purves was also guilty – aroused more concern
than those of racism and violence. Purves died before the issue was
resolved, but Dr Mackay had seen enough to resign from the society.

Missionary Imperialists

A Frenchman, Prosper Augouard

Lavigerie's diplomatic success at Rome on behalf of his White Fathers
provoked furious rivalry between the Catholic missionary orders. The
Holy Ghost Fathers had run Christian villages in the Gabon for almost
four decades without producing a single priest, and for a time it seemed
likely that the White Fathers might take over their work. This could
have happened if it had not been for a singular French Spiritian called
Philippe-Prosper Augouard.

As Bentley and Crudington were returning from Stanley Pool, they
met this young father travelling in the opposite direction. Augouard
combined an indestructible physique with a fiery temper with iron
will and he professed no affection for Africans. 'The black race', he
pronounced, 'is certainly the race of Ham, the race cursed by God.
This is not proved by anything in particular, but you feel it and see

it everywhere around you.'[16] Since talk of liberty, equality and fraternity only undermined the good order of God's universe, his lifetime objective was to instil the more-enduring virtues of obedience and duty.

Whether out of design or forgetfulness, the republican free-thinker Brazza had failed to tell this ultramontane priest that anybody who wished to negotiate at Stanley Pool must wear a cock's feather in his cap, and Augouard could not understand why he always received a poor reception in villages that were draped in French flags. Like Grenfell, he nursed a long-term objective to forge a link with co-religionists from Zanzibar, but for the time being, he left the two catechists at Stanley Pool and turned back towards the Atlantic. Over the coming months, he would travel across huge areas on both sides of the Congo, securing chiefs' signatures on forms of treaty with France. To get the governor's counter-signature would be, he thought, a *simple formalité!*'[17] Consequently, he felt bitterly betrayed when Republican politicians repudiated many of his treaties and ceded the lower river's south bank to Leopold II at the Congress of Berlin. Still, Augouard could reasonably claim to be father to the new colony of French Congo on the river's north bank and its hinterland, between the ocean and the Oubangui. The achievement made him a national hero. Bestowing on him the Légion d'Honneur, the public orator declared that 'Advancing into the barbarous regions of Africa, generally ahead of the explorers – cross in one hand and national flag in the other – Mgr Augouard conquered territory three times the size of the mother country for French civilisation. He qualifies as a great Frenchman because he never made any separation between his two faiths: God and country.'[18]

Four years after Pierre Savorgnan de Brazza was appointed colonial Governor of French Congo in 1886, Augouard accepted consecration to 'the world's most isolated and bizarre diocese', where cannibalism was reported to be widespread. Although no African missionary would ever suffer the indignity of being eaten, Augouard described how, every time a villager came close to stroke his white skin, he would imagine them thinking: 'that would taste good with bananas!' Even Leo XIII could not restrain his curiosity when 'the Bishop of the Cannibals' received a papal audience.

'Is it true', asked the Pope, 'that your blacks still eat each other?'

'Yes, holy father, every day.'

The Pope commented that not one of the holy martyrs had actually been eaten.

'Oh well, holy father', cried Mgr Augouard, 'I could try to put that right.'

'Certainly not!' replied Leo XIII quickly. 'I don't want that. The people in your diocese wouldn't leave us any relics.'[19]

Besides the fact that the issue of the cock's feather still remained unforgiven, the bishop also opposed what he perceived as Brazza's pro-Islamic policy. 'His first reaction', declared a later governor, 'was to fight everything that could slow or interfere with the execution of his plans.'[20]

Whether or not Brazza was as understanding to Africans as supporters made out at the time, his rule was certainly more humane than that of the Belgian king on the Congo's southern bank. Still, Augouard insisted that Leopold provided the better imperial model.

> I have promoted the extension of French influence for twenty
> consecutive years, and now I have to confess that I experience
> a deep pain to see our futile efforts and the vast sums that have
> been put out without return for anyone.... We have been in bitter
> competition with the Belgians and their efforts have been crowned
> with success. They have certainly harassed the people and
> committed acts of barbarism that are unworthy of a civilised
> nation; but haven't similar things been happening in the French
> Congo? It is better not to go too deeply into the matter and people
> in Europe will then never know what has happened and what still
> happens each day in this ever mysterious Africa.[21]

After waging a seven-year campaign of hatred, Augouard finally secured Brazza's dismissal. Conditions of life for Africans in the French Congo then deteriorated as rival French companies struggled to wring maximum profit out of their allotted territorial concessions.

An Italian, Guiseppe Sapeto

Lazarist monk Guiseppe Sapeto had always argued the case for greater European involvement in the Horn of Africa, but as long as his Italian homeland remained under Austrian rule, he felt forced to support the French cause. In middle life he followed news of the Italian *Risorgimento* with mounting excitement, and even when Garibaldi's red shirts entered the holy city of Rome, he could only rejoice that he was at last free to promote Italian interests. As Egyptian labourers finished their huge task of digging the Suez Canal, he knew that the eastern coast of Africa was about to gain a new strategic importance and he could not forget that his mission station now gave his country a strategic stake at the mouth of the Red Sea. Flushed with excitement, he withdrew from church work to devote his energies to the colonial cause. After prospecting both shores of the Red Sea, he decided that a new Italian colony should be sited at Assab, on the African side of the Bab el-Mandeb Strait, and sailed home to Italy, full of confidence that his 'patriotic ideal' would 'win the plaudits of all Italians'.[22] In chambers of commerce and government ministries, he promoted Assab as the ideal place for a coaling station for Italian ships and a commercial base for African and Arabian trade.

Returning to Africa believing that he had official authority to purchase the site for Italy, it came as a shock to discover that the government had committed no funds and the whole project had been handed over to a Genovese shipping magnate, Sr Ribattino. However, he reassured himself that the Italian government would support his colony with ships and troops, and he assumed secular power as 'Sultan of the Dinakii' – naively recording that his 'head swelled every day' as he sat in judgement on suppliants and supervised the building works of the new colony. He was right to assume the long-term support of the Italian government. Italy was then haemorrhaging migrants, and those who settled in foreign countries such as the United States were perceived as lost to national development. The Horn of Africa, in contrast, could become an Italian haven, where colonists would contribute to the wider national prosperity. This was only the beginning of Italian colonial efforts in the area. In later years, its soldiers would attempt to colonise Ethiopia. Emperor Menelik, who halted their forces at Adowa in 1896, might have recalled his predecessor Tewodros' warning: 'First they send the missionary, then the consul, then the soldier.'

A German, Felix Fabri

Missionaries of all nationalities had absorbed Buxton's and Livingstone's message that trade and religion must go hand in hand to achieve the conversion of Africa. By the mid-nineteenth century, the Rhenish mission was engaged in the painful transformation from a small organisation, centred on a single pietist congregation, into a larger and more-broadly based society. In 1857, a clique of wealthy men managed to secure the selection of a young chief inspector. Dr Friedrich Fabri was a man of new ideas. By his own admission, he approached the task with little theological background and no knowledge of missionary work. But he was a committed exponent of the new scientific racism, with a 'celestial bird's eye view of history' that identified a hierarchy within the world's population. At the summit were the 'Saxon races' of Germany and Britain, with the Latins some way below. People of colour, whom he named the 'red races', occupied the lowest rank; being by nature both lazy and improvident, they were destined to live forever under colonial rule.[23] After spectacular British colonial success in North America, Australia, New Zealand and India, Fabri believed that the time had come for the German-speaking peoples to take their proper place in the competitive business of colonisation.

Until then, the Germans had achieved little in the barren territory that John Philip had allocated to them. They worked in a land that suffered from an endemic three-cornered warfare between the agricultural Nama, the nomadic Herero and freebooting baastards of the Afrikaner clan. Under the aggressive leadership of Hugo Hahn, the Rhenish pastors turned their mission into a fourth force in local politics. Missionaries led their followers on punitive expeditions and those who chose to live within their communities had to obey Hahn's draconian laws. But still, after twenty years in the field, Hahn still could not claim a single convert.

Fabri understood that the imperial government would take no interest in African affairs until Germany had developed a significant economic interest in the continent. Following the example of Basel inspector Josenhans, he went into partnership with manufacturers to set up a company for trading with the Herero, with profits divided between the mission and shareholder. Infected by their inspector's enthusiasm, Hahn's clergy became increasingly involved in a plan to spread German influence across Tswana country, to link up with the Boers and create an outlet for German trade in the continental interior. At the time, there was a strong European demand for African ivory and ostrich feathers, and the Herero wanted firearms. Fabri's company duly obliged by importing weapons into South-West Africa on a massive scale, and the nomadic Herero began to settle round the German stations. Soon Hahn could watch catechumens tilling fields and tending the gardens that surrounded their rectangular houses. 'Who could have foreseen, a few years ago', he asked, 'that Hereros would come and order doors and windows with us on payment?'[24] In the longer term, however, Fabri's new trading initiatives brought only disaster. Although the weapons were officially designated as being for use in hunting, the Cape government became increasingly alarmed by this new proliferation of firearms across the southern part of the continent. The arid countryside was also being systematically swept clear of wildlife – first elephants, then ostriches – until high society ladies killed the trade in feathers almost overnight by deciding that they were no longer a fashionable adornment for their hats.

Fabri's company went bankrupt in 1880, carrying off investors' savings and bringing the mission to the edge of disaster. Undeterred, he founded the West German Society for Colonisation and Export with the objective of promoting trade and enlisting government support for the colonisation movement. Now dismissed from mission service, he continued to write and travel, proclaiming that Germany should take over selected areas in Africa and the Middle East – along with Samoa, New Guinea, Formosa, Madagascar and North Borneo.[25] With colonial hysteria growing, sympathetic politicians took up the argument that the German people needed to break out of their largely landlocked homeland, while industrialists demanded that the government must provide markets for their burgeoning industries. Bismarck finally gave way to the national mood, and in 1884, he instructed his commanders to annexe those African territories of South-West Africa, Togo and Cameroon where missionaries had already established a German presence. His action signalled the start of the European scramble for Africa.

A Briton, John Mackenzie

When Robert Moffat conducted his final service in Kuruman in 1870, it seemed as though the age of pioneers had reached its end. After half a century of work, his church had no African leadership, and even the most basic primary education remained sadly neglected. Education in general remained a contentious issue. When the old man's son John took over the work at Kuruman, he reacted with horror to the news that the directors were raising a fund in his father's honour to be used to endow a Moffat Institute of Higher Education in Tswana country. Like the Ploërmel fathers in Mother Javouhey's Senegal, John Moffat believed that the whole project of bringing higher education to Africans was a criminal waste of money. 'Let us first see what we can do with our elementary schools, which (I say it advisedly) are a shame and disgrace to our mission.'[26] In this, he was opposed by John Mackenzie, the man who had saved the Kololo mission survivors. It was the beginning of a lasting rivalry between the two men that would encompass much more than education.

The Cape Colony's northern frontier – up till now a remote, if violent, hinterland – was about to be transformed by two events into a major hot-spot of the global economy. Firstly, in 1871, diamonds were discovered in Griqua country, and later in the same year, the adventurer Cecil Rhodes would arrive in the area to start an operation that would grow into the De Beers Diamond Company. At the same time, the Westminster government suddenly rediscovered its interest in the northern frontier, and the diamond fields were promptly annexed for Britain. Secondly, another fourteen years on, a down-and-out miner in the Transvaal came upon a stone that carried golden markings, and the northern frontier quickly became the focus of a full-fledged gold rush.

Alienated from their own land's wealth, the resident Tswana now found themselves caught between the London government, the Transvaal Boers and the English-speaking settlers of the Cape Colony. Operating within the maelstrom of conflicting interests, Moffat and Mackenzie agreed that only the territorial ambitions of Boers on the east and Germans on the west had to be frustrated. Beyond that, the two men were at odds. While native South African Moffat insisted that the Africans' future was safe in the De Beers Company's hands, Scots incomer Mackenzie searched for ways to protect the Tswana from Cecil Rhodes's expansionist programme. Mackenzie looked to the Exeter Hall lobby for support, while Moffat prayed daily that God would frustrate the machinations of all 'sentimental philanthropists'. Both men started from imperialist assumptions; their irreconcilable difference was that Moffat wanted the new colonial structure to be based on the Cape, while Mackenzie was no less determined to ensure that it should answer to the imperial government in London.

Mackenzie's son assured mission supporters that his father was 'no indiscriminate lover of blacks, that he did not pet them or treat them with undue consideration'.[27] While recognising that settlers and indigenous inhabitants would inevitably compete for land, John Mackenzie saw no reason why this had to be an issue of concern. 'Why, in God's great garden should his flowers be kept to certain beds, while other flower beds have none?' Black farmers who were prepared to adopt western techniques had every right to keep possession of their land. 'Why should they be degraded as a class? They hold their fountains under some sort of tenure from their chiefs; let them continue to farm under such tenure as might be arranged.'[28] Others who failed to adapt would, however, have no place in this new world: 'let him sink to his own level among the

inferior labouring class'. Mackenzie argued that such a transformation
of society could only be achieved under benign imperial rule and he looked
forward to a time when 'natives' would welcome 'the helping hand
of a friendly English officer, living near their homes, who would listen
to their difficulties'. He therefore encouraged chiefs to cede sovereignty
to the British crown, holding out the hope that this might one day
be restored when Christianity and civilisation had finally taken root.[29]
In the words of modern anthropologists – 'here, then, is the ultimate
imperial hegemony, the culmination of the moral offensive launched
by the abolitionist movement and borne to Africa by the soldiers of the
Lord: overrule as a kindness to the colonised.'[30]

Mackenzie, the LMS missionary, sailed home in 1882 to plead the
cause of British involvement in Bechuanaland. With the help of dissident
Liberal and budding imperialist Joseph Chamberlain, who argued in
cabinet that 'the bitter cry of Bechuanaland had to be heard', he travelled
the country, railing against the way in which Gladstone's liberal
government had reneged on its most sacred obligations. When Paul Kruger
arrived in London to advance Boer claims, he was on hand to urge that
the government must stand firm: 'Let the Transvaal annex Bechuanaland
and the only available road into the interior is in her hands – the north
is before her.... Then England voluntarily shuts herself out of the fairest,
richest and most inviting part of southern Africa which has been opened
up by the enterprise of Englishmen.'[31] Between public meetings, John
Mackenzie even found time to write a rambling two-volume book that
he called *Austral Africa: Ruling It or Losing It*.

Soon LMS supporters learnt with joy that – in Gladstone's pragmatic
response to the arrival of German troops in South-West Africa – Britain
was preparing an expedition to bring northern Tswana country under
direct British rule. But Mackenzie's victory proved short lived. When
the military expedition turned out to be more expensive than had been
anticipated, Gladstone's Chancellor of the Exchequer set his face against
any further African venture at public expense, and from that time both
the risks and the profits of the scramble for Africa would be carried
by businessmen. This decision ushered in an age of commercial
exploitation. In 1886, 1888 and 1889, charters were granted to George
Taubman Goldie's Royal Niger Company, William Mackinnon's
Imperial British East Africa Company and Cecil Rhodes's British South
Africa Company. While Mackenzie could claim some credit for the
establishment of a protectorate in sparsely populated north of Tswana

Illustrations

1. Shipping slaves in Africa

2. Hannah Kilham

3. A Liberian settler

4. Thomas Birch Freeman

5. Jamaican missionary homes at Akropong

6. Johannes Zimmermann

7. CMS German David Hinderer and his English wife Anna Maria

8. CMS steamer Henry Venn on the river Niger

9. A liberated boy – a 'pawn'

10. Augustin Planque of the Lyons Fathers

11. LMS Pioneers Johannes Van Der Kemp and John Philip

12. Robert Moffat travelling by wagon with the Ndebele Chief Mzilikazi

13. David Livingstone mauled by a lion

14. Healthy South Africa – Daniel and Lucy Allen Lindley with their eleven children

15. Bishop John Coleso and his daughter Harriette

16. Daniele Comboni of the Lyons Fathers

17. Archbishop Charles Lavigerie of the White Fathers

18. A night stop on the trail to Uganda

19. Lovedale – integration; the College Band

20. Lovedale – segregation; the Work Party

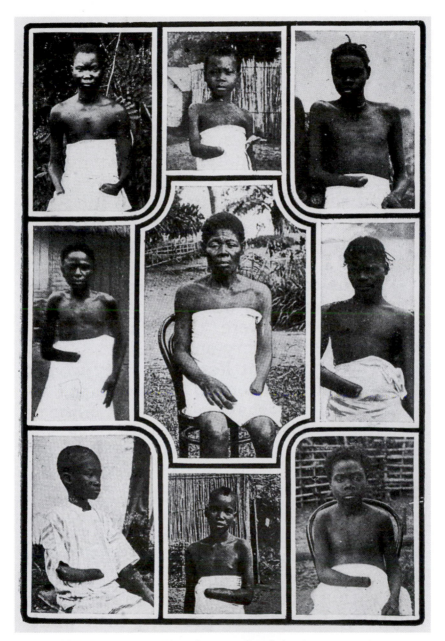

21. Leopold II's Congo victims. 'There they were, the right hands – I counted them, eighty-one in all.'

22. George Grenfell

23. Bishop Samuel Crowther

24. The Methodist Church at Cape Coast – Cradle of African nationalism

25. The Prophet Harris with his acolytes

26. Mary Slessor

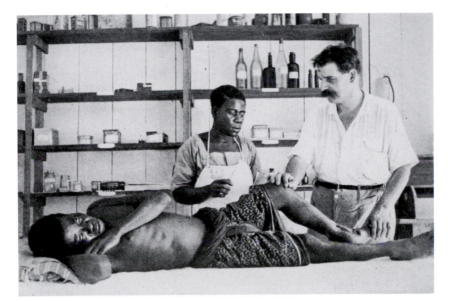

27. Albert Schweitzer operating at Lambarere

28. Please send us more missionary doctors

29. The Opening of Achimota College. Guggusberg has his hand on Aggrey's shoulder. Fraser (with hood) stands on the Governor's left.

country, the richer and more-densely populated southern region, where chiefs had stoutly defended their independence against all comers, was abandoned to the tender mercies of Cecil Rhodes. John Moffat lived long enough to be appalled by the outcome of the pro-Cape policy that he had once so enthusiastically promoted.

Missionaries in the Scramble for Africa

In 1889, church folk in Scotland gathered signatures on a petition demanding that the whole Shire Highland and the Lake Nyasa region should be designated an area of British influence. They were not silenced when experts advised that the whole Zambezi basin was now internationally recognised as Portuguese. Henry Drummond (who confessed that he could never understand why Africa should not belong to the Africans) argued that the graves of British missionaries gave Britain a stronger claim than Portugal. Little 'bantam cock' Harry Johnston, who had made his name as an empire builder in West Africa, was accordingly sent to Lisbon to negotiate a treaty for the division of land in Central Africa and returned with the news that the Portuguese would abandon any claim to the lake itself on condition that the Auld Kirk territory in the Shire Highlands be absorbed into Mozambique. As he explained this at an Edinburgh meeting, he noted how the rows of Scottish faces looking back at him were set like blocks of Aberdeen granite. The terms were not to their liking, and the Auld Kirk's public relations operation moved into action at once. The minister of St. George's Church in Edinburgh, who was chairman of the church's Africa committee, happened to have Cabinet member Lord Balfour as one of his elders and he took his seat in the House of Lords next day beside the new Prime Minister Lord Salisbury.

> 'My Lord', he said, 'my Scottish friends don't like the Portuguese terms'. 'Neither do I', was the reply, 'I don't want your Scottish friends to accept them. I want the Portuguese to know that I, too, have a strong public opinion behind me and I am sending their government a warning that they must not go too far.'[32]

Salisbury's freedom of movement was constrained by the fact that his Conservative Chancellor had not broken with his predecessor's policy of refusing to provide funds for African adventures, but Cecil Rhodes promised to pick up the bill and take over the troubled African Lakes Company's debts. With funding secure, Salisbury declared the British protectorate of Nyasaland and despatched Johnston to take up the post of consul. The Scots of the Auld Kirk accepted the decision as no more than their right. 'It was not to *make* a state that Harry Johnston was sent, but to deliver from Portuguese occupation a state already made.'[33]

Johnston sailed for the Zambezi with minister Alexander Hetherwick, who was returning to Blantyre from home leave. He would later become an outspoken opponent of company rule, and Johnston may not have enlightened his companion that he was no longer on the imperial government's payroll. As they travelled up the Shire River, the consul handed out flags, while the missionary explained to all those around that the great Queen had graciously agreed to take them under her protection. By the time the two men arrived at Blantyre, the stock of flags was exhausted. Hetherwick recalled the busy scene as Scottish wives made good the shortage.

> Yards on yards – hundreds of yards of calico – red, white and blue – were measured and cut and sewn into scores of emblems of British rule. Mornings and evenings, days and days, sewing machines went and rattled round the table. Ladies' deft fingers folded, hemmed and stitched without halt, and the rattle of machines on the table kept time to the music of the Empire, 'God Save our Gracious Queen'…. They were hoisted in many a village market-place – or in front of many a chief's hut. Probably few knew the meaning of it all – none knew that it was all a part of a great 'scramble for Africa' – but all knew that it was something from the white man's 'Queenie' – and in those pioneer days the white men were the best, and the 'Queenie' could only be a good Queen who loved the black men and women and would take care of them.[34]

After having been raised within a peripheral Christian cult, Harry Johnston had embraced militant atheism and was an unlikely friend of those religious ladies, but he gladly accepted help from the only people who could speak local languages to achieve Cecil Rhodes' objectives.

Travellers told how Katanga possessed abundant mineral resources, and Rhodes had deduced from this that a valuable band of metals must cross the continent, from the Rand, through Matabeleland and into Katanga; he meant to secure the whole rich seam for his company. The opportunity seemed to be there. Leopold had not yet secured any treaty with Swahili-Arab ruler Msiri, and Rhodes had no patience with agreements drawn up in distant European capitals. His second aim was to establish a link with CMS territory in Uganda, with a view to establishing a longitudinal railway line, which would one day link the Cape with Cairo without ever leaving British territory. To achieve this, he needed to secure the mountainous territories of Burundi and Rwanda. Again he chose to ignore the fact that the British government had agreed in principle that these territories would be German.

Johnston's deputy, Alfred Sharp, arrived in Katanga to find Plymouth Brother Charles Swan and one companion living in a 'state of degradation, unfitted to the dignity of a white man'. The Brethren were prohibited from taking any part in secular politics on pain of expulsion from the community and they refused to identify with the imperial cause. But when Swan chose instead to act as translator and adviser from behind Msiri's chair, Sharp soon discovered that he could achieve nothing without missionary support.

> On speaking to Msiri about treaties and concessions, he refused utterly. Said Mr Arnot had told him to have nothing to do with anyone who wanted him to sign papers as such people would only want to rule him and his country.... Missionaries appear to me to do much harm when they take upon themselves to advise the native chiefs on political matters.... It would be better for them to keep to their own sphere.[35]

Soon after Sharp left, mercenaries in Leopold's pay killed Msiri and secured Katanga for their master. In his despair, Cecil Rhodes declared that Britain could have secured the lion's share of Africa's wealth, if the Westminster government had only been less parsimonious.

There was, however, no expectation that missionaries who were prepared to act as agents for the colonial power should 'keep to their own sphere'. Even as Plymouth Brother Charles Swan was distancing himself from the imperial cause, LMS artisan and near namesake Alfred Swann was accepting the urgent commission to secure the twin territories of Rwanda and Burundi before the Germans arrived. 'Show my handwriting to no one, but go', urged Johnston. 'Go at once. I ask you because there is no one else who can assist me in this crisis, and I trust your connection with the London Missionary Society will prove no hindrance.'[36] After taking the mission steamer without consulting colleagues, Swann sailed the length of Lake Tanganyika and secured treaties that carried the marks of Burundi chiefs. Foreign office mandarins were scandalised that Johnston had resorted to 'treaty making by a missionary'. 'We have had the warm remonstrance of the LMS' wrote a senior official, 'and may have a still warmer one from the Germans'. But, though in public the LMS directors put on a disapproving face, in private some admitted that, had they been in Swann's place, they would probably have acted as he did. By the time that the official government rebuke arrived, Alfred Swann had already resigned from mission service to join Johnston's staff.

Since Cecil Rhodes had funded the forward movement in the Shire Highlands, he had good reason to expect that the Nyasaland protectorate would be consolidated with his other company territories. Johnston advised Rhodes that, while the Catholics, Anglo-Catholics and Scots Free Churchmen were either favourable or took a neutral position on whether the region should be ruled from Cape Town or Westminster, Auld Kirk missionaries were implacably opposed to company rule. 'A Chartered company is not a government and never can be' wrote moderator David Clement Scott. 'To be ruled by such is to be ruled for commercial ends by absentee directors and shareholders whose real interests are only served by tangible dividends.'[37] Assistant Alexander Hetherwick voiced the mission's opposition to the growing alienation of land for white settlement.

> Central Africa in no way can be regarded as a dwelling place for the white races; it is the home of the black man and of the black man alone. He alone can develop its resources under the guidance of the European. This is his place and sphere; ours is to govern him and teach him until he sees that his lot lies in his own home and on its soil and not in the mines of Kimberley.[38]

The Treaty-Makers

Zimbabwe (Matabeleland)

When ministers of the gospel sat down to negotiate treaties, illiterate chiefs had no way of knowing where their true loyalty lay. In 1887,

Rhodes heard with alarm that Lobengula had ceded mining rights to
the Boers, and with his grand design under threat, he recruited John
Moffat to negotiate on the company's behalf. When Lobengula's
former missionary presented himself at the royal kraal, the king
had no idea that he was now employed by a mining company. Moffat
convinced Lobengula to revoke his concession to the Boers and commit
his people to deal only with the British. In the following year, Rhodes
dispatched Charles Rudd with a more-carefully drafted document to
confirm the agreement, but now Lobengula was less sure. There was no
obvious reason why he should accept an agreement that ceded monopoly
rights for the exploitation of all his country's wealth in return for
a small annuity. Badly in need of help, Rudd went for help to senior
LMS missionary and the king's personal adviser Charles Helm. While
some have assumed that the other-worldly missionary was duped by
a worldly-wise operator, documents in fact show that Charles Helm
was a willing partner in the deception that became known as the Rudd
Concession.

After the agreement had been secured, a copy of the document came
into the hands of freelance miners, who had lost all their rights. Furious,
they went to Lobengula and explained, step by step, how he had sold
his country to a private company, which had power to dethrone him,
take his land and dig for gold – even within his own kraal. When
summoned to account for himself, Helm insisted that he had translated
the proceedings correctly. Keeping Helm shut up within the royal kraal,
Lobengula summoned his colleagues William Elliot and Bowen Rees and
ordered them to translate the document. Their words only confirmed the
miners' account. Confusion ensued, with Elliot and Rees trying to assure
Lobengula that any variance with Helm's translation was surely no more
than 'a difference of opinion between perfectly truthful men'. The truth
was that Helm had blatantly falsified his translation. But, reporting the
incident to London, Elliot and Rees took no issue with this; they were
merely irritated that Helm had placed them in an impossible situation
by failing to take them into his confidence. Elliot brushed the directors'
moral concerns aside:

> To talking as some do of filching the land from its rightful owners
> I regard this as pure unmitigated humbug. You look askance at the
> Co. and you know the home side of their affairs. We here hail them
> with joy, judging from what we hear and see on the spot. It is truly

a trifle startling to hear the Co. exists 'mainly in the interests of the
natives and the missionaries', but I presume nobody believes this.
I do believe however that their rule and opening up of the country
will be a prodigious advance on the old regime.[39]

Missionaries well understood that the terms of the Rudd Concession
must ultimately lead to conflict between company troops and
Lobengula's 'great and barbarous' kingdom. They justified coming
violence on the grounds that the Matabele were recent conquerors,
who had no ancient title to the land and that they also used force
to keep surrounding people in a state of subjection.

Zambia (Northern Rhodesia)

To the west, another missionary, Paris Evangelical François Coillard,
was responsible for interpreting when a young Englishman, Harry Ware,
negotiated for mining rights within the upper Zambezi territories
of Lekwanika, King of the Lozi (Barotse). Minerals were of no immediate
interest to these pastoral people, and the king and missionary negotiated
a reasonable 4 percent royalty on all minerals that would be extracted.
Having made his deal, Ware sold his rights for a profit, and after passing
through a number of hands, the concession ended up in the British
South Africa Company's hands. Refusing to countenance any idea of
paying a royalty, Rhodes dispatched Elliot Lochner with instructions
to renegotiate the deal. He arrived in Barotseland carrying a letter from
King Khama of the Bechuanaland Protectorate, addressed to brother
ruler Lekwanika: 'I have the People of the Great Queen with me and
I am glad that I have them. I live in peace with them, and I have no fear
of the Matabele or the Boers any longer attacking me.' For Coillard,
there was a letter from Khama's personal missionary, who wrote to
reassure him that 'one of the great objects before the Chartered Co.
is to combine commerce with philanthropy'. The administrator of
British Bechuanaland – a personal friend of Rhodes, who would later
be generously rewarded with company shares – also pointed out that
a member of the company's board was the Duke of Fife, recently married
to the Queen's granddaughter, meaning that the South Africa Company
could be presented as a royal organisation.

However, while Coillard and his Scottish wife Christina were happy
to promote British interests, they were reluctant to argue the case for a
commercial company and both also took an instant aversion to Lochner,

who had 'an invincible dislike for the natives'.[40] He did, however, manage to convince the missionaries that the British government had set its face against any further direct involvement in the area, and with Coillard's help, Lochner managed to replace the royalty with a flat payment of £2,000 a year, to be divided between the Lozi chiefs. After days of good-natured celebration, Lochner and Coillard stood witness as the king and his chiefs made their marks – in the full belief that they had concluded a treaty with the Great Queen, who had taken Khama under her protection. Lochner placed on record that the Company

> owed a great deal to all the missionaries of the Paris Evangelical Mission in the country: they helped the parley in every respect. I am sure that the Co. owes as much if not more to M. Collar [sic] than to myself in having secured the Barotse. He is heart and soul with the Co. and there need never be any fear of things going wrong as long as he takes the same interest in the Co.'s work as he has done.[41]

Rhodes had secured a momentous deal. According to the treaty's small print, at a cost of £2,000 a year, he had won control of all manufacturing, commercial and trading business; the mining of all diamonds, gold, precious stones and minerals; the control of all public works, transport and banking; and the right to create currency and to control all sales of arms and ammunition, not only in Lekwanika's country but for 'all allied tribes'. The last phrase was interpreted to include distant areas where the Lozi had never exercised any influence – so providing a veil of legality for the monopoly under which the South Africa Company would exploit the riches of the North Zambian Copper Belt for more than half a century. Lochner did accept a commitment that a British resident would settle in the region and that the company would take early action to set up schools, but neither promise was fulfilled.

It was of no concern to Cecil Rhodes that the missionary was left to face the fury of a deceived people. Coillard's artisan, George Middleton, who had set himself up as a trader, went through the treaty with Lekwanika before lodging a complaint with the Foreign Office at this 'gigantic monopoly of the entire natural resources of the country' as well as the cynical way in which the Duke of Fife's name had been used to give the proceedings a veneer of royal approval. Lekwanika's fury reached boiling point when he discovered that two handsome tusks, sent as

an ornament for the Great Queen's drawing room, adorned the South
Africa Company's board-room. He turned his fury on the missionaries,
who he held responsible for the deception. 'What do we want with that
rubbish-heap of fables that you call the Bible? What does your school
do for us? For you it is the trade you live by; for us it is purposeless and
profitless folly.'[42] Lekwanika did, however, understand that resistance
would only lead to the destruction of his people, and in 1902, he took
his place among colonial potentates as guest of the British nation at the
coronation of the Great Queen's son Edward VIII.[43]

A generation later one writer would acknowledge Britain's imperial
debt to the men of God: 'Pioneers for Christ these missionaries were;
pioneers for Empire they certainly became, often not willingly, but in the
end whole-heartedly and effectively. The record of this Empire service
is one of the romances alike of modern history and modern missions.'[44]

Namibia (South-West Africa)

In German South-West Africa, future Reichsmarshall's father, Dr Göering,
who had responsibility for negotiating 'protective treaties', discovered
early that pastors had few scruples about putting German interests ahead
of loyalty to the Africans who were supposed to be in their care. When
Johannes Bam provided interpreter services in the purchase of a strip
of land from a coastal tribe, the people only discovered too late that the
agreed price was to be paid in goods – at a valuation determined by the
supplier. Even more crucially, Bam failed to explain that the written
document used the uniquely German measurement of *geographical*
miles, which were 7.5 kilometres long, and instead of selling a barren
strip of coastal land, the chief had alienated all his people's territory.

Africans were not informed when C.G. Büttner, who had succeeded
Hahn as head of the Herero operation, left mission service to become
the government's chief agents for all negotiations with local people. He
confessed that there was 'not much evidence that the chiefs with whom
treaties are to be concluded are impatient to enter into agreements
with the German Reich', and asked for advice on what 'promises and
representations' he was permitted to make in order to exert the necessary
pressure.[45] Missionary Brincker even urged the authorities to abandon
the whole tiresome process of treaty-making.

> The German fatherland has a moral right to Damaraland for our
> Rhenish mission alone has expended thousands on it. Here lie the

graves of the missionaries who fell. I must stress that Damaraland
cannot be secured by treaties with chiefs. If we are to exploit its
treasures, there has to be a European power, with a militia of
at least 400 men and two batteries so that each case of arrogance
and injury of interests can be punished.[46]

As long as the Rhenish pastors lived beyond the colonial frontier, they
could make no sense of Luther's doctrine of the two kingdoms, which
placed them under an absolute obligation to obey the temporal power.
Only after a German Reich had been established across South-West
Africa did pastors again become comfortable with the proclamation that
subjects must obey their secular masters.

Chapter 10
If This Is Civilisation, What Is Barbarism?

Zimbabwe (Rhodesia)

In 1885, adventure writer H. Rider Haggard published his best-selling novel *King Solomon's Mines*. The title recalled ancient myths of the Queen of Sheba and of mineral wealth that was supposed to lie deep within the 'dark continent'. Since the time of the Californian forty-niners, there had been a series of gold rushes across North and South America, Australia and New Zealand; some generated more wealth than others, but the South African strikes of both diamonds and gold proved both profitable and enduring. Cecil Rhodes was convinced that the same seam ran north into Matabeleland, and by the time of the Rudd Concession, his mining interests had been generating cash for eight years. Now he planned to invest some of the profits into funding a move towards the north.

When facing shareholders, Rhodes took pride in the fact that not a penny of company money was spent on education and social services for the African population, but he also needed to placate the philanthropic lobby in Britain. From his viewpoint, it therefore made sense that he should take full advantage of missionary resources – and it cost him nothing to make free with promises of extensive mission farms in his prospective new territory. When accepting the offer, missionaries knew well enough that this land was currently grazed by great herds of cattle, but they took comfort from the expectation that, in that future colony, they would be able to shelter Africans from less scrupulous landlords. In 1890, news spread that Rhodes was putting together a force to move onto land that was home to the Shona people, who lived in subjugation to Mzikikazi's Ndebele, in the eastern part of modern Zimbabwe. Colleagues urged Anglican Bishop Knight-Bruce to grasp this unique opportunity: 'The church should be ready to accompany the troops if the Company will permit, or to follow closely in the rear. The Company is not prepared to subsidise any clergy, but intends to throw open all Mashunaland (*Shona country*) to all denominations of Christians.'[1]

Three Anglican chaplains travelled with the pioneer column, along with two Jesuits – elderly Englishman, Fr Prestage, and Austrian

Fr Hartman, who was just 5 feet tall and so stout that he could barely sit on a horse. As the wagons rolled through the Shona hills, young Methodist minister Isaac Shimmin caught glimpses of villages perched on the top of hills, and at times he could even hear the sounds of Shona daily life – 'mothers scolding, babies crying, men talking, boys and girls shouting and laughing'. He mused on how the fierce Ndebele could keep the countryside in such terror that people had to hide away, out of sight. Unknown to him, from those same hills the column was being watched by Shona spirit mediums, who also carried influence with the Ndebele, and they would advise the chiefs to welcome the white men, who would bring trade into the land.

It was of no consequence to the free-thinking Rhodes what brand of Christian message the preachers chose to deliver. A group of Dominican sisters from Natal, led by their young Irish prioress, Mother Patrick followed close behind the column. It was they who claimed the first Christian convert in the region, after baptising an old woman with a terrible cancer on her knee, whom they found on the road.[2] Trappists, Marists, Jesuits and White Fathers all claimed their share of land. At the other end of the ecclesiastical spectrum, Cecil Rhodes convinced General Booth that the Salvation Army should start work in the country: white settlers listened nostalgically as a brass band announced their arrival 'in typical Army fashion'. The leader of the American Seventh-Day Adventists thought it unlikely that Rhodes would be in sympathy with 'our kind of people', but the great man just scribbled on a piece of paper, 'put it in an envelope, sealed it, wrote an address on the outside, and gave it to me, saying, "Hand this over to Dr Jameson when you get to Bulawayo"',[3] and the Adventists duly received their land.

So long as prospectors continued to believe that riches lay under the earth, they had little interest in the farm-land that Rhodes was giving away with such abandon – the land itself would not become precious until it had become clear that the search for gold was fruitless. Shimmin was overcome with patriotic fervour as he 'beaconed out' his mission farm.

Surely the fact that our flag is now waving within a few days' journey of the Zambesi is sufficient to intensify the fervour of every earnest worker in the kingdom of Christ. Our flag is there and we must never desert it; rather we will fight up to it and beyond it until

we cross the Zambesi and join hands with the other great churches
in penetrating the darkest parts of the heart of this great continent.[4]

The time for such optimism ended one day in July 1893, when
Lobengula's warriors descended on Shona country to punish the Shona
for cattle stealing. The Ndebele young men were under strict instructions
not to harm whites, but some missionaries did have to watch as their own
servants were butchered. When Lobengula's war party finally returned
home, the 'Shonaland brethren' united to demand that the South Africa
Company destroy the bloody Ndebele kingdom once and for all.
As Dr Jameson's retaliatory force moved on Lobengula's kraal, Charles
Helm looked round at the peaceful Matabeleland countryside. 'Their
treatment of the Mashona and other tribes deserves punishment', he
admitted, 'but I wish we entered the war with clean hands.'[5] The fact
was that military and missionary advances often went hand in hand.
After Lobengula had been driven out to die beyond the Zambezi,
Matabeleland missionaries could at last report that Ndebele enquirers
were gathering around their stations and the fields were 'white for
harvest'.

While the Shonaland brethren on their scattered stations could not
be wholly blind to the abuses of company rule, only a tiny minority
registered any protest. Methodist George Eva described how he could
do nothing but stand and watch as seven innocent chiefs were snatched
from his church in reprisal for the death of a white policeman. His more
radically minded colleague John White described the process of tax
collection as no better than a cover for plunder. 'Very often great injustice
has been done to the Mashona people by the way in which the Hut Tax
has been collected. In the collecting of this rarely any attempt is made
to levy the charge equitably. This has had the tendency to make the
Mashona discontented and the Hut Tax hated.'

High Anglican Arthur Shearsby Cripps used poetry to express disgust
at a 400 percent tax increase:

O wise and most paternal State
His year of death to celebrate!
With four-fold taxings to redress
Your subjects' four fold emptiness ...
Go glean the fields of harvest bare,

From Famine meet a four-fold share!
Apply the text as best ye may -
From him that hath not, take away![6]

For all the bloodshed, Ndebele rule had at least left the basic structure
of society intact, but whites were now forcing both the Shona and the
Ndebele to accept a new role as landless labourers. When the Ndebele
young men rose for a second time in 1896, Shonaland whites rallied to
send help to hard-pressed Matabeleland settlers, but even as an armed
column was preparing to leave Fort Salisbury (modern Harare), mission
adherents were warning of trouble nearer to home. Salvation Army
Captain Cass died in the first Shona onslaught and other missionaries
took shelter in the laagers. As war fever grew, even the clergy became
militarised. Diminutive Anglican bishop, 'Billy' Gaul, took to wearing
a khaki episcopal apron and breeches, and Catholic Fr Barthelemy also
'donned the khaki uniform to minister as warrior-priest to the spiritual
and corporeal needs of the sick and dying'. Shimmin attributed the native
rebellion to that inveterate torpor common to all uncivilised people,
who longed to live in 'a savage paradise of perpetual laziness'. His letters
reveal the mixture of fear and excitement of any young man going to war.

> Fort Victoria under martial law, all the men enlisted either as
> volunteers or as burgers and all the inhabitants required to sleep
> in the fort at night. I got a hearty welcome from old friends and next
> day I was asked to join a party working the Gatling gun. I am also
> acting as chaplain to the force here so if there is going to be any
> fighting I am likely to be in the thick of it.... The issue of the
> struggle means a certain victory for the white man. In this time of
> plague and war we need the sympathy and prayers of all God's
> people.[7]

German Jesuit Fr Biehler, dispatching a stream of intelligence from
his station at Chishawasha, argued that the Shona had long experience
of holding out within their mountainous environment. 'It seems to me',
he advised, 'that the only way of doing anything at all with these natives
is to starve them, destroy their lands and kill all that can be killed.'[8]
Whether following his advice or on their own initiative, British troops
did indeed set about starving the Shona out of their mountain hideouts.
American Adventist Mrs Anderson recorded the operation's human cost:

Do you wonder that grey hairs are coming to our heads thick and fast? There are now five hungry women outside the door. Our native children, whom we have taken to save them from starving, cook their food about twelve feet from the kitchen door; yet we have to have someone watch it all the time to prevent the starving natives from stealing it out of the pot. Once they grabbed the kettle, and ran away with the food, kettle, and all. Imagine yourself compelled to treat all these cases with a stony heart, and act as if you did not care whether they lived or died, and you have our situation exactly. I had to stop writing just here, and drive a starving man from the door. He was determined to have some food.[9]

Native African evangelists and adherents found themselves caught between a two-sided fury; despised as apostates by their own people and yet hated by whites as untrustworthy 'mission boys'. 'Wherever the mission station is, there are the biggest blackguards', wrote one settler. 'So the best thing to do is to wipe them all out as far as one can – everything black.'[10] Every denomination would later construct its own hagiography of martyrs. While Jesuits gathered black orphans into their stations as the seed-corn of a new Christian generation, Catholic sisters were caring for white children in their Bulawayo convent, and with unexpected racial impartiality, company officials refused to contribute a penny towards the support of any bereaved children.

When both Matabeleland and Shonaland finally became quiet, church attendance rose and schools filled with children. Biehler also converted his Chishawasha station into a model community, where new generations of missionaries and settlers would be able to experience modern farming methods. As the land became increasingly prosperous, missionaries of all denominations discovered that they could trace the working of the hand of God, even through violence and starvation.

Tanzania (German East Africa)

While colonial excitement was spiralling out of control across Germany, the 'old prophet' Friedrich Fabri found himself challenged by a 'young prophet'. Karl Peters was the impoverished and rheumatic son of a Lower Saxony pastor. With a slight physique and *pince-nez* perched in front of short-sighted eyes, he may have looked more like a lecturer in

philosophy than a heroic builder of empires, but he combined a faith in the
destiny of his own 'master race' with a firm conviction that he possessed
the drive to lay his hands on the fabled 'gold of Ophir'. Although Bismarck
heartily detested Gladstone, the two men agreed that any colonial
expansion needed to be achieved at no cost to the domestic taxpayer, and
in 1885, the Chancellor sanctioned Peters to form his own German East
African Company. 'Let the Company take what it feels confident to take',
declared the Chancellor, 'Later we shall then see what we can officially
endorse.'[11] In private, Fabri confessed that nobody in his right mind would
entrust Peters with the leadership of any expedition, unless the objective
was to remove him as far from Berlin as possible, but in the interests
of colonial solidarity, he did agree to join the new company's board.

Peters travelled across huge areas of eastern Africa, from Portuguese
territory in the south to the borders of Somalia in the north, displaying
a level of brutality bordering on homicidal insanity, and shocking even
the home supporters. More seriously from their point of view, Africa's
fabled riches also proved elusive and, after just three years, Peters faced
the Bashiri revolt that could not be put down with his company's
limited resources. Germany's short-lived experiment in colonisation
by a commercial company ended when Bismarck mounted a state-funded
'punitive expedition', led by seasoned explorer and future colonial
governor Hermann von Wissman. Perhaps surprisingly, this German
expansion created no alarm in British government circles. 'If Germany
is to become a colonial power', announced the departing Gladstone, 'all
I say is God speed her', and his Conservative successor Lord Salisbury
went so far as to dispatch British ships to help crush the insurgents.
Von Wissman used simple methods to 'subdue the natives' – whenever a
column approached a village, the soldiers used their heaviest guns to fell
a tree and, if that did not bring instant submission, the weapons were
turned on the village. Those chiefs who submitted were given flags and
enrolled as servants of Germany, while those who resisted were hanged –
often alongside their headmen. Behind the armies came Catholic and
Protestant missionaries, whose competition for agreements with
surviving chiefs produced a checkerboard of religious affiliation within
the conquered territory.

* * *

During the decade when Bismarck was uniting the German people by
'blood and iron', the state and the Catholic Church had been engaged

in a bitter *kulturkampf* (culture struggle), which was to have an indirect effect on German missionary efforts in Africa. Partly a re-emergence of old enlightenment tensions, partly a conflict over the control of education, it resulted in German Catholics becoming increasingly isolated from the wider secular community. However, the situation had improved when Leo XIII succeeded the intractable Pius IX on the papal throne in 1878, and now the Benedictine abbot of St. Ottilen grasped the opportunity to put the argument to rest once for all on the mission field of German East Africa. Here his monks would show that Catholics were as loyal to the German state as any Protestant; operating under a rigid oath of obedience, priests, nuns and lay brothers would refrain from criticising the colonial occupation and promote German interests at all times. Following time-honoured Catholic strategy, orphans and ransomed slave children would be shut away in Benedictine *chrétientés*, to be prepared for service in the colonial army or as clerks in government and mission service.

Across the ecclesiastical divide, Lutheran societies held their own debate on how they should operate within a colonial society. Feelings ran high as traditional pietist Gustav Warneck challenged Freidrich Fabri's newfangled notions, arguing passionately that nationality had no bearing on how missionaries fulfilled their 'holy duty' of proclaiming the gospel. Those who wished to change hearts and lives, he argued, must not travel out as conquerors but must do so in a spirit of humility, respecting the traditions and culture of the people among whom they were set. Laying out the contrary position, Fabri argued that Protestant churches must fulfil their 'national duty' by ensuring that mission stations in German colonies were entirely staffed by Germans. On the day, Warneck's traditionalists outvoted Fabri's imperialists, and the conference sent a resolution to Bismarck demanding that the twin principles of freedom of labour and traditional land rights must be respected in the new colonial world. In the wider court of public opinion, however, Fabri's case carried the day, and across the German colonies, foreign missionaries found their work increasingly threatened. Seeing no future for their operation in German East Africa, LMS staff withdrew from their villages on the eastern shore of Lake Tanganyika and CMS clergy were expelled from stations in the fertile country below Mount Kilimanjaro. Only French Catholics and high church Anglicans invoked the freedom of religion that was promised at Berlin and held their ground. In Victoria, elderly West Indian James Fuller watched with disbelief as a Lutheran pastor from the Basel society took charge of the communion cups, and his fury erupted when he discovered that mission secretary Alfred Baynes had just sold the Baptist chapel for £100. 'Sir, we think that your committee is shaking off the very dust of the Kameroons from their feet by saying the chapel belongs to the Germans. We should like to know the meaning of the term £100. Is it to pay for the trouble which our fathers took to set up the place of worship?'[12]

Now openly at odds with traditional pietism, Fabri began to recruit both Lutheran and Calvinist ultra-nationalists from North Germany into his new Evangelical Missionary Society for German East Africa in Berlin, which – for ease of use and to separate it from two societies that were already operational in the city – became publicly known as Berlin III. To fill the post of Inspector, he recruited arch-nationalist C.G. Büttner who had by now completed his task of negotiating treaties in South-West Africa. But his new society remained both understaffed and under-funded, and even with the support of north German Lutherans from the Berlin Mission Society (Berlin I), his nationalists could not undertake the whole task. By his own definition, the despised pietists still remained German and two societies of the Warnek persuasion followed his nationalists into German East Africa.

The deep division that ran through German Protestantism was now exported to the mission field. On the one side, Berlin I and III workers set about imposing German culture and values by recruiting school children, who one day would find their niche within the colony. Berlin missionaries did not learn local languages, which were expected to wither rapidly away; all instruction was in German, or, if that was beyond resources, the coastal lingua franca of Swahili. Berlin stations were notoriously violent environments, where missionaries used the whip freely on young and old – but then, declared their pietist critics, 'nothing better could be expected from an enterprise that had come into being more from colonial enthusiasm than out of a spirit of prayer'.[13] On the other side, traditional pietists remained dedicated to the spirit of the *volk*, expressed in just those local languages that the colonisers so roundly despised. The clear educational advantage of teaching primary level children in tongues that they could understand did, however, have to be balanced by the fully intended side-effect that, as those children grew older, they were denied any grasp of Swahili or the European languages that brought advancement within the colonial economy.

* * *

Before the Germans arrived, British and French missionaries negotiated with local chiefs to raise labour for the construction of houses and churches, and since the money that passed hands rarely found its way to the workers, this must be seen as a form of forced labour. Indeed, under German rule, the whole colonial economy was based on compulsion. It wasn't long before one French Catholic noted a growing sense of discontent. 'The blacks must be very weary of paying dues and working in the cotton fields without any kind of salary.'[14] In July 1905, Christians at Berlin I's southern Maneromango station reported that local people were cursing their missionaries by name and whispering that the snake god had a medicine that would turn bullets to water. The message went round that after all whites had been consumed in a great flood – *Maji Maji* (water water) – life would return to the way that it had been before missionaries and soldiers arrived. With lives now at risk, Christian communities began to build fortifications and prepare for a siege. Soon there was a full-scale uprising. On one station, missionaries and adherents held off an assault for more than an hour, killing some thirty attackers at no loss to themselves. As Pastor Neuberg and his wife tried to cross the border into the Shire Highlands, they found themselves surrounded by armed men, but after being relieved of all their property, they were released when the attackers agreed that the pastor was 'a good man'.[15]

There was worse to come. Although both Berlin societies would later offer thanks that none of their missionaries had died during the troubles, the Benedictines were less fortunate. Before setting out on a journey with Mother Cordula, Sister Felicitas and Brothers Andreas and Gabriel, Bishop Spiss equipped his porters with six rifles and enough 'bullets to hold off an attack by a hundred Africans'. Once they were on their way, however, the porters quickly vanished, leaving five Europeans and three Africans face-to-face with Maji Maji rebels. As Spiss was trying to explain that they had only come to do good and to teach the children, a chief stuck a spear in his throat. The bodies of the five Benedictines and one of their African companions lay where they fell for more than a month.[16] Following the incident, other Benedictine stations were singled out for assault across the Southern Highlands: another priest was killed, two were wounded and a sister died from exhaustion. But missionary firearms certainly inflicted many times that number of casualties on the Maji Maji. Across the colony at Kiliminjaro, German Holy Ghost Fathers heard news of the Benedictine disaster without undue surprise;

in their eyes, African resistance to German rule was comparable to the struggle that their people had mounted against Napoleon's army.

German and English missionaries now abandoned their stations and retreated into the military forts as African warriors reclaimed large swathes of their homeland. One missionary recorded the fighting at Mahenge Fort, which took place in the morning of 30 August – just after a public hanging. Scarcely had the five victims been hauled up into the tree when groups of Maji Maji appeared from the bush: 'There must have been over a thousand men. Since they came to make an end of all of us, we had to defend ourselves and take part in the firing, which opened on the attackers at about 1,000 metres. Two machine-guns, Europeans and soldiers rained death and destruction among the ranks of the advancing enemy.'[17] The clergy shared the station commander's champagne when the last enemy retreated.

The defence of Mahenge Fort proved to be the turning point in a long war. Children would later recall how they were summoned to watch as chiefs and elders were hanged or shot through the back of the neck. Although none fought on with greater determination than the Ngoni warriors of the Southern Highlands, they too were finally defeated. Benedictine Johannes Hafliger agreed to give spiritual comfort to Chief Mputa Gama as he was hanged along with forty-seven of his elders. But he protested vigorously when the administrator unleashed a lawless band of 'auxiliaries' to burn houses and crops, steal food and rape Ngoni women. 'That's right', the administrator said to him, 'the fellows can just starve. We shall be sure to get food for ourselves. If I could, I would even prevent them from planting anything. This is the only way we can make the fellows sick of war'.[18] Hafliger sent a detailed indictment of German abuses to the new bishop, requesting that it be passed to the Governor. Criticism of the colonial power constituted a breach of his vow of obedience. Hafliger was moved from his station and his catalogue of abuses got no further than the bishop's file.

During the few remaining years before the outbreak of the First World War, a new German administration did set about making improvements. Efficient public health initiatives averted major epidemics and – in the teeth of settler opposition – reforming governors even tried to rebuild peasant agriculture. In this final decade of German rule, both Catholic and Protestant missionaries struggled to cope with an ever-growing work-load, as huge numbers of defeated and shattered Africans turned to their churches. They came to the missions with varied and mixed motives. Many were searching for some spiritual replacement for their lost religion and social bonds; others sought those western skills that would provide access to an alien but more prosperous world; some even hoped that, within the church environment, they might find some scope for that self-expression now denied to them in the secular world. Whatever the motive, here too missionaries reported that God was 'riding the storm' as he worked the divine purpose amongst violence, disease and suffering.

Rwanda and Burundi

By the time the nineteenth century drew towards its close, geographers had filled most of the blanks that had distorted their maps of Africa, but even at that late date, a few areas remained largely unknown to the industrialised world. Interest focused in particular on the fertile and densely populated twin kingdoms of Burundi and Rwanda, where there were supposedly enough riches to bring the whole Central African venture into profit. Leopold planned to export the region's wealth down the Congo to the Atlantic; Karl Peters dreamed of transporting it overland through German territory; Cecil Rhodes hoped to carry its products either north or south on his projected railway. But Lord Salisbury always suspected that plans for a Cape to Cairo railway lacked any contact with reality, and in 1890, he conceded Rwanda and Burundi to Germany as part of the same deal that secured Uganda for Britain.

In 1882, a party of White Fathers was wiped out while trying to enter Burundi from the south. Seven years later, Fr Alphonse Brard – renowned for his unique style of 'fisticuff evangelism' – led a party of heavily armed Ugandan Catholics into Rwanda. His caravan, which 'was not immediately identifiable as a team of peace-loving evangelists … left a trail of deposed chiefs and hurt feelings through the country, from Uganda to the Burundi border'.[19] Bishop Hirth followed next with an even larger force, believing that in this remote mission field he would, at last, be free to create a perfect society, based on the model of medieval Europe. 'If he had his way', reported one German officer, 'the government would go to hell and he would establish an African church-state.'[20]

Churchmen and soldiers alike found themselves in a land of extremes. Within this comparatively small region could be found both the tallest and the shortest people on earth and the population at first seemed to

divide easily by criteria of height and physical characteristics. When
Hirth presented himself to Musinga, King of Rwanda, he confronted
a thin lipped and long nosed man at least 2 metres tall, surrounded
by similarly built courtiers. These were the pastoral Tutsi, who had
established hegemony over the rest of the population. At the other end
of the scale, some Twa people of the upper Congo forest – known to the
world as Pygmies – scratched a living around the centres of population.
Between the extremes, the medium built majority –the Hutu – followed
an agricultural lifestyle. According to local legend, all three had been
descended from a common ancestor and the fathers would soon discover
that, outside the immediate environs of Musinga's court, lines of simple
demarcation between Hutu and Tutsi broke down. Most of the former
kept animals and many of the latter tilled fields; the two peoples were
largely indistinguishable physically, spoke the same language, frequently
intermarried and shared many customs. One White Father concluded
that the differences between the two groups 'had become so minimal that
one can speak of a common culture'.[21] At the same time, it suited those
officers who faced the challenging task of imposing German rule without
significant military support to exaggerate the division between ruling
Tutsi and subject Hutu. 'The policy of the imperial government', came
the order, 'has to be in all cases to strengthen … the authority of the
chiefs … even if this sometimes results in injustice to the Wahutu'.[22]
The governors of Rwanda and Burundi toured Catholic stations in their
areas, to reinforce the message that this key colonial policy had to be
obeyed 'without deviations'.

Lavigerie had left clear instructions that White Fathers must first focus
their attention on converting African rulers. Bishops and senior clergy –
who had themselves been raised within privileged society – therefore
focused their attention on the two royal courts, leaving the order's foot
soldiers – who had been born into rural deprivation and could be lightly
dismissed by their betters as 'peasant-like and cloddish' characters – to
make the best job they could of converting the Hutu.

Like Protestants Bowen and Krapf before them, members of the
Catholic hierarchy constructed theories based on the assumption that
'higher human characteristics' could not develop in sub-Saharan Africa.
But after Father Superior Léon Classe decided that he could detect
both Aryan and Semitic characteristics within the Tutsi, he concluded
that they had probably originated outside Africa and had once been
monotheists, and it followed that missionaries only had to strip away

layers of superstition that had accumulated through contact with the animist Bantu.[23] Colleagues tried to clothe his 'Hamitic myth' with some semblance of intellectual respectability. In a work of truly medieval pedagogy, Dutch-born Fr Van der Burgt piled up biblical and classical authorities to pour contempt on 'those fantasists ... who place, not only the origins of the negroes, but of the whole human race, in equatorial Africa, near the source of the Nile'. Brushing aside Harry Johnston's 'brutal assertion' that Africans could only be classified as 'fine animals', he insisted that the Tutsi were indeed a higher race. 'Everywhere you look, you can see evidence that these blacks once knew better days.'[24]

Academic theories did not translate into effective practical action. Far from being easy converts, upper-class Tutsi proved impervious to the Christian message, and at the outbreak of the First World War , the whole battery of higher clerics had failed to convert a single member of the Rwandan court. By this time, however, many of their 'peasant-like and cloddish' subordinates were ruling over burgeoning *chrétientés* across Hutu country. Looking at imposing churches and busy schools from the outside, frightened villagers told one another that the all-powerful White Fathers were dangerous sorcerers, and they beat any child who was caught wearing the sacred medals that the fathers handed out as incitements to draw them to the stations. Within traditional society, becoming a catechumen and receiving elementary Christian instruction was perceived as a formal act of submission to the invading power, and the very sound of a Fr Terebura's donkey's hooves was enough to make parents in his path hide children of school age.

In Rwanda at least, the image of a catechist as a devoted and peaceful black preacher concerned only with instructing his pupils was far from everyday reality. Men, who might combine the role of catechist and askari, would all too often travel the countryside, rounding up potential school pupils by force or invoking the fathers' authority to trade on their own account. The role of catechist could even serve as cover for simple plunder and sexual abuse. A bad situation became worse when bands of Ugandan 'brigand catechists and catechumens' began to roam the Rwandan countryside. Operating with some fifty followers from a base behind the Ugandan boarder, the notorious catechist and cattle thief Gabriel Madjasi terrorised the Rwandan countryside for some six years. Even after angry villagers had burnt his encampment, the fathers continued to extol his success in spreading the gospel, until they did finally get round to denouncing this Catholic protégé as 'a public scandal

to all Christians'.[25] As outlying fathers built up congregations among the
poor Hutu people, they took issue with their superiors' support for the
Tutsi hegemony. Priests who had themselves been raised in deep poverty
reminded their superiors that, although Jesus had preached to the poor
and the outcast, not to the powerful and wealthy, their Christian mission
was knowingly condoning injustice. While home on leave, the Alsatian,
Fr Gassldinger, went so far as to publish a sharp attack on German rule,
accusing administrators of failing in their civilising mission and being
content to rule over a people, who were filled only with 'sullen anger
and hate'.[26] The offending priest was refused leave to return and his
superior warned that any missionary who failed to support government
policy would be weeded out without compunction. 'Let those of our
missionaries who do not believe they can reconcile the apostolate with
the practice of our Rules look for a Society which has as its rule only the
caprice of its members.'[27] The outraged governor of Rwanda protested
that he could not establish settled government while the Hutu were being
encouraged to 'run to the mission' every time their Tutsi overlords had
cause to confiscate their cattle. As a warning to the White Fathers, he
invited their rivals, the pietists, to begin work in the country, but their
stay was short, because at the end of the First World War, the new Belgian
rulers expelled all German missionaries. It made little difference to the
people of the region. The new Belgian masters continued the policy of
divide and rule inherited from the Germans. During the post-war years,
the Tutsi people finally began to enter Catholic stations, but old divisions
survived and it was reported that 'even in the theological seminary, the
old antagonism, although dressed in Latin, could be felt as humiliating.
Tutsi dominance was complete but the Hutu fellow-students were not
likely to forget.'[28]

Namibia (South-West Africa)

While the small and remote states of Rwanda and Burundi were of only
marginal interest within the imperial reich, the Rhenish mission's
territory in South-West Africa was rapidly gaining in commercial and
strategic importance. When Franz Zahn took over as inspector after
Fabri's dismissal in 1880, he was quick to express shock at the colonial
apologists' apparent toleration of naked self-interest, going so far as
to question whether colonial conquest could ever be morally defensible.

Then, as conflict gathered, he began to change his tune, asking whether, in fact, God might be using a lesser evil to produce a higher good. Finally, he instructed his workers in South-West Africa to greet the German armies with joyful hearts and provide them with all possible help. Chiefs Samuel Herero and Hendrik Witbooi both looked on themselves as devout Christians, but they reacted to the arrival of German troops very differently. Even as Samuel delivered his people's submission, Hendrick was rallying his Nama to resist the white advance. Now purged of his earlier doubts, Zahn pressed the government, 'in the interest of our mission work, that this man should rapidly be paid the just reward of his criminal and arrogant deeds'.[29] As mission stations were converted into military posts, pastors found no difficulty in reconciling the role of chaplain to the German forces with that of missionary to the Nama.

> I certainly don't like war – even less my community involved in
> it – but this time it is inevitable and *additionally the right is on*
> *the German side....* Yesterday 18th April I held a service for the
> departing warriors. All of them were in a very serious mood, for
> they were well aware of the fact: *they are out to perform hard,*
> *bloody work, the success of which lastly belongs to the Lord.*
> I offered them a holy shield.[30]

The Lutheran pastors expressed no outrage when, in an outbreak of *furor germanicus*, seventy-eight women and children died in the storming of Witbooi's headquarters. After Nama resistance had finally been broken with great ferocity, a letter was received in Barmen, expressing the government's 'deep satisfaction that the missionaries of the Society have rendered us valuable services in informing the Imperial authorities ... sufficiently early about the movements of the rebellious Witboois'.[31]

Despite these valuable services, German settlers continued to mistrust missionary motives; they understood the process of colonisation in the simplest terms – the lower races had to give way before the higher, the black before the white and individual missionaries who dared to protest against the cruder manifestations of exploitation were derided as sickly sentimentalists and traitors:

> Whoever sets the inhabitants of Africa, by whatever means,
> a goal for external and internal development which is even near
> to that of the white race, does not belong with us, and he should

not complain if we treat him, according to our opposite moral conviction and our stronger political authority, on the same level as them. The key to the successful education of the negro is not learning, as the great part of our evangelical mission still believes, but discipline, authority and subordination.[32]

Early compliance bought the Herero no favours. As rapidly expanding white farms and endless fences severed their settlements from traditional pastures, the people faced the total destruction of their ancient way of life. The once-compliant Samuel Herero protested that his people's lives were now held of little account in the colonial capital. 'You know how many Hereros have been killed by white people, especially traders with rifles and in prison.... The blood of my people was always valued at no more than a few head of cattle.'[33] Rebellion was the outcome. Over 100 German soldiers and settlers died in the initial assault when the whole Herero nation rose in January 1904, though women, children and missionaries were, once again, generally spared, along with Boer and British men.

At a time when most of his colleagues were keeping silent, Pastor Kuhlmann of Otjimbingwe was prepared to stand up and defend the Herero in an open meeting. As settlers retailed stories of atrocity and depravity to the howling audience, he countered their accusations with tales of German atrocities against African women and children. While the vilification that was poured on him by the white press would have come as no surprise, Kuhlmann was surely ill prepared for the official reprimand that arrived from Barmen. He acquiesced with an ill grace: 'When here, far away, total silence has been imposed upon us, we must naturally keep it – and many will do so willingly for reasons I don't want to name – however whether this is beneficial to the worker and the work is another question.'[34]

Rhenish pastors on Herero stations watched in mounting horror as General von Trotha set about the systematic destruction of the rebel people. 'It was and remains my policy', he announced, 'to apply this force by unmitigated terrorism and even cruelty. I shall destroy the rebellious tribes by shedding rivers of blood and money.' At the battle of Waterberg, he laid his forces out in such a way that the western line of retreat lay enticingly open. Then, when the Herero accepted the bait, he set about driving the desperate people ever deeper into the Kalahari Desert. A German soldier described how he followed the shattered Herero into that arid country.

I saw tracks of innumerable children's feet, and among them those
of full-grown feet. Great troops of children led by their mothers had
passed over the road here to the north west.... How deeply this
wild, proud and sorrowful people had humbled themselves in the
terror of death: wherever I turned my eyes lay their goods in
quantities, oxen and horses, goats and dogs, blankets and skins.
A number of babies lay helplessly languishing by mothers whose
breasts hung down long and flabby. Others were lying alone, still
living with eyes and nose full of flies. Somebody sent out our black
drivers and I think they helped them to die.[35]

Historians describe this war as the twentieth century's first genocide.
Before its outbreak, the Herero population was estimated at about
80,000; of these, some 8,000 starving people found shelter on Rhenish
stations or with Catholics on the Orange River, and a few others
succeeded in crossing the desert to Bechuanaland. Since very few children
made it to safety, a whole generation was lost.

History does not record the emotions of surviving Herero
Christians, when they read the rebuke that arrived from Franz Zahn
in Barmen:

Dearly beloved in Christ Jesus.
    It is not easy for us to attach such a title to this letter. Our love for
you has suffered a rude shock on account of the terrible rebellion
in which so many of you took part and on account of the awful
bloodshed, as well as the many atrocities associated with the
rebellion, for which you also share at least co-responsibility, even
if we hope that only a few of you were directly involved in these
atrocious and murderous deeds.... It is in this spirit that we
continue to refer to you as 'dearly beloved in Christ Jesus'.
    We dare not conceal from you that you have made us very
unhappy and have caused us great sorrow. Our heart bleeds when
we think of you as the heart of the father bled when the prodigal
son turned his back on him. You too have set out on a path which
will inevitably lead you to misfortune, and you will perish miserably
unless you soon recognise your error and repent. You have raised
the sword against the government which God has placed over you
without considering that it is written, 'Whoever takes the sword
will also perish by the sword.'[36]

Although the surviving Herero and Nama did adopt Christianity with a new intensity, neither people ever forgave the Barmen missionaries for the support that they had given to the colonial power. Many switched their allegiance to untainted missionaries from Finland, who had been working in areas away from the centres of conflict.

Zaire (The Congo)

Throughout the 1890s, Leopold II was becoming increasingly desperate; lured on by dreams of untapped riches, he had for twenty years sunk large amounts of personal wealth into the Congo venture and got little in return. While Katanga was indeed mineral-rich, the task of exploiting the region's reserves of copper and cobalt would involve yet more investment, and in the end, base metals would prove no substitute for the diamonds and gold that had made Cecil Rhodes such a fabulously wealthy man. In January 1895, Leopold's forces finally managed to break Swahili-Arab power on the upper river, and in the same year, Belgian officers hanged ex-missionary Charles Stokes after a drumhead trial. The Stokes affair did arouse some concern that much must be wrong in the Leopold's Congo – if a white man could be treated with such scant regard to humanity, the situation for the native population could only be worse. Five years earlier, *Blackwoods Magazine* had published a story by a Polish-born sailor, who had worked on the river and now wrote under his Anglicised name of Joseph Conrad. His title, *Heart of Darkness*, turned a clichéd missionary phrase on its head. Livingstone had proclaimed that trade could bring civilisation to Central Africa; now, by Conrad's analysis, the deepest darkness lay in the hearts of those white traders. Belgium's own prime minister confirmed Conrad's diagnosis: 'The Congo state is said to be one vast factory.... No sooner do our Belgian officers touch African soil than they become a sort of bagmen.'[37]

Ivory had long been the staple forest export, but the newly invented high-quality bicycle and motor car tyres created a demand for the region's wild 'red rubber'. As the country was stripped bare of natural resources, first the ivory frontier and then the rubber frontier moved ever further eastwards. The worst abuses were perpetrated on the rubber frontier. The first impact of the collecting process had every characteristic of a slave raid: an armed force would descend on a village, inflict heavy casualties and carry off children for training in Catholic *chrétientés*.

An armed 'sentinel' would then be posted in the village to supervise the collection of the rubber quota, enforced by fearsome irregulars, known as the Zappu Zap, who were believed to have been recruited from cannibal tribes. Belgian officers demanded that the sentinels account for their expenditure of ammunition by bringing severed hands – many of which were said to have been cut from living people.

Under the traditional subsistence economy, each family supplemented the produce of a small agricultural plot with forest products, but the forest was now prohibited territory and villagers were allowed little time to tend their plots; anything that they did manage to produce was subject to state taxation. It is estimated that many more people died from starvation and disease than from state brutality; travellers told of how they found only ruin where there had once been thriving communities. But word was slow to get out, and when it did, it was not always believed. In London, the Anti-Slavery Society (ASS) was no more than a shadow of the organisation that had been led by Wilberforce and Buxton, and Secretary Henry Fox Bourne, though 'very active and zealous' was 'well stricken in years and tortured with asthma'. As information on abuses trickled into the ASS office, Leopold could counter every accusation with fulsome missionary endorsements of his enlightened rule. To Fox Bourne it appeared quite simply impossible that hundreds of Protestant and Catholic clergy, spread across the region, could be out of touch with the human tragedy that was happening on such a scale around their stations. Swedish evangelist E.V. Sjöblom, who had travelled to the Congo with the Livingstone Mission and now worked for the Northern Baptists at Bolenge, was the first to break the silence. He was preaching in a village in 1894 when the sentinel arrived and ordered everybody back to their work; then, when the people reacted slowly, he shot an old man and forced a child to cut off his right hand while he was still dying. 'Isn't this the height of cruelty', asked the Swede, 'and worse than slavery?'[38] Missionary colleagues Mr and Mrs Banks corroborated Sjöblom's next story. 'On the 14 December a sentinel passed our mission station, carrying a basket of hands. Mr and Mrs Banks, besides myself, went down to the road that they might count them. We counted eighteen right hands smoked, and from the size of the hands we could judge that they belonged to men, women and children.'[39]

When Mission Supervisor Aaron Sims, (an Englishman) heard that Sjöblom planned to send his story to the western press, he advised the mission secretary to bring this troublesome employee under control. 'The right thing to do is to expose whatever is wrong to the Governor General, or to the Secretary of State at Bruxelles, or through yourself to the King.'[40] But members of the home committee, who had never been fully convinced that they had acted wisely in taking over the LIM stations, printed the story in the society's magazine, from which it leaked into the Swedish and British press. In the Congo, Sjöblom and Banks were charged with the crime of telling lies about the state, which carried a penalty of five years in prison, but the charge was quietly dropped and Sjöblom was allowed to return to Europe on leave. As he passed through London, audiences sat riveted as this gaunt Swede recounted experiences on the river. Still Sims continued to oppose any suggestion that the society might align itself to the growing protest movement. 'I am much concerned in mind that you should not join the Congo Campaign.... I trust you will see the wisdom of confining your efforts to getting land leases – and as it were "minding one's own business" concerning the political questions, for if we do not, *we are certain* to be turned out.... The King, a hard man, never forgets and in time takes full revenge.'[41]

In a desperate attempt to deflect growing criticism, Leopold announced that he had appointed six missionaries to serve on a Commission for the Protection of the Natives. Catholics and Protestants were evenly balanced; on the Catholic side were the Vicar Apostolic, Mgr Van Ronslé; the Jesuit Superior, Fr Van Henxthoven; and Fr de Cleene of the Scheut Fathers, while, for the Protestants, Sims represented the American and Bentley and Grenfell the English Baptists. These six were scattered across a huge distance and the body never met. Grenfell confessed his cynicism in a letter to Bentley. 'What better way to allay the excitement than the appointment of a commission of missionaries? And what step could be taken that would interfere less with the powers that be out here?'[42] European editors were happy to bury a story that had 'lost its legs', and one editor closed his paper's coverage with the assurance: 'the British missionaries who have seats on this commission are pretty certain to see that its work is rendered efficient'. In practice, however, nobody seriously expected to hear tales of abuse from Catholics, who provided Leopold with so many recruits through their basic educational and training services. Children delivered to a *chrétienté* were refused permission to leave until they reached the age of twenty-five. With much of the day spent in military exercises, priests, brothers and nuns worked to convert their charges into 'non-commissioned officers in the army, artisans, store keepers and employees'.[43] 'Laziness is the sin beloved of the black race', reported Sister Amalia, 'so we have to use some severity to get our little savages working'.[44]

Despite the fact that hundreds of missionaries now worked within the Congo basin, the impetus for reform was generated within European secular society. At the turn of the century, shipping clerk Edmund Morel, who was of French and English descent and had access to Leopold's ledgers, noticed a gross inequality in the Congo trade. While ships on the return journey did, as expected, bring ivory, rubber and other raw materials, those sailing out carried only guns, chains and explosives, and from this he deduced that Leopold's whole business empire was founded on slave labour. American Southern Presbyterians on the Kasai River had kept to the policy of 'keeping as quiet as possible', but in 1903, news broke of a staggering atrocity. When a sentinel returned to his village to find everybody sitting on the ground and refusing to explain why they were not out working, he ordered his men to kill the whole population and cut off their right hands. From that time, mission superintendent William Morrison and African American missionary William H. Shepherd became passionate supporters of Morel's growing Congo Reform Association. Articles and lantern lectures were authenticated by harrowing photographs, provided by English missionary Alice Seeley Walker.

To make mission evidence truly credible, some confirmation needed to be provided by mainstream English Baptists, and three men – mission secretary Alfred Baynes, lower-river supervisor Holman Bentley and upper-river pioneer George Grenfell – were determined that this would not happen. All knew that, right across Africa, new colonial masters were expelling foreign missionaries from long-worked fields, and so, upholding first BMS secretary Andrew Fuller's rule that missionaries must never become embroiled in politics, they continued to cling desperately to the threadbare belief that Leopold had become involved in the Congo for philanthropic ends. A storm broke round Baynes's head in 1904 when he led a deputation to Brussels to present 'grovelling thanks' for a reduction in the mission's tax liability – during which he was once again reported to have congratulated Leopold on his 'enlightened rule on the Congo'. He defended the audience on the grounds that the delegation also took the opportunity to remind the king of the need for 'just and beneficent rule'. One critic was not impressed. 'It is unfortunate, however, that they disguised the hint so carefully that the King accepted it as a compliment, and that the King's friends have been parading it ever since as a certificate that the Baptist Missionary Society were thick and thin supporters of the abominations.'[45]

As a nervous, introverted man, Holman Bentley was most at ease doing language work with selected African advisers. Reformers were particularly scandalised that, in his two-volume autobiography *Pioneering on the Congo* (1900), praise for Leopold's civilising work was untempered by a single word of criticism. Bentley protested that he knew nothing of what was happening hundreds of miles upriver, but earlier correspondence does suggest that he was more aware of the abuses than he cared to admit.[46]

George Grenfell, in contrast, was only happy when he was on the move and commentators have always found it hard to understand how this charismatic and physically courageous man could have wilfully closed his eyes to the atrocities that were happening all around him. Devoted to a West Indian wife and mixed race children, he had always insisted that racism had no place within a Christian organisation and he had earlier drawn public attention to abuses by Stanley's expeditions. On his steamship *Peace*, Grenfell had sailed backwards and forwards across the ivory and rubber frontiers, and he had studied Sjöblom's reports before they ever appeared in print without ever challenging their accuracy. When colleague John Weekes returned from home leave, he sent Grenfell a copy of his protest to the governor over disasters that had overwhelmed his people in just a few short months.

> Last year the country all about here was flooded, yet you levied your cassava tax month after month upon the people in addition to your oil, fowl and goat tax etc. The people here had not enough to eat and, as their cassava was destroyed by the floods, they had to buy it at an exorbitant price from more fortunate districts. This year again the country is flooded and the farms spoilt, but I suppose you will enforce the cassava tax, and the people have to starve again. Why? To feed and strengthen State soldiers to raid them again in their weakness. You take away the sturdy young men leaving only the old people and children, so that every Steamer that stays here loots the town because the proper defenders have been carried off by the State.

His superior's only response was to send the governor an obsequious letter of apology and a sharp – if unconvincing – rebuke to a subordinate that his assertions were not subject to proof. 'You say: "Every steamer that stays here loots the town". This appears to me to be so serious that

I am induced to regard it as a relative generalisation rather than an absolute statement. Things have indeed come to a terrible pass if the State cannot convert exceptions.'[47]

Grenfell sailed the waterways in a single-minded attempt to bring Robert Arthington's millennial dream into reality. This work had at first been frustrated by Swahili-Arabs, whose lands straddled his route to the great lakes and upper Nile. When their power was finally broken, he rejoiced that the way into the continental heartland had at last opened and, in his excitement, he confessed that he could think of little else. As Arthington's disciple, he could only believe that the chaos that he saw around him might indeed be a harbinger of the last days and, as a committed Baptist and a competitive explorer, he could not bear the thought that Anglicans or Catholics might make the conjunction before him. With every year's delay, CMS catechists were pushing west from Uganda, while Belgian and French Catholics edged closer to meeting in the Rift Valley. Decorated by the king for his feats of exploration, Grenfell invented excuses for the obstructions he constantly experienced – that Leopold had undertaken an impossible task, that he was short of funds and that he was being badly served by officials who did not share his high ideals. When he finally reached the painful conclusion that Leopold had colluded with the Roman Catholic hierarchy to prevent Protestants from reaching the Rift Valley, he returned his medals to mission headquarters, along with a letter addressed to the King. After congratulating him for bringing civilisation and 'enlightened rule' to a barbarous country, Grenfell did admit that some of Leopold's agents had abused their trust, but insisted that he was only returning his medals because Leopold had frustrated his life work. 'Your Majesty will not be slow to recognise that it has been rendered impossible for me to continue to wear the insignia of the royal favour of the Sovereign whose will blocks the way to the realisation of the well known plans of our Society, plans that were formed before the State came into existence.'[48] Not yet ready to abandon hope, Baynes filed Grenfell's letter and put the medals into a drawer, where they were discovered when the mission moved premises over eighty years later.

By now, secular protest against the abuses in the Congo had gathered momentum. A motion presented in the British House of Commons demanded that the government confer with other signatories of the Berlin Act on how best to 'abate the evils' in the Congo. The proposer denied being 'one of those short-sighted philanthropists who thought that natives must be treated in all respects on equal terms with white men ...

but there were certain rights that were common to humanity.... If the administration of the Congo State was civilisation,' he asked, 'then what was barbarism?' Speakers noted with regret that the British societies' missionary still remained reticent on the issue.[49] After the motion was passed, the British government instructed its consul on the river to conduct an investigation. Protestant Irishman, Roger Casement (who would later be hanged for complicity in the Irish Easter Rising) had briefly worked on Bentley's station; now he travelled the upper river on the American Baptist boat, gathering copious evidence at mission stations. The publication of his report created a sensation as rumours were substantiated in an official document.

The great majority of Belgians found the whole affair very puzzling. Theirs was a small country, linked with just this single colony; Germany and France were expanding across Africa, the United States had occupied Mexican and Filipino land and Britain had coloured half the globe red. Alongside all these colonisers, could they be so uniquely wicked? Leopold reacted to world pressure by sending his own commission to investigate conditions on the Congo, but if he anticipated vindication, his hopes would be frustrated. The final document not only confirmed many of Casement's allegations but also criticised Catholic missions for the manner in which they recruited children and for their brutality. Now, at last, Catholic solidarity began to crumble. After Jesuit Fr Vermeersch published the first open criticism of Leopold's government from within the church, he received letters from the field, which demonstrated the extent to which the national consensus had broken down.

> Oh the state of the Congo! Who will deliver us? I no longer hope that Belgium will correct it.... Our Superior believes that we would be a hundred times better off under Protestant English rule.... I cannot shed the idea that our Catholic missions ought to be looking towards Protestant England to find that apostolic liberty that is our right and that we have been led to expect but have never been given.[50]

By the time that the Belgian state assumed responsibility for Leopold's discredited empire in 1908, Fox Bourne and Morel had found other campaigns to fight. For, inexcusably, colonial abuses continued, and the pattern set in British Rhodesia and German East Africa was repeated. Across the Congo basin those who had been stripped of tradition, wealth and self-respect turned to the churches in ever-increasing numbers.

Chapter 11
Black Men's God

West Africa

Young Purifiers on the Niger

A decade after Henry Venn died in office at the age of seventy-six, CMS activists were suggesting that the whole thrust of his policy had been an 'awful irremediable blunder'. A combination of influences, from scientific racism on the one side to the new millennial fundamentalism on the other, had made younger people impatient with his native church policy and dismissive of any suggestion that Africa would be converted by means of a marriage between religion, civilisation and legitimate trade. Concern increased as complaints about the behaviour of Crowther's agents began to arrive at mission headquarters. While one did, indeed, involve a grave crime, which Crowther had not handled well, most complaints were transparent attempts to discredit their African competitors by white commercial rivals.[1]

In 1882, twenty-four-year-old Cambridge graduate Alfred Robinson was appointed to the position of clerical secretary on the Niger. Having complete control over all mission funds and – at least by his interpretation – full powers to hire and fire staff, this young man had effectively been given seniority over a full diocesan bishop, who was more than fifty years his senior. He had been in his post just a year when twenty-two-year-old 'independent missionary' Graham Wilmot Brooke travelling from the Congo to Britain took the opportunity of going ashore to meet him. As the two young men talked late into the night, Brooke explained that he had explored different routes into the African interior. Since overland forays from Algiers and Senegal had proved fruitless and his latest trip up the Congo with Grenfell had also failed to produce results, his interest now focused on the Niger. Robinson briefed his new friend on the realities of life on the river. While the movement of people and goods was reasonably free as far as the confluence town of Lokoja, it was closed to whites beyond that point. North of Lokoja, the majority Hausa-speaking population were subject to emirs, who were descended from Uthman dan Fodio's devout Fulani followers. Working on the assumption that the Hausa must be tiring of Fulani oppression, the two young men worked out a strategy for the conversion of the Hausa. Young missionaries would settle in Lokoja, wearing Hausa clothes, eating Hausa food and living like the Hausa. Then, when the task of conversion was complete, the Hausa themselves would go out as missionaries to other races of the interior. Before the night was out, they had agreed that Brooke would submit this proposal to the CMS directors.

Wherever Brooke travelled, he carried books by US evangelist Charles Grandeson Finney, and he read and re-read the preacher's promises that nothing was impossible for those who could accept that the church must remain in a state of constant purification. Young disciples like Brooke nursed a particular horror of lukewarm Christians, who could not deliver personal testimony of conversion and were fit for nothing but to be 'spewed out of the mouth'. Before he made his presentation to the directors, Brooke had convinced himself that all the grassland country, from the Sahara in the north to the rain forest in the south, could be converted by Finney's methods within ten years. In due course, the gentlemen of the parent committee found themselves confronted by a young man whose eyes blazed with such passion that 'to see him was to love him'. Some were concerned at the ease with which he could brush aside all whose commitment did not match his own, but none could resist his enthusiasm, and it was agreed that Brooke and Robinson were to lead a group of 'young purifiers'. This team was young and inexperienced. The combined missionary experience of two Cambridge men – Keswick founder's son and newly qualified Doctor Charles Harford Battersby and his friend Eric Lewis – was limited to a few weeks, working with children on British holiday beaches, while Lewis's sister Lucy had campaigned with the Salvation Army. The oldest member, another Cambridge man, was serving vicar J.N. Eden, who was to take Robinson's place on the lower river. Eden also recruited his curate Henry Dobinson from Brasenose College, Oxford, which was then noted for sporting enthusiasm than for evangelical devotion (and his Cambridge companions treated him patronisingly as a very junior colleague). Brooke also travelled with his cousin and fiancé Margaret. Brooke rejected any suggestion that they were engaged in a 'civilising mission': 'Very much confusion is caused and very much nonsense talked by Evangelicals and Broad churchmen both confusing the work of saving men from the power of Satan, and that of building up political, commercial and social civilisation. I believe these two to be very frequently opposed and I know they are invariably distinct.'[2]

While Eden and Dobinson settled down to work in the delta, the main party continued upstream to Lokoja – where it quickly became clear that the task of converting the Muslim Hausa would be a great deal more challenging than anybody had anticipated. Impatient for rapid results, they turned their attention to the task of purifying Crowther's clergy and commercial agents, Brooke delivered a comprehensive assessment of the task ahead: 'The pastors must be changed, the communicants must be changed, the message preached must be changed, the time, mode and place of worship must be changed, the schoolchildren must be changed and the course in the schools must be changed.'[3]

Upper river archdeacon Henry 'Jerusalem' Johnson was summarily dismissed for his 'long and successful career of flagrant hypocrisy', and his training college was commandeered to become Battersby's hospital. Then, to the young doctor's fury, the joint leaders decided that having a hospital at all was only a distraction from the main task; when people arrived at the hospital, wrote Brooke, 'their amazement at the structure diverts their attention completely from our message and they begin to speculate as to its cost and the wealth of the White Mallams who own it'.[4] The building was sold without reference to London.

Dobinson, meanwhile, was reporting better news: 'The poor agents in the Delta district were quite cowed and distant, but Mr Eden left them in a different frame of mind, and learned very much of all the Mission work by simply taking time to listen to their stories and hear their troubles.'[5] But such reports only served to convince the two leaders that their downstream colleagues were content to lop off a few dead branches, when they needed to take the axe to the roots of the tree, and they called a formal meeting of the Finance Committee, to be held at Onitsha on 27 July 1890. Now they would have their chance to make a clean break with the past.

Hard evidence was of small interest to Brooke, who announced that he only had to look into any person's eyes to know whether they were saved, but the judicial process did need to be followed. After working day and night to glean every scrap of evidence against Crowther's agents, the two men arrived at the meeting with remarkably few issues of substance. First offender, David Anyaegbunam, faced the charge of having a loud and very public row with his wife, which had caused much merriment on the river. The couple had long been reconciled, but Eden's first inclination towards clemency was overruled and Anyaegbunam was dismissed. An unmarried clergyman was then accused of having two young female servants in his household; in the face of protests that his conscience was clear, it was considered enough that their presence could be misinterpreted, and he too was relieved of his duties. Then there followed an interminable debate over the fate of a single case of communion wine. Eventually, the young purifiers struck at Crowther's senior clergy. Rev Peters, who had built up a strong congregation in the delta port of Brass, was dismissed on a charge of smuggling. He fought furiously to clear his name, demanding that the case be brought to trial, but no evidence was ever delivered to the police. Finally, Eden announced that he could no longer work with the bishop's youngest son Dandeson as a Christian brother. It would later emerge that the two men had disagreed over some building work, and though no fault was suggested, Crowther's second archdeacon was dismissed. After following these proceedings in a state of mounting distress, Crowther refused to sign the minutes until his views had been recorded: 'Will you write down, say, please, Bishop Crowther expresses surprise at the statement of the Secretary that he has the power as the representative of the CMS to suspend any clergyman from his duty according to his power which he got. This is the first time I ever heard it. This report is correct, though I do not approve all the opinions expressed in it.'[6] At the end of the meeting, Robinson did express sadness that it had been necessary to humiliate such a pious old man.

After news of events on the Niger had spread along the coast, newspapers thundered denunciation, and whites found themselves being hissed at in the streets of Lagos. Protests from black and white poured into the London headquarters, and the CMS found itself embroiled in the most bitter controversy of its history. When Brooke returned home on sick leave, the mission's Africa committee gave him only a brief hearing before comprehensively repudiating the proceedings and restoring both archdeacons to their posts. Eden and Lewis resigned in anger. Brooke returned to Lokoka, where both he and Robinson died within two years. Sympathisers wondered whether repudiation had speeded their end, but Battersby commented that, in their determination to conform to native habits, his two colleagues had neglected the most elementary rules of good health. At around the age of eighty-five,[7] Samuel Crowther finally proposed that his Niger diocese should cut itself adrift from both the Anglican communion and the CMS which had nurtured him since

he landed as a recaptive child on the Freetown beach. He planned to
consecrate James 'Holy' Johnson, vicar of the Lagos parish of Breadfruit
and star performer at Keswick, as his assistant and successor and called
a meeting in the delta on 1 January 1892, but he died just hours before
it was due to take place.

Unbendingly puritan on moral issues and strictly conservative
in matters theological, Holy Johnson was now the most prominent
African clergyman on the coast, but this model Christian also nursed
a fierce black pride, and he looked towards the day when a single
African-led church would emerge out of fragmented Protestantism.
When the parent committee decided that whites only would be
appointed as diocesan bishops, with each supported by two black
suffragans, Johnson interpreted the idea that Africans could reach no
higher than 'half bishop' as a calculated racial insult: 'The delta church
had long been familiar with the government of an African independent
Bishop, and as the late departed Bishop had carried on the work in our
midst so faithfully, laboriously and successfully we could not submit
to have a white Bishop or Assistant Native Bishop, which would be
a retrograde step, as there are natives competent to fill with credit and
honour the post now vacant.'[8]

When a yellow fever epidemic scythed through the expatriate
community, killing the new Bishop Hill and members of his staff, the
mission found itself in the worst of all possible worlds; indigenous church
leaders were alienated and many of the whites who were supposed
to take their place were either dead or repatriated. Of all the 'young
purifiers', only Henry Dobinson continued to work happily on the Niger
at Onitsha – and he now asked why Africans should not take charge of
their own affairs. 'If they feel equal to standing alone let us encourage
them to do so if they can.... Let us not stand in the way, but say God
bless you go on and prosper, we will go to new places and get ready
for a similar movement in future years.'[9]

When Dobinson was returning from home leave in 1896, he was
invited to preach at the evening service in Freetown Cathedral. As his
sermon neared its end, 'I appealed for a renewal of the old feeling of close
union which existed in Bishop Crowther's days, and said how sincerely
I regretted the sad events of 1890, when many men were misjudged, and
had greatly suffered in consequence. I hope my words may not be in
vain.'[10] Though Dobinson was being sharply reminded from London
that he was 'in no position to speak for the society', the *Lagos Echo*

urged fellow Africans that the time had come to 'overlook, forgive and forget the sad and painful past'.[11]

Politics and Religion in the Gold Coast (Ghana)
After the death of Henry Wharton in 1873, the Methodist home committee came into line with other societies and abandoned its policy of black leadership for its Gold Coast church. From that time, its declared policy was to promote Africans to all positions short of general superintendent, but, in practice, discrimination went deeper as policy issues were increasingly resolved within an all-white missionary committee. Meetings of the multiracial synod could be turbulent, and visiting Basel missionaries were taken aback at the temerity with which members questioned the decisions of senior pastors. The same yellow fever epidemic that killed Bishop Hill and his colleagues in Nigeria also devastated the Gold Coast, and with white ministers either dead or invalided home, the position of general superintendent passed to another young man who had not long finished his college training. Dennis Kemp would have preferred to work in a tidy environment, in which the land was owned by white settlers, and Africans accepted orders with proper deference. 'It is said that the British territory at the Gold Coast is not really a colony. Truer words were never written – nor sadder. We have not colonised, so much the worse for that country.'[12] In the pews below him sat doctors and lawyers – many able to trace their ancestry back to original Gold Coast Society for the Propagation of the Gospel (SPCK) members – who bitterly opposed the way that this young man was now importing racial intolerance into what had previously been a relatively colour-blind community. When a series of Kemp's proposals were voted down in Synod, he poured his frustration into a letter to the mission secretary:

> If after carefully considering what is really best in the interests of the work I decide on a certain line of action am I to be dictated to by a people who, after making all charitable allowances for brotherhood etc. are at best only half a century removed from heathenism and have precious small minds into the bargain? ... I feel I must have the authority or be relieved of the charge of the District.[13]

Tension grew when Samuel Solomon returned from England as an ordained minister to become editor of *The Gold Coast Methodist Times*.

After resuming his Fanti name of Attoh Ahuma, he politicised the paper, directing 'fiery indignation' at the way in which the Crown Lands Bill was transferring ownership of forests and minerals from the people to the colonial government. Ahuma held his ground when Kemp insisted that the paper must return to its religious agenda. 'We have been indoctrinated as to how a religious paper should be conducted,' he insisted. 'We do not intend to wrap up our religion for Sunday use only.'[14]

Despite Kemp's efforts, his Cape Coast Methodist community was, under his eyes, turning into a breeding ground for what was arguably the first modern group of African political activists. London-trained barrister J.E. Casely Hayford used columns of the *Cape Coast Leader* to thunder against the whole colonial system, which imposed taxation without representation. Why, he asked, had the government concentrated monarchical power in the hands of a governor when such a thing had been inconceivable at home since the Glorious Revolution of 1688? James Small – a man 'tall and stalwart and black as ebony' – was another activist. After he had been discharged from the army in 1896, he travelled to the United States and joined the black American Methodist Episcopal Zion (AMEZ) Church, from where he returned with the title of Bishop to Africa, carrying a message for his people: 'The claims of Africa on all Christians, and particularly on those whose ancestors came from the densely populated continent, are too great and too urgent to turn over to others. Zion has hoisted her banner over the great continent whose sons made one of the largest contributions to the world's earliest civilisations and she must see to it that the banner is never hauled down or lowered.'[15] Small managed to recruit the patriarch's son, ordained minister Thomas Freeman, Jr, to his cause. His words to the AMEZ's inaugural meeting at Cape Coast illustrate how far the family had now become politicised: 'This church composed of Africans and entirely governed and worked by Africans was indeed, "bone of our bone and flesh of our flesh", which would naturally take a much greater interest in their missions in the motherland than can be possible with any missionary boards and missionaries of an alien race, who are not above the colour question.'[16]

Attention was once again focused on the relative importance of primary schooling and further education. While Kemp argued that an educated nation could only be constructed from the bottom upwards, his black critics protested that arguments for the priority of primary schooling were merely a device for denying Africans any higher qualifications. After establishing its secondary school in Cape

Coast, the AMEZ Church made an agreement to send its ablest boys to African-American colleges. Under this scheme, the promising Emmanuel Kwegyir Aggrey would remain in America for twenty years before returning to his land with a passionate commitment to higher education and the moderate political views of an instinctive peacemaker.

The Prophet Harris

By the beginning of the twentieth century, only Liberia and Ethiopia in the whole of sub-Saharan Africa remained under black rule. Despite massive and sustained assistance of American churches across the denominational spectrum, the expectations that Liberia would prove a springboard for the spread of Christianity had been sadly disappointed. Of forty-eight Methodist churches and fourteen preaching stations, not one was more than 5 miles from a centre of colonisation, and large areas had no school or church of any kind.[17] One writer constructed an imaginary conversation between a young missionary, fresh out from America, and more experienced colleagues:

'It seems strange to think', John exclaimed, 'that while there are almost 1.5 million native Liberian tribesmen, there should be only some 50,000 citizens. Aren't the natives allowed any of the privileges of citizenship?'

'No,' said Dr Howell, 'that wouldn't be possible. The natives are untrained. They have very few rights, and very little power.'

'They greatly outnumber the citizens, it is true', said one of the other missionaries, 'but they are given only as much authority and as many privileges as they are prepared to use.'[18]

Unorthodox clergyman, politician and pan-African enthusiast Edmund Blyden went so far as to argue that the mass of Liberian people would be better off under British rule. Taking a cue from him, a middle-aged teacher from the episcopal mission, William Wadé Harris, was arrested in 1910 while trying to raise the Union Jack at Cape Palmas. While behind bars, he claimed to have heard the voice of Gabriel saying, 'You are not in prison. God is coming to anoint you. You will be a prophet.' So began an unorthodox but highly successful one-man missionary movement. Like the reincarnation of some Old Testament prophet, Harris crossed the border into French-controlled Ivory Coast in July 1913 wearing a loose calico gown, a black tape round his neck and a flat white hat on his head. Behind him were two white-robed women, who served the prophet as acolytes and – it was said – wives. The younger, Helen Valentine, came from a Christian family, while the older, Mary Pioka, was of pagan background. At that time, traditional structures of life were coming under strain as French soldiers imprisoned chiefs and stripped warriors of their weapons, and the prophet's simple deal struck a chord with a defeated and confused people: those who worked diligently, were temperate, did not steal and submitted to the orders of the authorities would receive their reward in a marvellous afterlife. Harris travelled across the country, preaching, healing, destroying traditional shrines – sometimes converting whole villages at one time – and referring converts 'to be baptised and instructed by the Catholic and Protestant men of God'. Up to that time, some twenty-five Lyons priests, sisters and lay brothers had worked eight stations with very little success; now they were confronted by flocks of converts. 'On Sunday I saw him at Jacqueville where he attended the parish mass with all his wives, accompanied by almost all of the population.... At the end of mass he came to see me accompanied by the elders of the village, in order to decide to construct a more spacious church.'[19] When the priests tried to explain that catechumens must spend years under instruction before baptism, the prophet led his converts off and baptised them himself.

As Harris crossed into the Gold Coast, this vision of an indigenous prophet contrasted sharply with mission-trained teachers, who wore formal coats, glazed collars and starched cuffs, and even members of the AMEZ Church could not miss the message that this prophet took no inspiration from abroad. Caseley Hayford was profoundly impressed: 'This is not a revival. It is a Pentecost. Its orbit is world wide ... Men, women and children are drawn as by his irresistible power. And when he has done with them, they find their way to the churches of their own accord and remain there. It fills one with awe to hear some of those converts pray.'[20]

Catholic and Protestant clergy, who had watched the prophet's progress with grave misgivings, put their doubts aside as they struggled to cope with the flood of converts. But when Harris returned to the Ivory Coast, followed by a small army of traders and clerks, the French colonial authorities grew increasingly concerned as Methodist hymns and tracts began to circulate, first in Fanti and English, then in the Ivory Coast's indigenous languages. Finally their nerves snapped.

William Wadé Harris was 'apprehended without respect, stripped of his sacred staff and had his beautiful robe replaced by a common loincloth'. After he and the two women had received beatings (from which Helen Valentine died), the French set about suppressing the whole movement. It is estimated that in just seventeen months, Harris had converted some 200,000 people, of whom more than half were from the Ivory Coast. Some would later return to traditional ways, and others found a home in Catholicism, but a significant underground movement did survive. As miraculous stories were told about the Prophet, his continuing church became a focus of popular resistance to French rule. As word spread that Christianity could be an indigenous faith, a variety of self-governing independent churches appeared in British, French and Belgian territories. The message had now penetrated that – at least in religion – Africans no longer needed to give unquestioned allegiance to their new white masters.

Southern Africa

Religion and Poverty
The American Board missionary in charge of the Groutville Station could summon little optimism when he sat down to prepare his report for the mission's 1887 annual meeting. Tenants were deep in debt after mortgaging their homes at exorbitant rates of interest: 'There is now almost no sugar land under cultivation. The mill has long been lying idle, and it is doubtful if it will ever start again. The most fertile of the land is now leased to coolies. The church building is in a ruinous condition and sadly needs repairing. The bell is broken beyond redemption and no money can be raised to make these needed repairs. These are sad facts.'[21] His colleague at Amanzuinitote told a similar story, reminding his brethren that 'we awaken the natives to the needs and desires of Christian civilisation and yet we cannot furnish them with the means of satisfying those desires'.[22] Not everyone felt the same way. As the CMS on the Niger was falling into the hands of 'young purifiers', other followers of Charles Grandeson Finney were making a bid for control of the American Board's South African operation, and in their opinion, problems of human privation ranked low beside key issues of church discipline, such as sex and alcohol. Nevertheless, economics were now the key issue in South Africa.

As Anglican Charles Johnson looked over his Zulu congregation, he wondered how many had eaten that day. 'Not half of them; but a native can go a long time fasting. They all put on their best clothes in honour of the day, and the bright colours looked well in the bright sun.'[23] The headmaster of Lovedale College reminded his pupils that it served no purpose to lay the blame on the Europeans. 'If the white men had not come, the yellow men would have been there, for no race could hope to retain possession of the land except by their complete utilisation of it.' At least one agricultural expert took issue with such facile judgements, noting that the new intensive farming was creating widespread environmental degradation: 'Judging generally and from the evidence of crops produced, I am of the opinion that the archaic Kaffir is the best all-round cultivator of South Africa.'[24]

Political power was now the naked servant of economic self-interest. In Natal, for instance, the 21 percent white population controlled 99 percent of the votes and 92 percent of the colony's land, while the average white income stood at £124. 9s. 6d., against £3 18s. 6d. for a rural African. The tribal regions of southern Africa were seen as a sponge, storing and releasing labour for the mining industries. 'A man cannot go with his wife and children and his goods and chattels into the labour market,' declared senior official Sir Godfrey Langden. 'He must have a dumping ground. Every rabbit has a warren where he can live and burrow and feed, and every native must have a warren.'[25] Lagden advised fellow whites to support missionary efforts to raise the quality of the labour force and dampen disaffection. Clergy of all stripes converged on the minefields, where, once inside the compounds, they averted their eyes from the exploitation that surrounded them and launched into the endless struggle against alcohol and sins of the flesh. A proposal that 'the churches should do nothing that might disturb existing wage structures' was passed unchallenged at the Petoria Board of Missions. While one delegate pointed out that 'cheap labour has enabled in South Africa many developments which otherwise would have been left untouched', a second argued that 'it is not the duty of the church to civilise the native into an expensive worker', and a third insisted that the church should do everything in its power to bring the Lord's teaching 'and that only' home to the native.

Within church buildings, segregation increasingly reflected that which was found in society at large. In 1890, the Anglican parish priest of St. Cyprian, Durban, announced that coloured and white children

could no longer sit together in Sunday school. Since classification
was made based on levels of skin pigmentation, children of the same
family could be assigned seats in different parts of the church, and those
designated as 'coloured' were excluded from the higher classes. Outraged
parents protested to the Provincial House of Bishops that classification
by race had no place in the House of God. The unanimous response
marked a milestone in one church's journey to appeasement.

> We disapprove of anything like caste in the church of God, and
> should be grieved indeed at any course of action likely to promote
> its growth, but we trust that no such sad result will arise from that
> which you have represented to us.
>
> You must remember that the 'many nations, and kindreds and
> tongues' which are gathered into the Church of God by Holy
> Baptism differ greatly in characteristics, antecedents and education,
> and that time is required for the operation of the Good Spirit of
> God, in breaking down prejudices, and uprooting pride as well as
> in raising the depressed, and levelling distinctions, that all may be
> one in Christ Jesus, our King and Priest unto God. And you must
> not condemn your Pastor because in a matter so delicate he cannot
> work in the way which you would wish, and which he himself
> would wish, but has to consider the feelings of others as well
> as your own.[26]

Racial compromise was not confined to mainstream denominations.
Pentecostal preacher John G. Lake imported southern US practice and
prejudice into his Apostolic Faith Mission of South Africa. At baptism,
whites entered the water first, followed by coloureds and finally blacks;
services were segregated and full church membership accorded only to
whites. When invited to address the full South African parliament, Lake
delivered a lecture on the desirability of racial separation and later
claimed credit for 'setting the South Africa's racial policy on a sound
path'. 'I framed the policy in harmony with our American policy of
segregation of the Indian tribes, having as an example the mistakes
of the United States and other nations in regard to their handling of
the Native question.... This policy as outlined by me, was practically
adopted by the Boer party *in toto*.'[27]

The Independent Churches

In May 1890, US Hampton Institute graduate Orpheus Myron McAdoo brought his singing group on a nineteen-month tour of South Africa, and black South Africans had difficulty figuring out these exuberant young people, who travelled the country with all the privileges usually reserved for whites.

> Their admiration for their American cousins must have been great, for on the day the troupe left town, one of the classic crowd was heard to say in the deep drawling style – 'We shall never again hear such splendid singing until we go to heaven.'[28]

As the visitors sang of black sorrows, black experience and black piety to music that drew deep from African tradition, they laid down a challenge to those whites who denigrated all 'primitive' art and culture. After the visitors had left, a growing number of black choirs lent power to a wave of religious revival that was already running across the country.

Although mainstream churches still ordained few black clergy, their missionaries continued to preach from the text 'Let Ethiopia hasten to stretch out her hands to God' and link this with the story of how the Ethiopian eunuch read the *Book of Isaiah* and accepted the truth from the Apostle.[29] Within their congregations, the concept of Ethiopianism had developed political and religious overtones that were fundamentally different from anything intended in the white teachers' sermons. News of the Abyssinian victory over invading Italians at Adawa was greeted with rejoicing, and disputes that might have started as no more than a clash of personalities quickly gathered momentum. Across the southern part of the continent, missionaries were taken by surprise as they found themselves facing schism. American Board ministers were powerless as 'even the elect' left the parent church. On the Rand, the Methodist M.M. Makone took followers into his Ethiopian Church, and white clergy protested that their flock was being led astray by a lethal combination of African nationalism and empty promises from the New World. 'He is taking black missionary from America instead of white missionary from England. That is all the difference. He turns English Methodism out of the door to bring Negro Methodism down the chimney. He bites the white hand that has ministered for so many years to his spiritual destitution and kneels to kiss the black hand.'[30]

With ideas carried by fluid labour movements between South and Central Africa, it did not take long before the remote and authoritarian Scot William Elmslie was confronting the same problem in Nyasaland.

A vain fellow of the Ethiopian persuasion had been stirring up trouble around Ekwendeni and felt himself a match for Dr Elmslie. He wrote a long and laboured epistle, finishing with the triumphant challenge, 'Answer if you can.' No answer being received, he ventured to call on the doctor to complete his victory.

'What do you think of my letter?' he asked with impudent conceit.

'A piece of confounded impertinence', was the reply. 'Get out of here.' And the doctor rose to his full height threateningly.

'Oh, but-but', stammered the discomfited Ethiopian, as he hurriedly backed to the door, 'I did not wish to confound you.' There you have the spirit of it, mischievous childishness more than anything else, the natural conceit of a half-trained mind.[31]

This 'vain fellow' was probably local man Elliot Kamwana; after being trained by the Scots, he had moved to South Africa, where he came on the teachings of the Watch Tower Bible and Tract Society – later to be Jehovah's Witnesses. Kamwana's Watch Tower movement would remain largely separate from the American parent stem, to become – after only the Catholics – the largest Christian group in Northern Rhodesia (Zambia).

Protestant clergy in southern Africa – like the reformers before them – quickly discovered that, once the vernacular Bible was in the hands of 'common people', nobody could control how it was interpreted. Few missionaries had troubled converts with the disturbing images that were locked away in the last book of the Bible; now, as Africans faced their own apocalypse, African Christians concluded that the Book of Revelation must contain hidden messages from God. Missionaries who had thundered against polygamy also failed mention that the Old Testament patriarchs had all been polygamists. Missionaries, who had taught that every word of the Bible was the inspired word of God, now had to explain that a new dispensation had replaced the old and rules that might have applied to ancient Hebrews could have no place in a more-enlightened world.

Scholars have unravelled varied strands of the beliefs and practices that influenced different branches of the independence movement.[32] At one pole were churches that still sang from the old hymn books and remained faithful to the doctrines and practices of the mother church. At the other extreme were bodies that could not properly be called Christian. Between these two extremes lay the majority that imported some elements of traditional religion and laid a greater or lesser degree of emphasis on spiritual healing and on the casting out of evil spirits. After coming under pressure from indigenous churches, some missionaries understood that the old outright rejection of African culture needed re-examination. Some got the process embarrassingly wrong: if Africans had an inbuilt need to dance, they argued, and traditional movements were too sexually suggestive for Christian use, then it would do least harm for black children to be taught Scottish country dancing.

Rebellion

African scholar Margery Perham would later liken the Zulu nation to a steam engine that had been derailed and lay on its side, with all its latent power intact; the white population could not feel safe until that 'latent power' was neutralised. Settlers reserved their most unrelenting hatred for mission Africans, who nursed aspirations above their station and led their simpler brethren away from the path of unquestioning obedience. Although well accustomed to being howled down in public meetings, the old bishop's daughter Harriette Colenso continued to confront the vicious hysteria that she saw rising all around her, feeding information to the Exeter Hall lobby in London through a brother in London. When she became convinced that these letters were being opened by the authorities before leaving the country, she hid the information within a private family code.[33]

The hysteria soon escalated to violence. In 1905, an official (who had a history of violent racist behaviour) ordered his police to open fire on a Zulu crowd which had gathered to protest against the collection of a new poll tax. When the fighting died down, he was found dead, along with one policeman and two protestors. The ensuing investigation revealed that independent Presbyterian Church members had been involved in the riot, and fifteen of them were shot in retribution while others were sentenced to twenty years in prison. Troops rode through the country, killing all who offered the smallest resistance. White fury rose to fever pitch when it emerged that the London government had reacted to Colenso family lobbying by commuting all death sentences.[34]

Initially anxious to be identified as part of the white rather than the black population, young lawyer – now sergeant major – M.K. Gandhi led a party of twenty-five Indian stretcher bearers to the conflict-torn region. The future world leader described how his non-violent philosophy was forged out of his experiences in Natal. 'I then believed that the British Empire existed for the welfare of the world. A genuine sense of loyalty prevented me from ever wishing ill to the Empire. The rightness or wrongness of the "rebellion" was therefore not likely to affect my decision. . . . I considered myself a citizen of Natal.' He was shocked to discover the extent of white disrespect for African life, for, after nurses had refused to tend wounded Zulus, 'the white soldiers used to peep through the railings that separated us from them and tried to dissuade us from attending to the wounds'.[35] Once again black church mentors found themselves caught between the warring parties. While whites insisted that they, the African Christians, had fomented the whole uprising, their people despised them as loyalist traitors. While many Christians died alongside the traditionalist rebels, it seems likely that at least as many fought on the government side. Colenso opposed violence on the grounds that tribal armies were helpless against modern weapons; instead she urged those who had a grievance to prepare their case carefully and rely on the processes of law.

The Chilembwe Rising

In Melbourne, Australia, a heckler one day challenged street preacher Joseph Booth to sell all his possessions and go to preach to the heathen. Responding literally, he disposed of his business and left with his nine-year-old daughter Emily to set up an independent mission in the Shire Highlands of Nyasaland. When money ran low, he first joined the London-based Zambezi Industrial Mission and then the Seventh Day Adventists, before finally settling down with the Seventh Day Baptists. Booth's style of ministry presented a sharp contrast to that of the Auld Kirk *dominees* in Blantyre.

Candidly now, is it not a marvellous picture to see elegantly robed men, at some hundreds of pounds yearly cost, preaching a gospel of self-denial to men and women slaves, with only a very scrap of goat skin round their loins, compelled to work hard for six, but more often seven, days a week.... I have never felt so utterly ashamed of myself and my fellow countrymen as I have since coming here. Either we ought to stop spreading the Gospel or conform to its teaching amid such a needy cloud of witnesses as Central Africa presents.[36]

Not content to criticise colonial society, Booth actively worked to subvert it. He infuriated the Scots by paying his workers at above the market rate and encouraged those with potential to set up their own stations. Daughter Emily would later remember the impression that family servant John Chilembwe made on her young mind:

He had a great desire to learn to read and write, and to gain the truths of Christianity. Being a cook-boy was only a means to an end. While neither his cooking nor his English were astonishing in their perfection, they served both our needs and his.... Without his faithfulness I doubt very much if I could have survived.... A sick little girl could have been a great hindrance – but John was there.[37]

Booth sent Chilembwe to be trained for the ministry in an African-American college, and he returned 'a full-blown, round-collared, long-coated "Reverend" of the regulation type', and over the following years, his Providence Industrial Mission (PIM) prospered with financial and personnel support from black American Baptists. Settler concern grew as mission outstations began to draw in labourers who worked on their own ever-expanding holdings. To the north-east of Blantyre lay massive estates that had been built up by David Livingstone's son-in-law, mission director and businessman, Alexander Bruce. After Bruce's death, management of his vast estate passed to the great explorer's distant relative William Livingstone, and few disputed that Bruce Estate workers were exploited. When Chilembwe drew attention to this 'wicked abuse of power', and Livingstone retaliated by burning every PIM church on Bruce land.

Undeterred, Chilembwe continued to speak out. When large numbers of his church members were conscripted into the army on the outbreak of war in 1914, he responded by issuing a public manifesto: 'Let the rich man, bankers, titled men, storekeepers, farmers and landlords go to war and get shot. Instead the poor Africans who have nothing to own in this present world, who in death, leave only a long line of widows and orphans in utter want and dire distress are invited to die for a cause that is not theirs.'[38] Catholic fathers warned that an uprising was imminent, but nobody in authority was inclined to take the danger seriously. They should have done so. William Livingstone was killed on a Saturday night, and his head was displayed next day during Sunday service in Chilembwe's church. Rebels then mounted a surprise assault on a Catholic mission; after pausing to sing Protestant hymns in the church, they set fire to the thatch – unintentionally killing an orphan child – and left the only priest in residence for dead.

White men forgot their own differences in the face of this black peril, as German prisoners of war helped in the hunt for rebels and Portuguese soldiers patrolled the border to ensure that none could escape into Mozambique. Chilembwe died in action, and his fine church was levelled to the ground; those caught under arms were summarily shot, while others stood trial for treason. They faced their judges with defiance, quoting the Bible, 'Go to, ye rich men, howl and weep for the miseries that shall come upon you'.[39] The Scots were gravely embarrassed to discover that Chilembwe's second in command John Kufa had formerly been a respected elder at Blantyre. After recording the horrors in her diary, American Mary Bannister of the Churches of Christ took space to note the assault on tender missionary sensibilities. 'Six more of our teachers have been taken prisoner. I am so sorry for them all.... Flogging of prisoners goes on just the same. I do think they might have some consideration for us and punish them outside the place. A European ought not to be allowed to stay in a place like this. Sundays of all days is the worst.'[40]

The ageing Booth and three Americans were expelled from southern Africa, but in the court of white settler opinion, all missionaries should properly have been held responsible for creating a class of educated blacks with ideas above their station. For their part, Africans told their children that John Chilembwe would one day return to free his people from oppression.

Chapter 12
Keep the Flag Flying

Protestants and Catholics in Southern Nigeria

By 1880, the Scots of the United Free Church had become hopelessly
bogged down in the immediate neighbourhood of Calabar. From home,
journal editors begged missionaries in the field to send stories of heathen
excesses, like those that had rallied such support in the early days, but life
had somehow settled into normality and little newsworthy incidents
seemed to happen. Recruit Mary Slessor, who had learnt her religion
in the revivalist school, quickly lost patience with her colleagues'
methodical ways. After her superiors had tried in vain to break her
restless spirit – going so far as to lock her for days in a shed without
food – they finally allowed her to open her own station upriver among
the Okoyong. Never questioning the grounds of her own authority, she
dispensed a rough and ready discipline, under which a chief could receive
a cuff round the ear or a smack from her umbrella, and a man drinking
alcohol might be thrown to the ground and separated from his bottle.
When rival chiefs argued out an issue that might have ended in war, she
would sit between them, silently knitting for as long as it took emotions
to settle. Most important, she successfully promoted the Okoyong's right
to trade directly with the European ships, and in the end, the title *eka
kpukpro owo* (mother of all the people) was both given and received
with affection.

Even as Mary Slessor was consolidating her upriver work, barely
20 miles to the east, German soldiers were winning control over the
headwaters of the Efik River – thereby cutting Calabar traders' main
link to the interior. At the same time, some 150 miles to the west,
established African traders from the port of Brass on the Niger delta
were struggling to defend their palm-oil trade on the main river
against intruders from France and Britain. Around 1877, George
Taubman Goldie had systematically set about eliminating all those in
competition with his own National (later Royal) Africa Company –
buying out the French and, where necessary, starving out the Africans.
At this time, however, the 100 miles of coast that separated the Cross
and Niger rivers remained a colonial no-man's land. Scots missionaries

urged their consul to act boldly and bring the area under effective British control. In 1888, humanitarian consciences were eased when Scottish army soldier and pillar of the kirk Claude Macdonald was appointed British Commissioner for the Niger Coast Protectorate. Aware of Mary Slessor's reputation, he advised his young officers to call in at her new station in Ibibio country to draw on her insights into humane imperialism:

> If you can discriminate between fear and stubbornness you have won half the battle.... If you try to put yourself into these ignorant, besotted, cowed Ibibios' shoes you will see how much more likely they are to fear you than to give themselves over at once. Have patience. They are deceitful as a race, but I have many true and intelligent friends among them everywhere *and so shall you. Trust them and have patience.*[1]

When Macdonald appointed Mary Slessor as – reputedly the British Empire's first ever – woman magistrate, she used her position to promote the cause of women's rights. Three cases illustrate the complaints that came before her and the decisions that she handed down.

> Found guilty of brawling in market and taking by force 8 rods from a women's basket. *One month's hard labour.*
> Chasing a girl into the bush with intent to injure. *One month's hard labour.*
> Seizing a woman in the market. Chaining her for 14 days by neck and wrists. Throwing *mbiam* with intent to kill should she reveal it to white men. *Sentenced to six months' hard labour, and to be sent back on expiry of sentence to pay costs.*[2]

Most surprisingly, this ageing Scots lady developed an intense relationship with a colonial servant who was some thirty years her junior. Her uninhibited letters provide an insight into one missionary's conflicting attitudes and emotions at a time when colonial warfare was sweeping across the countryside. On the one hand she detested the punitive expeditions that passed her station, protesting especially bitterly when the British authorities offered policemen a bounty of £10 for every captive they brought in. 'And so the dogs of war were let loose on these poor villages with the result that there has been a reign of terror, every

chief insulted chained and tied up, women and men ... beaten and kept
in hunger and fear, the villages plundered clean of everything, and
all the time I had to wait and bear it, knowing that the DC [District
Commissioner] had given the order.'³ At the same time, she was anxious
to assist the consolidation of British rule by every means within her
power, and she gave her beloved boy strict maternal advice that he must
never travel in Ibibio country without a maxim gun.

* * *

The Macdonald regime turned out to be just a brief respite from
the brutal reality of conquest. By forcing Africans out of the Niger
trade, Goldie's company brought starvation to the delta, and the
London government recorded that his agents displayed 'an indifference
to African life which is the worst possible recommendation for an
extension of their power over new and more populous regions'.⁴
Many Africans died in jail, while others lost the will to live in forced
labour camps. Along the coast, Protestant missionaries enthusiastically
supported 'punitive expeditions' against the Western Ibo, the ancient
kingdom of Benin, the Yoruba Ijebu and the Efik Long Juju before
following the victorious armies into the conquered regions. The Scots
started at last to move inland from Calabar, Anglicans branched out
from their bases at Lagos and Abeokuta, Primitive Methodists based
operations on the delta and Ulster Presbyterians built stations on the
Qua Ibo River.⁵ They settled among a defeated and demoralised
people, given the choice of adjusting to the white men's ways or
perishing. As members of the wider community suffered conquest,
missionaries concentrated on the manageable task of defending the life
and liberty of their converts.

Goldie was still operating in competition with a number of smaller
French concerns, and Bishop Crowther still worked on the river from
his headquarters in Onitsha, with his authority as yet unchallenged,
when a lamentably prepared party of Holy Ghost Fathers landed at
Onitsha. Even after Crowther had received them courteously, none
of these Spiritians could understand how an African could have been
elevated to such high office. The old bishop, they decided, was clearly
'a poor soul, naturally innocent ... for how could he have distinguished
between right and wrong?'⁶ Without further ado, their leader Joseph
Lutz began to follow the order's traditional strategy in Africa, buying
slave children and decorating his makeshift church with lanterns

designed to entice the sick and outcasts into his *chrétienté*. But with medicines scarce and conditions appalling, life expectancy for the Spiritian priests and nuns was short; after surviving an unparalleled ten years on the river, Lutz was invalided home, with little achieved. With a huge red beard and hands that seemed better suited to holding a sword than a pen, his successor Joseph Lejeune appeared to be some kind of throw-back to his Norman crusading ancestors, but he did set about changing the traditional Holy Ghost mission policy. 'Slavery will never be abolished by the purchasing of slaves', he declared, 'but by evangelisation itself'. Instead of building communities of those excluded from society, he borrowed the White Father strategy of targeting the region's most influential chiefs. Lejeune was on his station when the British government bought out Goldie's interest and brought the Niger under direct imperial rule – but he refused to budge. Soon, administrative officers were complaining that the tricolour still hung over Holy Ghost stations. Lejeune gave no quarter to any who asked for a move into French territory. 'Leave your station? Never! I say *Never!* Keep the flag flying, *mon enfant.* The angels are on our side. The good God knows our sacrifices. One day he will give us victory. Fight on! I will never surrender to Satan a single foot of land we have gained for Christ.'[7]

It fell to Catholic magistrate Sir James Marshall to negotiate a solution. He submitted the case to Lejeune's superiors that 'because of the rivalry between the French and English, it is absolutely necessary to have English priests only in this territory'.[8] But although the Holy Ghost Fathers had no presence in England, they did in Ireland, and the Irish were still UK citizens. Joseph Shanahan duly arrived on the river in 1902, and when Lejeune was finally invalided home, French and Alsatian colleagues were outraged to hear that this young Irishman had been appointed mission superior over their heads.

Shanahan was impatient to confront the Protestants and prepared for battle by first putting his own operation in order, distributing regular doses of quinine and setting about building healthy living quarters. Although the Protestants had a long lead over their Catholic rivals, Shanahan could not miss the fact that his rivals were widely unpopular. The Anglicans, in particular, had also been seriously damaged by events on the Niger that ended in the public humiliation of Bishop Crowther. All white missionaries were also correctly seen as agents of white rule. Even in the old bad-company times, the CMS parent committee had instructed their agents that 'loyal obedience was due from all in the mission to the government, as the appointed representative power of the Crown, so that the presence of missionaries might be no embarrassment to the rulers'.[9] The hated company had gone, but one white man looked much like another to African eyes, and past sins remained unforgiven. For their part, the Irish priests and nuns, who had been reared on eyewitness accounts of the Great Famine, had no difficulty in identifying with the resentments of a conquered people. Consumed by their hatred of anything English, Shanahan's growing band of Irish workers exploited every opportunity to win back those Africans who had been 'lured into heresy'. With the backing of a growing band of catechists, they set about harnessing political discontent and emotional deprivation in their church's interests. Overwhelmed by this new popish threat, the Primitive Methodist Superintendent begged for reinforcements to help turn the Irish tide:

> I'm prepared to fight them with clenched fist and bite if need be like a bulldog.... We could have jogged along easily if they had kept their filthy hands off our territory. They are warriors I tell you. They are here not to save men but to defeat us and they will have a perfect and delirious delight in wrecking our peace.... Now if a Roman Catholic goes the first thing he does is to purchase a demijohn of rum and give all a drink. Then he makes other presents, eats their food and sleeps in their house at night, talks all kinds of lies about his power with the Government and there you are. He has his ends achieved.[10]

Most significantly for the long term, Shanahan recognised that, ever since Crowther's time, the Protestants had failed to address the growing African aspiration for western education, and he laid plans to establish a lead that the Protestants would never be able to win back. In common with other colonial administrations, the British rulers were anxious to fill the gaps in clerical and technical skills that were becoming ever more obvious within its new colony, and Shanahan instructed his workers to help improve the situation: 'Collaborate with all your power and where it is impossible for you to carry on both the immediate task of evangelisation and your educational work, neglect your churches in order to improve your schools.'[11]

It helped greatly that Catholics were not targeting individuals but whole communities. Shanahan's biographer described how the Catholics brought education to Ibibio country and beyond:

The impact of the school on paganism cannot be overstated. The whole town became interested because it was *their* school, built by *their* labour and engaged in training *their* children. The fathers never begged to take a school *please*; they just pointed out that it was a wonderful favour to have one and that if the people wanted it, they would have to build and support it, and if they refused, they would be laughed at by other towns for their backwardness.[12]

Joseph Shanahan would later be consecrated bishop, though his African career ended sadly when a Mother Superior from one of his orders lodged a complaint for sexual harassment against him. Even so, as he sailed home in disgrace, few questioned the scale of his achievement in making the Catholic Church a serious player in the affairs of South-Eastern Nigeria.

Government, Church and Islam

The Western Sudan
South of the Sahara Desert lay a belt of grassland that stretched from Senegal in the west to the borders of Ethiopia in the east, which was then all known as the Sudan (Soudan). Inside this area, a latitudinal boundary could be drawn – then known as the Fashoda Line – where the flat grasslands met with hilly country. To the north, the population was solidly Muslim; to the south lived the tribal people, most of whom still followed traditional beliefs. For centuries, Muslim raiders had crossed the border from north to south to plunder slaves, who would face a terrible journey on foot across the Sahara Desert to North Africa.

Ever since the beginning of the modern missionary movement, evangelicals had argued that it should be easier to convert Muslims, who had already taken the first step out of darkness, than pagans, who remained sunk in deepest darkness. For the better part of a century, therefore, missionaries had been struggling to break into this huge area. They had first sailed up the west-coast rivers in an attempt to reach the headwaters of the Niger, and then, when this proved impractical, they had explored the lower Niger and the distant Nile. By the end of the nineteenth century, every attempt to penetrate the mysterious Sudan had failed and some ninety million people still managed to survive in the area without the assistance of a single missionary. Within the millenarian community, word even passed that this vast un-evangelised region formed the greatest single obstacle in the way of Christ's second coming.[13]

By the end of the old century, Fulani rulers of Western Sudan had good cause to feel uneasy. As the French converged on Lake Chad in the north-east, the West African Frontier Force – now commanded by experienced empire-builder Frederick Lugard – was finishing the tasks of subduing southern Nigeria and gathering to move north of Lokoja. George Goldie, who was not renowned for piety, accepted the chair of a new Hausa Association, which was given a brief 'to carry on the work begun by the late John Alfred Robinson, by providing a scholarly study of the Hausa language, with a view to promoting the higher interests of that people, and of translating the Scriptures and other appropriate literature into their tongue'.[14] After making his case for a grant before the committee, John Robinson's younger brother Charles duly arrived in Lokoja – but the longer he stayed, the less he found that the Hausa people matched up to his dead brother's expectations: 'The discouraging thing about these Hausas is that, although they are outwardly more civilised than perhaps any other people in Central Africa, the civilisation they have would almost seem to have degraded them.'[15]

Back in England, however, he chose to deliver the old message that the region was ripe for conversion, and Bishop Tugwell decided to mount a more-ambitious expedition from clergy already working in his own Nigerian diocese. Communication would be greatly helped by the fact that the young Walter Miller was already a fluent Hausa speaker. By the time that they arrived at Lokoja in 1899, Lugard was already preparing his advance on the northern emirates, and he strongly recommended that they should go no further. Tugwell brushed the soldier's warnings aside – as also later those of the Emir of Zaria, who urged that going on to Kano would be dangerous. 'I am feeling exceedingly happy about our prospects', he declared. 'I think and believe we shall have a time of much blessing in Kano.'[16] His confidence was ill-founded. As soon as they entered the city, he and his party were imprisoned, while the Emir, his Waziri and some forty leading citizens debated their fate. Most supported the Emir's proposal that these strangers should be executed immediately, but the Waziri urged caution on the grounds that any killing of white men would surely provoke reprisals. After executing a Kano citizen who was adjudged to have greeted the foreigners too warmly, the Emir expelled the white men from his city. On the return journey they found that the gates of Zaria were also closed against them: 'After six years of waiting and then four and one-half months marching, tramp, tramp, sleeping at nights in huts, bush, upon the desert, night after night, at last we reached our destination so longed for, only to be kicked out. You cannot think what it meant, and now we are kicked out of Zaria and are practically fugitives, without home and living from day to day, never knowing what the next will bring.'[17]

They got no sympathy from Lugard, who exploded with rage, furious at the thought that imperial policy should be driven by a group of impetuous young men, who had taken it on themselves to court disaster. The Waziri had been right; had the missionaries been executed, Lugard would have felt compelled to restore the myth of white invincibility by mounting a major punitive expedition. In the event, he won control over the northern emirates in his own time with little bloodshed. For all his close encounter with death, Tugwell could now rejoice in the benefits that must flow from colonial rule:

> For many years earnest prayers have ascended from the lips of God's people that doors to these countries might be opened. Thank God their prayers have been answered, and the door stands now, not ajar, but wide open. Oppression, tyranny and the slave trade have received, we believe, their death blow, and an oppressed people is now free. But where is the army of occupation? The British force is in effective occupation; but what of the army of the Church of Christ?[18]

Even as Tugwell was summoning an army of occupation, American faith missionaries were independently laying down plans for converting Western Sudan. Canadian evangelist Albert Simpson was first converted by the preaching of Henry Grattan Guinness. After settling in New York, he established his own college where he taught his own four-fold gospel of 'Jesus our Saviour, Sanctifier, Healer and coming King'. Following Guinness' example, he set up a faith mission to the Congo, where his workers would demonstrate their faith in Jesus as healer in an absolutely literal manner. With the use of medicines forbidden, workers in other societies wrote home describing how they gave help to starving and

fever-ridden Simpson missionaries, before – predictably – the
whole operation collapsed in failure. In common with his Catholic
contemporary Augustin Planque, Albert Simpson could shrug off losses
like a general sending troops into battle, and it was not long before
he announced that he would next target the Western Sudan. Students
in New York sang his rallying hymn:

> Christ is coming to the dark Soudan,
> That lies by the Niger's shore,
> And the glory of the Son of man
> O'er its valleys and its plains shall pour,
> Land of deepest, darkest heathen night,
> Thou shalt yet be called the Land of Light;
> And in that millennial morn so bright
> Africa's sons at last shall weep no more.[19]

He planned that this next party of young people would follow the
difficult – even if apparently the most direct – route up the rivers of
Sierra Leone, across the Guinea watershed, to the headwaters of the
River Niger. They left America ill-prepared and poorly supplied – when
they unpacked a 'great saw' intended for cutting planks, they discovered
that all its teeth had been worn away before it had ever been packed.
Relying only on God and still eschewing all medicines, they doggedly
pushed on, preaching as they went that Jesus would soon return to judge
the world. As the pathfinders died or were invalided home, Simpson sent
out more to take their place. But when they finally reached the great river
they discovered that they could go no further. All had expected that they
might find the way forwards blocked by Muslim fanatics, but none had
anticipated that French officials would stop their journey forwards.

* * *

Nevertheless, other North Americans remained determined to break into
Sudan. One was Roland Bingham, an Englishman living in Canada. When
his father died in Sussex, England, his mother had struggled to raise
a large family on receipts from a tobacconist's shop. By the age of fifteen,
Roland was already lecturing her and the other family members on the
sin of making a living from the sale of such a wicked drug, and soon
afterwards – having made himself unwelcome at home – he emigrated
to Canada and started preaching his own millennial message in country

farm houses. On his travels, he met a young Canadian, Walter Cowans, who had studied in Simpson's college and still nursed ambitions to 'throw his own lance for his master' in Western Sudan. Finally joined by Thomas Kent, they somehow managed to scrape together money for a passage to Africa and, in 1893, disembarked in Lagos without funds or tropical equipment. Experienced churchmen urged them to return home: 'Young men, you will never see the Sudan; your children will never see the Sudan; your grandchildren may.'[20] Undeterred, the raw evangelists managed to get as far as Zaria, where both Cowans and Kent died. Roland Bingham returned alone to Canada, deeply puzzled by the ways of providence.

> My faith was shaken to the very foundation. First I had gone out, as I thought, trusting in the promises of healing that seemed plain, clear and explicit in the Bible, and yet I had left buried in the Sudan two of the most faithful Christians whom I had ever met.... It did not occur to me that my interpretation of the promises had been mistaken. Was the Bible merely an evolution of human thought, even biased thought, or was it a divine revelation?[21]

After a fruitless second trip, Roland Bingham returned to Nigeria a third time in 1900, and at last made a significant and unexpected advance. On his journey up-country, he met an army doctor, Ronald Ross, who had recently discovered the causes of malaria by uncovering the parasite's lifecycle within the body of the anopheles mosquito. Ross was a pious man, and as the two men sat together discussing the relationship of science, religion and disease, he managed to get over his message that, since science was a gift from God, every Christian had to take its findings seriously. To Simpson's eternal disgust, Bingham managed to absorb this new information into his rigid theology, and once convinced, he made it an inflexible rule that every worker on his newly established mission – the Sudan Interior Mission (SIM) – must take a daily prophylactic dose of quinine. Results were instantaneous. 'The death of Miss Clothier at Patigi was the last death from malaria on our Nigerian field. With our missionary force growing in the intervening thirty years until our permanent field staff now numbers almost four hundred, it can be seen what a tremendous debt we owe to science.'[22]

The SIM remained desperately short of money, but Bingham ensured that penury at headquarters need not inhibit expansion in the field by holding his recruits responsible for securing direct backing from their home churches. Converts lived to a strict regime, under which the consumption of tea and coffee brought rebuke and anything more serious evoked instant dismissal from communion. In common with millenarians before and since, Bingham placed little emphasis on the development of language skills or the study of African ways. Personally much attracted by the philosophy of the Plymouth Brethren, his mission increasingly assumed the character of a sect – to the extent that members of the neighbouring faith-based evangelicals of the Sudan United Mission (SUM) complained that they had more chance of sharing communion with Catholics than they did with Roland Bingham's SIM.[23]

After painful experiences with warring clergy in Uganda, Lugard had not the smallest intention of allowing Christians free rein to disrupt government within this newest part of the British Empire, and he forbade any kind of evangelical contact between missionaries and Muslims. Although Bishop Tugwell's fluent Hausa-speaker, Walter Miller, returned to establish the CMS headquarters in the partially Islamic city of Zaria, and some societies placed clinics and leprosy settlements on the grasslands as a symbol of the day when the Muslim lands would once again be open, the prohibition against evangelism remained in force through the whole period of British rule. Their main effort was concentrated to the south of the 'Fashoda line' where missionaries from a wide variety of societies planned to construct a *cordon sanitaire* to prevent any further southwards expansion of Islam. In practice, though, however eagerly Christians may have anticipated the arrival of British rule, the event turned out to be a disappointment. Those who had waited for the day when hated 'Fulani tyrants' would fall, could only watch as Muslim power became formalised and even reinforced, and the influence of Islam kept moving southwards.

Public-school-educated administrators in the northern cities were generally more comfortable playing polo with the sons of emirs than socialising with the clergymen who officiated at expatriate services and kept themselves away from white men's social clubs. Walter Miller believed that government policy was now being driven by British race and class attitudes, which were inhibiting the long-term development of Northern Nigeria.

> The majority of men who run the Civil Service ... have an
> instinctive leaning towards old families, good blood, good

manners, patriarchal-type rule of peasantry; are in fact middle class with a certain amount of snobbery. Following this instinct in Nigeria, power has been given to picturesque but often useless rulers, and concentrated in their hands, so that what was a very uncertain and unstable authority before our advent has been endowed with all the additional dignity and executive strength of the supreme authority – the British. In the North, consequent stagnation is general.[24]

At the time when Miller made this judgement, the Islamic emirates of Northern Nigeria had changed remarkably little from a century earlier, when explorers like Clapperton and Lander had travelled that way. Communication by road remained poor, not even the most skeletal system of health provision had been put in place, and primary and secondary education were both sketchy to non-existent.[25] When British rule ended in 1960, Northern Nigeria still lacked an indigenous educated class that could provide a sound base for independent government.

The Eastern Sudan

The vital link between Western and Eastern Sudan would remain severed as long as the Mahdi army continued to control the headwaters of the Nile, which is why, in 1898, Catholic and Protestant missionaries alike took such a keen interest in the progress of Major General Horatio Herbert Kitchener's combined British and Egyptian expeditionary force as it progressed up the Nile to confront the Mahdist forces, led by al-Khalifa Abdullahi. By the end of Friday, 2 September, more than 10,800 men lay dead on the plains of Omdurman – of which just forty-eight were Egyptian and British soldiers from Kitchener's army. Two days later, as many of the wounded still lay alive where they had fallen, Kitchener gathered his officers and men for a Sunday service of thanksgiving on the spot where General Gordon had died. After hymns and prayers, army chaplains of different denominations took turns to offer thanks for victory. With the 'fanatical dervishes' safely defeated, missionaries anticipated that they would be free at last to carry their message up the Nile and across the eastern grasslands. Like Lord Lugard to the west, however, British administrator Sir Evelyn Baring had other ideas. After receiving reports that young British evangelicals were fomenting trouble by preaching in the streets, and even the mosques, of Cairo, he determined that the process of restoration must not be compromised by religious confrontation. Catholics and Protestants were appalled to discover that a Christian government now planned to block 'the direct proclamation of Jesus Christ to all the races inhabiting the upper basis of the Nile'.[26] Anglican Bishop Gwynne – who, as a young man, had played professional football at centre forward for both Derby County and Nottingham Forest – listened aghast as Baring laid out government policy at a public dinner. 'It seemed to me at the time as if someone had smacked my face in public, only much more than that, it was as if He whom I serve was dishonoured at that table.... In my garden under the palm trees with the stars glistening above the trembling branches I poured out my soul, the despair and sorrow of it.'[27]

For a time it appeared that the rules were relaxing: Anglicans were allowed to build a cathedral in Omdurman to serve the growing expatriate population, and others were permitted to open medical and educational work with Muslims – on the strict condition that they had permission from the head of the household. But committed missionaries were always tempted to stretch the rules; Gwynne's medical colleague recorded with delight that two women had discussed religion with his wife while waiting for a consultation and an American Presbyterian started giving clandestine Bible teaching to Muslim children. A reaction was inevitable. The mission schools emptied within days when the chief Imam of Omdurman's great mosque thundered against Muslim men who had allowed their children to attend Christian schools and threatened that any man who failed to remove his children would be excommunicated and automatically divorced from his wives. Baring and Kitchener had other plans to 'lift their new colony out of ignorance'. Missionaries on the upper river would provide 'a certain number of trained artisans, carpenters, blacksmiths, etc., who in addition to the knowledge of their trade, should have a moderate knowledge of reading, writing and very simple arithmetic'.[28] At the same time, two colleges, based on the model of English public schools, would provide advanced studies to high-status Muslims. The Gordon Memorial College in Khartoum was a government institution, while the other – 'the Princes' College' at Wau – was entrusted to the Verona Fathers. To the evangelicals' fury, the government funded Muslim teachers of Arabic and the Islamic faith in both institutions. Here, the sons of Mahdist leaders – including no fewer than twenty of al-Khalifa Abdullahi's children – were trained to take up posts within the colonial administration and other responsible positions in public life.

As the modern country of Sudan established its identity on the Nile, so the name fell out of use to describe the larger geographical area in the continental interior. Sudan Political Service recruiters in London followed a policy of selecting gifted sportsmen from the old universities who in student days may even have run with those 'heavies' who enjoyed breaking up revivalist meetings. Like colleagues in Northern Nigeria, most were uncomfortable in the presence of missionaries, but surprisingly at ease with high-status Muslims, who kept their distance, never questioned their cultural values and had no wish to copy the white man's ways. In 1914, the governor general defended the administration's record before many Sudanese notables.

> God is my witness that we have never interfered with any man in the exercise of his religion. We have brought the Holy Places within a few days journey of Khartoum. We have subsidised and assisted the men of religion. We have built and given assistance for the building of new mosques all over the country. Finally the Kadis and others have received a free and thorough education in the Koran and in the tenets of the Mohammedan religion.[29]

The administration's concern that missionaries should not be let loose to behave as they wished was not without foundation. Those who question whether the stereotype of missionaries going out into the bush, without language skills or interpreters, to preach in a language that nobody could understand, has any foundation are answered by the account of Bishop Gwynne's expedition into Dinka country in 1905. When the Bishop suggested that his missionary party of millennial Anglicans should build a permanent mission station that would stand as a beacon of faith and civilisation in a pagan world, his younger companions rejected the idea outright. The missionary commandment stated that the gospel should be preached in every land – not that it should be preached in a comprehensible language. In the following weeks, Dinka tribes people tried to fathom out why shabby and half-starved white men, who had no apparent home, were trying to address them in a foreign language. After all the young hotheads had been invalided home, Gwynne could only abandon the project in disgust. Blame for the failure was, of course, apportioned to the Dinka: 'The mental capacity of a Denka [sic] at the present moment is very small and full of cow and corn. He cannot listen for more than a few moments and when you make him tell you back what you have told him he then asks for some corn or tobacco because hunger is hurting.'[30]

By the time the European war broke out in 1914, the time of mass conversion in southern Sudan still lay in the future, but the division of the country into mutually hostile northern and southern regions was already well advanced.

Kenya

Land and Labour

It is said that, after he had assumed authority as the first president of an independent Ghana, Kwame Nkrumah promised to build a statue to West Africa's saviour; when asked who could deserve such a honour, he replied 'the mosquito'. The area that had long been known as the white man's grave remained unattractive to settlers, and since those soldiers, government officials, traders and missionaries who did brave the climate planned to spend their retirement in their native countries, the alienation of African land had not become a major problem. The situation was very different in the area that would become known as the White Highlands of Kenya.

When the imperialists divided German from British East Africa, they drew a line on the map that still marks the boundary between the modern nations of Tanzania and Kenya. Starting at the Indian Ocean to the south of Mombassa, the border skirts the northern slopes of Mount Kilimanjaro before turning north-west to meet the eastern shore of Lake Victoria. For the better part of a generation, traders, soldiers and missionaries had followed this general direction on the long journey to Uganda. During the time that Karl Peters was staking a claim to German lands to the south, Mackinnon's Imperial British East Africa Company (IBEACo) was making little effort to exploit the territory that would later be named after its dominant natural feature, Mount Kenya. Travellers told of how they had crossed land claimed by warlike Maasai nomads, before emerging into the fertile central highlands farmed by the agrarian Kikuyu (Gikuyu). One described how he came upon a 'very enterprising people', who raised 'miles of (sweet) potato plantations ... alongside sugar cane, maize, millet, beans, yams, bananas, tobacco and oil-seed'.[31]

William Mackinnon's fragile IBEACo collapsed in 1893, soon after
its founder died and the imperial government had little option but
to accept responsibility for its African territory. In the American West,
new railroads had already reduced journey times, previously measured
in months or even years, to just days, and as a gesture of confidence in
the imperial future, Prime Minister Arthur Balfour determined to build
a railway that would open the area to trade and settlement. Indian
labourers started to lay the track out of Mombassa in 1896, and the first
section between the Indian Ocean and the railway depot of Nairobi in the
central highlands of Kenya opened to passengers and goods just six years
later. During those years of construction, poorly housed, under-paid and
half-starved workers destroyed wide areas of countryside looking for
building materials and food. It can be questioned whether this pillage
was the sole cause of the smallpox and famine that ravaged the country
during the last years of the nineteenth century, but it was estimated that,
during those years, up to half the population of the area died. According
to the terms of the 1902 Crown Land Ordinance, Africans could only
claim property rights over holdings that were 'clearly occupied', while
all other land – crucially including that which was grazed by animals –
was designated as crown property for distribution among settlers.
It suited the incomers that, in the wake of such major depopulation,
wide swathes of land could not be classified as 'clearly occupied'.

The first railway carriages to arrive in the central highlands of Kenya
were disproportionately filled with land-hungry missionaries. The new
British administration officially set a limit of 1,000 acres on all foreign
landholdings, but in these early years, when there was no rush of
settlers, this rule was loosely interpreted. In his ambition to establish
a self-sufficient base of the church's operations, ex–Blantyre Auld Kirk
minister Clement Scott lodged a claim for 3,000 acres of prime land
near Nairobi and this was approved – with 1,000 acres given in freehold
and the other 2,000 on a ninety-nine-year lease. According to Kikuyu
custom, land was held by families, rather than by the wider community,
as was common across the continent, but, writing seven decades later,
the mission's historian testifies that no record survives of any negotiation
with or compensation for the Mbari ya Hinga family which held rights
to the land by treaty and inter-marriage with the forest-dwelling Aathi.[32]

Close behind Clement Scott came the unrelated Peter Cameron Scott.
Born in Glasgow, he had emigrated to America and survived a spell with
Dr Simpson's disastrous venture on the Congo River. In 1903, he secured

665 acres of freehold land and 1,796 acres of leasehold land to the north-west of Nairobi for his own faith-based Africa Inland Mission (AIM) – before seizing a further strip 2 miles long and 200 yards wide, without anybody's permission. This mission's scholar again admits 'No inquiry was made into indigenous ownership. Should this have been done, the government would have found that one Kihehero, a Kikuyu pioneer, had established his Mbari long ago and laid claim to the land on which the AIM now held title from government.'[33]

Later trains carried members of the founder's family and many more AIM missionaries, recruited from across the US 'Bible Belt'. Scott's brother-in-law expressed concern that many recruits were 'extremely prejudiced and narrow-minded' and 'not the stamp of man that one would care to see exercising any considerable influence in this country'.[34] Since it was feared that book-knowledge would interfere with divine inspiration, few were educated above primary grades, and none had any training for mission work or plans to learn any African language. Many had only the most tenuous financial support from home churches, and when left destitute, some would drift into the settler population, while others became dependant on the charity of missionary colleagues.

As the London government publicised the opportunity to take up cheap land, administrative officers became increasingly alarmed at the number of evangelical societies jostling for a share of it. Evangelical Anglicans and Methodists, who had long been established on the coast, now moved the focus of their operations inland. First, Anglicans competed for territory with the Presbyterians; then, when they managed to reach a settlement, Methodists protested that they could not be expected to honour any agreement to which they had not been a party. Americans of the AIM also needed to be accommodated – and they would collaborate only with those who shared their fundamentalist beliefs.

Even after Protestants had reached some agreement, the fault line between Catholic and Protestant remained unbridgeable. Superior Fr Perlo regretted the church's fractured state: 'There is a man who respects the self sacrifice of the missionary, and again he who on the contrary sees nothing but the different sectarian authorities (too many indeed) hurling condemnation at one another, and exhausting themselves in personalities and futile theories.'[35]

Dividing the colony on the latitude of Mt Kenya, Propaganda allocated the southern half to the Holy Ghost Fathers and the northern half to the Italian fathers of the Consulata order. Catholics who could not rely on financial support from home needed to become quickly self-sufficient, and British missionaries soon became concerned at the Italians' apparently insatiable appetite for land. According to tradition, the Kikuyu proverb *gutiri mubia na muthungu* (there is no difference between a settler and a missionary) was first directed at these Italians. A Kikuyu writer would later recall how his grandfather rose and shook his stick at a Consulata father who happened to mention the word 'land'. 'You, Father Comorio, of all the people should be the last to tell me about land. Remember how your church took our land. They bribed Karuri wa Gakure with beads, your white brothers did. They looked like you. They dressed like you. And they sang in their houses like doves, never stopping. I hated them so much.'[36]

The use of forced labour for public works was a universal fact of life in early colonial Africa. Administrations of all nationalities also used taxation – that could only be paid in cash – as the device for forcing peasant farmers to become wage labourers within the wider private economy. Any use of forced labour 'for private profit' was, however, widely perceived as an exploitative step too far. Kenyan missionaries would, however, challenge even this limitation. After the First World War , the British government introduced a scheme for settling ex-service veterans in the White Highlands, and when taxation failed to deliver the required workforce, these new settlers demanded the government provide them with forced labour. In the face of outrage from home supporters and outspoken condemnation by missionaries working in other colonies, the Kenyan clergy stubbornly refused to speak out against the idea. One Scot insisted: 'I believe it is criminal of the government … to encourage settlers here and give them the land and not to see that there is an adequate labour supply for their needs. If this happens and the settlers rise up in arms against the government, is the government not to blame?'[37]

Presbyterian moderator John Arthur – who represented 'native interests' on the all-white Legislative Council – joined with two Anglican bishops to issue a formal statement supporting the principle that 'compulsory labour is not in itself an evil. We want the men to work, and after much consideration think that compulsory labour, with proper safeguards, will be better for the country and the natives. With regard to women and children, we have no objection to such going out voluntarily.'[38] The truly voluntary nature of female and child labour must be assessed against the declared administration policy of squeezing African landholdings to the minimum and increasing taxes 'up to the limit of endurance'.

The Customs

Missionary work also had a profound effect on Kikuyu customs. Anglican Harry Leakey – patriarch to the family of famous archaeologists – described how singing and preaching could draw great crowds of onlookers as if to some unknown kind of entertainment. Then, 'when at last it began to dawn on them that more than mere listening was expected of them which must of necessity mean a revolution in national custom was looked for by the missionary, they became violently opposed to his teaching'.[39] Once on their stations, new missionaries settled down to an existence separated from all that was going on around them, and they could only look on the behaviour of one American couple from the tiny Gospel Missionary Society with disapproval: 'Mrs Knapp's idea of hospitality coincided with traditional Kikuyu practice. No reputable caller left the household without being hospitably received – rough old men in skins, young bloods bedecked in red ochre and castor oil and Christian converts alike. The Knapps were the first missionaries I know to have Africans at their table.'[40]

In their attitudes to race relations, Kenyan clergy lagged significantly behind more progressive colleagues. By the time that Anglican Bishop Alfred Tucker of Uganda retired in 1910, he had taken his diocese some distance down the road to self-determination. In the face of opposition from subordinates, he had set up mixed-race councils from parish to diocesan level and even established a house of laity, with an African majority. Across the border in Kenya, in contrast, Protestant societies debated plans for combining missionary societies into a single Kenyan church without inviting a single African to take part in the meeting. Across the southern border in German territory, pietist Bruno Guttmann was thinking radically about how traditional culture could be absorbed into the Christian community. On his regular fraternal visits to Scottish stations in the White Highlands, Alexander Hetherwick from Blantyre also reminded colleagues that they must show at least elementary respect for local customs and never try to 'dis-Africanise' converts. Faced by such talk, the 'Kenyan brethren' could only conclude that Guttmann had plunged deep into heresy, and Hetherwick was talking liberal nonsense. Speaking at a joint conference of Ugandan and Kenyan

clergy, Archdeacon Walker heaped scorn on those who were tempted
to compromise with African ways.

> The native customs that could be redeemed were not very
> easily found. It was suggested that native dances, if purged of all
> immorality, might become useful calisthenics; and that drinking
> of native beer, if free from all intoxication, might become social
> gatherings or 'tea parties'. But I think many members of the
> Conference felt that dancing, merely for the sake of physical
> exercise, and drinking, merely for the sake of refreshment,
> would be something quite new, rather than a redemption of
> heathen custom.[41]

Throughout the pre-First World War years, Kenya, with a mere 5,000
converts shared between a welter of competing societies, remained one
of the least developed mission fields in sub-Saharan Africa. Whites might
take pride in the civilised appearance of those who had moved into their
orbit, but in the eyes of fellow country people, alien hair styles, western
clothing and the foul smell of soap could only serve to set converts apart
from decent society. Since beer flowed freely at all rites of passage,
stringent rules on the consumption of alcohol effectively separated
converts from their home communities. When the Americans proposed
that total abstinence should become a condition of membership across
the country, they found willing allies in the Scots – who created no little
alarm at home by demanding that total abstinence be written into Auld
Kirk's constitution. Anglicans, who refused to take this extreme position,
found other ways of imposing ferocious discipline. Douglas Hooper
forbade girls to wear corsets, use beads or plait their hair; on his station
converts could be flogged for moral offences such as 'filthiness, foolish
talking, jesting and all that is frivolous'.[42]

Early Protestant pioneers lodged objections against the practice of
circumcising both boys and girls at tribal initiation ceremonies. Taking
a contrary position, a Catholic priest described how the rite marked an
important turning point in the growing boy's life: 'a *kahee* or one who
is not circumcised, has no rights, he is not a man. He cannot take part
in a war and fight like other men.... He cannot walk with the warriors
or form a friendship with any of them.'[43] After theological debate over
the meaning of St. Paul's statement that in Christ there was no circumcision

or un-circumcision, objections against circumcising boys were dropped. Female clitoridectomy proved a much more difficult issue. A Scottish mission doctor first drew the attention of teachers Minnie Watson and Marion Stevenson to the fact that wounds incurred in the initiation ceremony could turn septic, bring pain, later problems in childbirth and occasional death. At first, traditional practitioners were invited to perform the operation hygienically within mission clinics, but – understandably – the doctors still found the whole process repellent. It was then laid down that any girl who subjected herself to, or woman who took part in, a clitoridectomy would be subject to the strictest discipline. In practice, this meant that a girl had to choose at puberty whether she would be remain a Kikuyu or become a Christian (and ever afterwards be treated as a prostitute and an outcast by her own people). The problem was made worse by the fact that Bible translators had used the word *muiriutu* – which in Kikuyu meant a circumcised but unmarried woman – to translate the Bible word *Virgin*. Why, asked adherents, could a Kikuyu girl not pass through a rite that had been acceptable for the mother of Jesus.

While the Catholics stood back and the Anglicans hesitated, the Scots and Americans were engulfed by the controversy. In 1928, there was a face-off between supporters and opponents. Mission readers combined to issue a declaration that female circumcision could not be stopped without undermining the very existence of the Kikuyu people, and ordained Scottish doctor John Arthur countered by proposing that all who wished to remain on mission land must repudiate the practice on oath. When American missionaries tried to enforce this rule, their stations plunged into schism.[44] While a minority of adherents – the *Kirore* – remained loyal to the missionaries, the majority – the *Aregi* – left to establish their independent churches and schools. In this bitter time, *Kirore* and *Aregi* would fight, shout abuse and even seek to disrupt each other's church services and school lessons. 'First the land has been taken from us, and now they attack our most sacred customs', protested the *Aregi*. 'What will they do next?'

The roots of the post–Second World War Mau Mau uprising can be traced to those divisions that tore the AIM apart. The *Aregi* independent school bodies – The Kikuyu Karinga Schools Association and the Kikuyu Independent Schools Association – fed radicalised young people into a variety of political organisations that formed the Kenyan African Union.

While the Mau Mau was certainly a war over the ownership of land, it was also a struggle for Kikuyu identity, of which female circumcision was an important part. First independent president Jomo Kenyatta, wrote that, by the mid-twentieth century, his people had become deeply suspicious of the white 'religious fanatics', who aimed 'to disintegrate social order and thereby hasten their Europeanisation'.[45]

Chapter 13

The Path in the Thicket

Albert Schweitzer and the Germans

As a boy, Albert Schweitzer had been introduced to the story of foreign missions as he listened to his father read Eugène Casalis' Basutoland letters from the pulpit in his church in Kyserberg Alsace, and it was to Casalis' Paris Evangelicals that, in 1905, he posted an application to work as missionary doctor in the French colony of Gabon. By this time, he had become one of the best-known churchmen in Europe; still only thirty years old, he was not only a respected theologian and teacher but also Europe's leading interpreter of the organ works of J.S. Bach. But his unorthodox views had already become so notorious that he had good cause to fear that the application would be rejected, and, indeed, he was accepted only after much heart-searching, on condition that he would never preach to Africans or enter into any religious discussion that might disturb his colleagues' more conservative faith.

Like some other pietists who, during the latter half of the nineteenth century, had separated themselves from the literalist mainstream, Schweitzer had subjected the Bible narrative to the full range of modern critical analysis. While Bishop Colenso had been content to analyse the book of Leviticus, Schweitzer turned the process on the life and teachings of Jesus himself. Even as he posted his letter to Paris, he was awaiting publication of *The Quest for the Historical Jesus*. Across the world, millenarians were warning Christians to prepare for the second coming, and Schweitzer agreed that Jesus had indeed presented an apocalyptic message – but the problem for literalists lay in the fact that he had clearly expected the end time to arrive within the lifetime of his own disciples. By demonstrating that Jesus had been 'capable of error', Schweitzer recognised that he had sawn off the branch on which he sat. 'The historical foundation of Christianity', he declared, 'as built up by rationalistic, by liberal, and by modern theology no longer exists.' The restrictions that the committee placed on his work in Africa created no problem because he no longer had anything to say; all that was left for him was to live out the Christian life as best he could.

Despite his other accomplishments, Schweitzer was no doctor; eight years of training were necessary before he and his new wife finally sailed for Lambaréné on the Gabon River in 1913. When war broke out in the following year, he did everything possible to shield the Africans from news of the terrible carnage that was taking place in the European homelands. Schweitzer's liberal creed was grounded in the Enlightenment belief in progress, and for him, if Christianity was not a force for the restoration of mankind, then it was nothing. As his whole religious and philosophical structure collapsed, he experienced a sense of 'wandering about in a thicket in which no path was to be found'. He described how he experienced his moment of revelation while travelling from Lambaréné by river:

Lost in thought I sat on the deck of the barge, struggling to find the elementary and universal conception of the ethical which I had not discovered in any philosophy. Sheet after sheet I covered with disconnected sentences, merely to keep myself concentrated on the problem. Late on the third day, at the very moment when, at sunset, we were making our way through a herd of hippopotamuses, there flashed upon my mind, unforeseen and unsought, the phrase, 'Reverence for Life'. The iron door had yielded: the path in the thicket had become visible.[1]

The same world war that left the liberal Schweitzer with no ethical compass only served to reinforce the increasing polarisation of twentieth-century Christianity. Through the decades before he died at Lambaréné in 1965 at the age of ninety, Schweitzer remained a Janus-like figure. He retained what some observers felt to be an alarmingly casual approach to modern medicine as well as a nineteenth-century attitude to those African people to whom he ministered: 'The negro is a child, and with children nothing can be done without the use of authority. We must, therefore, so arrange the circumstances of daily life that my natural authority can find expression. With regard to negroes, then, I have coined a formula: "I am your brother, it is true, but your elder brother." '[2] Against this, the twentieth-century Schweitzer – close relative of Jean Paul Sartre and confidant of Bertrand Russell – remained deeply critical of racial injustice and economic exploitation, a pacifist and strict vegetarian and early supporter of nuclear disarmament. His doctrine of reverence for life would provide a starting point for later generations, whose concerns focused on social justice and the environment rather than doctrinal belief.

* * *

As the war reached its bitter climax and half a million African conscripts drove German forces from the greater part of the fatherland's colonial possessions, Secretary of the World Missionary Conference Joseph Oldham grew increasingly concerned for the German missionaries who had been caught up in the conflict. Even during the pre-war years, colleagues had been impatient of the strident German nationalism that seemed so out of place in a missionary setting, but having studied in Germany, Oldham understood the divisions within the evangelical churches and was concerned that those who followed his old teacher Gustav Warneck should not be tarred with the same brush. The wider problem was well illustrated by tensions within the neighbouring British and German colonies of the Gold Coast and Togo. In the latter, although missionary work was officially run by the moderate Bremen society, most of its recruits came from the notoriously nationalistic area around Hamburg. Here school children worked in German, pledged allegiance to the German flag and spent many hours on military drill, it was only to be expected that the missionaries would be expelled when the colony fell to the allies. Across the border in the Gold Coast, the Basel workers – who answered to a neutral Swiss society – had long experience of working alongside British officials, who were inclined to prefer the structured Germanic organisation of the Basel workers to the democratic and sometimes chaotic ways of coastal Methodists – but at a time of war, they could not escape suspicion. The great majority were, after all, German, and the rest came from the German-speaking Switzerland, where support for the Kaiser's cause was strong. First, rumour spread that Basel stations were sending wireless messages to German submarines; then some Basel traders held a noisy party on the night that the large packet boat *Apapa* was sunk off Accra with much loss of life. While the Germans would claim that the event was a birthday party, others assumed that the revels had been held to celebrate the sinking. All German-born missionaries were expelled and Swiss-born staff quickly followed.[3] As similar incidents were replicated across the continent – and, indeed, the world – the whole German missionary

enterprise was being brought to an end. Oldham reminded his colleagues
what was involved:

> 'The missionaries who have been repatriated are men and women
> who have had their career cut short, who, in many instances, are
> face-to-face with the practical difficulty of earning a livelihood and
> who are facing the still severer trial of separation from the work to
> which the best years of their lives have been devoted and from those
> to whom they had become tied by ties of the deepest affection.'[4]

By the terms of the Versailles treaty, German colonies were distributed
to the victors under the League of Nations mandate: Tanganyika, Zanzibar
and part of Togo would go to Britain, most of Cameroon and the larger
part of Togo to France and Rwanda and Burundi to Belgium. The Cape
government had occupied German South-West Africa during the war and
this *fait accompli* was also legitimised (though a German community,
which had a long-standing affinity with the Boers, continued to flourish
alone). Some German missionaries would later find their way back to their
old stations, but they came to a strange world, in which they spoke the
wrong language and taught from the wrong history textbooks. Many now
had to answer for their actions to allied missionaries, such as the Scots
Presbyterians, who had the power of veto over all synod decisions in the
Basel area of the Gold Coast. It posed no great problem to the British
society to expand into the British Togo, though staffing the French area
proved more difficult. The Paris Evangelicals, who had taken over the Basel
work in Cameroon, could only express regret that they had no resources
for further expansion and the native church was finally left to its own
devices. When, four decades later, Swiss pastor Hans Debrunner visited the
area to see how this abandoned community had fared, he discovered that
a high proportion of the people attended church services regularly and still
considered themselves evangelical Christians. To his concern, however,
polygamists now held high positions within the church. With typical Swiss
thoroughness, he recorded that, in one evangelical village, 207 men had,
between them, contracted 463 marriages, and 58 percent of the 249
married women were living in polygamous relationships. He concluded
that a study of family relationships before the first missionary arrived
would probably have delivered similar statistics. But when Debrunner
questioned children about their people's past, he found that at least some
of nineteenth-century certainties had survived intact:

The traditions of the ancestors are all pagan and paganism is bad. If we held to the traditions of our ancestors we should not become civilised and barbarism would prevail for ever.

Our ancestors had lost their way to heaven.

Our ancestors were deluded by Satan, the church brings God's salvation.[5]

Revival

What had been achieved? By the early 1890s, Christian missionaries could only claim to have made significant inroads into traditional society in Uganda and perhaps Basutoland. Elsewhere church membership was largely restricted to purchased slaves, ransomed debtors, rescued twins and outcasts. In parts of West and South Africa, where the process of detribalisation had been well advanced before the first modern missionaries arrived, they had built strong Christian communities, but even here, Christians remained separate from wider society. In South Africa, for instance, there were 'red people' who lived in round huts, drank beer at festivals and whose women went bare breasted to market, and there were mission people, or *kholwa*, who lived in 'upright houses', wore white men's clothes, and were anxious to secure schooling for their children and make their living in the white man's world. Those converts, who had been fished out of the great ocean of heathenism 'with a line, not with a net', might serve as living proof that savages could be brought out of darkness into civilisation, but foreign missionaries still welcomed western armies because they alone could destroy those traditional societies that their own preaching had failed to penetrate. After the time of destruction, detribalised Africans who had lost land, status and all spiritual signposts, either flocked to the white men's missions or set up their independent churches; either way, the deity they found could no longer be mistaken for the white men's God.

Following the principle of reinforcing success, the CMS set about building up the work in Uganda and expanding into Rwanda. At the same time, however, serving missionaries were becoming increasingly concerned that the home officials were moving the CMS in a liberal direction. Determined to keep the Uganda operation pure, those in the field managed to loosen the ties with the home board and establish a recruiting link with Cambridge University's fundamentalist Christian union (CICCU). In the early 1930s, the white clergy became aware that an indigenous revival of Christian spirituality was being carried across east Africa by catechists and traders and even by railwaymen, who held meetings for prayer and testimony along the whole length of the line from Mombassa to Kampala. White workers, who had been taught how to control their emotions at public school and university, found some manifestations deeply disturbing.

> Strange things are happening in my church.... There is much conviction of sin by weeping and shaking. One woman has become dumb, and this is happening in three other churches.... A man began to howl at the top of his voice, I was alarmed and made people sit down. The man continued weeping lying on the floor.... I called him up to the chancel to say what he had experienced.... He stood beside me weeping and in halting words gave a moving testimony. He said he had seen a vision of Christ in the church and he saw the awful state of the lost and was overcome with grief for his own past.[6]

Clergy, who had long gone through the motions of praying for Christian revival, listened helplessly as senior church members confessed to sins of adultery and witchcraft. When they reprimanded their flock, they were reminded that such scenes were common in the early church and their doubts could only call into question whether they themselves had really been saved. As the bishop struggled to contain the movement within the Anglican fold, converts were indigenising worship to suit their culture.

> Syncopation began to appear in hymn tunes. For example the hymn, 'My hope is built on nothing less than Jesus blood and righteousness', with the 3/4 time of William Bradbury's tune, was sometimes sung nearly all night, more and more syncopated until the Africanised 6/8 time completely took the place of the original.[7]

Rwanda mission leader Joe Church recorded that, to his ears, the new rhythm fitted the vernacular words better than the western original, but many found any change to received practice disturbing. In racist Kenya, white clergy rejected the very idea that they might share a platform with Africans, and even in more flexible Rwanda, colleagues protested that 'no good at all would come from Mrs Guillebaud's habit of allowing

Africans to crowd into her house for hymn singing or Joe Church's custom of letting them sit in his room as equals and share news from his letters'. The practical problems of how mixed evangelical teams could be accommodated on their journeys proved insurmountable.

> Mr Clarke dared public opinion when he invited Blasio's team to lead the Mbarara mission, but he *could* not – no please he *could* not – invite them to eat in a European home! So they were sent to three small African homes, and Blasio wrote about it with characteristic meekness, 'We are not all staying at the same place. We are spread out all over Mbarara. We wanted to pray together hard, but God planned it differently. We tried to sleep in one place, but God did not wish it.'[8]

Africans now looked for a simple faith in which the Bible meant just what it said and, when J.C. Jones, principal of Kampala's Mokono Theological College, was judged to be delivering 'liberal' interpretations of what should be immutable truth, his whole final year walked out on the day before their final examination. Some would return later for ordination, but most continued to preach across East Africa as semi-detached lay evangelists or members of the independent Balokole (*Chosen Ones*) movement, which would carry the spirit of revival forward into the 1940s and later.[9]

The Medics

As fellow whites took up the task of administrating conquered colonies, missionaries withdrew from the political arena, in which so many had been active through the nineteenth century.[10] Through all the social distance and some mutual distrust, however, administrators and missionaries of the mainstream denominations discovered that they were joined in a symbiotic relationship. Since the imperial enterprise had never encompassed any vision for the building of medical and educational services for newly conquered countries, any advances in these areas would necessarily have to be delivered in partnership with mission agencies. Scottish universities had led the world in the study of medicine throughout most of the nineteenth century, and David Livingstone studied at Glasgow before starting work as Africa's first missionary with modern medical qualifications. As he travelled across southern Africa, his wagon was 'quite besieged by the blind, halt and lame', but still he remained uncertain about how to balance doctoring with his prime evangelistic responsibility: 'As I believe that the expenditure of much time on medicine is not the way in which I can do most for the Redeemer's glory, I usually decline treating any but the most urgent cases.'[11] Directors of the LMS clearly shared Livingstone's uncertainty, as he was not replaced. Nyasaland's clergymen-doctors Laws and Elmslie were the products of a joint course in the University of Edinburgh that was devised to provide medically trained ministers who could work in the remoter highlands and islands of Scotland. Not long after a UMCA lady worker would complain that Presbyterian doctors were 'as plentiful as blackberries', while her own society failed to provide even one.

To Catholics, who aimed to win the whole of society, the provision of medical services could be seen as a means of demonstrating Christian compassion within an unbelieving world, and a White Father working in the Rift Valley light-heartedly compared his arrival in an African settlement to the appearance of a medical charlatan in a French rural marketplace. Lavigerie set up a training school for medical catechists on the island of Malta, and seven of its graduates did arrive in East Africa, though only Adrien Aitman would stay the course, to work in the Catholic mission at Karema for an astonishing sixty-seven years: 'Each morning I visited the orphans and treated those who were ill. Persistent fevers were prevalent owning to lack of quinine.... Bandages were made from old clothes used by the orphans. Although washed they looked more like khaki than white materials.... In addition to medical treatment I gave religious instruction, taught in classes, and prepared the dying for baptism.'[12]

In the eyes of evangelicals like Wilmot Brooke, medical work was a distraction from the main task of bringing individuals to conversion. On its lowest level, however, healing could provide a valuable 'key to unlock the heart'. On the Lower Congo, medically untrained Baptist Holman Bentley would arrive in a village with a standard medicine chest containing 'glass stoppered bottles, with a drawer below for pestle and mortar and small boxes', followed closely by his wife at the head of a choir of mission boys. If the white man's medicines worked, hearts might indeed open; if not, they were likely to remain closed forever. Towards the end of the century, therefore, missionaries began to ask their societies to send out properly qualified doctors. Dr Albert Cook faced

outright hostility from evangelical colleagues when he arrived in Uganda
to set up the CMS flagship hospital at Mengo in 1897. Throughout his
long career, Cook insisted that his first priority as a missionary was to
lead Africans to conversion, but he saw no conflict of interest between
the twin tasks. 'To attempt to heal the suffering is much, to carry the
water of salvation is more, but to combine the two is the greatest work
that a man can hope.' After marrying the hospital's formidable matron
Katherine Timpson – whose rebukes could reduce white colleagues to
gibbering wrecks – and recruiting the help of his doctor brother Howard,
the family team set about the task of bringing western 'biomedicine'
to Uganda. Handing out drugs proved a poor substitute for the drama
of an operation, performed within the village setting.

> At Toro, the King begged to see an operation so, a suitable case
> appearing of a man with a large tumour on his back the size of two
> fists, we put him under chloroform and removed it. Fortunately for
> the credit of our medical work, it came out very nicely, and the
> wound healing quickly the man was soon all right. I think they were
> more astonished at the chloroform than the operation, the fact that
> the man suffering no pain being to them very extraordinary.[13]

Cataract operations also pulled great crowds, and as the patient walked
away with sight restored, no chance was lost to reinforce the message
that all healing was a gift from the Christian God. Healing went hand
in hand with converting. At evangelical hospitals across Africa, pagans
could expect to be harangued by catechists as they stood in line, to be
uplifted by religious pictures that decorated the hospital walls and to
learn from services delivered at the bedsides of converts, who had been
strategically placed around the ward. On occasion, a promising patient
might even be kept in hospital longer than medical need demanded until
the work of conversion had been brought to conclusion. Most of the
African orderlies were themselves ex-patients and John Arthur described
how he came to rely on their widening range of skills: 'They have been
trained to nurse cases, attend to proper feeding, take temperatures, apply
poultices, give enemas, inject stimulants hypodermically and go through
all the regular regime of a nurse's work at home.'[14]

Soon after the imperial wave had passed across sub-Saharan Africa,
it became all too clear that conquest had been achieved at a high cost
in African life. While many had been killed in direct military action, even

more had died of diseases – notably plague, smallpox, yaws and syphilis – carried across the continent by European armies and their African auxiliaries, carriers and labourers. The collapse of traditional society – so much welcomed by missionaries – also took a heavy toll on the life and health of people who struggled to adjust to new ways. Having no budget to set any basic health infrastructure in place, colonial administrators brought together mission and army medical teams and set them to deliver short-term assaults on the killer epidemics.

To everybody's concern it also began to appear that, far from improving, infant mortality rates were actually rising under colonial rule. Administrators, who had no means of reaching mothers, encouraged missionaries to run mother and child clinics and hold baby shows around the countryside. Encouraged by fashionable theories of eugenics, missionaries would often lend out western clothes, teach early weaning, discourage the carrying of babies on their mothers' backs and generally promote ideas of 'superior, monogamous and fertile families'.[15] Arriving in 1903 on her mission station 7 miles from Kampala, tiny Irish Sister Kevin had to accept that the Catholic effort lagged a generation behind the sophisticated facilities on offer at Protestant Mengo. Functioning within limited resources, she focused the mission's efforts on providing support for mothers within their own community. For this she needed both black and white female workers. 'There must be more sisters', declared her bishop, 'in fact the mission cannot survive without them.' Even after reinforcements arrived, Sr Kevin chaffed at the church's ruling that nuns must take no part in the painful and sweaty business of childbirth and concentrate their efforts on mother and child work within the villages. Protesting 'we can't build a living church on dead babies',[16] she set up a course for African midwives to operate in competition with the sophisticated programme that Katherine Cook now had in place at Mengo.

It has been estimated that, by the outbreak of the First World War, more women than men were working in the mission field, but with the single exception of the United Presbyterians in Calabar, women's work in Africa was rarely reported to home supporters or acknowledged to the wider world. On a photograph taken at Joseph Oldham's 1910 international mission conference, of the hundreds of (apparently all white) delegates packed into the Edinburgh Assembly Hall, one lady is taking notes at the front and a handful of others can be spotted at the back of the main hall, while others watch proceedings from the public gallery. African missionary effort had until now been overwhelmingly perceived as an operation directed at men by men. But, even as those solemn males filled the assembly hall, a significant change was taking place in the world outside. Euphemia Miller – Mammy Sutherland – had discovered that no man would ever gain entrance into those homes where the need was greatest, and half a century later, strategists began to repeat the slogan 'if you convert a man you have converted an individual, if you convert a woman you have converted a family'. Across Protestant Europe and America, evangelical societies within medical schools were flourishing, and overseas work was becoming attractive to women who had learnt to their cost that it was hard to forge a rewarding career in the male-dominated worlds of European and North American medicine. With hyperactive Bishop Shanahan in the lead, Catholics increasingly turned to Ireland for doctors and sisters to staff their hospitals and dispensaries across British-ruled Africa. Strategists were even beginning to recognise that it could only help if the home visitor was not only of the same sex but also spoke the same language, was of the same colour and had been raised within the same culture as the mother who looked to her for advice. Missionary societies that had previously focused solely on turning male converts into priests, ministers, catechists and hospital orderlies now realised that they must give high priority to the recruitment of both black and white women to work within the community as visitors, nurses and midwives.

The Teachers

At the end of the First World War, the northern American Baptists decided that the whole process of African education was in need of serious scrutiny. South of the Sahara, almost all schools that offered western education were in church hands. But, even in colonial times, few Protestants arrived in the country with any background in education, and ambitions remained limited to the provision of adequate literacy for the reading of Scripture, the training of catechists and the production of loyal subjects. Mission schools did provide practical skills, which was mainly aimed at keeping undesirable migrant workers out of the country. In the words of a Yale professor, education in Africa, reduced to its lowest level, could be seen as 'the process by which a human being is changed from what he is to something those in authority want him to be'.[17]

Some years earlier, philanthropically minded Caroline Phelps Stokes had bequeathed her large estate to a trust 'for the education of Negroes, both in Africa and the United States, North American Indians and needy and deserving white students'.[18] While her wishes had been carried out in North America, nobody had yet come up with any suggestion of how the trust might make a contribution to the education of Africans, and following a request from the Baptists, it was agreed that a commission should examine the state of education across the continent, both on mission stations and in government schools. Following his work with deprived communities in the United States, trust educational director Thomas Jesse Jones had developed his own model for the improvement of black education – identifying what he called four 'simples': The teaching of *Health* would include nutrition and sanitation as well as disease. The promotion of good health needs to become "the colouring of every subject, of every project and of the administrative provision from the lowest grades, through the activities of even colleges and universities".[19] Care for the *Environment* would run through all areas of social and scientific study, from geography to agriculture and nature study. Work in this area would involve a significant amount of 'learning by doing' and creative art: In the same way that the *Home* provided the centre for all human life, so it would underpin the school curriculum. Dr Jones was concerned at high African infant mortality rates and aimed to improve the status of women with 'courses in cooking, sewing and other household arts'. 'The perplexing problem of character training' would be addressed through *Recreation*. Every part of the school – playground, gymnasium, dormitory, laboratory, dining room, library, field and shop – needed to be designed with proper recreational facilities.

After Joseph Oldham had secured the collaboration of colonial governments and missionary societies, Jones recruited retired missionaries to travel with him on visits to anglophone countries across west, east and southern Africa. Dr Henry Hallenbeck had served with the American Board in Angola, while Mr and Mrs Arthur Wilkie were Scots who had worked in Calabar. Not everybody was happy that James Kwegir Aggrey was also included, but Jones insisted that the party must include one African.

As the commissioners visited schools, 'good, bad and indifferent', they discovered that neither mission nor government schools could deliver the four simples.

The children were asked, for example, to name the subjects taught in school. In the majority of the schools in the Gold Coast and Nigeria, English was named first, followed rapidly by arithmetic and writing. In many schools it required patience to discover that hygiene, nature study and agriculture were taught; and in many others patience was unavailing, for the subjects were not taught.[20]

Aggrey discovered that children, who could tell him what had happened in 1066, had no knowledge of their own history. When he found that children could sing *The British Grenadiers* and *Rule Britannia*, but knew no songs from their own tradition, he would strike up a Fanti folk song and tell them that they must be proud of 'everything that was good in their past'. In his analysis, African children 'were treated like empty jars to be filled with western learning, with not sufficient consideration for the immediate practical use of the learning in relation to the actual needs of the community'.[21] Educated African women were already complaining that members of their sex 'were nearly a century behind men in every respect',[22] and, indeed, Aggrey was shocked at the low number of girls that he found in classes across the continent. To make the point, he would first make the boys stand up and then the girls to demonstrate the difference, before urging the boys to bring their sisters to school.

This first serious study into African education did arouse significant interest. Strictures over the inadequacy of education for girls came as no surprise and both governments and missions began to search for women qualified to put a programme of education for girls in place. The Carnegie Foundation also agreed to fund a programme for peripatetic teachers in African schools, with a commission to introduce practical community skills. Under their guidance, 'girls were taught to sew, to mend their cloths and sew on buttons, and even to make their own dresses and to cook, while boys helped about the yard, brought in firewood, made mats of corn shucks and attended to any simple repair work that was needed'.[23] In the eyes of aspiring Africans, this system of 'learning by doing' might well have looked suspiciously like the regime imposed on the pupils of Dotheboys Hall by Charles Dickens' headmaster Wackford Squeers: 'We go upon the practical mode of teaching, Nickleby; the regular education system. C-l-e-a-n, clean, verb active, to make bright, to scour. W-i-n, win, d-e-r, der, winder, a casement. When the boy knows this out of book, he goes and does it.' As was obvious to the Africans, white administrative officers had not reached positions of power, white engineers had not learnt how to build docks and bridges and white doctors had not acquired the skills of modern medicine by making dresses and carrying firewood. However admirable in rural community terms, the Phelps-Stokes Commission had failed to emphasise that Africans needed to acquire higher skills if they were ever to achieve parity with their white masters.

During those interwar years, the same issue that had divided Mother Javouhey from the Ploërmel Fathers so many years ago came under debate. In 1922, the CMS opened a technical institute in Uganda designed to draw students from across East Africa and even the Upper Nile, which would later become Makerere University. Across the continent, the Gold Coast exchequer was benefiting from record prices for cocoa on the world market, while the post-war Governor Sir Hugh Clifford deplored the fact that the country's whole educational budget amounted to just a miserly £38,000 – and even that was not fully spent. His long-term aim was that every village would have a primary school, every province a teachers' training college and the nation itself would ultimately boast a Royal College of Higher Education.

Clifford's successor, Brigadier General Sir Gordon Guggisberg, decided to turn the timetable on its head and start the project by building a university at Achimota, near Accra. It did not help that, for all his high military rank, Guggisberg was a 'mere engineer' promoted over the heads of career administrative officers. As he faced up to critics who argued that Africans would never be fit for higher education, he was forced to agree to scale back his university to a flagship secondary school, integrated with a teachers' training college. But, in replying to his critics, he insisted that, since the Gold Coast would never be a white man's country, it was surely open to becoming a 'great field for the employment of all educated Africans', and he challenged them to say whether they were 'deliberately going to turn men who have an earnest desire for educational advancement – and some who have shown that they can benefit from it – into a race of malcontents by confining them to the subordinate work of trades and professions'.[24]

It was agreed that the new college would be a secular foundation, recruiting Christians of all kinds, as well as Muslims and traditional believers, who would work together within a broad Christian ethos. Ex-India Anglican missionary Alexander Fraser was recruited as first principal, with local educator and Phelps-Stokes commissioner James Kwegir Aggrey in support. The first problem that needed to be addressed was Aggrey's job description. As vice-principal, he would have to assume full responsibility whenever Fraser was away, but in the British Gold Coast, no African could hold authority over any white man.[25] Aggrey was therefore given the title Assistant Vice-Principal, which was deemed to carry no executive authority. Still, there would be many trials put upon him. When the Achimota advance party arrived in Accra, for instance, Fraser discovered that Aggrey had been provided with separate accommodation from the whites, a decision only reversed, amid loud complaint, after Fraser had threatened to take the next boat home.[26] Through all the racial insults, Aggrey remained a peacemaker and the college crest was designed to illustrate his parable of the piano keys. 'You can play a tune of sorts on the white keys and you can play a tune of sorts on the black keys. But for harmony you must use both the black and the white.'[27] It was not a message taken to heart by everyone. While the Gold Coast had more than its share of indigenous doctors and lawyers, the colony remained comparatively poor in qualified educators, and when Aggrey died in New York just three years later at the age of fifty-two, no black man was deemed worthy to take his place.

* * *

In 1919, Pope Benedict XV – 'the forgotten pope' – issued the encyclical *Maximum Illud* – with a title borrowed from the psalmist's words 'forget your nation and your ancestral home'. His successor Pius XI – 'the missionary pope' – reinforced the message in *Rerum Ecclesiae*. According to this new mission programme, brainchild of the Dutch head of Propaganda Willelm de Rossum, home-based orders needed to surrender control of missionary work to local dioceses, which would answer direct to Rome. Most radically, all white missionaries had to prepare African clergy to assume the responsibilities of diocesan bishop and had to establish indigenous religious orders for both men and women that would take over the bulk of work in local communities. White personnel would then support indigenous clergy in the great push for souls that would surely follow. Pius had no patience for those who muttered that the programme was premature and *Rerum Ecclesiae* was best interpreted as the pope's 'pious wish'. 'No,' he announced. 'It is our will and command.'

If the pope's demanding programme of reform was to be carried through, however, the whole structure of Catholic education needed to be overhauled. While evangelical Anglicans might ordain near-illiterate farmers after only a perfunctory training, potential Catholic priests needed to survive much sterner – and longer – preparation. After being identified and prepared in primary school, promising boys would spend the next fifteen years of their lives, first in junior and then in senior seminary, during which time they would never return to their villages or see their families. Immersed in Latin and church discipline, most would drop out, until perhaps as few as 1 in 20 might emerge as ordained priests at the end of the process. Having become strangers in their home community and perhaps even having lost their local dialect, they would then have to rely heavily on those African sisters and brothers, who had remained in contact with their people. Nevertheless, in 1939, Joseph Kaiwanika was finally consecrated bishop of Masaka, Uganda, overseeing a diocese containing 350,000 baptised Catholics, 90,000 catechumens, forty-six African priests and over 200 African sisters. Despite the fact that De Rossum's initiative lost impetus during the fascist era (when – in a return to the old, but now discredited, pattern of missionary behaviour – Italian clergy would follow Mussolini's invading forces into Ethiopia and even connive at the execution of the Orthodox patriarch), Kaiwanuka's consecration marked a new beginning.

* * *

With so much effort directed at the production of priests, Catholic secondary education could make little contribution to the training of those who would lead the new African nations. Apart from exceptions like the medical doctor Felix Houphouet-Boigny of the Ivory Coast, who rose through the French *école normale* system, Leopold Sénghor of Senegal, who was expelled from the Dakar seminary after protesting against racism, both within the institution and in the wider colonial society, and the Northern Nigerian Muslim Amadu Bello, most of sub-Saharan Africa's first generation of political leaders emerged from the Protestant missionary educational system. Other Catholics Kwame Nkrumah of Ghana and Julius Nyerere of Tanzania attended Protestant-influenced Achimota and Makerere, respectively, while Robert Mugabe of Zimbabwe went through both Catholic and Protestant schools. Protestants Jomo Kenyatta of Kenya, Kenneth Kaunda of Zambia and Hastings Banda of Malawi all came out off the Scots Presbyterian system. First Nigerian president Nnamdi Azikiwe attended Catholic, Anglican and Methodist institutions as well as the Presbyterian Hope Wadell College in Calabar and Lincoln College in America before setting up his own 'Zikist' philosophical cult. There was no provision for secondary education in the Belgian Congo outside the Catholic seminaries; after receiving primary schooling in both Protestant and Catholic schools, Patrice Lumumba could therefore aspire no further than to be trained as a post office clerk. At the time when these men took over the reins of office, programmes for African higher education were barely even in their infancy. In 1962 – 125 years after the CMS opened the Fourah Bay Institute of Higher Education in Freetown – UNESCO estimated that out of a relevant age group of (a probably underestimated) 13.2 million young people living in 'middle Africa', between the Sahara Desert and the Orange and Limpopo Rivers, only 46,000 or 0.35 percent were undertaking any kind of course of further education either in Africa or abroad, of which just 11,000, or 1:1200, were working to degree standard within their own country.[28]

Troublemakers

Through the missionary years, only a few Anglicans had challenged the racism that protected white minorities from black majority populations. The exceptions, like Arthur Shearsby Cripps, Walter Owen and the Colenso family, faced either apathy or blatant hostility from within their own communion. After the death of Harriette Colenso in 1932, the voice of protest appeared to have been finally extinguished, and African National Congress Chairman Albert Luthuli could only despair at the racism that appeared to run so deeply through that church's evangelical wing.[29] But new seeds of protest had been sown. Back in England, a small group of Anglo-Catholic priests had started preaching a radical message during the interwar years. Inspired by this, Michael Scott arrived in South Africa as a school leaver to work in a leper colony on Robben Island. After returning home for ordination, he made links with the communist party and became involved in tussles with black-shirt fascists in London's East End. After the war, he rejected the idea of becoming a monk – vows of poverty and chastity posed no problems, but obedience would surely prove an insuperable obstacle – and sailed again for South Africa, to embark on a life of direct action as priest and journalist on behalf of the dispossessed.[30] After being imprisoned for three months for joining an Indian community protest, he plunged into a life of enforced poverty, living in the heart of the 'pitiful patchwork of corrugated iron, planks and barrel staves' that was the black township of Torbuk.[31] Scott

worked to expose the appalling conditions of migrant workers in the
Transvaal and contract labourers in Namibia and helped raise political
opposition to the Central African Federation until he was finally
deported in 1953. Continuing his work in exile, Michael Scot, like John
Philip before him, never lost sight of the fact that South Africa's evils had
to be confronted on the political level.

> When all is said that ought to be said of missionaries and
> government servants who are giving such ungrudging service in
> the sphere of social welfare and health, the fact remains that their
> labour is being overborne by the consequences of artificially
> induced poverty and of a spiritual and economic frustration.[32]

At his colleague's funeral, Community of the Resurrection monk Trevor
Huddleston would acknowledge Scott's pioneering work: 'Although
Michael and I had come from the same English background and the
same ecclesiastical tradition: although within a fairly short time I could
not fail to recognise the marvellously rich human resources going to
waste through such dire poverty, it took me the best part of four years
to understand that it wasn't the symptoms but the disease itself that
had to be fought. It took Michael about four weeks.'[33]

Huddleston had responsibility for Johannesberg's black suburb
of Sophiatown during the period when the Afrikaans National Party
was giving a formal structure to the apartheid state. Under the guidance
of Heinrick Voerword (the son of a Dutch missionary, and Minister for
Native Affairs), Prime Minister and Dutch Reformed clergyman Daniel
Malan secured the passage of three acts of parliament. First, the Pass
Laws compelled non-whites to carry identification at all times, and
the Group Areas Act gave the government powers to deport whole
populations and flatten communities. Huddleston's outrage boiled
over when the Bantu Education Act of 1955 dismantled the structure
of church education by demanding that all non-white schools must
be surrendered into government control. From distant Rome, Pope
Pius XII decreed that the law must be defied and all Catholic schools
did, in practice, remain open, but many white Anglicans supported the
act and most church schools were handed into government control.
To Huddleston, it seemed clear that, from that time, Africans were to
be only offered 'education for servitude ... designed to condition native

children to the unalterable fact of the apartheid world, of the unalterable fact of white supremacy'.[34] After closing his beloved St Peter's school, he set about writing *Naught for Your Comfort*, which would become a worldwide bestseller and fatally wound the apartheid state. To forestall deportation, Huddleston's superiors recalled him to the community's parent house on the flimsy excuse that he alone could fill a vacant position supervising novice monks.

While both Scott and Huddleston had come from privileged backgrounds, Colin Winter took some pride in the fact that he alone among the high church clergy had experienced the problems of living with an outside pit lavatory in a deprived Potteries home. 'I was engulfed by a world of dirt, smoke and industrial pollution. It was a fight to get clean and to stay clean.'[35] Inspired by Huddleston's book, he and his wife Mary had planned to take on the challenge of work in South Africa, until they became convinced that the need in South-West Africa – which nationalists already called Namibia – was even more urgent. After arrival in 1964 and consecration as bishop in 1968, he quickly launched himself into the struggle to achieve a fair deal for contract workers. While his cathedral was in the capital city of Windhoek, most African Anglicans lived some 250 miles to the north in the native reserve of Ovamboland, which could only be entered by whites who held government permits. Basing his campaign on a report by Finnish lady missionary Rauha Voipio, he publicised the ways in which South African politicians were working to control the lives and working conditions of very poor people in collusion with chiefs and placemen. International corporations were caught up in the broad sweep of this bishop's condemnation: 'The Tswana Group, the largest single employer of black contract labour, offers wages which grievously exploits its adult labour force, is totally committed to the Vorster regime for obvious economic advantage and is a scandal to the name of America.'[36]

When South African newspapers carried reports of a speech by Winter in which he described conditions in Ovamboland as slavery, critics asked how could this be when slavery was based on compulsion and contract workers were free to leave their work whenever they liked. Accepting the challenge, Winter helped the workers call a strike, and the government responded by declaring a state of emergency, during which four strikers were shot dead on their way home from church. When the strikers were put on trial, the bishop raised funds for their defence and arranged for an

American judge to observe the proceedings. When he too was deported in 1972, church members begged him not to resign, but to continue to argue the Namibian case as bishop in exile.

* * *

New Zealand Church of Christ minister Garfield Todd applied for a teaching position in Southern Rhodesia in 1934 when he found that the great depression was damaging his prospects of getting work at home. On arrival with his forceful wife Grace at the Dadaya station in remote country to the north of Bulawayo, they found that there was not a single trained teacher in the whole area.

> The village school teachers, themselves having reached only standard two, three and four, had no timetable, no clock and no textbooks. Yet with absolutely no educational aids, they taught the children to read and write and all honour to them.[37]

Robert Mugabe, who was one of those teachers, would recall that the Todds were paid only £2 a month and Grace 'had at one point to sell her filing cabinet and a leopard skin to raise money for teachers' salaries because the total income from school fees only amounted to thirty shillings a year'.[38] Even as an old-fashioned headmaster, who was reported to have beaten 500 students, one after another, for complaining about the school food, Todd thought it nothing short of a national disgrace that the per capita educational budget for white children was fifty times larger than that for blacks. When pressed for improvement, Prime Minister Godfrey Huggins declared that the state could do no more than to educate a few natives, 'in the hope that they will pull the rest out of the mire'.[39] Huggins insisted that he did believe in racial partnership – that of horse and rider, with the whites as the rider and the blacks as the horse. In common with many liberal-minded people of the time, Todd ruled out the idea of majority rule, but he did want to see progress towards a constitution in which Africans would be involved in government on some kind of parity with whites. After standing for parliament, he was happy to serve as a loyal member of the Huggins government, and he supported the proposal for a federation with the British protectorates of Northern Rhodesia and Nyasaland that was so bitterly opposed by black nationalists. 'I told blacks that in Southern Rhodesia they outnumbered whites by 20:1, and in a federation it would

be something like 300:1. I thought this would dilute white power.
Of course', he confessed, 'I was wrong.'[40] When Huggins stepped up to
lead the larger federation, Garfield Todd inherited his position of Prime
Minister of Southern Rhodesia and he served in this role until he faced
a mass resignation of cabinet colleagues determined to preserve white
minority rule. When he appealed to the country over their heads in
a general election, he was heavily defeated by the all-white electorate.
Now knighted, Sir Garfield Todd served for five years in the Zimbabwean
senate. Deeply disillusioned by the Zanu government, he would then
resign when Shona President Mugabe unleashed his army in a brutal
settlement of old scores with the Ndebele-speaking minority.

By nature, Todd could never be a troublemaker, and more radical
politicians might cite his career as vindication of Michael Scott's dictum
that the problem with moderates was that they tended to be moderate
in their hatred of evil. In the beginning, however, the young Methodist
who arrived to take charge of a white free church on the neighbouring
copperbelt could even have been dismissed as an enemy of radical
politics. Colin Morris made no attempt to prevent members of his
congregation walking out when African representatives from a
neighbouring church took their places at his inauguration, and he would
later confess that 'during my first year of ministry, I saw to it that no
other African set foot in the church'. He even cast his vote in synod
against a motion calling for greater racial integration within the
Methodist communion.[41] Only slowly did he change his views. To begin
with, he was struck by the thought that virtually no European ever held
an intelligent conversation with any African:

> We must confess that we rarely allow an African to get close enough
> to us socially for us to be able to judge his educational standards. We
> cannot watch him eating in a hotel or train dining car because he is
> not allowed there. He cannot join any of the cultural organisations
> of our community (even those, strangely, whose membership address
> each other as 'brother'). The fact that he is an African is normally
> sufficient deterrent to prevent us from asking him into our house.[42]

When Morris made friends with the widely travelled journalist Sokota
Wina, he came to understand the depth of humiliation suffered by even
the most able and sophisticated Africans as soon as they set foot in their
own country.

Colin Morris's church emptied when he announced that nobody would be turned away on account of colour. This was a bold step for a free church minister as he could achieve nothing without the consent of his congregation. Morris would always insist that the real heroes of his story were the members of his church council, who backed his stand and held their nerve until the pews started to fill once more. Now widely reviled within the settler community as 'nothing more than a showman, a meddler in other people's affairs, a publicity minded parson', Colin Morris established a close relationship with resistance leader Kenneth Kaunda. The son of a Presbyterian clergyman and mission headmistress, Kaunda combined a fiery rhetoric of a resistance leader with a 'reassuringly Victorian' home life of daily prayers and hymn singing. In a published dialogue, Morris espoused the cause of black majority rule, while also pointing out that the way ahead would not be easy: 'It ought not to be forgotten that to a certain extent European living standards are symbol of achievement and contribution to society. They will have to mean the same thing to Africans if we are to have a thriving society.'[43]

The End of the Missionary Era?

Popes Benedict XV and Pius XI might have announced much earlier that the time of the missionary was over and that of the native church had arrived, but when John XXIII opened the Second Vatican Council, a great deal still needed to be achieved. As the bishops gathered in 1962, hardly one in four Tanzanian dioceses had a black bishop, but by the end of the century every one was African.[44] Even if Catholic progress in the first half of the century had been unspectacular, the Anglicans still lagged far behind, and three generations after Crowther's consecration, that church still had no black diocesan bishop on the African continent. Alexander Babatunde Akinyele was finally consecrated to the see of Ibadan in 1951, and a decade later, British Prime Minister Harold Macmillan toured British colonies, before finally addressing the Cape Town parliament. 'The wind of change is blowing through this continent', he declared. 'Whether we like it or not, this growth of national consciousness is a political fact.' As new nations came into being, the old colonial profile had to change, and when 735 bishops gathered for the 1998 Lambeth Conference, 224 were native Africans against just 130 from the host nation. The missionary tide then went into reverse when Ugandan John Sentamu was installed Archbishop of York in 2005. Throughout the twentieth century, the whole of Europe had been becoming increasingly secular, while sub-Saharan Africa was growing ever more Christian. In 1995, the CMS had made its concession to this changed world when it altered its name to Church Mission Society. Not everybody agreed that the missionary age was indeed over, and both the Australian and New Zealand branches declined to follow suit, but the most influential voices of dissent were heard in churches that had their origin in the United States of America.

Waves of Pentecostal revival had swept across sub-Saharan Africa during the years after 1910. While traditional denominations remained deeply tainted through association with colonial powers, this fresh generation of black and white American missionaries appeared to present a new and untainted message. In time, the Assemblies of God in Kenya and Zimbabwe, the Church of the Pentecost in Ghana and the Glad Tidings and Pentecostal Full Gospel churches in Uganda, as well as Elliot Kamwana's Watchtower Church and the New Apostolic Church in Zambia, began to overtake the more traditional Protestant denominations. For these believers, conventional missionary work was built into the fabric of faith. 'We believe that every Christian is called to be involved in missions either financially and prayerfully or by actually going to the field,' declares the Glad Tidings manifesto. Since the ruling did not apply only to foreigners, Africans also took the message to others within their own continent.[45] Millennial religion had long found a home within mainstream Protestantism and racially mixed teams now carried a distinctively East African emphasis on personal testimony to home churches in Europe and North America. By the late twentieth century, the great majority of African Protestants were happy to describe themselves as 'born again'. As had been Arthington's practice a century earlier, Bible-Belt Americans also began to list the world's disasters, not for targeting relief, but as data for a final countdown to the apocalypse. In the dying years of the twentieth century, they could record that the four riders of the apocalypse were carrying devastation across a small but beautiful country in the Rift Valley area of Central Africa.

Genocide and After

Less than a century after Bishop Hirth entered Rwanda, Catholic mission supporters could identify that country as a jewel in the missionary crown. In other sub-Saharan countries, the number of Christians – Catholic, Protestant and independent – rarely exceeded half of the total population, but in Rwanda Christians made up between 80 and 90 percent, and, of these, some 70 percent were Catholic. Even the Protestants found much to celebrate. Long-serving American missionary Gary Sheer described how he took pleasure in watching well-dressed groups of neighbours walking through the beautiful countryside to attend Sunday church services.[46] Here in Rwanda, at least, it did appear that the age of the missionary had indeed come to an end. Now, while Catholics and Protestants missionaries confined themselves to providing medical, technical and general support, while believers looked for guidance to African bishops, moderators or superintendents. But, despite all the progress towards self-government, old racial enmities still ran as deep within the church communities as they did in the wider society.

After the Belgians had driven the Germans out of the twin kingdoms of Rwanda and Burundi during the First World War, they continued the 'divide and rule' policy of keeping the majority Hutu population in subjection to the Tutsi elite. Despite its transparent absurdity, the Hamitic myth, which consigned the 'Bantu' Hutu to a lower level of human development than 'Semitic' pastoralists such as the Tutsi, continued to flourish deep into the twentieth century. By the mid-1950s, Hutu discontent was being reinforced by international pressure for colonial independence, based on the principle of majority rule. Before the Belgians granted independence to both states in 1962, they made a sharp reversal of policy and allowed the Hutus to share in the Rwandan administration. This colonial summersault proved to be a trigger for years of ethnic tension – when the Hutu massacred Tutsis in Rwanda and Tutsis massacred thousands of educated Hutus in Burundi. During this transitional period many Tutsis left Rwanda for neighbouring Uganda, where they would later support fellow 'Hamite' Yoweri Museveni's ultimately successful attempts to overthrow the two dictatorial Ugandan presidents, Idi Amin and Milton Obote.

The security situation in Rwanda did seem to improve after Hutu strongman Juvénal Habyarimana established dictatorial power in 1973. Even as he employed every device to build up his own cult of the personality, this new president continued to present himself as a pious son of the Catholic Church, visiting Rome regularly and stamping out birth-control campaigns that promoted the use of 'artificial' family planning. Catholic Archbishop Nsengiyumva prized his position as an active

member of the Central Committee of the ruling party, until Pope John
Paul finally issued a stern ultimatum that he had to choose between being
a churchman and a politician. Then, even after formally resigning from
the ruling body in obedience to the Pope's command, the archbishop
continued to take full part in state affairs.

Three events of the 1980s would, in retrospect, be seen as omens
of the disasters to come. In 1982, schoolgirls reported that the Virgin
had appeared and spoken to them in the corridor of their school in the
southern town on Kibeho. Initially they told only of warnings to the
unfaithful, but, as hysteria grew, devotees would report gruesome 'visions
of the crying Virgin, visions of people killed with machetes, of hills
covered with corpses', which would be seen as a foretelling of – and even
as divine approval for – genocide.[47] Then in 1986, leading churchmen
failed to lodge any protest when Habyarimana imprisoned and tortured
fringe Christians who refused to wear the presidential badge or take part
in events designed to celebrate the presidential personality cult.[48] During
this decade, a group of boys also came together as members of the
presidential football club.[49] Calling themselves the *interahamwe* (those
who act together), they formed themselves into a Hutu militia, that would
later provide the coordinators and storm troopers for genocide. Among
the earliest members was Robert, youngest son of Anglican teachers and
trusted missionary confidants, Marion and Eustace Kajuga.

In 1990, the Tutsi-dominated army of the Rwandan Patriotic
Front (RPF) crossed the border from Uganda, and two years later,
Habyarimana gave in to international pressure and signed a peace treaty,
under which exiled Tutsis would have the right to return home and even
take a share in government. Then, on the night of the 6 April 1994, the
presidential plane was hit by a ground-to-air missile and crashed –
killing, among others, both Habyarimana and President Ntaryamira
of Burundi. Debate continues over whether this atrocity was carried out
by members of the invading army or extremists within the president's
own ruling party. During the coming weeks, state broadcasters poured
out hatred, urging fellow Hutus to rally round the *interahamwe* to kill
all the Tutsi 'cockroaches'. 'The graves are half full', they announced.
'Who will fill them?' In this pre-industrial genocide, most victims died
slowly and painfully – often at the hands of their supposedly Christian
neighbours. Of the 900,000 Tutsi and moderate Hutu casualties, most
perished within just a 100 days of the presidential air crash. Apparently
blind to the growing bloodshed, Archbishop Nsengiyumva continued

to live within the ruling party compound and deliver his weekly address
to the nation. Lacking clear leadership from superiors, the lower clergy
responded very differently to the events in which they were now caught
up. Of about 200 priests who died, many were themselves Tutsi and
some Hutu priests died while trying to protect their flock. In the town
of Kibuye on the shores of Lake Kivu, Fr Senyenzi made every effort
to guard the Tutsis who had taken shelter in his church compound. After
pleading in vain with the governor (who in past times had been the
doctor in charge of the local hospital) this Hutu priest could only resign
himself to dying alongside his people. In just two days, the *interahamwe*
and its supporters killed some 21,000 men, women and children
in Kibuye alone.[50]

On the other side, survivors would tell how the Catholic nuns
Gertrude and Maria Kisito brought petrol to burn refugees out of their
convent's garage, and Fr Wenceslas was seen, wearing jeans and flack
jacket, with a pistol at his belt, handing out beer to the *interahamwe*.
Justifiably afraid for his life, Fr Wenceslas would later be smuggled into
France by priests, where he celebrated mass and carried out pastoral
duties until thirty-five massacre survivors published eyewitness accounts
of his complicity in atrocity.[51] When accused of 'providing killers with
lists of Tutsi in his church, flushing Tutsis out to be killed, attending
massacres without interfering, and coercing Tutsi girls to have sex with
him', he defended his actions vigorously. 'I didn't have a choice. It was
necessary to appear pro-militia. If I had had a different attitude, we
would all have disappeared.'[52] More than a decade later, his case had
still not been brought to court.[53] Less fortunate were Archbishop
Nsengiyumva, two other bishops and ten priests who were killed by RPF
soldiers, who had been charged with protecting them.

Across the ecclesiastical divide, Anglican Bishop Musabyimana was
charged, among other crimes, with 'actual and constructive knowledge
of the acts and omissions of Pastor Ngilinshuti (who had been spotted
helping soldiers and handing out weapons) and other unknown
pastors ... acting under his authority',[54] but his guilt remained unproven
as he died in custody while waiting for his case to be heard. Back in
England, retired Anglican missionaries Peter and Elizabeth Guillebaud
were watching the news on television when the president of the *intehamwe*
began to defend the killings, and to their horror, they recognised this
prime perpetrator of genocide as Robert, youngest son of Marion and
Eustace Kajuga. How, they asked could their own mission boy have

taken such a prominent part in bloodshed? Most movingly, an American reporter told how elderly Seventh Day Adventist superintendent Elizaphan Ntakirutimana (whose name translates as 'nothing is greater than God') received a letter from seven of his pastors. 'We wish to inform you that tomorrow we will be killed along with our families. We wish you to intervene on our behalf and talk to the Mayor. We believe that, with the help of God who entrusted you to the leadership of the flock which is going to be destroyed, your intervention will be highly appreciated, the same way as the Jews were saved by Esther.'[55]

Far from protecting his colleagues, Elizaphan and his doctor son Gérard appear to have taken part in the subsequent killing and both were later sentenced to twenty-five years imprisonment by an international court (of which the old man served only a small fraction). Their conviction prompted a formal statement from Adventist headquarters in Maryland, USA. 'We acknowledge with sadness that some of our church members turned against their fellow members and their neighbours. We are saddened that the accused did not act in harmony with the principles of their church. We offer an apology.'[56]

As the Hutu militia retreated into the Congo forests – where terrible violence still continues up to the time of this writing[57] – the balance sheet of heroism and blame attached to individual members of the clergy would slowly pale into insignificance beside the larger issue of how such events could occur in Africa's most Christian nation. A cardinal, who represented the Pope at a meeting of senior Rwandan priests, asked, 'are you saying, that the blood of tribalism is deeper than the waters of baptism?' – to which one church dignitary immediately replied 'yes it is!'[58] Despite the pervasive involvement of his own communion, Pope John Paul insisted that any blame must fall squarely on the individual offender. 'The church', he declared, 'cannot be held responsible for the guilt of its members that have acted against the evangelical law; they will be called to render account of their own actions.'[59]

While some Protestants were happy to ascribe all disasters to demonic possession, one observer recorded that the churches must face the 'haunting possibility' that something had gone drastically wrong with 'the Christianisation of the Rwandan people. A badly understood (Western?) Christianity broke down the norms of the traditional religion and culture, without establishing new accepted norms. Things just fell apart.'[60] Writing just months after the events, General Secretary of the Rwanda Bible Society Tharcisse Gatwa regretted the 'shallow foundations' of the famed East African Revival, which had carried evangelical Protestantism across the region. In his view, enthusiastic young missionaries had made the fundamental mistake of concentrating on the 'private, individual and familial context' of religion to the exclusion of the social gospel. In the same magazine, Anglican bishop – and present Archbishop of Rwanda – Emmanuel Kolini criticised those evangelical missionaries who had taught converts to shun the dirty game of politics – and therefore handed government to the forces of evil. 'The Protestants therefore had two stumbling blocks which made them ill-equipped to have practical political judgement – their supposedly biblical based beliefs that politics is evil and a low standard of education that reinforced a lack of understanding of political issues.' In a third article, Roger Bowen, past director of the Rwanda Mission, dismissed the kind of religion that placed an excessive emphasis on spiritual experience at the expense of hard teaching. Deprived of any solid underpinning of Christian knowledge, he argued that true revival had here degenerated into empty revivalism.[61]

Whether from the influence of past evangelical and ultramontane missionaries, or drawing from their indigenous inheritance, African Christians today overwhelmingly inhabit the conservative wings of their own confessions, and outside southern Africa, liberation theology has never established a foothold on the continent. As the Anglican communion falls apart over the exclusion of homosexual clergy, hard-line evangelicals in Britain and America – by whose criteria ordination would surely have been denied to both Trevor Huddleston and Arthur Shearsby Cripps – lay plans to place themselves under the authority of African bishops. At the same time, even as HIV/Aids advances across the continent, conservative popes rely on the support of an equally conservative Catholic hierarchy to enforce forms of sexual discipline on African women that have been widely rejected, even by the faithful, across the developed world. Partly through the fact that neither missionary societies nor colonial powers ever succeeded in laying a basis of sound all-round education, partly from post-colonial economic pressures and not a little through self-inflicted government failure and corruption, virtually all of the world's poorest countries can be found in 'middle Africa', where missionary activity was highest. Perhaps the saddest facts of all are that – whichever list you examine – Sierra Leone and Malawi, where English and Scots societies invested so much human and financial capital, currently occupy two of the five lowest places

among the world's most deprived nations and that Liberia – focus
of so much American effort – has been gravely damaged by civil war.

During the two centuries since Johannes van der Kemp and his
companions landed in South Africa, missionaries of all complexions
have dreamed of establishing new and vibrant churches with a level
of commitment that they found sadly lacking in their homelands.
The process took longer than any would have anticipated, but by the
beginning of the twenty-first century, it would be hard to argue that they
had failed. If any lessons can, however, be taken from the Rwandan
tragedy, it must surely be that fundamentalist faith – Catholic or
Protestant – which has been shorn of the social message that was
delivered by a small number of memorable pioneers, can offer little
of substance to the people of a continent who currently face a daunting
range of economic, social, political, medical and environmental
challenges.

Timeline

1701	Society for the Propagation of the Gospel founded
1732	First Moravians leave for the West Indies
1745	Thompson at Cape Coast Castle
1768	Sharp begins anti-slavery campaign
1787	First Sierra Leone settlement
1792	Nova Scotians land at Freetown
	France declared a republic
1792–1810	Early missionary societies founded
1799	Van der Kemp lands in South Africa
1807	British Atlantic slave trade abolished
1815	Basel college opened
1811	Cuffee's first visit to Sierra Leone
1816	American Colonization Society established
1819	Mr. Javouhey arrives in Senegal
1820	British settlers land at Algoa Bay, South Africa
1821	John Philip arrives in South Africa
	Ayres and Stockton acquire land for Liberian settlement
1822	The *Ilifaquane* arrives at Kuruman
1826	Fourah Bay College opens
1827	Basel missionaries arrive on the Gold Coast
1828	Buxton's Select Committee on Aboriginal Rights
1830	Gobat reaches Ethiopia
1833	Paris Evangelicals arrive in Thaba Bosiu
1834	British Act for the Emancipation of Slaves
	The Great Trek sets out
1835	American missionaries at Mzilikazi's kraal
1838	Freeman arrives on the Gold Coast
	Killing of Piet Retief and companions
1841	Failed Niger expedition
	Henry Venn appointed secretary of the CMS
	Livingstone arrives in Cape Town
1842	Krapf expelled from Shoa
	Barron sails for Liberia from the United States of America
1843	CMS Yoruba mission founded

1848	Libermann heads the Congregation of the Holy Ghost
1851	Dahomey assault on Abeokuta
	Livingstone reaches the Zambezi
1854	Baikie's successful expedition on the Niger
	Colenso tours the American Board stations
1856	Brésillac founds the Lyons Fathers
1856–1857	The Xhosa Cattle Killing
1857	Fabri appointed inspector of the Rhenish Mission
1860	Mackenzie's UMCA party on the Zambezi
1862	Colenso publishes his assault on biblical literalism
1863	Spiritans start work in East Africa
1864	Crowther consecrated bishop
1867	Lavigerie arrives in Algiers
1869	Suez Canal opens
1871	Diamonds found in Griqua country
1874	Livingstone's funeral in Westminster Abbey
1875	Scots arrive at Lake Nyasa
1876	Mahdi Uprising
1877	CMS reach Lake Victoria and Uganda
	John Mackenzie in London
1878	White Fathers start work in East Africa
	LIM and BMS arrive on the Congo
1876	Mary Slessor opens Okoyong station in Ibibo country
1885	Berlin General Act
	Spiritans arrive on the Niger
1886	Burning of the Christian pages in Uganda
1888	The Rudd Concession in Matabeleland
1890	'Young Purifiers' on the Niger
	McAdoo singers tour South Africa
1891	Bishop Crowther dies
1892	Missionaries follow German army into East Africa
	Battle of Mengo
1898	Battle of Omdurman
1900	Morel starts Congo atrocities campaign
1902	Mombassa to Nairobi railway opens
1905	Maji Maji uprising in German East Africa
1913	Harris enters the Ivory Coast
	Schweitzer arrives in Gabon

1914–1918	First World War
1919	Benedict XV delivers *Maximum Illud*
1920	Shanahan consecrated bishop
1924	The Phelps Stokes Commission
1927	Achimota opened
1939	Kaiwanika of Masaka first African Catholic bishop
1939–1945	Second World War
1953	Scott deported from South Africa
	Central African Federation formed
	Garfield Todd PM of Southern Rhodesia
1956	Huddleston publishes *Naught for Your Comfort*
1957	Kaunda and Morris publish *Black Government?*
1972	Winter deported from South-West Africa
1995	CMS changes its name from 'Missionary' to 'Mission'
2005	Ugandan-born Sentamu becomes Archbishop of York

Maps

AFRICA

EAST AFRICA, THE CONG

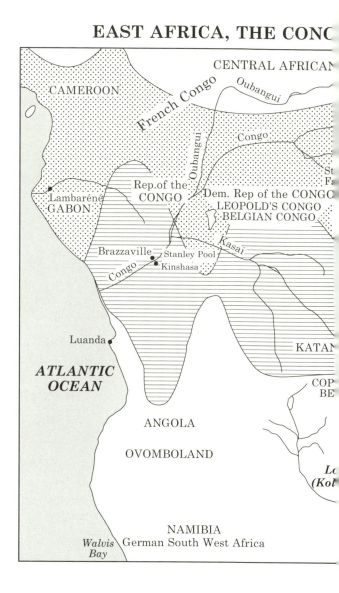

SIN AND THE RIFT VALLEY

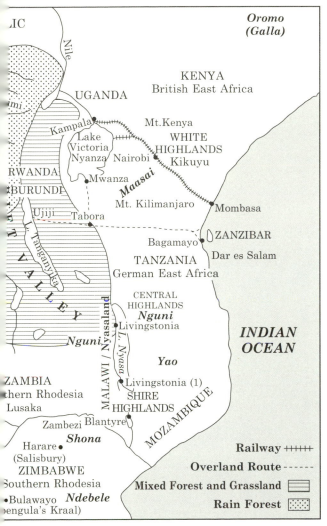

Oromo
(Galla)

LIC

Nile

KENYA
British East Africa

UGANDA

Kampala

Mt. Kenya

WHITE
HIGHLANDS

Lake
Victoria
Nyanza   Nairobi   Kikuyu

RWANDA

BURUNDI

Maasai

Mwanza

Ujiji   Tabora

Mt. Kilimanjaro   Mombasa

L. Tanganyika

ZANZIBAR

Bagamayo   Dar es Salam

TANZANIA
German East Africa

CENTRAL
HIGHLANDS
Nguni
Livingstonia

Nguni

INDIAN
OCEAN

MALAWI / Nyasaland

L. Nyasa

Yao

ZAMBIA
thern Rhodesia
Lusaka

Livingstonia (1)
SHIRE
HIGHLANDS

MOZAMBIQUE

Zambezi   Blantyre

Harare ●
(Salisbury)
ZIMBABWE
Southern Rhodesia

Shona

Bulawayo   Ndebele
engula's Kraal)

Railway +++++
Overland Route ------
Mixed Forest and Grassland ▤
Rain Forest ▦

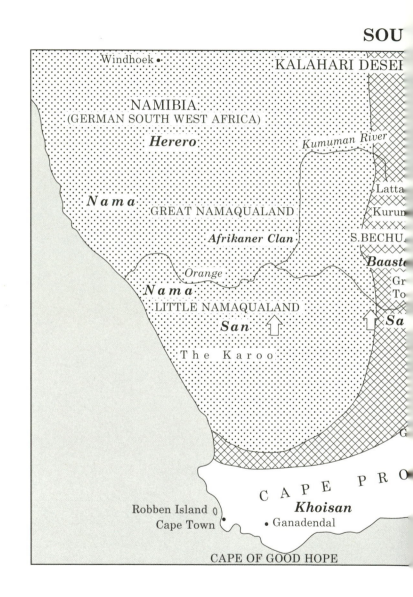

'RICA

BOTSWANA　　T R A N S V A A L
ECHUANALAND

　　　　　　　• Pretoria
　　　　　　• Mziliazi's Krall
　　　　　Johannesburg
　　　　　Rand goldfield

MOZAMBIQUE

DELAGOA BAY

ana　　　*Vaal*　　x VECHKOP

　　　　　　　　　　SWAZILAND

D　ORANGE FREE STATE　　ZULULAND
　　　　　Sotho　　　　x BLOOD RIVER
　　　　• Thaba Bosiu
Thaba Nehu　　　　　　　*Tugela*
•　　Leribe •　　LESOTHO
Kimberley　　• Morija　**Basutoland**
amond mines Beersheba　　　• **Durban**
Baastards　　　　　　　　(Port Natal)

　　　　　Orange　　NATAL
Bethulie

Khoisan　　　　　　　*Mfengu*

　　　Amatola Mts.
et •　Kat River
　　Settlement　Lovedale

N C E　　*X h o s a*　　*Kei*　　The Drakensberg Range

rahamstown •　　　　　　　Rainfall 0 – 10˝ per annum
thelsdorp •
　Elizabeth　ALGOA BAY　　Rainfall 10 – 20˝ per annum

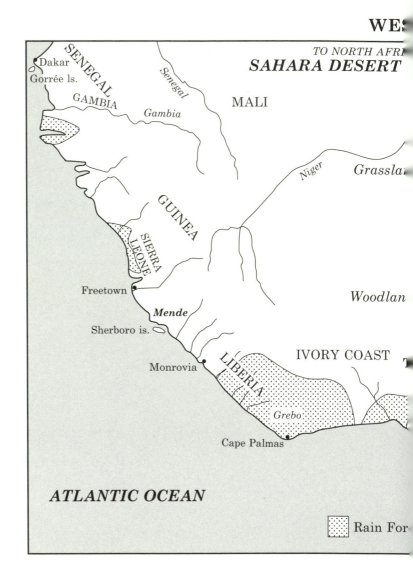

RICA

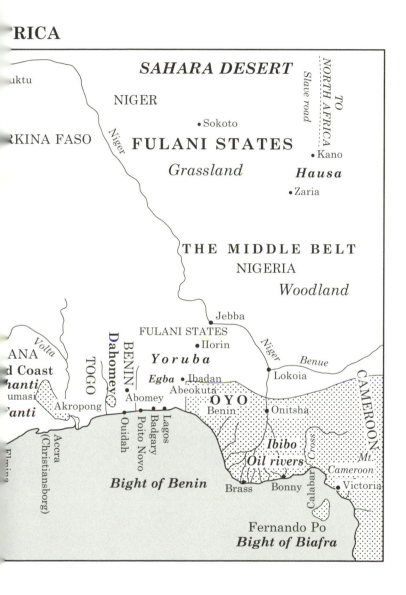

SAHARA DESERT

TO NORTH AFRICA

Slave road

NIGER

•Sokoto

RKINA FASO

FULANI STATES

Grassland

•Kano

Hausa

•Zaria

aktu

Niger

THE MIDDLE BELT

NIGERIA

Woodland

Jebba

FULANI STATES

•Ilorin

Niger

Benue

Volta

Yoruba

Lokoia

ANA

d Coast

hanti

Egba •Ibadan

Abeokuta

TOGO

BENIN

Dahomey

OYO

CAMEROON

umasi

Akropong

Abomey

anti

Benin

•Onitsha

Lagos

Badgary

Poito Novo

Ouidah

Ibibo

Oil rivers

Cross

Accra

(Christiansborg)

Bight of Benin

Brass

Bonny

Calabar

Mt.

Cameroon

•Victoria

Elmina

Fernando Po

Bight of Biafra

ETHIOPIA AND THE NILE

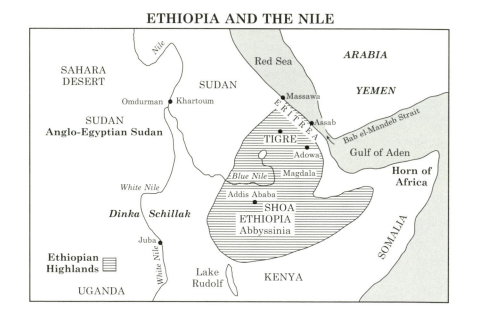

Bibliography

General

Anderson-Moreshead, A. E. M. 1897. *History of the Universities' Mission to Central Africa 1859–1896*. London.

Christensen, T., and W. R. Hutchinson. 1982. *Missionary Ideologies in the Imperial Era.* Aarhus.

Findlay, G. G., and W. W. Holdsworth. 1921. *The History of the Wesleyan Methodist Missionary Society*. London.

Groves, C. P. 1948. *The Planting of Christianity in Africa*. London.

Hastings, Adrian. 1994. *The Church in Africa 1450–1950*. Oxford.

Isichei, Elizabeth. 1995. *A History of Christianity in Africa: From Antiquity to the Present.* Grand Rapids.

Kalu, O. U., ed. 1980. *The History of Christianity in West Africa*. London.

Koren, H. J. 1958. *The Spiritans: A History of the Congregation of the Holy Ghost.* Pittsburgh.

Les Missions Catholiques (Lyons, from 1868).

Lovett, R. 1899. *The History of the London Missionary Society, 1795–1895*. London.

Mcleod, H. 2006. *The Cambridge History of Christianity*, vol.9. Cambridge.

Oliver, R. 1952. *The Missionary Factor in East Africa*. London.

Pakenham, T. 1991. *The Scramble for Africa: White Man's Conquest of the Dark Continent from 1876–1912*. London.

Porter, Andrew. 2004. *Religion versus Empire? British Protestant Missionaries and Overseas Expansion, 1700–1914*. Manchester.

Ruggieri, G., ed. 1988. *Église et Histoire de l'Église en Afrique*. Paris.

Stanley, Brian, ed. 1990. *The Bible and the Flag: Protestant Missions and British Imperialism in the 19th and 20th Centuries*. Leicester.

Stanley, Brian. 1992. *History of the Baptist Missionary Society 1792–1992*. London.

Stock, E. 1899. *History of the Church Missionary Society*. London.

Sundkler, B., and C. Steed. 2000. *A History of the Church in Africa*. Cambridge.

Warneck, G. 1906. *Outline of a History of Protestant Missions from the Reformation to the Present Time*. Edinburgh.

Chapter 1: The White Men's God

Atkins, J. 1737. *A Voyage to Guinea, Brasil and the West Indies*. London.

Brookes, G. S. 1937. *Friend Anthony Benezet*. Philadelphia.

Carey, S. P. 1934. *William Carey*. London.

Equiano, Olaudah. 1789. *Interesting Narrative of the Life of Olaudah Equiano, or Gustavus Vassa, the African*. London.

Fyfe, C. 1964. *Sierra Leone Inheritance*. London.

Hoare, P. 1820. *Memoirs of Granville Sharp Esq.* London.

Horne, M. 1794. *Letters on Missions*. Bristol.

Kruger, B. 1966. *The Pear Tree Blossoms*. Genadendal.

Lewis, A. J. 1960. *Zinzendorf, the Ecumenical Pioneer: A Study in the Moravian Contribution to Christian Mission and Unity*. London.

Meachan, S. 1964. *Henry Thornton of Clapham, 1760–1815*. Cambridge, MA.

Morris, J. W. 1826. *Memoirs of the Life and Writings of the Rev. Andrew Fuller*. London.

Newton, J. 1925. *Out of the Depths*. London.

Sharp, G. 1773. *An Essay on Slavery*. London.

Spangenberg, A. G. 1838. *The Life of Nicholas Lewis Count Zinzendorf*. London.

Stanley, B., ed. 2001. *Christian Missions and the Enlightenment*. Grand Rapids.

Thompson, T. 1758. *An Account of Two Missionary Voyages: By the Appointment of the Society of the Gospel in Foreign Parts*. London.

Wadstrom, C. B. 1789. *Observations on the Slave Trade and a Description of Some Parts of the Coast of Guinea*. London.

Chapter 2: The Foundation of Happiness

Ashmun, J. 1921. *Memoir of the Life and Character of the Rev. Samuel Bacon*. Washington, DC.

Bane, M. J. 1956. *Catholic Pioneers in West Africa*. Dublin.

Biller, S. 1837. *Memoir of the Late Hannah Kilham*. London.

Birks, T. R. 1852. *Memoir of the Rev. Edward Bickersteth*. London.

Cable, M. 1971; repr. 1977. *Black Odyssey: The Case of the Slave Ship Amistad*. New York; London.

Campbell, P. 1971. *Maryland in Africa: The Maryland State Colonization Society, 1831–1857*. Chicago.

Coker, D. 1810. *A Dialogue between a Virginian and an African Minister*. Baltimore.

Crooks, J. J. 1903. *A History of the Colony of Sierra Leone*. Dublin.

Cuffe, P. 1812. *A Brief Account of the Settlement and Present Situation of the Colony of Sierra Leone*. New York.

Dunn, D. E. 1992. *A History of the Episcopal Church in Liberia, 1821–1980*. Metuchen, NJ.

Falconbridge, A. M. 1802. *Narrative of Two Voyages to the River Sierra Leone*. London.

Fisher, M. M. 1982. 'Lott Cary: The Colonizing Missionary'. In *Black Apostles at Home and Abroad: Afro-Americans and the Christian Mission from the Revolution to Reconstruction*. Edited by D. W. Wills and R. Newman. Boston.

Flickinger, D. F. 1907. *Fifty-Five Years of Active Ministerial Life*. Dayton.

Fyfe, C. 1962. *A History of Sierra Leone*. London.

Fyfe, C. 1964. *Sierra Leone Inheritance*. London.

Fyfe, C., and E. Jones, eds. 1968. *Freetown: A Symposium*. Freetown.

Gurley, R. R. 1971. *Life of Jehudi Ashmun, Late Colonial Agent in Liberia: With an Appendix, Containing Extracts from His Journal and Other Writings; with a Brief Sketch of the Life of the Rev. Lott Cary*. New York.

Harris, K. 1985. *African and American Values: Liberia and West Africa*. Lanham, MD.

Hennell, M. 1958. *John Venn and the Clapham Sect*. London.

Huberich, C. H. 1947. *The Political and Legislative History of Liberia*, 2 vols. New York.

Jakobsson, S. 1972. *Am I Not a Man and a Brother?* Uppsala.

Kilhman, H. 1830. *The Claims to West Africans to Christian Instruction through the Native Languages*. London.

Knutsford, Viscountess. 1900. *Life and Letters of Zachary Macaulay*. London.

Kup, A. P. 1961. *A History of Sierra Leone: 1400–1787*. Cambridge.

Liebenow, J. G. 1987. *Liberia: The Quest for Democracy*. Bloomington.

Lynch, H. R. 1980. 'The Native Pastorate Controversy and Cultural Ethno-centrism in Sierra Leone 1871–1874'. Pp.270–292 in *The History of Christianity in West Africa*. Edited by O. U. Kalu. London.

Macaulay, K. 1827. *The Colony of Sierra Leone Vindicated from the Misrepresentations of Mr. Macqueen of Glasgow*. London.

Martin, C. 1970. *The Amistad Affair*. New York and London.

Martin, Jane. 1968. 'The Dual Legacy: Government Authority and Mission Influence among the Glebo of Eastern Liberia, 1834–1910'. Ph.D. Thesis. Boston University.

Meacham, S. 1964. *Henry Thornton of Clapham, 1760–1815*. Cambridge, MA.

Morgan, J. 1864. *Reminiscences of the Founding of a Christian Mission on the Gambia*. London.

Moses, W. J. 1989. *Alexander Crummell: A Study of Civilization and Discontent*. New York.

Nash, G. B. 1988. *Forging Freedom: The Formation of Philadelphia's Black Community, 1720–1840*. Cambridge, MA.

Olson, G. W. 1969. *Church Growth in Sierra Leone: A Study of Church Growth in Africa's Oldest Protestant Mission Field*. Grand Rapids.

Owens, W. A. 1953. *Slave Mutiny: The Revolt on the Schooner Amistad*. London.

Pierson, A. T. 1897. *Seven Years in Sierra Leone*. London.

Schama, Simon. 2005. *Rough Crossings*. London.

Shick, T. W. 1980. *Behold the Promised Land: A History of Afro-American Settler Society in Nineteenth-Century Liberia*. Baltimore.

Smith, J. W. 1987. *Sojourners in Search of Freedom: The Settlement of Liberia by Black Americans*. Lanham.

Staudenraus, P. J. 1961. *The African Colonization Movement, 1816–1865*. New York.

Thompson, G. 1852. *Thompson in Africa: Or, an Account of the Missionary Labors, Sufferings, Travels, and Observations*. New York.

Thompson, G. 1858. *The Palm-Land of West Africa*. Cincinnati.

Walker, J. W. St. G. 1976. *The Black Loyalists: The Search for a Promised Land in Nova Scotia and Sierra Leone 1783–1870*. London.

Walls, A. F. 1959. 'The Nova Scotian Settlers and Their Religion'. *Sierra Leone Bulletin of Religion* 19–31.

Walls, A. F. 2008. 'The Influence of Sierra Leone on Methodist Mission Thought and Practice'. Henry Martin Centre Lecture, 14 February.

Williams, P., Jr. 1817. *A Discourse Delivered on the Death of Paul Cuffe, before the New York African Institution, in the African Methodist Episcopal Zion Church*. October 21, 1817.

Wilson, C. M. 1971. *Liberia: Black Africa in Microcosm*. New York.

Chapter 3: Knowing One's Place as a Negro

Ajayi, J. F. A. 1965. *Christian Missions in Nigeria 1841–1891*. London.

Ajayi, J. F. A. 1980. 'Henry Venn and the Policy of Development'. In *The History of Christianity in West Africa*. Edited by O. U. Kalu. London.

Ajayi, W. O. 1980. 'Christian Involvement in the Ijaye War'. Pp.200–214 in *The History of Christianity in West Africa*. Edited by O. U. Kalu. London.

Ayandele, E. A. 1966. *The Missionary Impact on Modern Nigeria 1842–1914: A Political and Social Analysis*. London.

Barnard, F. M. 1965. *Herder's Social and Political Thought*. Oxford.

Bartels, F. L. 1965. *The Roots of Ghana Methodism*. Cambridge.

Beecham, J. 1841. *Ashantee and the Gold Coast: Being a Sketch of the History, Social State, and Superstitions of the Inhabitants of Those Countries: With a Notice of the State and Prospects of Christianity among Them*. London.

Bowen, T. J. 1857. *Central Africa: Adventures and Missionary Labors in Several Countries in the Interior of Africa from 1849–1856*. Charleston.

Buxton, T. F. 1840. *The African Slave Trade and Its Remedy*. London.

Clark, J. 1850. *Memoirs of R. & J. Merrick*. London.

Crowther, S. 1855. *Journal of an Expedition up the Niger and Tshadda Rivers*. London.

Crowther, S., and J. C. Taylor. 1859. *The Gospel on the Banks of the Niger*. London.

Curtin, P. D. 1965. *Images of Africa*. London.

Debrunner, H. W. 1965. *A Church between Colonial Powers: A Study of the Church in Togo*. London.

Debrunner, H. W. 1967. *A History of Christianity in Ghana*. Accra.

Delaney, M. R., and Campbell. 1969. *Search for a Place: Black Separatism and Africa, 1860*. Ann Arbor.

Fiedler, K. 1996. *Christianity and African Culture*. Leiden.

Freeman, T. B. 1843. *Journal of Two Visits to the Kingdom of Ashanti, in Western Africa.* London.

Hackett, R. 1989. *Religion in Calabar: The Religious Life and History of a Nigerian Town.* Mouton de Gruyer.

Hinderer, A. 1872. *Seventeen Years in the Yoruba Country: Memorials of Anna Hinderer.* London.

Innes, A. 1862. *Cruelties Committed on the West Coast of Africa by an Agent of the Baptist Mission.* London.

Kimble, D. 1973. *A Political History of the Gold Coast, 1850–1928.* Oxford.

Lander, Richard, and John Lander. 1832. *Journal of an Expedition to Explore the Course and Termination of the Niger.* London.

McFarlan, D. 1946. *Calabar: The Church of Scotland Mission.* London.

Mobley, H. W. 1970. *The Ghanaian's Image of the Missionary.* Leiden.

Moister, W. 1875. *Memoir of the Rev. Henry Wharton.* London.

Page, J. 1908. *The Black Bishop, Samuel Adjai Crowther.* London.

Ramseyer, F. A., and S. J. Kühne. 1875. *Four Years in Ashantee.* London.

Rennsitch, K. 1982. 'The Understanding of Mission, Civilization and Colonialism in the Basel Mission'. Pp.94–103 in *Missionary Ideologies in the Imperial Era: 1880–1920.* Edited by T. Christensen and W. R. Hutchinson. Aarhus.

Schön, J. F., and S. A. Crowther. 1842. *The Journals of the Rev James Frederick Schön and Mr. Samuel Crowther.* London.

Smith, N. 1966. *The Presbyterian Church of Ghana, 1835–1960.* Accra.

Taylor, W. H. 1996. *A Mission to Educate: A History of the Educational Work of the Scottish Presbyterian Mission in East Nigeria 1846–1960.* Leiden.

Townsend, G. 1887. *Memoir of Rev. Henry Townsend.* London.

Underhill, E. B. 1884. *Alfred Saker: A Biography.* London.

Venn, H. 1971. *To Apply the Gospel: Selection from the Writings of Henry Venn.* Grand Rapids.

Waddell, A. 1883. *Memorials of Mrs. Sutherland, Missionary, Old Calabar.* Paisley.

Waddell, H. M. 1863. *Twenty Nine Years in the West Indies and Central Africa.* London.

Ward, W. E. F. 1949. *A History of the Gold Coast.* London.

Wiltgen, R. M. 1956. *Gold Coat Mission History, 1471–1880.* Techny, IL.

Yates, T. E. 1978. *Venn and Victorian Bishops Abroad.* Uppsala.

Chapter 4: A Crucifix and a Breviary

Ajayi, J. F. A. 1965. *Christian Missions in Nigeria 1841–1891.* London.

Coulon, P., and P. Brasseur. 1988. *Libermann 1802–1852.* Paris.

Cullen, J. B. 1912. *Life of Venerable Mother Javouhey.* Dublin.

Gadille, J. 1988. 'Idéology des Missions Catholique en Afrique Francophone'. Pp.43–61 in *Église et Histoire de L'Église en Afrique.* Edited by G. Ruggieri. Paris.

Hogan, E. M. 1981. *Catholic Missionaries and Liberia.* Cork.

Isichei, E. 1982. 'An Obscure Man. Pa Antonio in Lagos'. Pp.28–33 in *Varieties of Christian Experience in Nigeria.* Edited by E. Isichei. London.

Jones, D. H. 1980. 'The Catholic Mission and Some Aspects of Assimilation in Senegal, 1817–1852'. *Journal of African History* 21.3.

Koren, H. J. 1958. *The Spiritans: A History of the Congregation of the Holy Ghost.* Pittsburgh.

Les Missions Catholiques. Tome 9 (Lyons, 1877).

O'Carroll, M. 1982. *Francis Libermann: Apostle of Africa.* London.

Ruggieri, G., ed. 1988. *Église et Histoire d'Église en Afrique.* Paris.

The Irish Province of the Society of African Missions. 1956. *100 Years of Achievement.* Cork.

Todd, J. M. 1962. *African Mission*. London.

Tucker, J. T. 1933. *Angola, the Land of the Blacksmith Prince*. London, p.32.

Chapter 5: Stolen Country

Ayliff, J., and J. Whiteside. 1902. *History of the Abambo, Generally known as the Fingos*. Cape Town.

Benham, M. S. 1896. *Henry Callaway: First Bishop for Kaffraria*. London, p.58.

Broadbent, S. 1865. *Narrative of the First Introduction of Christianity amongst the Barolong Tribe*. London.

Brown, G. 1855. *Personal Adventure in South Africa*. London.

Brownlee, C. 1896. *Reminiscences of Kaffir Life and History*. Lovedale.

Calderwood, H. 1858. *Caffres and Caffre Missions*. London.

Cobbing, Julian. 1988. 'The Mfecane as Alibi'. *Journal of African History* 487–519.

Cochrane, J. R. 1987. *Servants of Power: The Role of the English-Speaking Churches in South Africa, 1903–1930*. Johannesburg.

Comaroff, Jean, and John Comaroff. 1991. *Of Revelation and Revolution*, 2 vols. Chicago.

le Cordeur, B., and C. Saunders, eds. 1976. *The Kitchingman Papers*. Johannesburg.

Davies, H., and R. H. W. Shepherd. 1954. *South African Missions: An Anthology*. London, p.100.

Dugmore, H. H. 1958. *The Reminiscences of an Albany Settler*. Grahamstown.

Enklaar, I. H. 1988. *Life and Work of Dr. J. Th. van der Kemp 1747–1811*. Cape Town.

Etherington, N. 1978. *Preachers, Peasants and Politics in South East Africa, 1835–1880*. London.

Eveleigh, W. 1920. *The Settlers and Methodism*. Cape Town.

Godlonton, R., and Irving. 1851. *A Narrative of the Kaffir War of 1850–1851*. London.

Holt, B. 1954. *John Williams and the Pioneer Mission to the South Eastern Bantu*. Lovedale.

Lakeman, Sir S. 1880. *What I Saw in Kaffirland*. London.

Lichtenstein, H. 1815. *Travels in the Southern Africa*. London.

Lovett, R. 1899. *History of the London Missionary Society*. London.

MacCrone, I. D. 1937. *Race Attitudes in South Africa*. Johannesburg.

Majeke, N. n.d. *The Role of the Missionaries in Conquest*. Johannesburg.

Merriman, N. 1854. *Passages of Missionary Life from the Journals of the Venerable Archdeacon Merriman*. London.

Mostert, N. 1993. *Frontiers*. London.

Peires, J. B. 1982. *The House of Phalo: A History of the Xhosa People in the Days of Their Independence*. Berkeley.

Peires, J. B. 1989. *The Dead Will Arise: Nongqawuse and the Great Xhosa Cattle-Killing*. Johannesburg.

Philip, J. 1828. *Researches in South Africa*. London.

Ricards, J. D. 1880. *The Catholic Church and the Kaffirs*. London.

Ross, A. C. 1986. *John Philip 1775–1851: Missions, Race and Politics in South Africa*. Aberdeen.

Ross, R. 1976. *Adam Kok's Griquas*. Cambridge.

Sadler, C., ed. 1967. *Never a Young Man: Letters and Journals of the Rev. William Shaw*. Cape Town.

Sayles, J. 1975. *Mission Stations and the Coloured Communities of the Eastern Cape, 1800–1852*. Cape Town.

Shaw, W. 1974. *Memoir of the Rev. W. Shaw*. London.

Shrewsbury, J. V. B. 1867. *Memorials of the Rev. William J. Shrewsbury*. London.

Templin, J. A. 1984. *Ideology on a Frontier: The Theological Foundation of Afrikaner Nationalism, 1652–1910*. Westport, CT.

Wells, J. 1909. *Stewart of Lovedale: The Life of James Stewart*. London.

Whiteside, J. 1906. *The History of the Wesleyan Methodist Church in South Africa*. London, p.187.

Williams, D. 1978. *Umfundisi: A Biography of Tiyo Soga*. Lovedale.

Chapter 6: The Cheapest and Best Military Posts

Booth, A. R. 1976. *The United States' Experience in South Africa*. Cape Town.

Broadbent, S. 1865. *The Barolongs of South Africa*. London.

Brown, W. E. 1960. *The Catholic Church in South Africa*. London.

Campbell, J. 1918. *Travels in South Africa*. London.

Casalis, E. 1861. *The Basutos*. London.

Casalis, E. 1889. *My Life in Basutoland*. London.

Champion, G. 1967. *The Journal of an American Missionary in the Cape Colony*. Cape Town.

Colenso, J. W. 1855. *Ten Weeks in Natal*. Cambridge.

Colenso, J. W. 1863a. *The Pentateuch and Book of Joshua Critically Examined*. London.

Colenso, J. W. 1863b. *The Trial of the Bishop of Natal for Erroneous Teaching*. Cape Town.

Comaroff, Jean, and John Comaroff. 1991. *Of Revelation and Revolution*. Chicago.

Cory, G. E., ed. 1926. *The Diary of the Rev. Francis Owen, Missionary with Dingaan in 1837–1838*. Cape Town.

Ellenburger, V. 1938. *A Century of Mission Work in Basutoland*. Morija.

Germond, R. C. 1967. *Chronicles of Basutoland*. Morija.

Gray, C. 1876. *Life of Robert Gray*. London.

Guy, J. 1983. *The Heretic: A Study of the Life of John William Colenso, 1814–1883*. Pietermaritzburg.

Haggard, H. Ryder. 1882. *Cetywayo and His White Neighbours*. London.

Hance, G. R. 1916. *The Zulu Yesterday and Today*. New York.

Jeal, T. 1973. *Livingstone*. London.

Kotzé, D. J. 1950. *Letters of the American Missionaries, 1835–1838*, vol.31. Cape Town.

Livingstone, D. 1857. *Missionary Travels and Researches in South Africa*. London.

Malan, C. H. 1876. *South African Missions*. London.

Moffat, R. 1842. *Missionary Labours*. London.

Moffat, R. 1976. *The Matabele Journals of Robert Moffat*. London.

Moffat, R., and M. Moffat. 1962. *Apprenticeship at Kuruman*. London.

Northcott, C. 1961. *Robert Moffatt, Pioneer in Africa*. London.

Parsons, J. W. 1997. *The Livingstones at Kolobeng, 1847–1857*. Gaborone, Botswana.

du Plessis, J. 1911. *A History of Christian Missions in South Africa*. London.

Price, E. L. 1956. *The Journal of Elizabeth Lees Price*. London.

Rees, W., ed. 1958. *Colenso Letters from Natal*. Pietermaritzburg.

Ross, R. J. 1976. *Adam Kok's Griquas: A Study in the Development of Stratification in South Africa*. Cambridge.

Sanders, P. 1975. *Moshoeshoe: Chief of the Sotho*. London.

Schapera, I., ed. 1974. *David Livingstone's South African Papers, 1849–1853*. Cape Town.

Simensen, J., ed. 1986. *Norwegian Missions in African History*. London.

Smit, E. 1972. *The Diary of Erasmus Smith*. Cape Town.

Smith, E. W. 1949. *The Life and Times of Daniel Lindley*. London.

Tyler, J. 1971. *Forty Years among the Zulus*. Cape Town.

Vijn, C. 1988. *Cetshwayo's Dutchman*. London.

Welsh, D. 1971. *The Roots of Segregation*. Cape Town.

Chapter 7: The Rewards of Great Sanctity

de Arteche, J. 1964. *The Cardinal of Africa*. London.

Bakke, J. 1987. *Christian Ministry: Patterns and Functions within the Ethiopian Evangelical Church Mekane Yesus*. Oslo.

Bouniol, J. 1929. *The White Fathers and Their Missions*. London.

Burridge, W. 1966. *Destiny Africa: Cardinal Lavigerie and the Making of the White Fathers*. London.

Cohen, W. B. 1980. *The French Encounter with Africans: White Response to Blacks, 1530–1880*. Bloomington and London.

Crummey, D. 1972. *Priests and Politicians: Protestant and Catholic Missions in Orthodox Ethiopia, 1830–1868*. Oxford.

Cuoq, J. 1986. *Lavigerie, les Pères Blancs et les Musulmans*. Rome.

Fowler, M. 1901. *Christian Egypt*. London.

Gobat, S. 1847. *Journal of Three Years Residence in Abyssinia*. London.

Gobat, S. 1884. *His Life and Works: A Biographical Sketch Chiefly from His Own Journals*. London.

Groves, C. P. 1948. *The Planting of Christianity in Africa*. London.

Hastings, Adrian. 1994. *The Church in Africa, 1450-1950*. Oxford.

Herbert, Lady M. E. 1867. *Abyssinia and Its Apostle*. London.

Isenberg, C. W., and J. L. Krapf. 1968. *The Journals of C. W. Isenberg and J. L. Krapf*. London.

Krapf, J. L. 1860. *Travels, Researches and Missionary Labours*. London.

McEwan, D. A. 1987. *Catholic Sudan: Dream, Mission, Reality*. Rome.

Mondini, A. G. 1964. *Africa or Death*. Boston.

Montclos, X. 1965. *Lavigerie; Le Saint-Siège et l'Église*. Paris.

New, C. 1971. *Life Wanderings and Labours in Eastern Africa*. London.

O'Donnell, J. D. 1979. *Lavigerie in Tunisia: The Interplay of Imperialist and Missionary*. Athens, GA.

Pearce, N. 1831. *The Life and Adventures of Nathaniel Pearce: Written by Himself*. London.

Petherick, J. 1861. *Egypt, the Sudan and Central Africa*. Edinburgh.

Renault, F. 1994. *Cardinal Lavigerie, Churchman, Prophet and Missionary*. London.

Riley, G. 1972. *No Drums at Dawn*. Melbourne.

Slade, R. M. 1959. *English-Speaking Missions in the Congo Independent State (1878–1908)*. Brussels.

Storme, M. 1957. *Rapports du Père Planque, de Mgr Lavigerie et de Mgr Comboni sur l'Association Internationale Africaine*. Brussels.

Tonilo, E., and R. Hill. 1974. *The Opening of the Nile Basin*. London.

Vantini, G. 1981. *Christianity in the Sudan*. Bologna.

Waldmeier, T. 1886. *The Autobiography of Theophilus Waldmeier*. London.

Chapter 8: Pitching Tents in the Interior

Anonymous. 1884. *A L'Assault des Pays Negrès. Journal des Missionaires d'Alger dans l'Afrique Equitoriale*. Paris.

Anonymous. 1892. *L.Ouganda et les Agissements de la Companie Anglaise 'East Africa'*. Paris.

Arnoux, M. 1947. *Les Pères Blanc au Aources du Nil*. Namur.

Ashe, R. P. 1894. *Chronicles of Uganda*. London.

Awdry, F. 1904. *An Elder Sister*. London.

Baskerville, G. K., and G. L. Pilkington. 1896. *The Gospel in Uganda*. London.

Beach, D. N. 1973. 'The Initial Impact of Christianity on the Shona'. Pp.25–40 in *Christianity South of the Zambezi*. Edited by A. J. Dachs. Gwelo.

Bentley, H. M. W. 1907. *Holman Bentley: Life and Labours of a Congo Pioneer*. London.

Boeder, R. B. 1981. *Alfred Sharp of Nyasaland*. Blantyre.

Buchanan, J. 1885. *The Shire Highlands*. Edinburgh.

Chadwick, Owen. 1959. *Mackenzie's Grave*. London.

Coillard, F. 1897. *On the Threshold of Central Africa*. London.

Cussac, J. 1955. *Évêque et Pionnier, Mgr. Streicher*. Paris.

Elmslie, W. A. 1899. *Among the Wild Ngoni*. Edinburgh.

Gale, H. P. 1959. *Uganda and the Mill Hill Fathers*. London.

Guinness, H. G. 1890. *The New World of Central Africa*. London.

Hansen, H. B. 1984. *Mission, Church and State in a Colonial Setting*. London.

Harrison, J. W. 1890. *A.M. Mackay: Pioneer Missionary of the Church Missionary Society to Uganda*. London.

Hawker, G. 1909. *The Life of George Grenfell*. London.

Helgesson, A. 1994. *Church, State and People in Mozambique*. Uppsala.

Hellberg, C. J. 1965. *Mission on a Colonial Frontier West of Lake Victoria*. Uppsala.

Hore, E. C. 1970. *Missionary to Tanganyika, 1877–1888*. London.

Kieran, J. A. P. 1966. 'The Holy Ghost Fathers in East Africa'. Ph.D. Thesis. University of London.

Leblond, G. 1942. *Le Père Auguste Achte*. Algiers.

Lechaptois, A. 1913. *Aux Rives du Tanganyika*. Algiers.

Livingstone, W. P. 1921. *Laws of Livingstonia*. London.

Lovett, R. 1899. *History of the London Missionary Society*. London.

Lugard, F. 1892. 'British Officials and French Accusations'. *Fortnightly Review*, November.

Lugard, F. 1893. *The Rise of Our East African Empire*. London.

Mackintosh, C. W. 1907. *Coillard of the Zambezi*. London.

McCracken, J. 1977. *Politics and Christianity in Malawi, 1875–1940*. Cambridge.

Moffat, R. 1945. *The Matabele Journals of Robert Moffat, 1829–1860*. London.

Oded, A. 1974. *Islam in Uganda*. Jerusalem.

Pirouet, M. L. 1978. *Black Evangelists*. London.

Pirouet, M. L. 1982. 'Women Missionaries of the Church Missionary Society in Uganda, 1896–1920'. Pp.231–242 in *Missionary Ideologies in the Imperial Era*. Edited by T. Christensen and W. R. Hutchinson. Aarhus.

Rowe, J. A. 1964. 'The Purge of Christians at Mwanga's Court'. *Journal of African History* 5: 55–72.

Rowley, H. 1867. *Story of the Universities' Mission to Central Africa*. London.

Sedgwick, A., and W. Monk, eds. *Dr. Livingstone's Cambridge Lectures*. Cambridge.

Slade, R. M. 1959. *English-Speaking Missions in the Congo Independent State (1878–1908)*. Brussels.

Stewart, J. 1894. *Lovedale*. Edinburgh.

Thomas, T. M. 1872. *Eleven Years in Central South Africa*. London.

Thompson, J. T. 1995. *Christianity in Northern Malawi*. Leiden.

Thoonen, J. P. 1941. *Black Martyrs*. London.

Tiberondwa, A. K. 1978. *Missionary Teachers as Agents of Colonialism*. Lusaka.

Tucker, A. R. 1911. *Eighteen Years in Uganda*. London.

Twaddle, M. 1993. *Kakungulu and the Creation of Uganda, 1868–1928*. London.

Waliggo, J. M. 1976. 'The Catholic Church in the Buddu Province of Buganda'. Ph.D. Thesis. University of Cambridge.

Waller, H., ed. 1974. *The Last Journals of David Livingstone in Central Africa*. London.

Wallis, J. P. R., ed. 1952a. *The Matabele Mission*. London.

Wallis, J. P. R., ed. 1952b. *The Zambezi Journals of James Stewart*. London.

Wells, J. 1909. *Stewart of Lovedale*. London.

Young, E. D. 1887. *Nyassa: A Journey of Adventures*. London.

Chapter 9: Losing It or Ruling It

Arnold, W. E. 1985. *Here to Stay: The History of the Anglican Church in Zimbabwe*. Lewes.

Arnot, F. S. 1889. *Garenganze: Or, Seven Years Pioneer Mission Work in Central Africa.* London.

Augouard, P. 1905. *28 Annés au Congo.* Poitiers.

Cairns, H. A. C. 1965. *Prelude to Imperialism: British Reactions to Central African Society, 1840–1890.* London.

Chirnside, A. 1880. *The Blantyre Missionaries: Discreditable Disclosures.* London.

Comaroff, Jean, and John Comaroff. 1991. *Of Revelation and Revolution,* vol.1. Chicago.

Crawford, D. 1912. *Thinking Black.* London.

Dreschler, H. 1980. *Let Us Die Fighting.* London.

Drummond, H. 1888. *Tropical Africa.* London.

Gorjou, J. 1926. *En Zigzags en travers l'Urundi.* Namur.

Goyau, G. 1926. *Monseigneur Augouard.* Paris.

Halldén, E. 1968. *The Culture Policy of the Basel Mission in the Cameroons.* Lund.

Hanna, A. J. 1956. *The Beginnings of Nyasaland and North Eastern Rhodesia.* Oxford.

Herman, Arthur. 2001. *The Scottish Enlightenment.* London.

Knight-Bruce, G. W. H. 1895. *Memories of Mashonaland.* London.

Livingstone, W. P. 1931. *A Prince of Missionaries.* London.

Loth, H. 1963. *Die Christliche Mission in Sudwestafrika.* Berlin.

Mackenzie, J. 1887. *Austral Africa,* vol.1. London.

Mackenzie, W. 1902. *Douglas, John Mackenzie, South African Missionary and Statesman.* London.

Mackintosh, C. W. 1907. *Coillard of the Zambezi.* London.

Mullins, J. 1877. 'A New Route and Mode of Travel'. *Proceedings of the Royal Geographical Society,* 26 February.

Ogilvie, J. N. 1923. *Our Empire's Debt to Missions.* London.

Oliver, R. 1957. *Sir Harry Johnston and the Scramble for Africa.* London.

Oliver, R. 1965. *The Missionary Factor in East Africa.* London.

Perham, M. 1956. *Lugard: The Years of Adventure.* London.

Prins, G. 1980. *The Hidden Hippopotamus.* Cambridge.

Rabut, E. 1989. *Brazza, Commissaire Général. Le Congo Français 1886–1897.* Paris.

Ross, A. C. 1996. *Blantyre Mission and the Making of Modern Malawi.* Blantyre.

Rotberg, R. I. 1964. 'Plymouth Brethren and the Occupation of Katanga, 1886–1907'. *Journal of African History* 2: 285–297.

Rotberg, R. I. 1965. *Christian Missionaries and the Creation of Northern Rhodesia.* Princeton.

Sapeto, G. 1879. *Assab e suoi Critici.* Genoa.

Sillery, A. 1971. *John Mackenzie of Bechuanaland: A Study in Humanitarian Imperialism.* Cape Town.

Steere, D. V. 1973. *God's Irregular: Arthur Shearly Cripps.* London.

Swann, A. J. 1969. *Fighting Slave-Hunters in Central Africa.* London.

Temu, A. J. 1972. *British Protestant Missions.* London.

de Vries, J. L. 1978. *Mission and Colonialism in Namibia.* Johannesburg.

Watt, S. 1923. *In the Heart of Savagedom.* London.

Whitford, J. 1867. *Trading Life in Western and Central Africa.* Liverpool.

de Witte, Baron J. 1924. *Monseigneur Augouard.* Paris.

Chapter 10: If This Is Civilisation, What Is Barbarism?

Alexis, F. 1894. *Soldats et Missionaires au Congo.* Brussels.

Anderson, W. H. 1919. *On the Trail of Livingstone.* Mountain View, CA.

Andrews, C. F. 1935. *John White of Mashonaland.* London.

Anonymous. 1947. 'A Dominican Sister': *In God's White Robed Army.* Cape Town.

Arnoux, A. 1947. *Les Pères Blancs aux Sources du Nil.* Namur.

Beach, D. N. 1973. 'The Initial Impact of Christianity on the Shon'. Pp.25–40 in *Christianity South of the Zambezi*, vol.1. Edited by A. J. Dachs. Gwelo.

Beidelman, T. O. 1981. *Colonial Evangelism*. Bloomington.

Benedetto, R. 1996. *Presbyterian Reformers in Central Africa*. Leiden.

Bennett, N. R. 1964. 'The British on Kilimanjaro'. *Tanganyika Notes and Records* No 63: 229–240.

Bentley, W. H. 1887. *Life on the Congo*. London.

Bentley, W. H. 1900. *Pioneering on the Congo*. London.

Bhebe, N. 1979. *Christianity and Traditional Religion in Western Zimbabwe 1859–1923*. London.

Bindseil, R. 1998. *Le Rwanda et l'Allemagne depuis le temps de Richard Kandt*. Berlin.

Bley, H. 1971. *South West Africa under German Rule*. London.

Boulger, D. C. 1903. *The Congo State Is Not a Slave State*. London.

Chanatwa, D. 1981. *The Occupation of Southern Rhodesia*. Nairobi.

Chrétien, J. P. 1993. *Burundi, l'histoire retrouvée: Vingt-cinq ans de métier d'historien en Afrique*. Paris.

Cocks, F. S., and E. D. Morel. 1920. *The Man and His Work*. London.

Conrad, J. 1899. *Heart of Darkness*. London.

Dachs, A. J., and W. F. Rea. 1979. *The Catholic Church and Zimbabwe, 1879–1979*. Gwelo.

Doerr, L. 1969. 'The Relationship between the Benedictine Mission and the German Colonial Authorities'. *Dini na Milla*. Kampala.

Enquist, Roy, J. 1990. *Namibia, Land of Tears, Land of Promise*. Selinsgrove.

Fox Bourne, H. R. 1903. *Civilization in Congoland*. London.

Fripp, C. E. 1949. *Gold and the Gospel in Mashonaland: The Mashona Mission of Bishop Knight-Bruce*. London.

Genichen, H. W. 1982. 'German Protestant Missions'. Pp.181–190 in *Missionary Ideologies in the Imperial Era*. Edited by T. Christensen and W. R. Hutchinson. Aarhus.

Goldblatt, L. 1971. *History of South West Africa*. Cape Town.

Guinness, F. E. 1890. *The New World of Central Africa*. London.

Guinness, H. G. 1904. *Congo Slavery*. London.

Gwassa, G. C. K., and J. Iliffe. 1967. 'Records of the Maji Maji Rising'. *Historical Association of Tanzania*. Paper No. 4.

Hassing, P. 1970. 'German Missions and the Maji-Maji Risings'. *African Historical Studies* 3: 373–389.

Johanssen, D. 1935. *Führung und Erfahrung in 40 jahrigem Missionsdienst*. Bethel, Bielefeld.

Koponen, J. 1994. *Development for Exploitation*. Helsinki and Hamburg.

Lagergren, D. 1970. *Mission and State in the Congo*. Uppsala.

Lemarchand, R. 1974. *Rwanda and Burundi*. Cambridge.

Linden, I. 1977. *Church and Revolution in Rwanda*. Manchester.

Loth, H. 1963. *Die Christliche Mission in Südwestafrika*. Berlin.

Louis, W. M. R. 1963. *Ruanda-Urundi, 1884–1919*. Oxford.

Louis, W. R. 1964. 'Roger Casement and the Congo'. *Journal of African History*, 99–120.

Louis, W. R. 1965. 'The Stokes Affair'. *Revue Belge de Philologie et d'Histoire*. Tome. XLIII, pp.572–584.

MacDonald, F. W. 1893. *The Story of Mashonaland and the Mission Pioneers*. London.

Maples, E. 1899. *Journals and Papers of Chauncy Maples*. London.

Markowitz, M. D. 1973. *Cross and Sword: The Political Role of Christian Missions in the Belgian Congo, 1908–1960*. Stanford, CA.

Masson, J. 1944. *Les Missionaires Belges de 1804 Jusqu'a Nos Jours*. Brussels.

Maynard Smith, H. 1926. *Frank: Bishop of Zanzibar*. London.

Merensky, A. 1894. *Deutsche Arbeit am Njassa, Deutsch-Ostafrika*. Berlin.

Morel, E. D. 1909. *Great Britain and the Congo*. London.

Peters, C. 1891. *New Light in Dark Africa*. London.

Poewe, K. 1987. *The Namibian Herero*. Lewiston.

Ranger, T. O. 1923. *The African Voice in Southern Rhodesia, 1898–1930*. London.

Ranger, T. O. 1967. *Revolt in Southern Rhodesia*. London.

Sheppard, W. H. 1917. *Presbyterian Pioneers in the Congo*. Richmond.

Sicard, S. Von. 1970. *The Lutheran Church on the Coast of Tanzania*. Uppsala.

Slade, R. 1957. 'King Leopold II and the Attitude of English and American Catholics towards the Anti-Congolese Campaign'. *Zaire* 11.

Slade, R. M. 1959. *English-Speaking Missions in the Congo Independent State (1878–1908)*. Brussels.

Smith, E. W. 1928. *The Way of White Fields in Rhodesia*. London.

Starr, F. 1907. *The Truth about the Congo*. London.

Stoecker, H. 1986. *German Imperialism in Africa*. London.

Storme, M. 1952. 'Leopold, Les Missions du Congo et la Fondation du seminaire Africaine de Louvain'. *Zaire – Revue Congolaise*.

Stuart, C. H. 1969. 'The Lower Congo and the American Baptist Mission to 1910'. Ph.D. Thesis. Boston University.

Tibbault, E. 1910. *Nos Missionaires au Congo*. Société Belge d' Études Coloniales.

Van der Burgt, J. M. M. 1903. *Un Grand Peuple do l'Afrique Équitoriale*. Bois-le-Duc.

de Vries, J. L. 1978. *Mission and Colonialism in Namibia*. Johannesburg.

Wright, M. 1971. *German Missions in Tanganyika*. Oxford.

Wright, M. 1972. 'Nyakyusa Cults and Politics in the Later Nineteenth Century'. In *The Historical Study of African Religion*. Edited by T. O. Ranger and I. N. Kimambo. London.

Zvobgo, C. J. M. 1991. *The Wesleyan Methodist Mission in Zimbabwe*. Harare.

Chapter 11: Black Men's God

Ajayi, J. F. A. 1965. *Christian Missions in Nigeria 1841–1891*. London.

Anderson, A. 2000. *Zion and Pentecost*. Pretoria.

Ayandele, E. A. 1966. *The Missionary Impact on Modern Nigeria*. London.

Ayandele, E. A. 1970. *Holy Johnson: Pioneer of African Nationalism, 1856–1917*. London.

Chirenje, J. M. 1987. *Ethiopianism and Afro-Americans in Southern Africa, 1883–1916*. Baton Rouge.

Cochrane, J. R. 1987. *Servants of Power: The Role of the English-Speaking Churches in South Africa: 1903–1930*. Johannesburg.

Colenso, Harriette. 1895. *The Present Position among the Zulus*. London.

Daneel, L. 1987. *Quest for Belonging*. Gweru.

Dobinson, H. H. 1899. *Letters of Henry Hughes Dobinson*. London.

Ekechi, F. K. 1971. *Missionary Enterprise and Rivalry in Igboland*. London.

Flora, G. R. 1945. *New Turns on the Liberia Road*. Baltimore.

Ghandi, M. K. 1949. *An Autobiography or the Story of My Experiments with the Truth*. London.

Guy, Jeff. 2002. *The View across the River: Harriette Colenso and the Zulu Struggle against Imperialism*. Oxford.

Haliburton, G. M. 1971. *The Prophet Harris*. London.

Hayford, J. E. Caseley. 1915. *William Waddy Harris: The West African Reformer*. London.

Kemp, D. 1898. *Nine Years at the Gold Coast*. London.

Kimble, D. 1973. *A Political History of Ghana: The Rise of Gold Coast Nationalism, 1850–1928*. Oxford.

Langworthy, E. B. 1952. *This Africa Was Mine*. Sterling.

Lee, A. W. 1930. *Charles Johnson of Zululand*. London.
Lynch, H. R. 1967. *Edward Wilmot Blyden: Pan-Negro Patriot 1832–1912*. London.
Marks, S. 1963. 'Harriet Colenso and the Zulus'. *Journal of African History* 4.
Maxwell, D. 1997. 'Rethinking Christian Independency: The Southern African Pentecostal Movement ca. 1908–1960'. Ph.D. Thesis. University of Keele.
Morrison, J. H. 1919. *Streams in the Desert*. London.
Mostert, N. 1992. *Frontiers*. London.
Page, J. 1908. *The Black Bishop*. London.
Pauw, B. A. 1960. *Religion in a Tswana Chiefdom*. London.
Porter, A. 'The Career of G.W. Brooke'. *Journal of Imperial and Commonwealth History* 6/1: 23–46.
Shank, D. A. 1994. *Prophet Harris: The 'Black Elijah' of West Africa*. Leiden.
Shepperson, G. A., and Thomas Price. 1958. *Independent African*. Edinburgh.
Sundkler, B. 1961. *Bantu Prophets in South Africa*. London.
Sundkler, B. 1976. *Zulu Zion and Some Swazi Zionists*. London.
Walker, S. S. 1983. *The Religious Revolution in the Ivory Coast*. Chapel Hill.
Walls, W. J. 1974. *The African Methodist Episcopal Zion Church*. Charlotte.
Whiteside, J. 1906. *The History of the Wesleyan Methodist Church in South Africa*. London.
Williams, W. L. 1982. *Black Americans and the Evangelisation of Africa*. Madison.

Chapter 12: Keep the Flag Flying

Al-Rashim, A. 1969. *Imperialism and Nationalism in the Sudan*. Oxford.
Arén, G. 1978. *Evangelical Pioneers in Ethiopia*. Stockholm.
Baldwin, A. F. 1973. 'The Impact of American Missionaries on the Bura People of Nigeria'. Ph.D. Thesis. Ball State University.
Bashir, M. O. 1968. *The Southern Sudan: Background to Conflict*. London.
Bewes, T. F. C. 1953. *Mau Mau and the Christian Witness*. London.
Bingham, R. W. 1943. *Seven Sevens of Years and a Jubilee: The Story of the Sudan Interior Mission*. Toronto.
Bittinger, D. W. 1938. *The Sudan's Second Sunup*. Elgin, IL.
Boer, J. H. 1979. *Missionary Messengers of Liberation in a Colonial Context*. Amsterdam.
Bottignole, S. 1984. *Kikuyu Traditional Culture and Christianity*. Nairobi.
Brown, G. G. 1973. *Christian Response to Change in East African Traditional Societies*. London.
Cagnolo, C. 1933. *The Akikuyu*. Nyeri.
Clarke, P. B. 1978. 'The Methods and Ideology of the Holy Ghost Fathers in Eastern Nigeria'. P.41 in *Christianity in West Africa: The Nigerian Story*. Edited by O. U. Kalu. Ibadan.
Collins, R. O., and F. M. Deng. 1984. *The British in the Sudan*. London.
Crampton, E. P. T. 1975. *Christianity in Northern Nigeria*. Zaria.
Ekechi, F. K. 1971. *Missionary Enterprise and Rivalry in Igboland*. London.
Flint, T. E. 1960. *Sir George Goldie and the Making of Modern Nigeria*. London.
Forristal, D. 1990. *The Second Burial of Bishop Shanahan*. Dublin.
Gogarty, H. A. 1920. *In the Land of the Kikuyus*. Dublin.
Graham, S. F. 1966. *Government and Mission Education in Northern Nigeria*. Ibadan.
Hooper, H. D. 1921. *Leading Strings*. London.
Hotchkiss, W. R. 1937. *Then and Now in Kenya Colony*. London.
Hunter, J. H. 1961. *A Flame of Fire*. Toronto.
Jackson, H. C. 1960. *Pastor on the Nile*. London.
Jornan, J. F. 1948. *Bishop Shanahan of Southern Nigeria*. Dublin.
Kenyatta, J. 1938. *Facing Mount Kenya*. London.
Kumm, K. W. 1907. *The Sudan*. London.

Leakey, L. S. B. 1952. *Mau Mau and the Kikuyu*. London.
Mackenzie, A. F. D. 1998. *Land, Ecology and Resistance*. Edinburgh.
Macpherson, R. 1970. *The Presbyterian Church in Kenya*. Nairobi.
Miller, W. R. S. 1947. *Have We Failed in Nigeria?* London.
Munro, J. F. 1975. *Colonial Rule and the Kamba*. Oxford.
Niblock, T. 1987. *Class and Power in the Sudan*. Albany.
Raum, O. 1937. 'Dr. Guttmann's Work on Kiliminjaro'. *International Review of Missions* 1–24.
Richardson, K. 1968. *Garden of Miracles*. London.
Robinson, F. 1928. *Charles H. Robinson*. London.
Roseberry, R. S. c.1937. *The Niger Vision*. Harrisburg, PA.
Rubingh, E. 1969. *Sons of Tiv*. Grand Rapids.
Sanderson, L. M. P., and N. Sanderson. 1981. *Education, Religion and Politics in Southern Sudan 1899–1964*. London and Khartoum.
Sandgren, D. P. 1989. *Christianity and the Kikuyu*. New York.
Shao, M. F. 1990. *Bruno Gutmann's Missionary Method*. Erlangen.
Sharkey, H. 2003. *Living with Colonialism*. Berkeley.
Shields, R. F. 1936. *Behind the Garden of Allah*. Philadelphia.
Strayer, R. W. 1978. *The Making of Mission Communities in East Africa*. Albany.
Temu, A. J. 1978. *British Protestant Missions*. London.
Tett, M. E. 1969. *The Road to Freedom*. Sidcup.
Trimingham, J. S. 1948. *Christian Approach to Islam in the Sudan*. London.
Udo, E. A. 1980. 'The Missionary Scramble for Spheres of Influence in South-Eastern Nigeria 1900–1952'. Pp.151–181 in *The History of Christianity in West Africa*. Edited by O. U. Kalu. London.
Vantiti, G. 1981. *Christianity in the Sudan*. Bologna.
Ward, K. 1976. 'The Development of Christianity in Kenya 1910–1950'. Ph.D. Thesis. University of Cambridge.
Wray, J. A. 1928. *Kenya: Our Newest Colony*. London.

Chapter 13: The Path in the Thicket

Anonymous. 1935. *Village Education in Africa*. Report of a Meeting of 'Janes' Teachers in Salisbury Rhodesia. Lovedale.
Burke, J. F. 2001. *These Catholic Sisters Are All Mamas*. Brill.
Burr, E. 1956. *Annals of Old Hill*. London.
Church, J. E. 1981. *Quest for the Highest*. Exeter.
Clements, K. W. 1999. *Faith on the Frontier: A Life of J. H. Oldham*. Edinburgh.
Comaroff, Jean, and John Comaroff. 1997. *On Reason and Revelation*, vol.2. Chicago.
Cromwell, Adelaide. 1986. *An African Victorian Feminist*. London.
Dallaire, R. 2003. *Shake Hands with the Devil*. Toronto and London.
Debrunner, H. W. 1965. *A Church between Colonial Powers*. London.
Debrunner, H. W. 1967. *A History of Christianity in Ghana*. Accra.
Denniston, R. 1999. *Trevor Huddleston: A Life*. London.
Forristal, D. 1994. *Edel Quinn*. Dublin.
Gatwa, T. 2001. *Rwanda: Eglises, Victimes ou Coupables?* Yaoundé.
Gatwa, T., E. Kolmi, and Bowen. 1995. *Transformations* 12.2.
Gourevitch, P. 1999. *We Wish to Inform You that Tomorrow We Will Be Killed with Our Families*. New York.
Guggisberg, G. 1924. *The Keystone*. London.
Guillebaud, L. 1941. *A Grain of Mustard Seed*. London.
Guillebaud, Meg. 2002. *The Land that God Forgot*. London and Grand Rapids.
Hardiman, David, ed. 2006. *Healing Bodies Saving Souls*. Amsterdam.

Hastings, Adrian. 1979. *A History of African Christianity, 1950–1975*. Cambridge.

Huddleston, T. 1956. *Naught for Your Comfort*. London.

Hunt, Nancy Rose. 1999. *A Colonial Lexicon of Birth Ritual, Medicalization, and Mobility in the Congo*. Durham.

Iliffe, J. 1998. *East African Doctor*. Cambridge.

Jones, T. J. 1926. *The Four Essentials of Education*. New York.

Kalu, O. U. 2006. 'African Christianity from the World Wars to Decolonisation'. Pp.197–218 in *The Cambridge History of Christianity*, vol.9. Edited by H. McLeod. Cambridge.

Kaunda, K., and C. Morris. 1960. *Black Government? A Dialogue*. Lusaka.

Lewis, L. J. 1962. *The Phelps-Stokes Reports on Education in Africa*. London.

Louis, Sr. O. F. S. 1964. *Love Is the Answer*. Dublin.

Maxwell, D. 2006. 'Post Colonial Christianity in Africa'. Pp.401–421 in *The Cambridge History of Christianity*, vol.9. Edited by H. McLeod, Cambridge.

Morris, Colin. 1958. *Anything but This*. London.

Morris, Colin. 1961. *The Hour after Midnight*. London.

Mungazi, D. A. 1999. *The Last British Liberals in Africa*. Westport.

Mwaura, P. N. 2005. 'Pentecostal Missionary Enterprise in Kenya'. Pp.246–264 in *Religion, History, and Politics in Nigeria*. Edited by C. J. Korieh and G. U. Nwokeji. Lanham.

Oldham, J. H. 1924. *Christian Education in Africa and the East*. London.

Schweitzer, Albert. 1931. *My Life and Thought*. London.

Schweitzer, Albert. 1953. *On the Edge of the Primeval Forest*. London.

Scott, M. 1958. *A Time to Speak*. London.

Shaw, Mabel. 1936. *God's Candlelight*. London.

Smith, E. W. 1929. *Aggrey of Africa*. London.

St. John, Patricia. 1971. *Breath of Life*. London.

Sundkler, B., and C. Steed. 2000. *A History of the Church in Africa*. Cambridge.

UNESCO. 1963. *The Development of Higher Education in Africa*.

Vaughan, Megan. 1991. *Curing Their Ills*. Cambridge.

Ward, K. 2006. 'Christianity, Colonialism and Mission'. Pp. 71–88 in *The Cambridge History of Christianity*, vol.9. Edited by H. McLeod. Cambridge.

Ward, W. E. F. 1965. *Fraser of Trinity and Achimota*. Accra and Oxford.

Weiss, R. 1999. *Sir Garfield Todd and the Making of Zimbabwe*. London.

Winter, Colin. 1977. *Namibia*. London.

Winter, Colin. 1981. *The Breaking Process*. London.

Yates, A., and Lewis Chester. 2006. *The Troublemaker*. London.

Archives Consulted

Houghton Library, Harvard University. Also on microfilm in Dale Mission Library, Yale
    American Board of Commissioners of Foreign Missions (ABCFM), Newbury, Oxon
Valley Forge, PA
    American Baptist Foreign Missionary Society
Regents Park College, Oxford
    Baptist Missionary Society (BMS)
University of Birmingham
    Church Missionary Society
Episcopal Seminary, Austin, TX
    Protestant Episcopal Church
National Library of Scotland, Edinburgh
    Scottish Presbyterian Free and Church of Scotland, including manuscripts of Duff
        Macdonald diary and R. Keymer, *Establishment and Evolution of the Livingstonia
        Mission*, 1964. (Some papers were destroyed in the Second World War)
New College, Edinburgh
    Regions Beyond Centre – Sudan United Mission (faith missions were generally not in the
        business of keeping records)
School of Oriental and African Studies (SOAS), London
    London Missionary Society (Manuscripts labelled CWM)
    Wesleyan Methodist Missionary Society (WMMS)
    Primitive Methodist Missionary Society
Cambridge University Library
    British and Foreign Bible Society
Royal Commonwealth Society Collection in Cambridge University Library
    Van der Kemp, Memoir and attachment – see chapter 5, n.5
    CMS instructions – see chapter 9, n.5
    Coillard papers
Rhodes House, Oxford
    Anti-Slavery Society Papers
    Society for the Propagation of the Gospel (SPG)
    Harriette Colenso papers
Dundee Museum
    Correspondence of Mary Slessor
Dundee Central Library
    Mary Slessor Partridge correspondence
Newbury, Berks
    African Evangelical Fellowship

Notes

Preface

1. Adrian Hastings, *The Church in Africa 1450–1950* (Oxford University Press, 1994), pp.83–84. Chapters 3 and 4 provide the authoritative source for the Catholic 'antiqa missio'.

2. John K. Thornton, *The Kongolese Saint Anthony: Dona Beatriz Kimpa Vita and the Antonian movement, 1684–1706* (Cambridge University Press, 1998), pp.115–128.

3. J. A. Atkins, *Voyage to Guinea, Brasil and the West Indies* (London, 1737).

4. J. Newton, *Out of the Depths* (London, 1925), p.126.

5. Newton wrote his most famous hymn at Olney, before Wilberforce convinced him of the evils of slavery. The words express standard evangelical piety.

6. David Brion Davis, 'Slavery and Emancipation in Western Culture', http://www.yale.edu/glc/aces/germantown.htm (cited 26 May 2008).

Chapter 1: The White Men's God

1. A. J. Lewis, *Zinzendorf: The Ecumenical Pioneer* (London, 1960), p.80.

2. E. L. Price, *The Journal of Elizabeth Lees Price* (London, 1956), p.113.

3. T. Thompson, *An Account of Two Missionary Voyages: By the Appointment of the Society of the Gospel in Foreign Parts* (London, 1758), pp.37–38.

4. G. Sharp, *An Essay on Slavery* (London, 1773).

5. G. S. Brookes, *Friend Anthony Benezet* (Philadelphia, 1937), p.417.

6. Olaudah Equiano, *Interesting Narrative of the Life of Olaudah Equiano, or Gustavus Vassa, the African* (London, 1789).

7. P. Hoare, *Memoirs of Granville Sharp, Esq.* (London, 1920), p.239.

8. K. B. Wadstrom, *Observations on the Slave Trade and a Description of Some Parts of the Coast of Guinea* (London, 1789).

9. C. Fyfe, *Sierra Leone Inheritance* (London, 1964), pp.116–118.

10. M. Horne, *Letters on Missions* (Bristol, 1794), pp.vi–vii.

11. Ibid. pp.60–61.

12. S. P. Carey, *William Carey* (London, 1934), p.92.

13. The Congregationalists have joined with the English Presbyterians to form the United Free Church.

14. E.g. Brian Stanley, ed., *Christian Missions and the Enlightenment* (Grand Rapids, 2001).

15. J. W. Colenso, *The Pentateuch and Book of Joshua Critically Examined*, vol.1 (London, 1863).

16. This generalisation is supported by information gleaned from a wide range of missionary bodies. The most compelling evidence lies in the sudden ending of malaria deaths after Ross's research on the life cycle of the malaria parasite gained general acceptance during the period 1905–1910.

17. H. Masters and W. E. Masters, *In Wild Rhodesia* (London, 1920), pp.198–199.

Chapter 2: The Foundation of Happiness

1. Simon Schama, *Rough Crossings* (London, 2005), draws on John Clarkson's unpublished diaries. I wrote a book for young people about these events: Martin Ballard, *Benjie's Portion* (London, 1969).

2. C. Fyfe, *Sierra Leone Inheritance* (London, 1964), p. 120.

3. The only surviving Connexion congregations can be found in Sierra Leone.

4. Viscountess Knutsford, *Life and Letters of Zacharay Macaulay* (London, 1900), p.8. Compare Christopher Fyfe in his standard work, *The History of Sierra Leone*. 'Disgusted by employment as overseer on a Jamaican slave plantation, he turned in revulsion to a colony where slaves had become free' (p.48). This sanitised account is still widely followed.

5. S. Jakobsson, *Am I Not a Man and a Brother?* (Uppsala, 1972), p.125.

6. Charles Grandeson Finney and W. W. Holdsworth, *The History of the Wesleyan Methodist Missionary Society,* vol.4 (London, 1921), p.84.

7. J. Morgan, *Reminiscences of the Founding of a Christian Mission on the Gambia* (London, 1864).

8. A. F. Walls, 'The Nova Scotian Settlers and Their Religion'. *Sierra Leone Bulletin of Religion* (1959): 19–31.

9. CMS Proceedings, 1820–1821, p.80.

10. C. Fyfe, *A History of Sierra Leone* (London, 1962), p.131.

11. A. T. Pierson, *Seven Years in Sierra Leone* (London, 1897), p.18.

12. Andrew Walls, 'The Influence of Sierra Leone on Methodist Mission Thought and Practice', Henry Martin Centre Lecture, 14 February 2008.

13. H. Kilham, *The Claims of West Africans to Christian Instruction through the Native Languages* (London, 1830), p.5.

14. P. Williams Jr., *A Discourse Delivered on the Death of Paul Cuffee* (New York, 1817). See also S. H. Haris, *Paul Cuffee: Black America and the African Return* (New York, 1972).

15. P. Cuffee, *A Brief Account of the Settlement and Present Situation of the Colony of Sierra Leone* (New York, 1812).

16. C. M. Wilson, *Liberia: Black Africa in Microcosm* (New York, 1971), p.4.

17. C. H. Huberich, *The Political and Legislative History of Liberia,* vol.1 (New York, 1947), p.123.

18. Ibid. p.191.

19. M. M. Fisher, *Lott Cary: The Colonizing Missionary* (Boston: From Black Apostles, 1982), p.218. See also *Sketch of the Life of Lott Cary*, appendix to R. R. Gurley, *The Life of Yehudi Ashmun* (New York, 1971).

20. The more comfortable story that the Monrovia colonists were fighting off slave traders is not supported by any evidence.

21. J. W. Smith, *Sojourners in Search of Freedom: The Settlement of Liberia by Black Americans* (Lanham, 1987), p.59.

22. John Leighton Wilson, Archives of the ABCFM, Houghton Library, Harvard University. Box 15.2.49.

23. W. J. Moses, *Alexander Crummell: A Study of Civilization and Discontent* (New York, 1989), pp.95, 99.

24. Jane Martin, 'The Dual Legacy: Government Authority and Mission Influence among the Glebo of Eastern Liberia', Ph.D. Thesis, Boston University, 1968. The rest of this chapter draws on her unpublished work.

25. G. Thompson, *Thompson in Africa* (New York, 1852), pp.32, 81.

26. G. Thompson, *The Palm-Land of West Africa* (Cincinnati, 1858), p.113.

Chapter 3: Knowing One's Place as a Negro

1. F. M. Bartels, *The Roots of Ghana Methodism* (Cambridge, 1965), p.10.

2. Wesleyan Methodist Missionary Society, Archive, School of Oriental and African Studies (London, Box 258/1109 Wrigley. 20.2.37).

3. Thomas B. Freeman, *Journal of Two Visits to the Kingdom of Ashanti* (London, 1843), pp.24–25.

4. C. A. Gordon, *Life on the Gold Coast* (London, 1874), pp.79–80.

5. J. F. A. Ajayi, *Christian Missions in Nigeria 1841–1891* (London, 1965), p.14.

6. H. W. Debrunner, *A Church between Colonial Powers* (London, 1965), p.87.

7. H. W. Debrunner, 'The Moses of the Ghana Presbyterian Church'. *Ghana Bulletin of Theology* 1/4 (1958): 12–18.

8. F. M. Barnard, *Herder's Social and Political Thought* (Oxford, 1965), p.57. For a brief but clear analysis of the interaction of German romanticism, pietism and language theory, see K. Fiedler, *Christianity and African Culture* (Leiden, 1996), pp.12 ff.

9. H. W. Debrunner, *A History of Christianity in Ghana* (Accra, 1967), p.173.

10. A. Innes, *Cruelties Committed on the West Coast of Africa by an Agent of the Baptist Mission* (London, 1862). Virtually all Saker's correspondence has been 'weeded' out of the BMS files.

11. D. McFarlan, *Calabar: The Church of Scotland Mission* (London, 1946), p.7.

12. H. Waddell, *Twenty-Nine Years in the West Indies and Central Africa* (London, 1863), p.337.

13. A. Waddell, *Memorials of Mrs. Sutherland* (Paisley, 1883), p.78.

14. J. F. Schön and S. Crowther, *The Journals of the Rev J. F. Schön and Mr. Samuel Crowther* (London, 1842), p.163. See also C. C. Ifemesia, 'The Civilizing Mission of 1841'. Pp.81–102, in *The History of Christianity in West Africa*, ed. O. U. Kalu (London, 1980).

15. T. J. Bowen, *Central Africa* (Charleston, 1857), p.94.

16. L. E. Meyer, 'T. J. Bowen and Central Africa: A Nineteenth-Century Missionary Delusion'. *International Journal of African Historical Studies* 15 (1982): 247 ff.

17. G. Townsend, *Memoir of Henry Townsend* (London, 1887), p.85.

18. Church Missionary Society, Archive, University of Birmingham, Townsend to Venn, 5 February 1860.

19. E. A. Ayandele, *The Missionary Impact on Modern Nigeria* (London, 1966), p.11.

20. Ibid. p.8.

21. Op. cit., n.5, pp.76–77.

22. A. Hinderer, *Seventeen Years in Yoruba Country* (London, 1872), pp.133–134.

23. CMS Anna Hinderer to Venn. CA.2.049. e.g. 23.5.1854.

24. Op. cit., n.5, p.181.

25. J. Page, *The Black Bishop* (London, 1908), p.369.

Chapter 4: A Crucifix and a Breviary

1. J. B. Cullen, *Life of the Venerable Mother Javouhey* (Dublin, 1912), p.154.

2. D. H. Jones, 'The Catholic Mission and Some Aspects of Assimilation in Senegal'. *Journal of African History* 21/3 (1980): 327.

3. E. M. Hogan, *Catholic Missionaries and Liberia* (Cork, 1981), p.14.

4. H. J. Koren, *The Spiritans: A History of the Congregation of the Holy Ghost* (Pittsburgh, 1958), p.81.

5. Ibid. pp.182, 504.

6. A. Hastings, *The Church in Africa 1450–1950* (Oxford, 1996), p.296.

7. G. Ruggieri, ed., *Église et Histoire d'Église en Afrique* (Paris, 1988), p.52.

8. Op. cit., n.4, p.173.

9. J. M. Todd, *African Mission* (London, 1962), p.29.

10. Ibid. p.28.

11. Ibid. p.44.

12. Ibid. p.72.

13. E. Isichei, 'An Obscure Man: Pa Antonio in Lagos'. P.30, in *Varieties of Christian Experiences in Nigeria* (London, 1982).

14. The Irish Province of the Society of African Missions, *100 Years of Achievement* (Cork, 1956), p.30.

15. *Les Missions Catholiques*. Tome. 9. (1877): 124.

16. Ibid. Tome. 13. (1881): 442.

17. J. F. A. Ajayi, *Christian Missions in Nigeria 1841–1891* (London, 1965), p.116.

Chapter 5: Stolen Country

1. School of Oriental and African Studies, London Missionary Society, South African Incoming Correspondence. Book 1. Folder 1. Jacket A.

2. I. D. MacCrone, *Race Attitudes in South Africa* (Johannesburg, 1937), p.83. Captain Dampier's description.

3. J. A. Templin, *Ideology on a Frontier* (Westport, CT, 1984), p.37.

4. London Missionary Society papers. South Africa, Incoming Letters. Box 1. Folder 3. Jacket A.

5. 'An Account of the Religion, Customs, Population, Government, Language, History and Natural Resources of Caffaria'. Typed copy, bound with Memoir of Van der Kemp. RCS Collection, Cambridge University Library.

6. B. Le Cordeur and C. Saunders, eds., *The Kitchingman Paper* (Johannesburg, 1976), p.210.

7. H. Lichtenstein, *Travels in the Southern Part of Africa* (London, 1815). Van Riebeck Society Reprint, vol.1 (Cape Town, 1930), p.294.

8. N. Mostert, *Frontiers* (London, 1993), pp.453–454.

9. R. Lovett, *History of the London Missionary Society* (London, 1899). The official author's sometimes racy narrative created outrage at the time of publication. Other societies' documents would be exhaustively 'weeded' to eliminate anything that could 'cause embarrassment to family members'.

10. J. Sayles, *Mission Stations and Coloured Communities of the East Cape* (Cape Town, 1975), pp.83 ff.

11. J. Philip, *Researches in South Africa*, vol.1 (London, 1828), p.369.

12. Op. cit., n.8, p.739.

13. W. Shaw, *Memoir of the Rev. W. Shaw* (London, 1974), p.95.

14. Ibid. p.113.

15. J. Comaroff and J. Comaroff, *Of Revelation and Revolution*, vol.1 (Chicago, 1991), p.167; Julian Cobbing, 'The Mfecane as Alibi'. *Journal of African History* 29 (1988): 487 ff.

16. Andrew Porter, *Religion versus Empire* (Manchester, 2004), p.147.

17. J. R. Cochrane, *Servants of Power* (Johannesburg, 1987), p.22.

18. J. B. Pieres, *The House of Phalo: A History of the Xhosa People in the Days of Their Independence* (Berkeley, 1982), p.128.

19. Op. cit., n.8, p.738.

20. Ibid. pp.612–621.

21. J. V. B. Shrewsbury, *Memorials of William J. Shrewsbury* (London, 1867), pp.232–233. As a young man, Shrewsbury was expelled from the West Indies under the accusation of being over-sympathetic to slaves. His position appears to have changed on arrival in South Africa.

22. J. Ayliff and J. Whiteside, *History of the Abambo – Generally Known as the Fingos* (Cape Town, 1902), pp.24–26.

23. J. D. Ricards, *The Catholic Church and the Kaffirs* (London, 1880), pp.19–20.

24. Sir S. Lakeman, *What I Saw in Kaffirland* (London, 1880), p.94.

25. H. Calderwood, *Caffres and Caffre Missions* (London, 1858), p.55.

26. G. Brown, *Personal Adventure in South Africa* (London, 1855), p.135.

27. Williams, *Umfundisi. The Biography of Tio Soga* (Lovedale, 1978), p.47.

28. B. le Cordeur and C. Saunders, *The Kitchingman Papers* (Johannesburg, 1976), p.138.

29. J. B. Peires, *The Dead Will Arise: Nongqawuse and the Great Xhosa Cattle-Killing* (Johannesburg, 1989), p.79.

30. Ibid. p.157.

31. Charles Brownlee, *Reminiscences of Kaffir Life and History* (Lovedale, 1896), p.136.

32. See Mike Davis, *Late Victorian Holocausts* (London and New York, 2001), for examples of how the same doctrine would exacerbate larger famines in British India.

33. Op. cit., n.29, pp.232 ff.

34. J(anet) Hodgson, *Princess Emma* (Craighill, South Africa, 1987), p.54.

35. T. Gusche, *The Bishop's Lady* (Cape Town, n.d.).

36. M. S. Benham, *Henry Callaway: First Bishop for Kaffaria* (London, 1896), p.58.

Chapter 6: The Cheapest and Best Military Posts

1. R. Lovett, *History of the London Missionary Society*, vol.1 (London, 1899), p.58.

2. Ibid. pp.520–521.

3. B. Le Cordeur and C. Saunders, eds., *The Kitchingman Papers* (Johannesburg, 1976), p.529.

4. Missionary sources generally use the Tswana spelling, Moselekatse.

5. S. Broadbent, *The Barolongs of South Africa* (London, 1865), p.XXX.

6. R. Moffat and M. Moffat, *Apprenticeship at Kuruman* (London, 1962), p.94.

7. R. Philip, *Researches in South Africa*, vol.1 (London, 1828), p.227.

8. D. J. Kotzé, *Letters of the American Missionaries*, vol.31 of van Reibeeck Society Publications (Cape Town, 1950), p.120.

9. J. Du Plessis, *Christian Missions in South Africa* (London, 1911), p.220.

10. G. Champion, *The Journal of an American Missionary in the Cape Colony* (Cape Town, 1967), p.ix.

11. A. R. Booth, *The United States' Experience in South Africa* (Cape Town, 1976), p.56.

12. Op. cit., n.8, p.174.

13. A. R. Booth, ed., *The Journal of George Champion* (Cape Town, 1967), pp.34–35.

14. Op. cit., n.11, p.69.

15. C. F. J. Muller, *A Pictorial History of the Great Trek* (Taffelberg, 1978), p.54.

16. G. E. Cory, ed., *The Diary of the Rev. Francis Owen, Missionary with Dingaan in 1837–1838* (Cape Town, 1926), pp.107, 157–158.

17. E. Smit, *The Diary of Erasmus Smit* (Cape Town, 1972), p.90.

18. E. W. Smith, *The Life and Times of Daniel Lindley* (London, 1949), p.156.

19. J. Tyler, *Forty Years among the Zulus* (Cape Town, 1971), p.52.

20. Op. cit., n.18, p.240.

21. J. W. Colenso, *Ten Weeks in Natal* (Cambridge, 1855), p.236.

22. J. Guy, *The Heretic. Study of the Life of John William Colenso* (Johannesburg, 1983), p.237.

23. SPG Papers. Rhodes House, Oxford. Natal Diocese. Letters Received, CLR 138, 12 December 1980, p.251.

24. C. Vijn, *Cetswayo's Dutchman* (London, 1988), p.99.

25. H. Ryder Haggard, *Cetywayo and His White Neighbours* (London, 1882), p.11.

26. E. Casalis, *My Life in Basutoland* (London, 1889), p.176.

27. E. Casalis, *The Basutos* (London, 1861), p.78. Since he would become Moshoeshoe I of the Lesotho line, the work 'king' is certainly applicable.

28. P. Sanders, *Moshoeshoe: Chief of the Sotho* (London, 1975), p.125.

29. R. C. Germond, *Chronicles of Basutoland* (Morija, 1967), p.279.

30. Op. cit., n.28, p.154.

31. V. A. Ellenburger, *Century of Mission Work in Basutoland* (Morija, 1938), pp.90–91.

32. Op. cit., n.28, p.101.

33. Op. cit., n.29, p.223.

34. WMMS Bechuana Correspondence, 132. J. Cameron. November 1852.

35. W. E. Brown, *The Catholic Church in South Africa* (London, 1960), p.217.

36. T. Jeal, *Livingstone* (London, 1985), p.35.

37. J. W. Parsons, *The Livingstones at Kolombeng 1847–1857* (Gaborone, Botswana, 1997), p.55.

38. D. Livingstone, *Missionary Travels and Researches in South Africa* (London, 1857), p.20.

39. Op. cit., n.37, p.78.

40. I. Schapera, ed., *David Livingstone's South African Papers, 1849–1853* (Cape Town, 1974), p.9.

41. J. Comaroff and J. Comaroff, *Of Revelation and Revolution* (Chicago, 1991), p.276.

42. J. P. R. Wallis, ed., *The Matabele Journals of Robert Moffat 1829–1860*, vol.1 (London, 1976), p.377.

43. Op. cit., n.38, p.114.

Chapter 7: The Rewards of Great Sanctity

1. Adrian Hastings, *The Church in Africa 1450–1950* (Oxford, 1994), p.XXX.

2. Report of the British and Foreign Bible Society, vol.4, 1820–1821, p.162.

3. N. Pearce, *The Life and Adventures of Nathaniel Pearce, Written by Himself*, vol.1 (London, 1831), p.323.

4. C. W. Isenberg and J. L. Krapf, *The Journals of Isenberg and Krapf* (London, 1968), p.162.

5. J. L. Krapf, *Travels, Researches and Missionary Labours* (London, 1860), p.72.

6. M. E. Lady Herbert, *Abyssinia and Its Apostle* (London, 1867), p.56.

7. Ibid. pp.32–33.

8. Ibid. pp.111–112.

9. D. Crummey, *Priests and Politicians: Protestant and Catholic Missions in Orthodox Ethiopia 1830–1868* (Oxford, 1972), p.80.

10. C. P. Grove, *The Planting of Christianity in Africa*, vol.2 (London, 1948), p.90.

11. C. New, *Life Wanderings and Labours in East Africa* (London, 1971), p.250. See also A. J. Hopkins, *Trail Blazers and Road Makers* (London, 1928).

12. Op. cit., n.6, p.163.

13. Op. cit., n.10, p.83.

14. J. Petherick, *Egypt, the Sudan and Central Africa* (Edinburgh, 1861), p.131.

15. A. G. Mondini, *Africa or Death* (Boston, 1964), p.65.

16. Ibid. p.72.

17. E. Tonilo and R. Hill, *The Opening of the Nile Basin* (London, 1974), p.82.

18. G. Vantini, *Christianity in the Sudan* (Bologna, 1981), p.241.

19. Ibid. p.195.

20. *Les Missions Catholique*. Tome 13 (Lyons, 1881), p. 257.

21. B. Choen William, *The French Encounter with Africa* (Bloomington and London, 1980), p.276.

22. J. de Arteche, *The Cardinal of Africa* (London, 1964), p.59.

23. J. Bouniol, *The White Fathers and Their Missions* (London, 1929), p.42.

24. Ibid. p.158.

25. W. Burrifge, *Destiny Africa. Cardinal Lavigerie and the Making of the White Fathers* (London, 1966), p.122.

26. T. Pakenham, *The Scramble for Africa* (London, 1991), p.21.

27. R. M. Slade, *English-Speaking Missions in the Congo Independent State (1878–1908)* (Brussels, 1959), p.62 n.

28. R. P. M. Storme, *Rapports du Père Planque, de Mgr Lavigerie et de Mgr Comboni sur l'Association Internationale Africaine* (Brussels, 1957), Planque's letter, pp.12–15.

29. Ibid. p.131.

30. F. Renault, *Cardinal Lavigerie, Churchman, Prophet and Missionary* (London, 1994), p.225.

31. J. Cuoq, *Lavigerie, les Pères Blancs et les Musulmans* (Rome, 1986), p.60.

32. Ibid. p.31.

Chapter 8: Pitching Tents in the Interior

1. CWM, Lizzie to Olive Helmore, 4 December 1860; CWM, Africa Personal Box. Helmore Papers No. 27.

2. J. P. R. Wallis, ed., *The Matabele Mission* (London, 1952), p.75.

3. F. Coillard, *On the Threshold of Central Africa* (London, 1897), p.44.

4. Ngwabi Bhebe, *Christianity and Traditional Religion* (London, 1979), p.59.

5. T. O. Ranger, *Revolt in Southern Rhodesia* (London, 1967), p.38.

6. A. Sedgwick and W. Monk, eds., *Dr. Livingstone's Cambridge Lectures* (Cambridge, 1860), pp.165–167.

7. H. Rowley, *The Story of the Universities' Mission to Central Africa* (London, 1867), p.112.

8. Ibid.

9. Ibid. p.185.

10. F. Awdry, *An Elder Sister*, 3rd ed. (London, 1904), p.238.

11. Stewart's editor notes that he tried to obliterate the title, but it still remains visible.

12. J. P. R. Wallis, ed., *The Zambezi Journals of James Stewart* (London, 1952), p.190.

13. Owen Chadwick, *Mackenzie's Grave* (London, 1959), p.192.

14. E. D. Young, *Nyassa: A Journal of Adventures* (London, 1887), p.59.

15. W. P. Livingstone, *Laws of Livingstonia* (London, 1921), p.214.

16. J. T. Thompson, *Christianity in Northern Malawi* (Leiden, 1995), p.47.

17. J. M. McCracken, *Politics and Christianity in Malawi* (Cambridge, 1977), p.161.

18. W. A. Elmslie, *Among the Wild Ngoni* (Edinburgh, 1977), p.47.

19. Op. cit., n.15, p.118.

20. BMS, Western Sub-Committee Minute Books, 22 September 1903.

21. This was a time of great bitterness between established and nonconformist churches, and Arthington denied that he had made the donation. While mission historians find it hard to accept that such a pious man could have been 'economical with the truth', no other likely donor has been identified. His obituary, written by a close confidant of his later years, also records that he did fund 'Church of England Missionary Societies'. *Friends Quarterly Examiner* 35 (1901): 281.

22. E. Stock, *History of the Church Missionary Society*, vol.3 (London, 1899), p.95.

23. Ibid. p.102.

24. *A L'Assault des Pays Negrès. Journal des Missionaires d'Alger dans l'Afrique Equitoriale* (Paris, 1884).

25. R. P. Ashe, *Chronicles of Uganda* (London, 1894), p.64.

26. Op. cit., n.22, p.415.

27. J. A. Rowe, 'The Purge of Christians at Mwanga's Court'. *Journal of African History* 5 (1964): 55 ff.

28. J. P. Thoonen, *Black Martyrs* (London, 1941), p.172.

29. F. Lugard, 'British Officials and French Accusations'. *Fortnightly Review*, November 1892.

30. Op. cit., n.25, pp.154–155.

31. Ibid. p.57.

32. *L.Ouganda et les Agissements de la Companie Anglaise 'East Africa'* (Paris, 1892), p.48.

33. M. Twaddle, *Kagungulu and the Creation of Uganda* (London, 1993), p.72.

34. F. Lugard, *The Rise of Our East African Empire*, vol.2 (London, 1893), p.453.

35. L. Pirouet, 'Women Missionaries of the Church Missionary Society in Uganda, 1896–1920'. Pp.231–242, in *Missionary Ideologies in the Imperial Era*, ed. T. Christensen and W. R. Hutchinson (Aarhus, 1982).

36. Grenfell's biographers maintained the fiction. The true story was uncovered by Brian Stanley, the society's most recent historian.

37. H. G. Guinness, *The New World of Central Africa* (London, 1890), p.180.

38. H. M. W. Bentley, *Holman Bentley: Life and Labours of a Congo Pioneer* (London, 1907), p.59.

39. J. O. Mearns, 'The Proposed Mission in Central Africa', ABCFM paper, Cambridge, MA, 1879.

40. *The Times*, 14 April 1884.

41. T. Packenham, *The Scramble for Africa* (London, 1992), p.247.

42. R. M. Slade, *English-Speaking Missions in the Congo Independent State (1878–1908)* (Brussels, 1959), p.142.

43. F. Alexis, *Soldats et Missionaies au Congo* (Brussels, 1894), p.237. (The society's directors anticipated that Belgian employees of the AIA would.)

Chapter 9: Losing It or Ruling It

1. J. Whitford, *Trading Life in Western and Central Africa* (Liverpool, 1867), pp.71–72.

2. Arthur Herman, *The Scottish Enlightenment: The Scot's Invention of the Modern World* (London, 2001), p.364.

3. W. E. Arnold, *Here to Stay: The Story of the Anglican Church in Zimbabwe* (Lewes, 1985), p.37.

4. G. W. H. Knight-Bruce, *Memories of Mashonaland* (London, 1895), p.144.

5. G. A. Duncan, *Lovedale – Coercive Agency: Power and Resistance in Mission Education* (Pietermaritzburg, 2003), p.159.

6. Instructions Issued in 1876 and 1878 to the Pioneer CMS parties to Kagawe and Uganda. TSS, RCS collection, Cambridge University Library.

7. J. A. Mullins, 'New Route and Mode of Travelling into Central Africa', *Proceedings of the Royal Geographical Society*, 26 February 1877, p.235.

8. H. A. C. Cairns, *Prelude to Imperialism: British Reactions to Central African Society* (London, 1965), p.41.

9. Rachel S. Watt, *In the Heart of Savagedom* (London, 1923), p.85.

10. Daniel Crawford, *Thinking Black: 22 Years without a Break in the Long Grass of Central Africa* (London, 1912), p.324.

11. A. J. Hanna, *The Beginnings of Nyasaland and North-Eastern Rhodesia, 1859–1895* (Oxford, 1956), p.26.

12. A. Chirnside, *The Blantyre Missionaries: Discreditable Disclosures* (London, 1880), p.14.

13. A. J. Temu, *British Protestant Missions* (London, 1972), pp.18–19.

14. CWM Central Africa. Mackay. 6 August 1898. Box 10. Folder 1. Jacket D.

15. Ibid. Box 10. Folder 3. Jacket D. 5 June 1899. Box 28. p.420; Thompson. 6 January 1900.

16. P. Augouard, *28 Annés au Congo*, vol.1 (Poitiers, 1905), p.77.

17. Ibid. p.55.

18. G. Goyau, *Monseigneur Augouard* (Paris, 1926), p.121.

19. Ibid. p.119.

20. www.brazza.culture.fr/en/pop_up/prosper_augouard.htm (cited 10 June 2008).

21. E. Rabut, *Brazza Commissaire Général: Le Congo Français 1886–1897* (Paris, 1989), p.148.

22. G. Sapeto, *Assab e suoi Critici* (Genova, 1879), pp.14–47.

23. K. J. Bade, *Friedrich Fabri und der imperialism us der Bismarckzeit* (1975), p.68.

24. J. L. de Vries, *Mission and Colonialism in Namibia* (Johannesburg, 1978), p.121.

25. H. Loth, *Die Christliche Mission in Sudwestafrika* (Berlin, 1963), p.145.

26. J. Moffat, 7 September 1876. CEM Box 38. Folder 3. Jacket C.

27. W. Douglas Mackenzie, *John Mackenzie: South African Missionary and Statesman* (London, 1902).

28. J. Mackenzie, *Austral Africa: Losing It or Ruling It*, vol.1 (London, 1887), p.9.

29. Ibid. p.122.

30. Jean Comaroff and John Comaroff, *Of Revelation and Revolution: Christianity, Colonialism and Consciousness in South Africa*, vol.1 (Chicago, 1991), p.308.

31. A. Sillery, *John Mackenzie of Bechuanaland, 1835–1899: A Study of Humanitarian Imperialism* (Cape Town, 1971), p.77.

32. W. P. Livingstone, *A Prince of Missionaries* (London, 1931), p.52.

33. J. M. McCracken, *Politics and Christianity in Malawi* (Cambridge, 1977), p.165.

34. W. P. Livingstone, *Mary Slessor of Calabar* (London, 1916), p.55.

35. IBEAC papers. SOAS. London. Sharp to Mackinnon, 26 February 1991. Box 76. File 59.

36. R. A. Oliver, *The Missionary Factor in East Africa* (London, 1965), pp.172–173.

37. A. C. Ross, *Blantyre Mission and the Making of Modern Malawi* (Blantyre, 1996), p.113.

38. Op. cit., n.32, p.106.

39. CWM. Matabele Mission. Box 1. Folder 4. Jacket C. Elliot. 19 February 1990.

40. G. Prins, *The Hidden Hippopotamus* (Cambridge, 1980), p.217.

41. Coillard papers. Royal Commonwealth Society collection, Cambridge University Library. Box MSS 52. No 86. When Coillard's British niece came to research her uncle's tombstone biography, she unearthed the papers that told the treaty's full story. After writing what was expected of her, she deposited the papers for the benefit of future historians.

42. C. E. Mackintosh, *Coillard of the Zambezi* (London, 1907), p.393.

43. Op. cit., n.41, No 122.

44. J. N. Ogilvie, *Our Empire's Debt to Missions: The Duff Missionary Lectures* (London, 1923), p.27.

45. H. Dreschler, *Let Us Die Fighting* (London, 1980), p.27.

46. H. Loth, *Die Christliche Mission in Südwestafrika* (Berlin, 1963), p.160.

Chapter 10: If This Is Civilisation, What Is Barbarism?

1. C. E. Fripp, *Gold and the Gospel in Mashonaland: The Mashona Mission of Bishop Knight-Bruce* (London, 1949), p.141.

2. 'A Dominican Sister': *In God's White Robed Army* (Cape Town, 1947), p.65.

3. W. H. Anderson, *On the Trail of Livingstone* (Mountain View, CA, 1919), p.66.

4. C. J. M. Zvbogo, *The Wesleyan Methodist Mission in Zimbabwe* (Harare, 1991), p.30.

5. CWM, Matabeleland. Box 1. Folder 5. Jacket A. Helm. 9 October 1993.

6. D. S. Steere, *God's Irregular* (London, 1973), p.47.

7. MMS Rhodesia correspondence. Box 333. Folder 3. Letter 32. 19 May 1996. Shimmin.

8. Ibid. p.295.

9. Op. cit., n.3, p.117.

10. T. O. Ranger, *Revolt in S. Rhodesia 1896–1897* (London, 1967), p.236.

11. J. Koponen, *Development for Exploitation* (Helsinki and Hamburg, 1994), p.72.

12. BMS papers. Fuller to Baynes. 21 April 1988. A/5.

13. H. Johanssen, *Führung und Erfahrung in jahrigem Missionsdient*, vol.1 (Bethel bie Bielfeld, 1935), p.38.

14. J. A. P. Kiernan, 'The Holy Ghost Fathers in East Africa', Ph.D. Thesis, 1966, p.313.

15. P. Hassing, 'German Missions and the Maji-Maji Risings'. *African Historical Studies* 3 (1970): 375.

16. *Passionsblumen aus den fernen Süden* (Tutzing, 1906), p.46.

17. G. C. K. Gwassa and J. Iliffe, 'Records of the Maji Maji Rising'. *Historical Association of Tanzania*. Paper No.4 (1967): 21.

18. Ibid. p.27.

19. I. Linden, *Church and Revolution in Rwanda* (Manchester, 1977), p.32.

20. W. M. R. Louis, *Rwanda–Burundi* (Oxford, 1963), p.176.

21. R. Lemarchaud, *Burundi* (Cambridge, 1974), p.14.

22. Op. cit., n.19, p.97.

23. J. P. Chrétien, *Burundi, l'histoire retrouvée: Vingt-cinq ans de métier d'historien en Afrique* (Paris, 1993), pp.345 ff.

24. J. M. M. Van der Burgt, *Un Grand Peuple do l'Afrique Équitoriale* (Bois-le-Duc, 1903), p.LXXVIII. The author reinforces his medieval credentials by using Roman numerals!

25. P. Rutayisiré, 'L'Africanisation du Christianisme et la Pratique Missionaire en Réference a la Christianisation du Burundi'. P.14, in *Église et Histoire de l'Église en Afrique*, ed. G. Ruggieri (Paris, 1988); R. Lemarchand, *Rwanda and Burundi* (Cambridge, 1974).

26. Op. cit., n.20, p.140.

27. Ibid. p.73.

28. B. Sudkler and C. Steed, *A History of the Church in Africa* (Cambridge, 2000), p.862.

29. H. Loth, *Die Christliche Mission in Südwestafrika* (Berlin, 1963), p.165.

30. J. L. de Vries, *Mission and Colonialism in Namibia* (Johannesburg, 1978), p.163.

31. Ibid. p.74.

32. Ibid. p.6.

33. http://web.jjay.cuny.edu/~jobrien/reference/ob22.html.

34. H. Bley, *South West Africa under German Rule* (London, 1971), p.178.

35. K. Powe, *The Namibian Herero* (Lewiston, 1987), pp.69–71.

36. Roy J. Enquist, *Namibia: Land of Tears* (Selinsgrove, c.1990), p.57.

37. Anti-Slavery Society Papers. Rhodes House, Oxford. MSS. Brit. Emp.S22.G261, vol.1, issue no.1.

38. D. Lagergren, *Mission and State in the Congo* (Uppsala, 1970), pp.118 ff.

39. H. R. Fox Bourne, *Civilization in Congoland* (London, 1903), p.216.

40. ABFMS. Group 1. Box 77. Sims. 10 June 1896.

41. Ibid. Sims. 29 August 1904.

42. R. M. Slade, *English-Speaking Missions in the Congo Independent State (1878–1908)* (Brussels, 1959), pp.248–249.

43. J. Masson, *Les Missionaires Belges de 1804 Jusqu'a Nos Jours* (Brussels, 1944), p.117.

44. F. Alexis, *Soldats et Missionaires au Congo* (Brussels, 1894), p.211.

45. Anti-Slavery Society Papers, vol.1, no.21. 20 March–24 March 1903.

46. H. M. Bentley, *The Life and Labours of a Congo Pioneer* (London, 1907), p.293.

47. BMS papers. Box 20. Grenfell. 31 January 1898.

48. BMS papers. Grenfell. 10 August 1903.

49. Parliamentary papers. 20 May 1903. pp.1289 ff.

50. R. Slade, 'King Leopold II and the Attitude of English and American Catholics towards the Anti-Congolese Campaign'. *Zaire* 11 (1957): 611.

Chapter 11: Black Men's God

1. J. F. A. Ajayi, *Christian Missions in Nigeria 1841–1891: The Making of a New Elite* (London, 1965), p.261.

2. A. Porter, 'Evangelical Enthusiasm, Missionary Motivation, and West Africa in the Late Nineteenth Century: The Career of G. W. Brooke'. *Journal of Imperial and Commonwealth History* 6/1 (October 1977): 23–46.

3. F. K. Ekechi, *Missionary Enterprise and Rivalry in Igboland 1857–1914* (London, 1971), p.13.

4. CMS G3/A3/O/1890/78.

5. H. H. Dobinson, *Letters of Henry Hughes Dobinson* (London, 1899), p.56.

6. For the minutes, see CMS G3/A3/O/1890/165.

7. Crowther never knew his date of birth, but biographers place it in 1806.

8. CMS G3/A3/O/1893/72.

9. CMS G3/A3/O/1894/37; cf. also G. O. M. Tasie, *Christian Missionary Enterprise in the Niger Delta* (Leiden, 1978), p.151.

10. Op. cit., n.5, p.195.

11. F. K. Ekechi, *Missionary Rivalry Igboland 1857–1914* (London, 1971), pp.68–69.

12. D. Kemp, *Nine Years at the Gold Coast* (London, 1898), p.155.

13. WMMS Archive. SOAS, London. Box 269/134. Kemp/Hartley. 20 February 1994.

14. D. Kimble, *A Political History of Ghana: The Rise of Gold Coast Nationalism, 1850–1928* (Oxford, 1973), p.348.

15. W. J. Walls, *The African Methodist Episcopal Zion Church* (Charlotte, 1974), p.238.

16. Op. cit., n.14, p.163.

17. E. Lyon, 'The American Methodist Episcopal Church in Liberia'. *Liberia* Bulletin (30 November 1907): 28–36.

18. G. K. Flora, *New Turns on the Liberia Road* (Baltimore, 1945), p.30.

19. D. A. Shank, *Prophet Harris, the 'Black Elijah' of West Africa* (Leiden, 1994), p.8. See also S. S. Walker, *The Religious Revolution in the Ivory Coast: The Prophet Harris and the Harrist Church* (Chapel Hill, 1983) and G. M. Haliburton, *The Prophet Harris* (London, 1971).

20. J. E. Casely Hayford, *William Waddy Harris, the West African Reformer* (London, 1915).

21. ABC. 5/4/12/75.

22. ABC. 5/4/12/64.

23. A. W. Lee, *Charles Johnson of Zululand* (London, 1930), p.195.

24. N. Mostert, *Frontiers: The Epic of South Africa's Creation and the Tragedy of the Xhosa People* (London, 1992), p.1267.

25. J. R. Cochrane, *Servants of Power: The Role of English-Speaking Churches in South Africa: 1903–1930* (Johannesburg, 1987), p.72.

26. Rhodes House, Oxford. Anti-Slavery Papers. Fox-Bourne. C.150. p. 148.

27. D. Maxwell, 'Rethinking African Independency: The Southern African Pentecostal Movement ca. 1908–1960', unpublished thesis, University of Keele, 1997. Copy in Henry Martin Library, Cambridge, p.54.

28. J. M. Chirenje, *Ethiopianism and Afro-Americans in Southern Africa, 1883–1916* (Baton Rouge, 1987), p.35.

29. Psalm 68 31 Acts 8 27–8.39.

30. B. A. Pauw, *Religion in a Tswana Chiefdom* (London, 1960), p.67.

31. J. H. Morrison, *Streams in the Desert* (London, 1919), p.57.

32. I. Daneel, *Quest for Belonging* (Gweru, 1987), pp.38 ff.

33. See Colenso Papers. Rhodes House, Oxford.

34. For the war, see S. Marks, 'Harriet Colenso and the Zulus'. *Journal of African History* 4 (1963): 403–411.

35. M. K. Gandhi, *An Autobiography: The Story of My Experiments with Truth* (London, 1949), pp.261–262.

36. G. A. Shepperson and T. Price, *Independent African* (Edinburgh, 1958), p.33.

37. E. B. Langworthy, *This Africa Was Mine* (Stirling, 1952), p.40.

38. Op. cit., n.36, p.235.

39. *Epistle of St. James*, p.51.

40. Op. cit., n.37, pp.347–348.

Chapter 12: Keep the Flag Flying

1. Dundee Central Library. Partridge Letters. No. 1. 5 June 1905. These letters, which were one side of a long correspondence, were deposited in the library by Partridge before he died in the 1950s.

2. W. P. Livingstone, *Mary Slessor of Calabar* (London, 1916), p.232.

3. Op. cit., n.1, No. 53. For further background see also Nos 2, 25, 28, 31, 40, 41, 46 and 49.

4. J. E. Flint, *Sir George Goldie and the Making of Modern Nigeria* (London, 1960), p.148.

5. E. A. Udo, 'The Missionary Scramble for Spheres of Influence in South-Eastern Nigeria 1900–1952'. Pp.159–181, in *The History of Christianity in West Africa*, ed. O. U. Kalu (London, 1980).

6. P. B. Clarke, 'The Methods and Ideology of the Holy Ghost Fathers in Eastern Nigeria'. P.41, in *Christianity in West Africa: The Nigerian Story*, ed. O. U. Kalu (Ibadan, 1978).

7. D. Forristal, *The Second Burial of Bishop Shanahan* (Dublin, 1990), p.53.

8. Ibid. p.40.

9. F. K. Ekechi, *Missionary Enterprise and Rivalry in Igboland, 1857–1914* (London, 1971), p.103.

10. Primitive Methodist papers. SOAS, London. Christie to Pickett, 2 September 1907. Box 1162, p.289.

11. K. Ward, 'Christianity, Colonialism and Mission'. P.78, in *The Cambridge History of Christianity*, vol.9, ed. H. Mcleod (Cambridge, 2006).

12. J. P. Jordan, *Bishop Shanahan of Southern Nigeria* (Dublin, 1948), p.96.

13. As stressed to aspiring missionaries in Albert Simpson's New York College.

14. F. Robinson, *Charles H. Robinson* (London, 1928), p.51.

15. Ibid. p.91.

16. CMS Archive G3/A9/1900 27.

17. CMS Archive G3/A9/1900 29.

18. H. K. W. Kumm, *The Sudan: A Short Compendium of Facts and Figures about the Land of Darkness* (London, 1907), p.64.

19. R. S. Roseberry, *The Niger Vision* (Harrisburg, PA, 1934), p.6.

20. R. V. Bingham, *Seven Sevens of Years and a Jubilee: The Story of the Sudan Interior Mission* (Toronto, 1943), p.19.

21. J. H. Hunter, *A Flame of Fire: The Life and Work of R. V. Bingham*, foreword by Donald M. Fleming and introduction by Albert D. Helser (Canada, 1961), p.65.

22. Op. cit., n.20, p.33.

23. As said by an SUM missionary to the author,

24. Walter R. Miller, *Have We Failed in Nigeria?* (London, 1947), p.277.

25. To flesh out this statement: the province of Bornu (where the present writer worked in the 1950s) had a population of over 1.5 million and a land area more than half the size of England. All health needs were served by one government hospital, in the provincial capital of Maiduguri, which had just one doctor. Protestant missionaries ran two remote hospitals and one leprosy settlement. Very few rural children had any access to Western-style education; there was a single government-run secondary school for boys and one for girls, but no provision for further or higher education.

26. M. O. Beshir, *The Southern Sudan: Background to Conflict* (London, 1968), p.22.

27. H. C. Jackson, *Pastor on the Nile* (London, 1960), p.64.

28. Heather J. Sharkey, *Living with Colonialism: Nationalism and Culture in the Anglo-Egyptian Sudan* (Berkeley, 2003), p.22.

29. Trimingham, op. cit., p.26.

30. R. O. Collins and F. M. Deng, *The British in the Sudan, 1898–1956* (London, 1984), p.179.

31. J. R. L. Macdonald, *Soldiering and Surveying in British East Africa, 1891–1894* (London, 1897), p.109.

32. R. Macpherson, *The Presbyterian Church in Kenya* (Nairobi, 1970), p.35.

33. D. P. Sandgren, *Christianity and the Kikuyu* (New York, 1989), p.32.

34. J. F. Munro, *Colonial Rule and the Kamba: Social Change in the Kenya Highlands, 1889–1939* (Oxford, 1975), p.105.

35. C. Cagnolo, *The Akikuyu, Their Customs, Traditions and Folklore* (Nyeri, 1933), p.260.

36. S. Bottignole, *Kikuyu Traditional Culture and Christianity: Self Examination of an African Church* (Nairobi, 1984), p.56.

37. A. J. Temu, *British Protestant Missions* (London, 1978), pp.121–122.

38. Ibid. chapter 6.

39. Ibid. p.110.

40. Op. cit., n.32, p.90.

41. K. Ward, 'The Development of Protestant Christianity in Kenya 1910–1950', Ph.D. Thesis, University of Cambridge, 1976, pp.88 ff.

42. R. W. Strayer, *The Making of Mission Communities in East Africa* (Albany, 1978), p.56.

43. H. A. Gogarty, Dublin, 1920, pp.28–29.

44. Op. cit., n.33, chapters 4 and 5.

45. J. Kenyatta, *Facing Mount Kenya, 1938* (London, 1979), p.135.

Chapter 13: The Path in the Thicket

1. Albert Schweitzer, *Out of My Life and Thought* (London, 1931), p.185.

2. Albert Schweitzer, *On the Edge of the Primeval Forest and More from the Primeval Forest* (London, 1953), p.95.

3. H. W. Debrunner, *A History of Christianity in Ghana* (Accra, 1967), p.287.

4. K. Clements, *Faith on the Frontier: A Life of J.H. Oldham* (Edinburgh, 1999), pp.147–148.

5. H. W. Debrunner, *A Church between Colonial Powers: A Study of the Church in Togo* (London, 1965), p.297.

6. J. E. Church, *Quest for the Highest* (Exeter, 1981), pp.125 ff.

7. Ibid. p.131.

8. Patricia Mary St. John, *Breath of Life: The Story of the Ruanda Mission* (London, 1971).

9. B. Sundkler and C. Steed, *A History of the Church in Africa* (Cambridge, 2000), p.857.

10. Adrian Hastings, *A History of African Christianity 1950–1975* (Cambridge, 1979), p.21.

11. Jean Comaroff and John L. Comaroff, *Of Revelation and Revolution*, vol.2 (Chicago, 1997), pp.338 ff.

12. J. Iliffe, *East African Doctors: A History of the Modern Profession* (Cambridge, 1998), p.17.

13. Megan Vaughan, *Curing Their Ills: Colonial Power and African Illness* (Cambridge, 1991), p.58.

14. Op. cit., n.12, p.22.

15. David Hardiman, ed., *Healing Bodies, Saving Souls: Medical Missions in Asia and Africa* (Amsterdam, 2006), pp.225 ff.

16. O. S. F. Louis, *Love Is the Answer: The Story of Mother Kevin* (Dublin, 1964), p.100.

17. *Village Education in Africa. Report of a 10 Day Conference of 'Janes' Teachers* (Salisbury, Lovedale, 1935), p.7.

18. E. W. Smith, *Aggrey of Africa: A Study in Black and White* (London, 1929), p.145.

19. T. Jesse Jones, *Four Essentials of Education* (New York, 1926), pp.20 ff.

20. L. J. Lewis, *Phelps-Stokes Reports on Education in Africa* (London, 1962), p.5.

21. Ibid. pp.149–150.

22. Adelaide M. Cromwell, *An African Victorian Feminist: The Life and Times of Adelaide Smith Casely Hayford, 1868–1960* (London, 1986), p.19.

23. Op. cit., n.18, p.11.

24. G. Guggisberg, *The Keystone* (London, 1924), pp.5–9.

25. In 1949, I was stationed near Accra as a sergeant on national service. Although straight from school, I was deemed senior to two experienced Africans – an RSM and a CSM – who both later became generals in the Ghanian army.

26. W. E. F. Ward, *Fraser of Trinity and Achimota* (Accra and Oxford, 1965), pp.183–185.

27. Op. cit., n.19, p.123.

28. UNESCO, *The Development of Higher Education in Africa* (UNESCO, 1963), p.22.

29. O. U. Kalu, 'African Christianity from the World Wars to Decolonisation'. P.201, in *The Cambridge History of Christianity*, vol.9, ed. H. McLeod (Cambridge, 2006).

30. A. Yates and L. Chester, *The Troublemaker* (London, 2006), p.20.

31. Op. cit., n.19, p.61.

32. Michael Scott, *A Time to Speak* (London, 1958), p.110.

33. Op. cit., n.31, p.37.

34. R. Denniston, *Trevor Huddleston: A Life* (London, 1999), pp.47–48.

35. Colin Winter, *The Breaking Process* (London, 1981), p.1.

36. Colin Winter, *Namibia: The Colin Winter Story* (London, 1977), p.13.

37. R. Weiss, *Sir Garfield Todd and the Making of Zimbabwe* (London, 1999), p.36.

38. www.rhodesiana.com/rsr/rsr3-005.html (cited 13 June 2008).

39. D. A. Mungazi, *The Last British Liberals in Africa* (Westport, CT, 1999), p.126.

40. Op. cit., n.38, p.67.

41. Colin Morris, *The Hour after Midnight* (London, 1961), p.21.

42. Colin Morris, *Anything but This: The Challenge of Race in Central Africa* (London, 1958), p.11.

43. Kenneth Kaunda and Colin Morris, *Black Government? A Discussion between Kenneth Kaunda and Colin Morris* (Lusaka, 1960).

44. Kevin Ward, 'Christianity, Colonialism and Mission'. P.87, in *The Cambridge History of Christianity*, vol.9, ed. H. McLeod (Cambridge, 2006).

45. C. J. Korieh and G. U. Nwokeji, *Religion, History, and Politics in Nigeria: Essays in Honor of Ogbu U. Kalu* (Lanham, MD, 2005).

46. J. J. Kritzinger, 'The Rwandan Tragedy as Public Indictment against Christian Mission', http://www.geocities.com/missionalia/rwanda1.htm?200829 (cited 13 June 2008).

47. P. Gourevitch, *We Wish to Inform You that Tomorrow We Will Be Killed with Our Families* (New York, 1999), p.79.

48. T. Gatwa, *Rwanda: Eglises Victimes ou Coupables?* (Yaounde, 2001), p.120.

49. Meg Guillebaud, *Rwanda. The Land that God Forgot* (Grand Rapids and London, 2002), p.206.

50. Chris McGreal, 'Rwanda – 10 Years on', http://www.guardian.co.uk/world/2004/mar/29/rwanda.chrismcgreal (cited 13 June 2008).

51. *African Rights*, Issue 9, 1998.

52. Op. cit., n.48, pp.135–136.

53. http://www.fidh.org/spip.php?article4467 (cited 13 June 2008).

54. International Criminal Tribunal for Rwanda Indictment. Case No. ICTR-2001-62-1.

55. Op. cit., n.48, p.42.

56. http://news.adventist.org/data/2003/1045672278/index.html.en (cited 13 June 2008).

57. Chris McGreal, 'We Have to Kill Tutsis Wherever They Are', http://www.guardian.co.uk/world/2008/may/16/congo.rwanda (cited 16 May 2008).

58. Op. cit., n.47, p.5.

59. http://www.afrol.com/Countries/Rwanda/backgr_cross_genocide.htm (cited 13 June 2008).

60. Op. cit., n.47, p.8.

61. 'Transformation'. *Journal of the World Evangelical Fellowship* 12/2 (1995): 4–8 (Gatwa); 12–14 (Kolini); 15–18 (Bowen).

About the Author

Martin Ballard was a scholar of St. Paul's School and of Jesus College, Cambridge. He first landed in modern Ghana as a national serviceman, and, while travelling through Freetown and staying in Accra, he took the opportunity of visiting both Fourah Bay and Achimota colleges. After taking his degree in history, he returned to Africa for two tours as a member of the Northern Nigerian colonial service. During this time, in Bornu Province, he made friends with British missionaries and received medical treatment in a remote American hospital.

He later taught history in his native city of Bristol and had to face up to the history of slavery while researching his first book *Bristol Seaport City*. This was followed by other works of fiction and non-fiction for young readers, some of which have African themes. He also edited *New Movements in the Study and Teaching of History* (Temple Smith). Martin Ballard has studied theology and has many years of experience in the publishing industry.

Index